THE

Devil's Pulpit.

CONTAINING TWENTY-THREE

ASTRONOMICO-THEOLOGICAL DISCOURSES,

BY THE

Rev. ROBERT TAYLOR, B.A.,

Of St. John's College, Cambridge; Member of the Royal College of Surgeons; Author of the Diegesis, &c., &c.

WITH

A SKETCH OF HIS LIFE.

VOL. II.

THE BOOK TREE
San Diego, California

This edition
Originally published
1882
Freethought Publishing Company
London

New material, revisions and cover
© 2015
The Book Tree
All rights reserved

ISBN 978-1-58509-361-8

Cover Layout
Mike Sparrow

Published by
The Book Tree
P O Box 16476
San Diego, CA 92176
www.thebooktree.com

We provide fascinating and educational products to help awaken the public to new ideas and information that would not be available otherwise.
Call 1 (800) 700-8733 for our *FREE BOOK TREE CATALOG*.

FOREWORD

This book is the second volume in a collection of sermons presented by Rev. Robert Taylor – sermons that stirred up more trouble in England than most anything else during this time. Taylor was ordained in 1813 and spent five years preaching standard Christianity before meeting an "infidel," who opened Taylor's mind. Taylor began researching and questioning everything in the Christian faith that seemed deceitful and disgusting, which was being supported and praised by the standard fanatics in the faith that surrounded him.

While seeking the true meaning and origins of the scriptures, he was shunned by family and friends, and ousted by the Church. He was jailed on more than one occasion, due to his oratory skills and winning many debates against those supporting standard religious dogmas. His time in prison was always put to good use through the many written works that he produced. This work was originally published in 1832, then again in 1882. Volume One was reprinted by The Book Tree in 2006, with this rare Volume Two now joining it in 2015. Volume Two includes the complete overview or "Memoir" of Taylor's life. In the older, previous printings it was divided between volumes, but no part of it was included in Book Tree's Volume One reprint due to its incompleteness at the time, and we never knew if we could find its missing section. His complete Memoir is now found in its entirety here.

Subjects covered in this volume include The Dangers of Belief, The Origins and Purpose of the Devil, the Zodiac and the Old Testament, Lying Spirits, the Fall of Man, Noah, Who Was Abraham?, Melchisedec, Origins of the Lord God, the Twelve Patriarchs, Who is the Lord?, Exodus, Miriam, and much more. Robert Taylor was one of the first insiders of the faith to start thinking for oneself and questioning things that needed questioning, despite the heavy price that he had to pay. He could have buckled under and quit from the pressure and jail time, but sharing the truth was more important to him. As a result, his writings continue to inspire readers to think for themselves and to question the powers that be.

Publisher's Note: At the end of some chapters, page numbers will sometimes jump forward either two or four pages, giving the impression that there may be some missing information. These pages were merely blank, so in order to save space we chose not to print them.

MEMOIR

Of the REVEREND ROBERT TAYLOR, *who received from* H. HUNT *the title of "The Devil's Chaplain."*

ROBERT was the sixth son of John and Elizabeth Taylor, born at the village of Edmonton, on the north-east side of London, in the Walnut Tree House, adjoining the wooden bridge over the pond, at 3 o'clock p.m. of Wednesday, August 18th, 1784. His parents were highly respectable, and of ample fortune; but its division among seven sons and a daughter left no more to each than the nucleus of a fortune to be acquired by the pursuit of some profession. Robert was first educated at the boarding-school adjoining the Bell Inn, Fore-street, and subsequently under Mr. Thomson, of Ponders End. His father died while he was yet young; and, after a long visit to his uncle and guardian, Edward Farmer Taylor, Esq., of Chicken Hall, near Bridgnorth, he was articled as house pupil to Mr. Samuel Partridge, surgeon, resident in the General Hospital, near Birmingham. In the year 1805 he walked Guy's and St. Thomas's Hospitals, under Sir Astley Cooper and Mr. Cline, and passed the College of Surgeons with great applause in 1807.

Being unsettled as to his views and prospects in life, Mr. Taylor imbibed very strong religious feelings from his intimacy with the Rev. Thomas Cotterell, then minister of Lane End, in Staffordshire, a clergyman of the Established Church of high evangelical principles. That reverend gentleman, seeing in his young friend a strong natural eloquence combined with strong religious feelings, persuaded him to seek holy orders in the Established Church.

In October, 1809, Mr. Taylor matriculated, and instantly became Queen Margaret's Foundation scholar at St. John's College, Cambridge. During his residence in the University he was a constant hearer of the Rev. C. Simeon, whose hearers were distinguished by the name of *Simeonites*, and was by that gentleman instructed in the art of *sermon-making*, in which art Mr. Simeon distinguished him as the *facile princeps* and *incomparabilis* of his class.

In January, 1813, Mr. Taylor took his degree of Bachelor

of Arts, purposely refusing his chance of the *inferior* honors of the Tripos. He was complimented by the Master of St. John's College as a singular honor to the University in his scholarship such as Cambridge had not for some time known; and in all his scholastic struggles for superiority under competition he was never second. The present Mr. Herschel, son of Dr. Herschel, the astronomer, was his compeer and competitor.

The Rev. Richard Lloyd, Rector of St. Dunstan's and of Midhurst, in the county of Sussex, wanting a curate for the latter place, wrote to the Rev. Mr. Simeon, of Cambridge, requesting him to pick out the cleverest and most religious young man at the University for that vacancy. The choice of the Professor fell on Mr. Taylor, who, having no objection to embrace that opportunity of entering upon holy orders, was ordained Deacon by the Bishop of Chichester (Buckner) on Sunday, March 14, 1831, at St. James's Piccadilly. He subsequently received the order of the priesthood. On the same day that he was ordained Deacon he preached his maiden sermon at St. Dunstan's, Fleet Street.

From March 1813 to the summer of 1818 he continued a zealous and highly evangelical preacher at Midhurst, and obtained from Mr. Poyntz, a gentleman of that neighborhood, a *brown-coat rectory.**

About the commencement of the year 1818, the Rev. Mr. Taylor became acquainted with a tradesman at Midhurst who was an infidel. Having neither hypocrisy nor scepticism in himself, and despising the hypocrisy of others, he was open to the arguments of the infidel and of infidel authors, and soon found that they were not deficient of weight. Here began the struggle in his mind of virtue with the hypocrisy of the world. On the Trinity Sunday he preached a sermon which gave offence to the more orthodox part of his congregation. The scepticism which thus began, and which had for six months been fermenting in his mind, derived strength and growth from the disgust he had conceived at the bitter spirit and *deceitful practices* of the

---

* *A brown-coat rectory* is a very significant Church phrase. It means a rectory or church living in which the patron, as Mr. Poyntz was on this occasion, pockets the hundreds or thousands that it may produce, and gives a black-coated curate a mere twenty pounds a-year for his occasional services.

fanatics by whom he was surrounded; and he wrote to his Diocesan, Dr. Buckner, Bishop of Chichester, tendering the resignation of his little preferment, on the alleged ground of the insupportable pain of conscience he felt in continuing to preach that which he had ceased to believe. It was at this time that Dr. Buckner, the Bishop of Chichester, remonstrated with him on the folly of relinquishing his prospects in the Church because he ceased to think with the orthodox, described the Christian religion as a Promethean nose of wax, and declared that he would not have ordained him if he could have imagined that he, Mr. Taylor, would have turned out such a fool as to entertain such silly scruples. This sort of appeal startled our young philosophising divine, and he began to feel an inclination to remain in the Church; but he had so far committed himself that atonement was necessary, some apology, and something in the shape of recantation of infidel principles must be made; and for this purpose it was agreed between the Bishop, Dr. Buckner, the Rector, Mr. Lloyd, and the Rev. Mr. Taylor, that the latter should retire from Sussex, or from his then appointments, be secluded for a time, and be brought out again in the first good living at the disposal of the Bishop. The Bishop of London was privy to this arrangement.

Mrs. Elizabeth Taylor, the widowed mother of our young sceptical divine, was a very religious woman and prided herself much in having so promising a son in the Church. The shock of his removal from Midhurst was to her, consequently, great and almost fatal. It brought her on a bed of sickness, and on an apparent death-bed. In an agony of mental conflict with filial affection, the hero of our memoir rushed to relieve the mind of his agonised mother, and, in a delirium of grief, he was ready to recant, to avow, or to publish anything that should be called for. This for a moment assuaged the anger of his family, but added nothing to the fame, while it has been a thorn in the side of the reverend gentleman. Dr. Gaskin, of Newington, of orthodox celebrity, undertook the purification of the mentally wavering apostate. But *infidelity is knowledge;* and though it may be concealed, or perverted, or debased, it can never be converted. He was allowed to officiate in the churches of Edmonton, Tottenham and Newington as an assistant; but he became impatient of the *little while* that was required for his retirement and the subsiding of the excitement produced by his singular apostacy, and unhallowed, though well-meant, recantation. He wrote to the Bishop of London, requesting speedy restoration to the bosom of the Church which he had offended, but for which offence he thought he had made due atonement. The Bishop answered in a most sarcastic tone that the circumstances required all the patience that should evince a humility, a penitence, and a sincerity becoming a Christian minister under affliction, to the satisfaction and judgment of the heads of the Church, and that enough of the necessary proof had not yet been obtained. Our mortified aspirant then wrote to the Bishop of Chichester in claim of the promised preferment, and was answered most insolently and significantly by his former Rector, the Rev. Mr. Lloyd, in nearly the following words—" *My dear Taylor, the background is the place for you.*" This was not to be mistaken. There was no further hope in the Church. Other means of living must be sought.

Our baffled, wavering, but growing hero, having a few hundred pounds at command, sought its employment, backed by his brighter talents, in the possession of a school. An advertisement brought him acquainted with a Bristol family of the name of May, which professed to have a suitable school for his purpose. He embarked the remains of his little fortune with them. They found him uninitiated into any of the tricks of commerce, and getting his loose cash, as well as his acceptance to a hundred pound bill, they soon proved to be swindlers, and his title to the school was not worth a shilling. Wright, the Bristol Quaker banker, had some transactions with those Mays, and seven years afterwards prosecuted a claim for the acceptance of the hundred pound bill, which drove our unchurched, unsuspecting, and impoverished dupe to a relief from prison by the Insolvent Debtors' Court. One of the Mays was hanged at Newgate for forgery; and, if the Rev. Mr. Taylor's account of the story be correct, the Quaker banker rather deserved a prosecution for a conspiracy to defraud than to be considered a legal creditor.

In distress, and shunned by his family, he obtained, through the kindness of an old friend, the curacy of Yardley, near Birmingham, and hoped to purge himself here of the sin of avowed scepticism by an orthodox life and a strictly ceremonial service in this secluded church. The Bishop of Worcester discovered the intruder among his flock, was peremptory in his demand for dismissal and departure, rejected all proposed terms and all sufficiency of recantation, and, by dint of persecution, produced a reaction in the mind of our clerical transgressor, who used the time which custom allowed him to have for his quittance in the preaching of Deism in the parish church of Yardley, by which the churchwardens and most of the parishioners were converted. It is but just to observe, *en passant*, that his moral character was *exemplary*, and his practical habits highly calculated to win the esteem of those who knew him, and who were too wise to be offended by his lapse and relapse in doctrine, or too ignorant to be conscious of the meaning.

In this predicament his brothers consented to make him a monthly allowance if he would quit England. Not knowing what else to do, he retired to the Isle of Man. The first month's promised allowance was duly paid, but either the second or the third was peremptorily refused without any assigned reason. Thrown on his own resources in the Isle of Man, he sought literary employment with the two newspapers of the Island; but on writing an article in justification of suicide, he was summoned before the Bishop, who had traced the character of the new inhabitant, and warned that if he did not quickly leave the Island the Bishop had power to imprison him for life without being accountable to anyone. If this be true, it is time that it should cease to be so. Moneyless and friendless, scouted by his family, our hapless hero landed at Whitehaven, in the best conveyance in which he could get away from the alleged absolute power of the Bishop of Sodor and Man. His last resource was his old friend, Mr. Partridge, from whom he obtained a ten pound note, and having paid about three pounds of debt incurred at Whitehaven, he sailed for Dublin with remainder to seek a living in a hoped retirement in Ireland.

The clerical errant succeeded by an advertisement in getting a situation in the school of a Mr. Jones, to the best of our recollection, at Rathfarnham; and so striking were his talents that it was not long before he was the admired preacher in the parish church and the favorite of all the respectable families of the neighborhood. The *odium theologicum* was lynx-eyed and inexorable; Archbishop Magee, of

Dublin, discovered the refugee, thundered forth his anathema, and no one connected with the church or with a school dared to give shelter to the excommunicated offender, whose entreaties for new trial were received with scorn. Thrown again on his wits, he tried his talent publicly in Dublin by the publication of several tracts, under the title of "The Clerical Review," in which he introduced a Middletonian style of assailing the church. Such a Deism as that of Conyers Middleton was the extreme of his acquirement up to the year 1824. In that year his leanings were rather to the Christian religion than to Deism, and it is to his persecution by the Church that we owe the noble and measurelessly important character to which he has now arrived. His Dublin publications brought him the acquaintance of Archibald Hamilton Rowan, of a Mr. Jessop, of Mr. Shaw, the printer and bookseller, and of many respectable persons of Dublin, one of whom was Lord Dillon. Under their auspices he projected a public association for the inculcation of morals only in preaching under the title of "The Society of Universal Benevolence." This was prospectively, though not avowedly, a Deistical association. Obtaining the use of a small theatre for his lectures, the bigotry of the Dublin Protestants was roused, the students of the Trinity College flocked to the Sunday morning's lecture, commenced an outrageous violence by cries of blasphemy, almost destroyed the theatre, and put his life in danger. His friends subscribed him the means of a journey to London under this frightful aspect of affairs in Dublin, with a hope and calculation that his projected association for universal benevolence would better suit this metropolis. He reached London in the summer of 1824, and having made a few friends, one of whom was in himself a host of public virtue, on the 24th of November he held the first meeting of his Christian Evidence Society under the principles of the Association of Universal Benevolence, free enquiry and fair discussion. His talents and wants necessarily brought his professional character under the double head of being a private teacher of the classics and a public lecturer. He began the latter as the founder of the Christian Evidence Society, at the "Globe Tavern" in Fleet Street, and continued it at the "Crown and Anchor Tavern" in the Strand, at the Crown and Rolls Room in Chancery Lane, at

Mitchell's Room in Portugal Street, Lincoln's Inn Fields; at the "Paul's Head," Cateaton Street; at the Founder's Hall Chapel, Cannon Street. There were ninety-five public meetings of this association, the purpose and business of which was to discuss the merits of all the writings which were, by Christians, deemed standard evidences of the goodness of religion, such as those of Lardner, Addison, Leslie, Paley, Doddridge, Hall, Chalmers, and others. The business of a public meeting was opened with a reading of a portion of one of those authors. The Rev. Mr. Taylor delivered an oration on the merits of the matter read; after which, any competent person present was allowed to address the chairman in answer to the objections which had been taken, and the rev. orator closed the business with a general reply to all that had been advanced against his oration. Ninety-five of these discussions were held and so many orations delivered by the rev. gentleman, three only of which have been printed; the Introductory Lecture, the 44th, and the 93rd. The others are preserved for the convenience of putting them to press in a regular way, to be made into two or three volumes.

The Christian Evidence Society was so well supported, that a great desire was expressed for the possession of a chapel, in which one or more discourses should be delivered on the Sunday. And here was the first successful attempt openly to assail the Christian faith on the Sunday. An old chapel was obtained, in an old building, called Founder's Hall, Lothbury, in the spring of 1826. In this chapel there was a most respectable congregation; the business was confined to a morning's discourse, and the previous reading of a Liturgy prepared for the occasion.

The success of the chapel in Founder's Hall induced the purchase of a more elegant chapel in Salter's Hall, Cannon Street, to the particulars of which we shall, by and bye come.

MEMOIR.

The Sunday morning discourses were ethical treatises, thirty-eight in number, the whole of which have been printed in a periodical work, entitled *The Lion*, and are intended to form a separate volume. These, with a dozen discourses on various subjects, four of which are in succession of those published in the two volumes of "The Devil's Pulpit," make up the labors of the rev. gentleman, on infidel discourses, to the time of his confinement in Horsemonger-lane Gaol. There are six discourses on the evidences of the Christian religion not printed, and two printed, under the head of "Missionary Orations." His present labor is bestowed on an improved series of discourses, developing the astronomical allegory of the sacred scriptures, and perhaps the world will be more speedily made the wiser on this subject through his present confinement.

The years 1825 and 1826 were triumphant years for the reverend orator. He went on gathering strength; and a conspiracy was laid in the spring of 1827 to get him into gaol. The Government was at the bottom of this; but the prominent acting persons were the Aldermen of the City of London, and more particularly Brown, the Mayor, and Atkins. Early in the year he was arrested on a Saturday evening, and thrown into Giltspur Street Compter. This arrest was made so as to interrupt the Sunday's proceedings at the chapel. The charge was that of having delivered a blasphemous discourse in the Cannon Street Chapel. An indictment was obtained at the January sessions, and notice of trial given for those ensuing; but at the last moment a writ of *certiorari* was brought by the prosecutors to remove the trial from the Old Bailey to the Court of King's Bench.

While this indictment was pending, Wright, the Bristol Quaker banker, prosecuted his claim on the hundred pounds acceptance to a judgment, and threw the reverend gentleman into the King's Bench prison, on an arrest for the assumed debt; from whence, after a few months' confinement, he was released by the Insolvent Debtors' Court.

In the spring of 1827 an indictment was also obtained, at the instance of the same prosecutors, against the Rev. Mr.

Taylor, and five others, Messrs. Saul, Brooks, Brushfield, Roome, and Hanger, for a conspiracy to overthrow the Christian religion; and under this state of things, Mr. Roome, who was the principal in trust for the Salters' Hall Chapel, brought it to sale, and a fine theatre of free discussion was thus sacrificed to the manes of despotism. The chapel had been purchased by £5 shares, and by loans of money: and it was sold again for a sum of money within one hundred and fifty pounds of the original cost. That loss was divided among the shareholders at the rate of £1 8s. per share; while the landholders were paid in full, with interest. This division caused much dissatisfaction; more particularly as many shares were not at all accounted for, and never have been accounted for to this day, through the alleged concealment of Mr. Robert Brown, the secretary of the society. Mr. Roome acquitted himself honorably in the disbursements, if the payment of the loans with interest, when the shares were deteriorated, can be justified.

On the 24th October, 1827, the Rev. Mr. Taylor was brought to trial at the Guildhall Court of King's Bench, in the City of London, before Lord Chief Justice Tenterden; and, after a splendid defence, which lasted above three hours, an ever-stupid and barbarous religious jury said "Guilty." This defence, and a speech on receiving judgment, is printed.

In January, 1828, an attempt was made to bring on the trial for conspiracy; but it failed through the absence of the special jurymen, and the evident disinclination of the Lord Chief Justice to entertain the case. It has not been since heard of.

On the 7th of February, 1828, the Court of King's Bench gave judgment on the conviction of the 24th of October, that the reverend defendant should be imprisoned one year in Oakham Gaol, and should give recognisance for his good behaviour for five years, himself in five hundred pounds, and two others in two hundred and fifty pounds each.

In the night of the 7th he was hurried off to Oakham Goal, without being able to take a change of linen with him.

In this most solitary confinement—for Oakham Goal had never above half-a-dozen prisoners—and seeing but few friends, in consequence of the distance from London, our reverend author produced his pamphlet entitled "Syntagma," and also that fine volume "The Diegesis," besides a good weekly letter, published in "The Lion." "Syntagma" was a reply to Dr. John Pye Smith; and "The Diegesis" is an historical work, showing that the Christian religion did not originate according to the narrative of the gospels, but was more ancient.

It is worthy of mention, in contrast with the present imprisonment in Horsemonger Lane Gaol, that the Rev. Mr. Taylor never had the least disagreement with Mr. Orridge, the keeper, or with any person, during his confinement in Oakham Gaol. He had the free range of the gaol, and gave no offence, excepting a little liberty taken, in writing a few notes, in Hebrew, in the chaplain's Book of Common Prayer, as a reproach to his fondness for reading the commination service so often to half-a-dozen prisoners.

Mr. Carlile's close acquaintance with the Rev. Mr. Taylor was begun on the occasion of his being sent to Oakham Gaol. Before that they were not acting together. Mr. Carlile knew how apt the best of friends are to weary of supporting a public cause; and fearing the Rev. Mr. Taylor would not be otherwise well supported in Oakham Gaol, he managed the subscription in such a way as to leave nothing that was desirable unprovided. A similar effort has been successfully made, up to this time, with regard to the present confinement: but there is not that necessary balance in hand which ensures prospective comfort, as there was throughout the confinement in Oakham Gaol.

It was the wish of many of the Rev. Mr. Taylor's friends, that he should refuse to give the required recognisance for his liberation, and his own inclinations were for a short time up to this point; but they failed when he became a prisoner of choice, and Mr. Carlile and a friend became his bail.

On his return to town, in February, 1829, the rev. gentleman officiated a little in the large room of Mr. Carlile's house in Fleet Street, and occasionally at the Universalist's Chapel in Windmill Street, Finsbury Square, preparatory to an infidel mission, through the North of England, with Mr. Carlile. The mission was entered upon in May, and begun at Cambridge, by a general challenge to that University, in the most formal and most complete way in which it could be made, to the public defence of the Christian religion.

The only answer given to this challenge was in the persecution of Mr. Smith, of Rose Crescent, the print-seller and lodging-house keeper, for lodging the infidel missionaries. Waiting near a week at Cambridge to no purpose, but with some threats of personal violence from the members of the University, the mission proceeded to Wisbeach, to Stamford, and to Nottingham, without being able to get standing room under a roof of an audience, but not without formally challenging the priests by a printed circular. From Nottingham a movement was made to Leeds; and here the fine Music Hall was obtained for one night; but the Mayor interfering, in the least possible offensive way, the use of the hall for the purpose of their discussions could not be continued. Another place was obtained, but it was inconvenient; and on finding that it was to be used on the Sunday, a magisterial interference again took place, and Leeds was left to its superlative bigotry and native darkness, a complete specimen of the prostration of mind to large masses of wealth. From Leeds a movement was made to Bradford and to Manchester, in neither of which places was there any success worthy of mention. Ashton-under-Lyne and Bolton afforded more game; but at Liverpool the mission was crowned with success and glory, by the Rev. Mr. Thom stepping forward to accept the challenge of the missionaries. Here Christianity, as it is in common practice, was completely put to trial and as completely failed. The Mayor (Robinson) blustered forth his magisterial authority and hunted the engagement for a theatre from place to place, and when the fine room of the shipwrights was at last secured, the Rev. Mr. Thom, after one night's attempt, refused all further invitation to keep his ground. A Unitarian printer of the name of Wright made a similar attempt, and came on twice, but to little purpose. The agitation of Liverpool has done a deal of good, for it has been the means of bringing forth the "LADY FROM THE COUNTRY," who is now about to lecture at the Rotunda. It was the general shrinking of the Christians there that first raised a doubt in her most sincerely religious mind.

From Liverpool the mission proceeded to Wigan, Blackburn, Bury, Hyde, and to Huddersfield in Yorkshire, having profitably spent some days in Stockport, before going to Liverpool. At Huddersfield a powerful effect was produced, and, after four months' absence from London, and the approach of winter, a return was made to town.

It was an intention to have kept up the mission every summer; but in the ensuing May (1830) the taking of the Rotunda, Blackfriars Road, opened a new scene of action, and the French revolution, of July in that year, became a new feature in the political world.

The effect produced at the Rotunda from May, 1830, to July, 1831, was prodigious. It is now felt throughout the country, notwithstanding the second imprisonment of both Mr. Carlile and the Rev. Mr. Taylor; and in spite of all natural or supernatural power, the Rotunda will go on to moralise the country, and to give the people the necessary knowledge. The best of political, and moral and anti-theological sentiments have been there uttered, heard and cherished by thousands and tens of thousands of persons. It should be nationally consecrated as the first public building fairly appropriated to the whole principle of free discussion. The Government was alarmed, and absolutely removed Mr. Carlile on the 10th of January, 1831, and the Rev. Mr. Taylor on the 4th of July. Still the spirit of the Rotunda lives, and will live for ever, in this country. The steps gained within the last two years cannot be retracted. It opens with new spirit, with new attraction with all that is lovely and virtuous in woman to grace it, on the anniversary of the birth of Thomas Paine, the 29th of January, and as a proper succession to the close of the second volume of "The Devil's Pulpit."

HORSEMONGER LANE GAOL.

The second prosecution of the Rev. Mr. Taylor was managed by a society professing to associate for the suppression of vice; but whose first principle, for thirty years, has been, to protect the superstition of the country against all the inroads of reason. The mock trial came on on the 4th of July, sorry anniversary of American independence; and, in the night of that day, the fascinating orator was in the hands of religious ruffians, who treated him with all the barbarity they could think of or durst venture on. Robert Hedger was the chairman of the Court of Sessions—a man whom no good man calls friend or companion; a man who has emanated from one of the vilest hot-beds of vice that this metropolis ever contained, and who retains the character and the habits that were there generated. Such was the magistrate who sentenced the virtuous and talented Robert Taylor to two years' imprisonment and to felons' treatment. Such is a fair sample of the Surrey magistrates' bigotry, encouraging in those of better morals what vice produces in the others.

To detail the treatment suffered in Horsemonger Lane Gaol, had better be reserved until the treatment is at an end. Suffice it here to say, that it has been most atrocious and novel in England, and has had the full sanction of the Patriot King and his Whig Ministers.

But there is one thing connected with that treatment, that here requires explanation, and that is the

BRANDY BOTTLE AFFAIR AND THE ALLEGED ATTEMPT TO STAB.

Whenever any complaints are made to Lord Melbourne, or George Lamb, his brother, at the Home Department, there is the cuckoo or parrot cry set up of Mr. Taylor's having attempted to kill the gaoler. Now the public should know that this is a fabricated story, and the upshot of a conspiracy between the Whig Ministers, the Surrey Magistrates, and the gaoler, to find some excuse for their wickedness and persecution towards the reverend gentleman. Lord Melbourne is notoriously not a man of honor and sincerity of character, or he would have had this affair sifted by competent evidence and judgment; but it has been, his lordship well knows, a stratagem to cover a wickedness on the part of his administration. It is utterly a lie to say that the Rev. Mr. Taylor attempted to stab Walter, the gaoler. In the first place he had no weapon; a clasp dinner knife, which was not presented in any way whatever, as a weapon, on the occasion of the scuffle alluded to, was not visible or thought of. The only knife at hand was a small buckhorn penknife, which no man bent on destruction would have thought of as a sufficient weapon. The case is simply this:—

The Rev. Mr. Taylor is not a dram drinker, and is very abstemious in the use of wine or grog, when it is in abundance about him. He has never been seen overcome with the spirit of intoxicating liquor. But still he is just of that temperament to crave and weakly to long for any article of use that should be withheld from him. He craved a small quantity of brandy. His desire for it was expressed in such a style of anxiety and seriousness that two or three of his friends hazarded the introduction of a small bottle-full to him. Such was his weakness or incautiousness on the subject that, on receiving a visit from Mr. Briscoe, the magistrate and member for the county, the gaoler being in attendance, the reverend gentleman jocosely asked them to bury all grievances over a glass of grog, and mentioned that he had a bottle of brandy in the cell. The bottle was of flat stone, and might have contained, when full, something about a half-pint; certainly not more. The magistrate and gaoler smiled, and there was an impression left on the mind of the prisoner that so long as no abuses arose from his possession of a little brandy it would not be objected to. This happened on a Thursday or Friday evening. On the Wednesday morning following the gaoler entered the cell in a very insolent manner and demanded the brandy bottle. He came bent on mischief. Mr. Taylor had very foolishly threatened him, on the subject of having his letters broken open, before this; the gaoler knew how to play on such a temperament; knew that there was a wide difference between a little theatrical vaunting and a resolute man bent on revenge. The walls of the metropolis had been powerfully crying *murder* against the authorities for the treatment inflicted on the prisoner, a strong sympathy was gathering even in the obduracy of bigot bosoms, and it was to destroy this sympathy that the conspiracy was laid and the assault committed on the prisoner instead of any assault committed by him on the gaoler. The Canadian Missionary Ourangoutang Osgood was hired to be the trumpeter of the alleged fray. Everything was planned. The Union Hall magistrate, Chambers, was told of it nobody knows how. He sent for the very reluctant gaoler to have the story told, that it might be reported from the Union Hall as a police case. There was nothing but *ex parte* evidence heard on the subject, and the plot failed in everything but in the attempt to smother the cry of murder against the authorities. In that it succeeded; and now it is the excuse for all atrocities practised before and after upon the reverend prisoner. Such is the character of religious persecution during the reign of William the Fourth, and the Administration of Grey, Brougham, and Althorp.

The Devil's Pulpit.

"AND A BONNIE PULPIT IT IS."—*Allan Cunningham.*

No. 1.—Vol. II.]   [Price 2*d.*

BELIEF, *NOT* THE SAFE SIDE:

An Oration,

DELIVERED BY THE REV. ROBERT TAYLOR, B.A.

IN THE UNIVERSALISTS' CHAPEL, WINDMILL STREET, FINSBURY SQUARE, FEB. 11, 1830.

"*Ye blind guides, which strain at a gnat and swallow a camel.*"
—MATTHEW xxiii. 24.

THE gentlemen who distribute religious tracts, the general body of dissenting preachers, and almost all persons engaged in the trade of religion, imagine themselves to have a mighty advantage against infidels, upon the strength of that last and reckless argument,—that whether the Christian religion be true or false, there can be no *harm* in believing; and that belief is, at any rate, the safe side.

Now, to say nothing of this old Popish argument, which a sensible man must see is the very essence of Popery, and would oblige us to believe all the absurdities and nonsense in the world: inasmuch as if there be no harm in believing, and there *be* some harm and danger in *not* believing, the more we believe, the better: and all the argument necessary for any religion whatever would be, that it should frighten us out of our wits: the more terrible, the more true: and it would be our duty to become the converts of that religion, whatever it might be, whose priests could swear the loudest, and damn and curse the fiercest.

But I am *here*, to grapple with this Popery, in disguise, this wolfish argument in sheepish clothing, upon scriptural ground, and on scriptural ground only; taking the scriptures of the Old and New Testament, for this argument's sake, to be of divine authority.

The question proposed is, ' Whether is the believer or the unbeliever the more likely to be saved, taking the scriptures to be of divine authority?' And I stand here, on this divine authority, to prove that the unbeliever is the more likely to be saved: that unbelief, and *not* belief, is the safe side: and that a man is more likely to be damned for believing the gospel, and *because* of his having believed it, than for rejecting and despising it, as I do.

I propose to sift this question, with most careful diligence, and to bring all its merits before you, with the utmost fairness, candour, and truth, taking words and meanings in their most ordinary acceptation, submitting the result to the judgments of your own minds, no judgment of mine withstanding. Let your good patience hear,—let such conviction as shall follow on your patient hearing, decide.

But, if such a patient hearing be more than good Christians be minded to give us, when thus I advance to meet them on their own ground, their impatience and intolerance itself will supply the evidence and demonstration of the fact, that, after *all*, they dare not stand to the text of their own book, that it is not the Bible that they go by, nor God whom they regard: but that they want to be *God-a'-mighties* themselves, and would have us take *their* words for God's word: you must read it as *they* read it, and understand it as they understand it; you must '*skip, and go on*,' just where a hard word comes in the way of the sense *they* choose to put upon't: you must believe what the book contains, what you see with your own eyes that it does *not* contain: you must shut your eyes, and not see what it *does* contain; or you'll be none the nearer the mark of *their* liking, though you should "from the table of your memory" wipe away all trivial fond records,

> All saws of books, all forms, all pressures past,
> That youth and observation copied there,
> And God's commandment, it alone should live
> Within the book and volume of your brain,
> Unmixed with baser matter.

And though you should be ' a scholar, and a ripe and good one,' with all advantages that education and learning can confer on man, as familiar with the text of the original

Greek, as with your mother tongue, the most illiterate bungling ass, the smutched artificer, the dirty kern, the cobbler from his lapstone, the weaver from his loom, having once given his mind to religion, will expect that *your* understanding should submit to *his;* and 'that' you should receive not merely the text he quotes, but whatever sense he chooses to understand, or to misunderstand, from it. So that the Sun itself is not more apparent in the Heavens, than is the fact, that religion is nothing more than the moody melancholy of an overbearing and tyrannical disposition; and your religious man, nothing more than an usurping saucy knave, who wants to be your master.

> 'How calm and sweet the victories of life!
> How terrorless the triumph of the grave!
> How ludicrous the priests' dogmatic roar,
> The weight of his exterminating curse,
> How light! and his affected charity,
> To suit the pressure of the changing times,
> With palpable deceit! but for *thy* aid,
> Religion! But for thee, prolific fiend,
> That peoplest earth with demons, hell with men,
> And Heaven with slaves!'
> *Shelley's Queen Mab.*

Hear the pulpit, Sirs! and their word of God, to be sure, is all joy and peace in believing,—mild, as if blest voices uttering praise,—soft, as the down upon the ring-dove's breast,—'sweet, as the south wind that breathes upon a bank of violets, stealing and giving odours.' Hear *itself*, Sirs! the gospel itself! uncommented by any gloss of mine; and

'The word of God is quick and powerful, and sharper than any two-edged sword, piercing even to the dividing asunder of soul and spirit, and of the joints and marrow.' Heb. iv. 12. What is hypocrisy? What is deceit? if greater hypocrisy and deceit can be, or be conceived, than that men should put Heaven in their shop windows, when Hell is in the shop? that they should 'cry peace! peace! when there is no peace;' and call their gospel 'glad tidings of great joy,' which, when we come to look into't, presents descriptions of grief, and woe, and pain, the bare imagining of which doth blanch the cheek of health to ashy paleness: and 'makes the seated heart knock at the ribs against the use of nature.'

> 'Regions of sorrow, doleful shades, where peace
> And rest can never dwell; hope never comes

That comes at all; but torture without end,
And pain of inextinguishable fire
Still urges, and a fiery deluge fed
With ever-burning sulphur unconsumed.'

And are THESE 'glad tidings of great joy?' Is the liabilty which Christian men stand in, if the gospel be true, of being infinitely and eternally miserable, so tempting as to tempt a man to *wish* that it may be true; when that liability, if the gospel be true, and the scriptures, from Genesis to Revelation, be of divine authority, impends *more* over the believer than the unbeliever; and that the unbeliever is more likely to be saved in consequence of his unbelief, and by virtue of his unbelief: and the believer more likely to be lost and damned to all eternity, because he *did* believe, and in consequence of his having believed?

Taking the authority of Scripture, for this argument's sake, to be decisive, I address the believer who would give himself airs of superiority, would chuckle in an imaginary safety in believing, and presume to threaten the unbeliever as being in a worse case, or more dangerous plight than *he*. 'Hast thou no fears for thy presumptuous self?' when on the showing of thine *own* book, the safety (if safety there be), is *all* on the unbelieving side. When for any one text that can be produced, seeming to hold out any advantage or safety in believing, we can produce *two*, in which the better hope is held out to the *unbeliever*. For any one apparent exhortation to believe, we can produce two *forbiddances* to believe, and many threatenings of God's vengeance, *to*, and *for* the crime and folly of believing. To this proof I proceed, by showing you:

1st. What the denunciations of God's vengeance are: with no comment of mine, but in the words of the text itself.

2nd. That these dreadful denunciations are threatened to believers: and that they are *not* threatened to unbelievers: and

3rd. That all possible advantages and safety, which believing could confer on any man, are likely, and *more* likely to be conferred on the unbeliever, than on the believer.

That the danger of the believer is *so* extreme, that no greater danger can possibly be.

1st. What are the denunciations of God's vengeance? 'There are,' (says the holy Revelation, xiv. 10), ' who shall drink of the wine of the wrath of God, which is poured out without mixture into the cup of his indignation, and shall be tormented with fire and brimstone, and the smoke of their torment ascendeth up for ever and ever: and they have no rest day nor night.' There's 'glad tidings of great joy' for you. The Christian may get over the terror of this denunciation by the selfish and ungenerous chuckle of his 'Ah! well, these were very wicked people, and must have deserved their doom; it need not alarm us: it doesn't apply to us.' But good-hearted men would rather say, 'It *does* apply. We cannot be indifferent to the misery of our fellow-creatures. The self-same Heaven that frowns on them, looks lowering upon us.' And who were they? and what was *their* offence? Was it Atheism? was it Deism? was it Infidelity? No! It was for church and chapel-going; it was for adoring, believing, and worshipping. They worshipped the beast: I know not what beast they worshipped; but I know, that if you go into any of our churches and chapels at this day, you will find them worshipping *the Lamb;* and if worshipping a *lamb* be not most suspiciously like worshipping a *beast,* you may keep the colour in your cheeks, while mine are blanched with fear. The unbeliever only can be absolutely safe from this danger. He only who has no religion at all, is sure not to be of the wrong religion. He who worships neither God nor Devil, is sure not to mistake one of those gentlemen for the other.

But will it be pretended that these are only metaphors of speech, that the thing said is not the thing that's *meant.* Why, then, they are very ugly metaphors. And what is saying that which you don't mean, and meaning the contrary to what you say, but LYING?*

And what worse can become of the Infidel, who makes it the rule of his life 'to hear and speak the plain and simple

---

* But if the Christian hath a right to say that there are some parts, and even *many* parts of Scripture, which are not to be taken as strictly and literally *true;* but which must be understood as *metaphors* and *allegories:* what right can he have to dispute our right to maintain, that the whole gospel story is a metaphor and an allegory from first to last; that there is not a word of truth in it: that it was not written to pass for truth; but only as a vehicle to convey moral instruction, after the well-known Oriental style; a fable with a moral to it: of which the duller wit of these western nations forgot the moral, and ran away with the fable?

truth,' than of the Christian, whose religion itself is a system of metaphors and allegories, of double meanings, of quirks and quiddities, in dread defiance of the text that warns him, that 'All liars shall have their part in the lake which burneth with fire and brimstone.' Rev. xxi. 8.

Is it a parable that a man may merely entertain his imagination withal, and think no more on't,—though not a word be hinted about a parabolical signification; and the text stands in the mouth of him, who, we are told, was the truth itself. And *he* it is who brought life and immortality to light, that hath described in the 16th of Luke, such an immortality as that of one who was a sincere believer,—a son of Abraham, who took the Bible for the rule of his life; and was anxious to promote the salvation of his brethren, yet found for himself no saviour, no salvation; but, 'In Hell he lifted up his eyes, being in torment: and saith, Father Abraham, have mercy on me, and send Lazarus, that he may dip the tip of his finger in water, and cool my tongue, for I am tormented in this flame.' But that request was refused. 'Then he said, I pray thee, therefore, Father, that thou wouldest send him to my father's house; for I have five brethren, that he may testify unto them, lest they also come to his place of torment.' But that request was refused. There's 'glad tidings of great joy' for you.

That the believer's danger of coming or going into that place of torment is so great, that greater cannot possibly be: and that his belief will stand him in no stead at all, but make his plight a thousand times worse than if he had not been a believer; and that unbelief is the safer side,—Christ himself being judge,—I quote no words but his to prove.

Is the believer concerned to save his soul, then shall he most assuredly be damned for being so concerned: for Christ hath said, 'Whosoever will save his soul shall lose it.' Matthew xvi. 25.

Is the believer a complete beggar? If he be not so,—if he hath a rag that he doth call his own, he will be damned to all eternity. For Christ hath said, 'Whosoever he be of you who forsaketh not all that he hath, he cannot be my disciple.' Luke xiv. 33.

Is the believer a rich man? and dreams *he* of going to Heaven? 'It is easier for a camel to go through the eye of a needle.' Matthew xix. 24. Is he a man at all, then he cannot be saved: for Christ hath said, 'Thou believest that there is one God;' saith St. James, 'Thou dost well, the devils also believe and tremble.' 2 James 19. And so much good, and no more, than comes to damned spirits in the flames of Hell, is all the good that ever did and can come of believing. 'For though thou hadst all faith, so that thou couldst remove mountains,' saith St. Paul, 'It should profit thee nothing.' I Cor. xiii. 2.

Well, then! let the good Christian try what saying his prayers will do for him: *this* is the good that they'll do for him; and he hath Christ's own word to comfort him in't, 'He shall receive the greater damnation.' Luke xx. 47.

Well, then, since believing will not save him, since faith will not save him, since prayer will not save him, but all, so positively make things all the worse, and none the better, there's one other chance for him. Let him go and receive the Sacrament, the most comfortable Sacrament, you know, 'of the body and blood of Christ,' remembering, as all good communicants should, 'that he is not worthy so much as to gather up the crumbs that fall from that table.' 'Truth, Lord! But the dogs eat of the crumbs that fall from their master's table;' O what happy dogs. But let those dogs remember, that it is also *truth*, that he that eateth and drinketh unworthily, eateth and drinketh damnation to himself.' 1 Cor. xvi. 29. O what precious eating and drinking.

> 'My God! and is thy table spread;
> And doth thy cup with love o'erflow?
> Thither be all thy children led,
> And let them all thy sweetness know.'

That table is a snare, that cup is deadly poison, that bread shall send thy soul to Hell.

Well, then! try again, believer: perhaps you had better join the Missionary society, and subscribe to send these glad tidings of these blessed privileges, and this jolly eating and drinking, to the Heathen.

Why, then, you have Christ's own assurance, that when you shall have made one proselyte, you shall just have done him the kindness of making him twofold more the child of Hell than yourself. Matt. xxiii. 15.

Is the believer liable to the ordinary gusts of passion, and in a passion shall he drop the hasty word, 'thou fool:'

for that one word 'he shall be in danger of Hell fire.' Matt. v. 22.*

Nay, Sirs! this isn't the worst of the believer's danger. Would he but keep his legs and arms together, and spare his own eyes and limbs; he doth by that very mercy to himself damn his eyes and limbs, and hath Christ's assurance that it would have been profitable for him rather to have plucked out his eyes, and chopt off his limbs, and so to have wriggled and groped his way through the 'Straight gate and the narrow way that leadeth unto life,' than having two eyes and two arms, or two legs, to be cast into Hell, into the fire that never shall be quenched, where their 'worm dieth not, and the fire is not quenched.' Mark ix. 43.

Well, then! will the believer say, what were all the miracles and prophecies of both the Old and the New Testament *for?* those unquestionable miracles, and clearly accomplished prophecies, if it were not that men should believe? Why, absolutely, they were the very arguments appointed by God himself to show us that men should not believe; but that damnation should be their punishment if they did believe. 'To the law and the testimony,' Sirs! These are the very words: 'Of miracles,' saith God's word, 'They are the spirits of devils, that work miracles.' Rev. xvi. 14. And it is the Devil who 'deceiveth them which dwell on the earth, by means of those miracles which he hath power to do.' Rev. xiii. 14. So much for miracles.

Is it on the score of prophets and prophecies, then, that you will take believing to be the safe side? Then 'thus saith the Lord of Hosts, the God of Israel, the prophets prophesy falsely, and the priests bear rule by their means.' Jer. v. 31. 'The prophet is a fool: the spiritual man is mad.' Hosea i. 7. 'Thus saith the Lord of Hosts, hearken not unto the prophets.' Jer. xxiii. 15. 'O Israel, thy prophets are like the foxes of the desert.' Ezekiel xiii. 4. 'They lie unto thee.' Jer. xiv. 14. 'And they shall be tormented day and night for ever and ever.' Rev. xx. 10. 'And the punishment of the prophet shall be even as the punishment of him that seeketh unto him.' Ezekiel xiv. 10.

Nay more, *then*, it is, when God hath determined to damn men, that he, in every instance, causeth them to become

---

* Ενοχος εσται εις την γεενναν του πυρος.

believers, and to have faith in divine Revelation, in order that they may be damned. Believers, and none but believers, becoming liable to damnation; believers, and none but believers, being capable of committing that unpardonable sin against the Holy Ghost, which hath never forgiveness, neither in this world, nor in that which is to come. 'Whereas all other kinds of blasphemy shall be forgiven unto men, and all sorts of blasphemy wherewith so ever they shall blaspheme. But there is no forgiveness for believers.' Mark iii. 28. For it is written, 'For this cause God shall send them strong delusion, that they should believe a lie: that they all might be damned.' 2 Thess. ii. 11.*

So when it was determined by God that the wicked Ahab should perish, the means to bring him to destruction, both of body and soul, was to make him become a believer. I offer no comment of my own on words so sacred; but those are the words: 'Hear thou, therefore, the word of the Lord. I saw the Lord sitting upon his throne, and all the hosts of Heaven standing by him on his right hand and on his left. And the Lord said, who shall persuade Ahab that he may go up and fall at Ramoth Gilead? and one said on this manner, and another said on that manner. And there stood forth a spirit, and stood before the Lord, and said: I will persuade him. And the Lord said unto him wherewith? And he said, I will go forth, and I will be a lying spirit in the mouth of all his prophets. And he said thou shalt persuade him, and prevail also. Go forth and do so. Now, therefore, behold the Lord hath put a lying spirit in the mouth of all thy prophets.' 1 Kings xxii. 22. There were 400 of 'em; they were 'the goodly fellowship of the prophets for you; all of them inspired by the spirit from on high, and all of them lying as fast as they could lie.

So much for getting on the safe side by believing. Had Ahab been an Infidel, he would have saved his soul alive. As it was, we may address him in the words of St. Paul to just such another fool, 'King Ahab, believest thou the prophets? I know that thou believest: but not better than I know, that for that very belief, fell slaughter on thy soul:

---

* If, then, the evidence of the Christian religion were as strong as you please: where would be your evidence to show that that evidence itself was not strong delusion? And if God doth send men strong delusion, I guess the delusion is likely to be strong enough.

and where thou soughtest to be saved by believing, it was by believing that thou wert damned.'

So when Elijah had succeeded in converting the 450 worshippers of Baal, who had been safe enough while they were Infidels, and they began crying 'the Lord He is God, the Lord He is God:' the moment they got into the right faith, they found themselves in the wrong box: and the prophet, by the command of God, put a stop to their *Lord-Godding*, by cutting their throats for 'em. 'Elijah brought them down to the brook of Kishon, and slew them there.' 1 Kings xviii. 40. O what a blessed thing! ye see, to be converted to the true faith.*

Thus all the sins and crimes that have been committed in the world, and all God's judgments upon sin and sinners have been the consequence of religion, and faith, and believing.

What was the first sin committed in the world? It was believing. Had our great mother Eve not been a believing credulous fool, she would not have been in the transgression. Who was the first reverend divine that began preaching about God and immortality? It was the Devil. What was the first *lie* that was ever told, the very damning and damnable lie? It was the lie told to make folks believe that they would not be dead when they were dead, that they should not surely die, but that they should be as gods, and live in a future state of existence. When God himself hath declared, that there is no future state of existence: that 'Dust thou art, and unto dust shalt thou return.' Who is it, then, that prefers believing in the Devil rather than in God, but the believer? And from whom is the hope of a future state derived, but from the father of lies?—the Devil. But

If in defiance of so positive a declaration of Almighty God, men will have it that there is a future state of existence, after death, who are they who shall sit down with Abraham, and Isaac, and Jacob, in the Kingdom of Heaven, but unbelievers, let 'em come from the north, from the south, from the east, or from the west? And who are they that shall be cast out, but believers, 'the children of the kingdom?'

---

* He brought them to the brook, ye know, for the convenience of baptising and killing them at the same time. I suppose they were on the safe side of the brook.

As St. Peter very charitably calls them, 'cursed children.' 2 Peter ii. 14. That is, I suppose, children with beards, children that never grew to sense enough to put away childish things, but did in gawky manhood, like new-born babes, desire the pure milk and lollipop of the gospel. 'For of such is the Kingdom of Heaven.'

And who are they whom Christ will set upon his right hand, and to whom he will say. 'Come ye blessed of my Father!' but unbelievers, who never troubled their minds about religion, and never darkened the doors of a gospel shop. But who are they to whom he will say, 'Depart ye cursed into everlasting fire, prepared for the devil and his angels, but believers, every one of them believers, chapel-going folks, Christ's blood-men, and incorrigible bigots, that had been bothering him all their days with their 'Lord, Lord!' to come off at last with no better reward of their faith than that he will protest unto them, I never knew ye.

One text there is, and only one, against ten thousand of a contrary significancy: which, being garbled and torn from its context, seems, for a moment, to give the advantage to the believer: the celebrated 16th chapter of Mark, xvi 16: 'He that believeth, and is baptised, shall be saved; but he that believeth not shall be damned.' But little will this serve the deceitful hope of the Christian, for it is immediately added: 'And these signs shall follow them that believe; in my name shall they cast out devils; they shall speak with new tongues; they shall take up serpents; and if they drink any deadly things, it shall not hurt them; they shall lay hands on the sick, and they shall recover.' Can the Christian show these signs, or any of them? Will he dare to take up a serpent, or drink prussic acid? If he hesitate he is not a believer, and his profession of belief is a falsehood. Let belief confer what privilege it may, he hath no part nor lot in the matter: the threat which he denounces against infidels hangs over himself, and he hath no sign of salvation to show.

Believing the gospel, then, (or rather, I should say, *professing* to believe it, for I need not tell you that there's a great deal more professing to believe, than believing), instead of making a man the more likely to be saved, doubles his danger of damnation, inasmuch as Christ hath said, that, 'the last state of that man shall be worse than the first.'

Luke xi. 26. And his holy apostle Peter addeth, ' It would have been better for them not to have known the way (2 Peter ii. 21) of righteousness.' The sin of believing makes all other sins that a man can commit so much the more heinous and offensive in the sight of God, inasmuch as they are sins against light and knowledge: and ' the servant who knew his Lord's will, and did it not, he shall be beaten with many stripes.' Luke xii. 47. While unbelief is not only innocent in itself, but so highly pleasing to Almighty God, that it is represented as the cause of his forgiveness of things which otherwise would not be forgiven. Thus St. Paul, who had been a blasphemer, a persecutor, and injurious, assures us that it was for this cause that he obtained mercy, ' because he did it ignorantly in unbelief. 1 Tim. i. 13. Had he been a believer, he would as surely have been damned as his name was Paul. And 'tis the gist of his whole argument, and the express words of the 11th of the Epistle to the Romans, that ' God included them all in unbelief, that he might have mercy upon all.* Unbelief being the essential qualification and recommendation to God's mercy: not without good reason was it that the pious father of the boy that had the Devil in him, when he had need of Christ's mercy, and knew that unbelief would be the best title to it, cried out and said with tears, ' Lord, I believe, help thou mine unbelief!' Mark ix. 24.

While the apostles themselves, who were most immediately near and dear to Christ, no more believed the gospel than I do: and for all they have said and preached about it, they never believed it themselves, as Christ told 'em that they hadn't so much faith as a grain of mustard seed. And the evangelist John, bears them record, to their immortal honour, that ' though Christ had done so many miracles among them, yet believed they not.' John xii. 37.

And the same divine authority assures us that, ' neither

---

* It is said of Abraham himself, that ' he staggered not at the promises of God, through unbelief.' Romans iv. 20. It being nothing but belief that sets men staggering. And when the whole Jewish nation became unbelievers, God was so pleased with them for it, that he actually saved the whole gentile world in compliment to them: they have been the most money-getting people ever since. And it is expressly declared, that the Gentiles obtained mercy through unbelief. Romans xi. 30.

did his brethren believe in him.' John vii. 5. Which then is 'the safe side,' Sirs, on the showing of the record itself? On the unbelieving side, the Infidel stands in the glorious company of the apostles, in the immediate family of Christ: and hath no fear, while the believer doth as well and no better, than the Devils in Hell, who believe and tremble.*

If there were in reason any danger or guilt in being an unbeliever: if it could be thought or feared for a moment that God would punish a man for being an Infidel—that is, for the mere error of his thought, if an error it be—the mere mistake of a mind, made by God himself liable to be mistaken; what chance, what hope, what dream of salvation, could exist for the believer? The chance of salvation is a chance not worth having; it is a madman's dream. It is a hope but as of a man who is to be hanged. It is a gallows hope: for if the righteous scarcely be saved, where shall the ungodly and the sinner appear?'

But let not the sinner be cheated by the belief, that belief will keep him safe from any denunciation threatened against unbelief. His very belief itself is *founded* upon unbelief. He cannot maintain his notion of being accountable to God, and that he shall exist in a future state, without flying in the face of his own Bible, making it a nose of wax, twisting it to his own conceit, taking the part he likes, and in the sense he likes it, but rejecting what likes not him, (Does the Infidel do more than this?) Does his brain-sick vanity lead him to think that he is of so much consequence, that his every thought, word, and deed, is registered in Heaven, and that an accusing angel flits up to Heaven's chancery to insult the majesty of God, with an account how a beggar's callet stole a cabbage net?

And doth he not, by that very vanity, as much trample upon the word of God, as ever did an Infidel, where that word hath said, 'Is it any pleasure to the Almighty that thou art righteous? Or is it gain to him that thou makest thy way perfect?' Job xxii. 3. 'And if thou sinnest, what

---

* While the first believers of Christianity,---the martyrs as they would pretend to be, who are said to have sealed the truth with their blood, had the seal of God's providence upon them---that it was a lie that they sealed with their blood: for how could God's providence express his displeasure and indignation against believers more strongly than by bringing them to a bad end?

dost thou unto him? or, if thy transgressions be multiplied, what dost thou unto him?' Job xxxv. 6.

Dreams the crackt fool of his superiority to the brute creation, and that when he dies there shall not be as sheer and final an end of him as them? And is he not himself an Infidel, and an unbeliever in that very text of God's word, which saith, and which hath the testimony of his own reason, and of his own senses, and of all nature, and the experience of all time, and of all places, and of all men in the world, in attestation of what it saith? That which befalleth the sons of men, befalleth beasts; even one thing which befalleth them. 'As the one dieth so dieth the other: yea, they have all one breath: so that a man hath no pre-eminence above a beast: all go unto one place: all are of the dust: and all turn to dust again.' Eccles. iii. 19.

Well, then, Sirs! What comes of their appeal to reason, as to belief being the safe side? What comes of their appeal to Scripture as to belief being the safe side? Their ground fails them on every side.

In what then originated the mighty hue and cry against unbelief, and the exceeding bitterness of the saints against unbelievers? How comes the free exercise of our thoughts, which should be as free as air, and our free speech as free as our free thoughts, to be so grievous to the clergy, from the proud prelate who swells in the throne of a cathedral to the ragamuffin that sweeps the hayloft of God-a-mighty's second wife, mother Soapsuds and her little Shiloh? It spoils their trade: it crosses the paths of their ambition.

Should men become unbelievers, and act and reason like men.

'Othello's occupation's gone!'

The craft, Sirs; the most gainful craft going,—the craftiest of all crafts, would be in danger: the craft that makes men fools to make them slaves, and promises them a Heaven of pappiness to reconcile them to a world of misery. All the trick of all the religion that ever was in the world, on the part of those who have not themselves been the dupes and tools of others, have never been aught else than a scheming, greedy, grasping at unrighteous gain, and a tyrannous usurpation of an undue influence over the minds that could be easily cajoled and terrified.

The whole argument, then, of terror and danger, which

the priests denounce against unbelievers, is the danger and terror to themselves. Their 'He that believeth not shall be damned,' when interpreted to its real meaning, means no more than d——n them that don't deal at our shop.

And, as you value real happiness, and solid substantial peace of mind, don't go to their shops,—avoid them as you would a pestilence. In infidelity, in unbelief, let me not be misunderstood, in that entire scorn, that total rejection, contempt, and hatred of the gospel, which is my pride and boast, to exhibit to the world, you will enjoy a reality of safety which the dupes of faith do only dream of. You will be safe from those imaginary terrors that alarm the guilty mind: you will be safe from those chimerical dreams of a kingdom of heaven, like unto a grain of mustard seed, that you must get through a needle's eye first,—the straight gate, the narrow way, of which you have to be sure the blessed assurance, that if you should seek to enter in you should not be able. You will be safe from those bad feelings and angry passions which you see dim the faces of religious people. You will be safe from that bad heart, and remorseless and vindictive temper, by which alone a man could bear to believe in such accursed trash as all false religion is. By rejecting religion altogether, you will save yourselves from that liability to madness, and that crackiness and confusion about the brains, which you see with your own eyes, that all religious people are so peculiarly subject to. I speak this upon my right to have an opinion on this subject, as being, as I am, a member of the Royal College of Surgeons, and having made the structure and philosophy of the human brain matter of my particular study. I speak what I do know, and testify what I have seen. Religion is poison of the brain: by rejecting religion altogether, you will be safe from all cares and anxieties, but for your well being, and well doing in life; and in death without a fear, without a doubt, without a wish, will resign your being into the hands of the good and gracious Father of us all. In a word, to be an Infidel is to be on the safe side: to be an Infidel is the highest style, the noblest privilege, the greatest happiness of man. Let me die the death of an Infidel, and let my last end be like his. And *down*, I say! DOWN WITH PRIESTCRAFT.

END OF THE DISCOURSE ON BELIEF, *NOT* THE SAFE SIDE.

The Devil's Pulpit.

"AND A BONNIE PULPIT IT IS."—*Allan Cunningham.*

No. 2.—Vol. II.] [Price 2*d*.

THE RESURRECTION OF LAZARUS:

A Discourse,

ON THE ELEVENTH CHAPTER OF ST. JOHN,
DELIVERED BY THE REV. ROBERT TAYLOR, B.A.

AT HIS CHAPEL IN FLEET STREET

THE subject on which I would now engage your attention, the resurrection of Lazarus, bears a solemn, serious, and affecting character: and admits, therefore, of being treated with corresponding seriousness on our part. I have purposely chosen it, in order to supply a demonstration to the public, that my manner of treating a subject has ever been suitable to the nature of that subject: and that I have only used the arguments of burlesque and ridicule on such subjects as would not admit of a serious consideration. I pledge myself now to surrender every argument I have ever adduced against the evidences of Christianity, and to admit that all such arguments have been a tissue of sophistication, foolery, and falsehood, if any argument which I shall now adduce shall, in the judgment of any good and conscientious man, admit of a more fair, more serious, or less offensive way of being stated by any man on earth. I solemnly call on every professing Christian who would wish to persuade his fellow men that the faith of Christ is 'worthy of all men to be received,' to submit the things of which he would have men be persuaded to the test of a fair and impartial examination.

Let him reject that which shall appear to be false: let him embrace that which shall appear to be true: let him 'prove all things, and hold fast that which is good:' let him treat his fellow man with the respect with which *he* would wish to be treated: and accept with kindness the kindest offer man can make to man—' Come now and let us reason together.'

It is only in the gospel according to St. John, in the chapter which I have now read, and in four disgregated sentences in the chapter which follows, that there is any mention of this miracle. ' 1. Lazarus was one of them which sat at the table with him. 2. Much people came that they might see Lazarus also, whom he had raised from the dead. 3. But the chief priests consulted, that they might put Lazarus also to death, because that, by reason of him many of the Jews went away, and believed on Jesus. 4. The people, therefore, that was with him when he called Lazarus out of his grave, and raised him from the dead, bear record.'

The name of Lazarus occurs nowhere else but in a parable, which stands as an episode in the 16th of Luke's gospel, where it is the name of *a beggar*, and used as applicable to any infirm, or sick and poor person, as Cruden gives the derivative significancy of the word Lazarus, the *help of God* —that is, one whom God alone can relieve.

It must occur to every mind capable of dealing honestly with its own faculties, that it is at least wonderful that the other evangelists, though they have each their distinctive narratives of far less striking and consequential miracles, have not taken notice of this. While the epistle of the New Testament abound with expressions which must necessarily be false, if this miracle were true. For absolute contradictions, I hope, cannot both be true. It cannot be true, as St. Paul has said, that ' Now is Christ risen from the dead, and become the first fruits of them that slept:' if that be true, which St. John hath reported, that Lazarus had risen from the dead before him.

Neither can the great inference of the Christian's ground of faith and hope, on the score of the resurrection of Jesus, be at all tenable, if any other person, or many other persons, had risen as well as he.

But weighing this stupendous miracle by its own intrinsic and internal character, and independently of all apparent inferences and consequences which must follow from it.

if I rob them of their faith (which God forgive me for being devilishly like to do,) what will I give them in its stead?" I answer, I will give them learning in its stead—I will set before them the treasures of science and knowledge, to no worse effect than to create in them an appetite for extended information, whose cravings shall never more be satisfied with the baby's lesson, nor content with eternal repetitions of what they knew before; but shall demand continual supplies of what they did not know before; such supplies as shall increase the store of their intellectual wealth, improve their minds, enlarge their hearts, and free them from the yoke of priestcraft. As now, sirs, ye shall see the use of so much learning, in the learned languages, as shall not cost you the expense of a classical education, nor the labour of your whole life to attain; but as, by your few hours of diligent attention to these lectures, even with your pleasure and entertainment, you shall find yourselves to have acquired; till there shall not be an individual of competent faculties that had been fairly applied to these studies, but who shall be a better scholar than any clergyman or preacher of the gospel, if he be dunce enough to believe the gospel himself, can possibly be. See now, sirs, how we advance! As, would not a man who had but the reason and proper spirit of a man, put to himself the question,—If these so called *sacred* writings of the Old and New Testament were written, as indeed they purport to be, and most certainly were, " in ages long ago betid," in conformity to the notions of men who have long ago ceased to exist, and in languages which have long ceased to be spoken; who but the sheerest idiot and booby would dream of the possibility of a translation of them into a modern language; or that a sense of them, according to the sense, or nonsense of modern notions, could possibly come even within a guess at their original significancy? But with the simple data of our admissions, as the axioms and postulates of this science: 1. That men, ten thousand years ag , were of the same nature as they are at present; their heads grew upon their shoulders, I suppose; and they had ears, eyes, nose, and mouth in them,— that is, they had the same sources and means of acquiring ideas. 2. They had but the same, and no other means and ways of communicating the ideas they had acquired. 3. The same things made the same impressions. 4. And the yet St. Luke is so far from suggesting to us that Jesus had any such friend, that he informs us, that when he was told that his mother and brethren were enquiring for him, he answered, that *his* nearest and dearest friends and relations were his disciples, who heard the word of God and obeyed it.

Secondly, our Lord repeatedly declared, that no man was worthy of him, who did not forsake family, friends, and all that he had, for *his* sake and the gospels. Yet Lazarus never forsook his family, and abode at Bethany, (and never took any part in the promulgation of the gospel.)

Thirdly, 'He whom God raised up, saw no corruption:' but of Lazarus, we are informed, that he had lain in the grave four days, and that his body was already putrified.

Now for what purpose is this greatest of all such miracles supposed to be wrought? The Almighty is here introduced as enabling Jesus to perform the greatest miracle imaginable, for no kind of purpose whatsoever

Such, and still stronger expressions of unbelief, and disgust at this miracle, have fallen from the pen of the learned Christian divine, Edward Evanson, his professed and firm faith in the divinity of the Christian Revelation, notwithstanding.

It is then nothing but sheer intolerance, and a wicked and cruel usurpation of a tyrannous infallibility, in *any man*, to refuse his *fair* consideration to the calm and sober principles of rational criticism, applied to this subject, as they ought to be applied to every subject proposed to the human mind.

I submit, then, to every mind that hath not renounced the use of reason altogether. All the reasons that can possibly be applied to this case; which are:

1st. Reasons for considering it to be true.
2nd. Reasons for considering it to be false.
3rd. Reasons for considering it to be neither true nor false; but allegorical.

I. *The Reasons for considering it to be true are:*

1st. All the reasons, whatever they be, and how strong or weak soever, which men *have*, or can pretend to have, for believing the gospel, or any part of it, to be true: there absolutely being no reason *left*, why any part of the gospel should be believed to be true, if this be false.

2nd. The narrative is told with such solemnity, such

minuteness of circumstance, such an appearance of artlessness and simplicity, and so tender a vein of human gentleness and love, that our feelings betray our judgment, and it must cost any man an effort, to break the charm thrown over his faculties, and to pronounce *that* to be fiction which is so agreeable to imagination and so affecting to sentiment.

3rd. No appearance of a bad or wicked design is traceable in any part of this gospel: yet, if it *were* false, it is hard to conceive how its author could have had any other than a bad and wicked design.

4th. Even the statistical inaccuracies which a severe criticism may detect in the detail of this miracle, admit of an apology honourable to the veracity of the evangelist: since it may be maintained that they are not more, nor other, than such as a mind absorbed in the substantive *truth* of the great fact itself might naturally fall into: and such as a mind engaged only in giving plausibility to a fiction, would have been more likely to have avoided, than to have committed.

II. *The Reasons for considering the miracles to be false are:*

1st. The want of corroboration of the single testimony of this one man by any other testimony whatever.

2nd. The appearance of collusion between all the parties concerned in it.

3rd. The appearance of theatrical exhibition.

4th. The intermixture of repeated declarations, which can by no possibility have had any other than a scenic or dramatical propriety.

5th. The outrage on all the known laws of nature, and of the character of man, involved in any attempted understanding of it, as other than a dramatic representation.

6th. The insignificancy and uselessness of the miracle to any end that could be proposed by it.

7th. The monstrous absurdity of the supposition, that the miracle should have been real: and not have commanded the belief of the whole world.

8th. Its obvious subjectness to the unanswerable questions.

1st. Why is the whole affair got up in the private circle of Jesus's immediate friends?

2nd. Why waits Jesus till arrangements are made for his appearance?

3rd. Why *quibbles* he with his disciples on so serious a subject, in such a string of riddles and conundrums, as that

Lazarus was sick, but 'not unto death,'—then, that he was only *asleep*, and he was going to awake him out of sleep: and then, that his friend Lazarus was dead, and he was glad of it?

4th. How comes Martha, the sister of Lazarus, to run out to meet Jesus in public, at a particular place?

5th. How comes she to *anticipate* that Jesus was going to raise her brother from the dead?

6th. How comes she to be so perfectly acquainted with the doctrine of the resurrection at the last day, before Jesus had taught any such doctrine, or any Jew or Jewess upon earth had ever dreamed of such a doctrine?

7th. How came Jesus to say that he *was* ' the resurrection and the life,' as a way for saying, that he was the author of the resurrection, and the giver of life: and then to propose such a monstrous conundrum as—that a man might be a believer, though he was dead; and though he was dead, might yet be alive; and though he was alive, might never die: and then, to ask a poor young woman, who was already half out of her mind with grief, whether she believed it? and so she said, ' Yes, my Lord.'

She believed everything; and had no doubt that he was the most extraordinary personage that ever lived, the Christ, the Son of God, which should come into the world. Whereupon she sets off with a falsehood in her mouth, to run and fetch her sister to come and see the performance.

Her sister, upon arrival at the place of exhibition, repeats the speech of Martha, only giving it more effect by falling down at Jesus's feet. An act, for which no propriety but that of dramatic effect can be imagined.

' When Jesus therefore saw her weeping, and the Jews also weeping.' Why! he wept too. He groaned in spirit, ενεβριμησατο τω πνευματι—that is, he made a noise with his breath: and *was troubled*, και εταραξεν εαυτον, and shook himself. But wherefore? in the name of God, I ask, wherefore? And,

' He said, where have ye laid him?' How came he not to know? and where else could he think that they had laid him, but in the church-yard?

' Jesus wept:' then said the Jews (who, it is to be observed, were *weeping also*), ' Behold, how he loved him!' Now what is this, but the language of the *chorus* of a tragedy, calling upon the spectators to observe the process of the scene?

Why, after all this weeping and groaning, must the scene be changed to the church-yard, as if Jesus could not have raised him so well without going near enough, and ordering the tomb-stone to be taken away, and calling with 'a loud voice,' that the dead man might be the more likely to hear him?

How comes Martha, who, in the 22nd verse, had discovered that she was aware of the intended miracle, upon the taking away of the stone, for the convenience of the dead man's hearing, when Jesus called him, to endeavour to magnify the miracle by remonstrating, 'Lord, by this time he stinketh, for he hath been dead four days.'

Why did Jesus make a speech to God, and tell God that it was only because of the people that stood by that he spoke it?

Why did he 'lift up his eyes' to God, who is invisible?

Why did he call with a loud voice to Lazarus, when a whisper in his ear would have done as well?

How came Lazarus to come forth, when he was 'bound hand and foot with grave clothes?'

How came his face to be bound with a napkin, σουδαριω—a sudary, a *pocket handkerchief?* when the use of such an article was not known, and had never been heard of, till many hundreds of years after this gospel should have been written?

How came Jesus to say, 'loose him and let him go?' Where did he go to?

How came some of the Jews, who saw this miracle, to have gone and represented it to the chief priests and pharisees as an imposture?

How is it, that Lazarus himself never attempted to vindicate the reality of the miracle, and that we have no account of what became of him afterwards?

These, and many other similar queries, which every rational mind must suggest, and no rational mind ever did, or can attempt to answer, lie a dead weight in the scale of reasons, why this miracle should be pronounced *a falsehood.*

But, in bar of such a judgment, stands the alternative of the possibility of its being neither true nor false, but allegorical.

III. *Reasons for considering this miracle to be allegorical*

1st. The relief which the admission of an allegorical sense affords to the *moral* character of the evangelist, who will not appear to have been so bad a man, and does not, from any part of his writings, appear to have been so bad a man, as, beyond all doubt he must have been, had he intended to have palmed off this story as an historical truth.

2nd. There is nothing more certainly known of ancient times than that the first priests were *players;* that the first mode of instructing mankind was by shows and pantomimes; and the earliest types of the religions of all nations were pictures of the operations of nature.

When the people began to apply themselves to agriculture, the formation of *a rural calendar*, requiring a continued series of astronomical observations, it became necessary to appoint certain individuals charged with the functions of watching the appearance and disappearance of certain stars, to foretell the return of the inundation, of certain winds, of the rainy season, and the proper time to sow every kind of grain. These men, on account of their services, were exempt from common labour, and the society provided for their maintenance.

The name of *Bishops*, retained to this day,—the *Episcopacy*, the *Diocese*, the *See*, are all derived from that function of *seeing*, or *looking out*; to observe the phenomena of the visible heavens, which was their appointed duty.

The natural stupidity and dulness of the people, the difficulty of oral communication, and the importance of impressing the mind as much as possible, led these astrologers to convey their instructions by pantomimic and hieroglyphical actions. They personated the elements, the winds, the seasons, the sun, the moon, the stars, the months, the days, and so forth; and dressed themselves in emblematical devices, stoles, rochets, tonsures, black gowns and white, and performed tragedies,—such as this of 'the Resurrection of Lazarus' appears to be.

The names of the priests themselves, who had been peculiarly successful in these exhibitions, would often come to supersede the proper dramatical names,—what had been shown upon a stage, would come to be spoken of, as having really happened. The very excellence of the performance would but strengthen the delusion: and as it has been played off on the mind from its infancy, when the deepest impressions are most easily made, not one mind in a hundred thousand would be likely to acquire sufficient vigour afterwards, as to care, or to endure to be informed of the original significancy.

Yet the literal text itself of this miracle, most literally adhered to, discovers that it *was* an allegorical tragedy: and an absolute violence must be done to the text, and words inserted that are no part of it, and words omitted which *are* a part of it, to make it appear any thing else than such a tragedy.

The tragedy really is, the *tragedy of Bethany*—that is, of *the House of Affliction*. Its meaning is, the Death and Resurrection of THE YEAR. The DRAMATIS PERSONÆ are the *year*, represented by Lazarus.

The two winter months, *December* and *January*, represented by *Martha* and *Mary*, the two sister attendants on the dying and reviving *Lazarus*.

The *Sun*, represented by the *Lord*, or manager himself.

The *Chorus*, the attendant Jews, endeavouring to comfort the two winter months, concerning the death of their brother, the *year*.

The CLUE TO THE ALLEGORICAL SENSE is,—the *Sun* withdraws himself, and the *year*, which he loves, is sick.

The *two winter months*, the youngest and oldest sisters of the *year*, to which the *Sun* is *equally* attached, send to *the Sun*, to inform him of the declining state of their brother, *the year*. Upon which the *manager*, or chief performer in the tragedy, kindly informs the audience, that 'this sickness is not unto death'—that is (than which no sense ever conveyed by words could be plainer), that there was no real death, and consequently no real resurrection, and no reality of any sort intended, but 'for the glory of God'—that is, literally, *under the brightness of God*. 'that the Son of God might be glorified thereby'—that is, the whole matter was intended as an hieroglyphical exhibition of the power of the Sun on vegetative nature.

If it were not for a false collocation of the words,—the very first words of this chapter would at once discover its *theatrical* character. For it is *not* in the Greek text, as in our deceitful translation, 'Now, a certain man was sick, named Lazarus:' But, *Now Lazarus was any sick*—that is, not that there was any *man* in the case,—for *that* word is expressly excluded: but Lazarus represented the character of the sick,—the sick any thing—the sick and debile year: and the probability is, that this part was acted by a doll, or puppet, let down, and pulled up, by a string: as there was no speech or action of any sort for Lazarus to perform. The term, THE LORD, in the second sentence, 'It was that Mary, which anointed the Lord with ointment, and wiped his feet with her hair,' is of a purely astrological significancy. It could not have been applied to any real personage: it could not have been used by an historian of real events: it could not have been devised, till after the established prevalence of all the notions which it involves.

The *Kurios*, or person who was to represent the *Sun*, in this famous tragedy, having spoken the prologue in explanation of its allegorical meaning, falls at once into the *corps de ballet*, and speaks and acts in his *character* of THE SUN throughout; and churlishly answers the remonstrances of *the days*, who want to be longer than he finds it convenient to wait on them, 'Don't I give you twelve hours a-piece? what would you have? And as for our friend, *the year*— 'Tis, if he has any day at all to walk in, he is right enough; because he has all the light that my arrangements can afford him.'

Recovering his temper, however, he adds, 'Our friend Tis —that is, the *year*, sleepeth, but I shall go and wake him out of sleep.' 'If he sleepeth he shall do well, say *the days*, for he has been in a declining condition a long while.'

Then saith *Jesus*—that is, *the Sun*, in a PARRHESIA— that is, in the figure of rhetoric, called a *parrhesia*, a poetical license in the confidence of its figurative character being understood,—*Lazarus is dead*—poor Lazarus. In a figure of speech, *Lazarus is dead*—that is, by a *parrhesia*, *Lazarus is dead*. This word, *parrhesia*, positively asserting the figurative sense, and binding on us an obligation to understand what is said, in *none other* than a figurative sense, escapes the discovery of the mere English reader, by standing in that most wickedly false translation, 'Then saith Jesus unto them PLAINLY, Lazarus is dead.' Why then! says Thomas—that is, the 21st of December, always given to gloom and despair,

> 'Tis done, dread winter spreads his latest gloom,
> And reigns tremendous o'er the conquered year.

How dead the vegetable kingdom lies;
How dumb the tuneful! Horror wide extends
His desolate domain.'

'If the *year* be dead, let us, *the days*, die with him,' saith Thomas, which is called Didymus—that is a TWIN, which cannot but remind us of the sign of the Zodiac, *Gemini*, the Twins; to his fellow-disciples, τοις συμμαθηταις, to his *fellow-pupils*. It is truly astonishing that the sense of this word should never have startled the slumber of Christian credulity into a sufficient discovery of the allegorical character of the whole system. A Μαθητης literally signifies *a learner of the mathematics*, a *pupil*, a *scholar* to some mystic art; which cannot be supposed for a moment to apply to the followers of a man who certainly was no professor of any art; but strikingly suits a company of amateur comedians, under the management of an *old stager*, learning the art of acting.

The *Sun*—that is, the *manager*, personating the Sun, finds his friend, *the year*, to have been in the sepulchre four days —that is, during the 21st, 22nd, 23rd, and 24th of December. The Jews, who are the *chorus*, as was usual in all ancient tragedies, are introduced as *comforting* Martha and Mary— that is, December and January, concerning the death of their brother, *the year*. Here again, the word for *comforting* literally asserts, that the whole affair was a *mythology*, or fable; and that this *chorus* of Jews were to *mythologize* with the mythological Martha and Mary.

Martha, in her mythological character, tells *the Sun*, that if he had been present, her brother (the year) had not died: which astronomical truism is repeated by her sister month.

The *Sun* assures her, that it will soon be *new year's day*,— her brother shall rise again.

'Yes,' she replies in character, 'in a month or two,— next spring,—in *the last day*, when you cannot for shame refuse to shine upon us, the year *will* rise again.'

'I am the spring,—my presence recalls *the year*,—whatever depends on my exhilarating beam, though it seems to die in winter, yet shall live: and nothing that exists, however it may change its form and circumstance, shall ever be annihilated.'

'New Jesus was not yet come into the town, but was in that place were Martha met him.' v. 30.

Here is another stage direction, an evident instruction to

the scene-shifters, as to the order in which the scenes were to succeed each other; and to the performers, as to the positions they were to take fronting the audience.

Scene, a distant view of the town of Bethany; Jesus standing on the right; enter, from the left, Mary, who falls down at Jesus's feet; Jesus, deeply affected, groans in spirit. Scene changes to the church yard, the tomb of Lazarus. 'It was a cave, and a stone lay upon it'—v. 38—that is, precisely the same scene as the tomb of Jesus, used in the tragedy of the Resurrection of the Sun, which was also 'a cave, and a stone lay upon it.'

In this tragedy of *the resurrection of the year*, the allegorical personages, Mary and Martha, or, as it is too carelessly directed, 'THEY took away the stone from the place where the dead was laid.' v. 41. But in the tragedy of the Resurrection of the Sun, which was a great improvement upon this, the machinery was much improved; and the same allegorical personages, Mary Magdalene and the other Mary, are represented as asking, 'Who shall roll us away the stone from the door of the sepulchre?' Mark 16. 'And when they looked, they saw that the stone WAS rolled away: for it was very great'—17—that is, it rolled itself away, for it was very great. It was a very particular stone indeed. It became animated,—it came to life: and when *coming to life* was the order of the day, you know, it was quite as likely that a stone should come to life, as a corpse: for if the corpse had not been quite as dead as the stone, there could have been no miracle at all in the case.

Nay, far greater authority is there, both of the Old and New Testament, to lead us to believe that it was the tombstone that came to life, and not the corpse. For we are nowhere told that the corpse was in anything different from other corpses; but we are most expressly told, that the stone was a very great stone.

There is no prophesy in the Old Testament of the resurrection, either of Jesus or of Lazarus; but there are the clearest predictions of the resurrection of a stone. 'Thus saith the Lord God, Behold I lay in Zion for a foundation stone, a precious corner stone, a sure foundation.' Isaiah 28. 'The same stone which the builders rejected,' saith the Psalmist, 'has become the head of the corner; this is the Lord's doing, and it is marvellous in our eyes.'

Now what stone could be more marvellous in our eyes, than a stone that came to life, and was also a very great stone?

But the New Testament is still more explicit in laying it down, that it was the tombstone, and not the corpse, that was raised.

St. Peter, who was the first of all the disciples, in eagerness to visit the sepulchre, and to ascertain everything that had taken place, is expressly said to have seen the stone that was rolled away from the door of the sepulchre. And he saw and believed, but he saw nothing of the corpse: and, consequently, in his first epistles, it is not in the living corpse which he requires us to believe, but in the living *stone* (1 Peter 2—4). A living corpse, we know, is no corpse at all, and, therefore, could have nothing marvellous in it. But *a living stone* would, indeed, be something for a man to believe in, and supply some sort of foundation for our faith.

It is altogether monstrous and inconceivable that dead men should come to life again. But we have the positive assurance of Christ himself, that it would be nothing out of the course of nature for the stones to become animated, and that if the children that cried after him as he rode through the streets upon a Jerusalem pony, should have held their peace, the stones would immediately have cried out. Luke xix. 40.

God, we know, is able of the stones to raise up children unto Abraham.

The term *laity*, by which the clergy designate the common people, is derived from λαος, a stone, which signifies that the laity, in the judgment of the clergy, are little better than stones made to be trod on, made to lie in the dirt, or to be chiselled into blocks and pedestals to support the church. A compliment which we see paid to true believers (and than which they deserve not better) by the apostle himself. 'Ye also, as lively stones,' says he, 'are built up a spiritual house' (a house for the priesthood.) As much as to say, ye blocks, ye stones, ye fools, alive indeed,—but with no more wit than blocks and stones : nothing can be too gross for you. A sarcasm, which, if it had not been deserved, would not have escaped detection, since we find him laying it on again, in the same connection. 'As new born babes desire the sincere milk of the world,' the pap, the lollipop, the tapioca of the gospel,—suck it in, ye squalling babes of grace; you shall see the show, and it shall all be right earnest; and you shall see Lazarus come out of his grave, and you shall see Jesus come out of his.

Such, I am sure, is the significancy, and none other than such, of the passages I have read.

I am not more sure of my own existence, than I am of the fact, that not a single individual who can read the original text, not one on earth, of whom every sensible man would not, the moment he saw him, say, *that man is labouring under mental insanity*, who would, in any company whatever, seriously maintain that he believed in the resurrection of Lazarus.

Is it not, then, my brethren, a cruel wrong? is it not an outrageous tyranny—is it not a grievous oppression, that our understandings are to be insulted, and our moral feeling trampled in the dust, for the keeping up this system of hypocrisy: and that we must pay the respect, due alone to wisdom and virtue, to a system that there is not a rational man on earth that believes, nor one on earth who would dare to say that he believed, anywhere but where he might be neither questioned nor answered?

END OF THE DISCOURSE ON THE RESURRECTION OF LAZARUS.

The Devil's Pulpit.

"AND A BONNIE PULPIT IT IS."—*Allan Cunningham.*

No. 3.—Vol. II.] [Price 2*d*.

THE UNJUST STEWARD:

A Discourse,

DELIVERED BY THE REV. ROBERT TAYLOR, B.A.
AT THE ROTUNDA, BLACKFRIARS ROAD. OCT. 3, 1830.

'For that which is highly esteemed among men is abomination in the sight of God.'—LUKE xvi. 15.

IN a former discourse, I treated that most important and characteristic passage of this holy gospel, which bears in the gospel, without any note or comment of mine, the avowed character of 'the parable of the Unjust Judge.' I come now to the consideration of the no less important counterpart of that parable, which, in the same gospel, and in like manner without any note or comment of mine, bears the title of 'the parable of the Unjust Steward.'

The two parables together are essential parts and pillars of the great fabric of the morality of the gospel. They constitute its moral: they both of them purport to be propounded by Christ himself, to instruct us in the most important lessons in which man is interested: the one exhibiting to us the character of God, the other exhibiting to us what *is*, or ought to be, the character of man—that is, of a

---

* The Church of England appoints this parable of the Unjust Steward to be read every ninth Sunday after Trinity, and prefaces it with the collect: 'Grant to us, Lord, we beseech thee, the Spirit to think and do always such things as be rightful, that we who cannot do anything that is good without thee, may by thee be enabled to live according to thy will, through Jesus Christ our Lord.'

Christian man, a true disciple and follower of the blessed Jesus, the only man you know worthy the name of man. In the parable of the Unjust Judge, we are instructed upon what principle it is that God will act towards us all: and in the parable of the Unjust Steward, we are instructed how it is that we ought to act all towards one another. So that these two unjust characters, the Unjust Judge that executed people first and tried 'em afterwards, and the unjust servant that robbed his master, are the divinely selected specimens of the moral perfections of both God and man.

The gospel, ye see, my brethren, contains the purest system of morals ever propounded to man. It *has* its difficulties and its mysteries, it must be allowed. But look at its morals! its morals! for God's sake look at its morals; and then let any man say if such a perfect, such a beautiful code of morals, could possibly have emanated from any other source than divine inspiration?

If there were no other world than, this to look to, no hereafter, no future state; yet 'Godliness has the promise of the life which now is, as well as of that which is to come:' and a man, making the morals of the gospel the rule of his life, and acting on the principles here laid down, would hardly fail of promoting his best worldly interests. 'He would be,' as our blessed Saviour says, 'wise in his generation,' and his Lord would commend him for his honest, honest rascality. That there may be no possible danger of misunderstanding the moral instruction, laid down in this divine parable of the Unjust Steward, whom his Lord commended, because he had done wisely; we have the same moral lesson laid down in the parable of *the steward who was not unjust*, but returned his Lord's money, without letting a halfpenny of it stick to his fingers, whom his Lord commanded to be bound hand and foot, and cast into utter darkness, because he had not done wisely. *His* account with his master enabled him to answer the call at any moment that it might be made, with a 'Lo, there thou hast that is thine.' But, 'O thou wicked servant, said his master, why haven't ye brought me more than was mine for it? *Usury!* interest! cent. per cent., two for one, four for two, and ten for five.' So the poor fool was hanged for it, though not a sixpence, not a halfpenny had he detained, even to pay the rent of the bag that he had kept it in. But the other fellow, who had contrived that his reckoning should come in to the tune of minus 20*l.* out of the 100*l.*, and minus 50*l.* out of another, was a gentleman to the back bone, established in a circle of the most respectable connections; and his example is propounded by Christ himself, as that which all good Christians ought to imitate—the grand pattern and paragon of Christian honesty. It is the more important that these moral excellencies should be pointed out, and set in full view, inasmuch as we are continually encountered by the favourite argument of a particular sort of Infidels, who, while they hesitate not to own that they do not believe the doctrines of Christianity, yet assert that it ought to be supported, on account of the moral excellencies of the system merely.

What! say our conscientious lawyers (our Attorney-Generals, our *Scarlet* counsellors, and *Brown* mayors, whose morality is all of the gospel school,—all of this Unjust Judge and Unjust Steward character), would you do away with a system that restrains men from the commission of crimes, which proposes such beautiful examples to their imitation, holds out such animating prospects to their hopes: and would you open the flood-gates of vice and immorality which would deluge society, if once men were to set the gospel aside, and begin to act like rational creatures.

So, my brethren, all I say is, let us examine this precious morality, and see how far we may improve upon the mere guidance of unassisted reason, by setting these beautiful examples before us, and conforming our conduct to the principles proposed.

Of these principles, the first and paramount principle is, the sheer summerset and *upsy-turvy* of all notions of right and wrong, and of all distinctions between good and evil, which our unassisted reason would suggest, and natural conscience approve. For the principle laid down by Christ himself, and which must never be out of observance as the guide and rule of all Christian morality, is here in specific terms avowed, 'that which is highly esteemed among men, is an abomination in the sight of God;' of which, the co-essential and necessary converse is, that that which is abomination in the sight of men, is highly esteemed by God. Our meat is God's poison, and that which is vice with us is virtue with *him*.

So that, upon gospel principles, the man whom all the world, and all wise and good men in the world, had known to be the blackest scoundrel, thief, and murderer, that ever breathed, may, for all we know, be an angel of light, and the paragon of innocence all the while.

Who shall condemn when God acquits? Who can acquit when God condemns? If God be for us, who can be against us?

For, on the other hand, my brethren, we may all of us deserve to go to Hell without knowing what we've been doing. We may be miserable sinners, without ever having so much as said our souls were our own. The Rev. Dr. John Pye Smith, for instance, a very particular friend of mine, and the Rev. Dr. Bennett, who are particularly skilled in the morals of the gospel, and have got just the right way of applying gospel principles, would take such a man as your humble servant, well enough as the world wags, and show him up in such colours, that the dearest friend he had on earth should be frightened at him. Innocent gentlemen, be perfectly innocent. God, Sirs, that's of no use at all. You'll be all the blacker for being all the whiter, and all the worse for being all the better: your innocence will be the proof of your guilt, your not having done what they lay to your charge, will be the very proof that you *did* do it: your spotless virtue, your unwarped integrity, will only serve to show what abominable creatures you are in the sight of God, and all your righteousnesses are as filthy rags.

Right's right! we used to say in the corrupted currents of this world, but when we come to gospel morality, we find that right's wrong, and it's ten to one if we don't find ourselves in Hell at last, by means of the very virtues with which we had hoped to pay the turnpike into Heaven.

Where, for instance, could there have been danger of a more fatal mistake, than *that* we were likely to have fallen into in forming a judgment of the character of this Unjust Steward, whom our blessed Saviour proposes as an example for our imitation. We should have thought the man no better than he ought to have been. We should have thought that when his master caught him altering the sums set down in the ledger, and truckling with the debtors to let 'em off, with half, and three parts payments, that *he* might go snacks in the difference; his master would have said, O, you rascal!

It would be an injury to society to let you escape unhanged! But nothing of the kind, said *he*. His master was delighted with him: said he was the cleverest man he had ever had in his service, took him into partnership, I dare say, on that very account, in hopes that he might bring the same adroitness of cheating to the benefit of the common concern,—while our blessed Saviour (just as honest as both of them), instructs us all to act on the same (if not) swindling and rascally, perfectly evangelical principle. 'And I say unto you, make to yourselves friends of the mammon of unrighteousness'—that is, Cheat! swindle! rob! and steal! clap your hands deep enough into your master's bag. Put money into thy purse, as honest *Iago* says to *Roderigo*: put money into thy purse, and then whatever purse it came out of, it will be sure to make friends for you. Make to yourself friends of the mammon of unrighteousness.

MAMMON is an undefinable Syriac word for *money*. The mammon of the righteousness, therefore, means only money unrighteously obtained. So that the only moral sense that can be given to this passage, amounts to no more than the Catholic principles, that the end justifies the means: we are to do evil that good may come: to get money by deceiving and robbing those who trust us, and when we have got it, to make the best friends we can with it. Rem facias: rem si possis recte: si non quocunque modo rem.*

In vain do we look for an ironical sense in the commendation of this fraudulent conduct, and still more in vain, for any alleviating sense of the apparent proposal of it to our imitation by Christ himself. Should we suppose the injured Lord to have condescended to treat a matter of the most atrocious fraud, as a mere exploit of shrewdness, to put up with his injury, and to have meant no more by commending the Unjust Steward, because he had done wisely, than that he commended him because he had done shrewdly, wisely for his own interest, however traitorously and villanously for his master, the moral would not be at all mended: it

---

* Get money, if you can get it honestly; but if you cannot, get it as the Devil may help you to it. Nay, the command goes further than this. For if the mammon were not unrighteously obtained, it could in no sense be called the mammon of unrighteousness. So that a command to do something with the mammon of unrighteousness involves a command to get mammon unrighteously.

would only leave us to doubt, whether the master or the man were the greater knave.

' Shall we suppose our blessed Saviour, in propounding this example to us, to have meant, that it was only the shrewdness and foresight of this Unjust Steward, that should be imitated, and not his unjust conduct: and thus the utmost extent of the moral lesson intended was, that Christians (the children of light) ought to be as politic, shrewd, and actively on the look-out, for the furtherance of their heavenly and immortal objects, as knaves and tricksters (the children of this world) are, for the promotion of their worldly and unjust purposes? Yet,

If it were so (and be it so), I challenge the last particle of common sense and common honesty that Christianity hath left in any Christian heart, to say, if this be not the most equivocal, suspicious, and dangerous way of inculcating a moral lesson, that ever a viciously disposed mind, and a bad heart, could have devised. Here's a lesson of moral virtue set before us in an example of a dashing stroke of villainy : we're to go to school to learn honesty from a pickpocket: to pluck the jewel virtue out of the mire of iniquity to go to Heaven by way of Hell, and to be as true and just in all our dealings as it is like we shall be, when we have taken a lesson from the man that robbed his master.

Excellent morality this ! The more one studies it, the more it improves upon us. It is the shrewdness of the act, and not the act that we are to imitate. It is the foresight, the precaution, the acumen, the intellectual energy, the ingenuity of resource, the skill of contrivance, the calculation of results, the ! the ! what *d'ye call it*, that is proposed as an example to us, in which respects, indeed, it is a matter of just reproof, that Christians should suffer themselves to be outdone by the mere worldly wisdom of those whose objects and pursuits are confined to the purposes of this transitory world: only the Devil on't is, to find out, after a man shall have learnt this moral lesson, and have become a perfect adept in the shrewdness, the foresight, the ingenuity, and all the other virtues which our blessed Saviour was so anxious to inculcate, what should hinder him from taking a benefit occasionally. How long will a man meddle with pitch, and keep his hands unsoiled? and study the elegant arts and evangelical sciences of bilking creditors, picking locks, and forging bills, only for the sake of being able to show that he could do such a thing, if his conscience would let him. But it is not alone the difficulty of the moral problem, which should engage our study in this parable: it presents a difficulty of a critical character of still more absorbing interest, a difficulty, which Christians have found it more expedient to skip and pass over, than fairly to grapple with. For here, Sirs, is another of those ten thousand indications of monkish and monastic fabrication, which betray the true character and origin of your whole gospel mystery. If these sanctified examples of unjust judges, unjust stewards, unjust masters, unjust servants, an unjust God, and unjust men, have left a particle of honesty remaining in the creature of these examples. Look ye here, Sirs, look ye here.

'I say unto you, make to yourselves friends of the mammon of unrighteousness, that when ye fail, they may receive ye into everlasting habitations.'

Καγω υμιν λεγω ποιησατε εαυτοίς φιλους, εκ του μαμωνα της αδικίας, ινα, οταν εκλιπητε, δέξωνται υμας εις τας αιωνίους σκηνυς. Οταν εκλιπητε—that is, when ye fail—that is, when ye fall short of your reckoning, when ye shall have robbed your masters, and are FOUND OUT, THEY—that is, the *friends* which you shall have made, at your master's expense, may receive you into the Aionian habitations.

Now where is the Christian man who has ever done his own reason the justice to ask for the meaning of all this? or who hasn't rather shut his eyes and run away from his reason for fear his reason should bring his faith to justice, and cry stop thief! FRIENDS! made your friends by the mammon of unrighteousness. What honest friends are they? bought friends, bought by money, bought by money unrighteously obtained, friends for whom you robbed your master to give to them?

'That they may receive ye unto the Aionian habitations.' What habitations are they? for which you must pay rent before hand, and purchase your right to be admitted by an annual insurance fee, to be raised (no matter how it was to be raised), it was to be raised. The revenues of the church must be raised, or the church will raise the Devil: beg it, fetch it, steal, starve, or die,—but you must raise the revenues of the church.

And is it, Sirs, because it hath never been possible that

there could have been such a thing as a gang of thieves in such an honest world as ours is, never any universities, or colleges, or monastries, or nunneries, or corporate bodies of congregated knaves, monks, friars, black, white, and grey, Dominican, Benedictine, Franciscan, Augustinian, that we must look for these friends of the mammon of unrighteousness in some other world? In Heaven, you know! in glory, I suppose? These friends of the mammon of unrighteousness are the souls of the poor saints, whom you shall have relieved by your charitable bounties upon earth, and who, having gone to Heaven before you, when you shall go after them, will fly with open arms (that is, with open wings) to meet you, and cry, 'Ah! what are you come, 'twas the best thing you ever did in your life, when you robbed your employers to give it us.' Come in, my boy! here's the best lodging in the whole sky for you: we're all of the same kidney here. Character, reputation, good name in man or woman. Really, you would not have been in the wrong box, if you had never cared a rush for your character, 'for that which is highly esteemed among men, is an abomination in the sight of God.' He hates an honest man, as the Devil hates holy water! And that's gospel morality again. So sublime, ye see! so exalted, so superior to anything that can be found in the moral precepts of any of the sages and philosophers of antiquity, whose precepts, though discovering here and there a ray of dim light borrowed from the Shekinah of the Jews, yet never shone with the lustre, never exhibited that beauty of example, that simplicity of illustration, and that grandeur of moral excellence, which appears in every one of the parables, doctrines, and precepts of our blessed Saviour.

But this bright concentration of moral perfection cannot fairly be estimated by partial views, or by taking merely distinct parts of the system. It is the result of the harmonious whole: and ere we presume to give our judgment on the moral tendencies and aspects of any particular parable of this divine collection, we should bring to it the light derived from all the other parables, and from the whole history, life, and conduct of that divine teacher who did not come to plagiarise and adopt the moral precepts of the Pagan philosophers, but 'who spake as never man spake,' and laid down a system of morals, not only opposed to the natural dictates of the human heart, but at war with all the conceptions of the human understanding.

The philosophers of old, ye see, had laid it down, that honesty was the best policy: and Cicero has gone so far as to insinuate, that if a man should put his hand in a gentleman's pocket, and rob Peter to pay Paul, though Paul might have no objection to it, it wouldn't be quite right; but our blessed Saviour has taught us, that there's nothing like making friends of the mammon of unrighteousness.

The philosophers of old, again, were so loose in their notions of moral propriety, that they were of opinion, that if a man had stolen anything, he ought to return what he had stolen back every farthing of it to its rightful owner, without making any allowance for human depravity whereas, the only rule laid down by the apostle is, 'Let him that stole, steal no more, which, if a man steals as he ought to do when he's about it, he'll have no occasion to do. But if he were to give it back, he might as well have been doing nothing, he will have lost not only all the advantage of that shrewdness, adroitness, ingenuity of resource, and skill of contrivance, which our blessed Saviour recommends, but he will have lost also the means of making friends of the mammon of unrighteousness.

On which considerations, our blessed Saviour not only set us an example of the most perfect righteousness, by never returning the ass, and the colt, the foal of the ass, which he stole himself, because he had need of them: but he has left us the most unqualified and positive precept to guide our conduct in similar cases: 'He that is unjust,' says he, 'let him be unjust still.' Or, as it stands in our text, though somewhat more ambiguously, 'He that is unjust in the least, is unjust also in much;' which is as much as to say, you should always steal by wholesale when you're about it: which, again, is not more than the holy apostle, St. James has said, 'For whosoever shall keep the whole law, and yet offend in one point, he is guilty of all,' (2 James), which is precisely what may be called gallows morality, which, in like manner, inculcates that a man might as well be hanged for an ox as a sheep.

As our blessed Saviour, who was the friend of sinners and hypocrites, and knaves and swindlers, and thieves and impostors, and all other *unfortunate gentlefolks*,—and, as the apostle says, 'could have compassion on them that were out of the way, inasmuch as he himself was touched with a feeling of their infirmities,'—gives them the kindest and most affectionate moral instruction that was ever given to man : 'Ye hypocrites,' says he, 'ye serpents, ye generations of vipers, fill ye up the measure of your sins.'

And that there be no possible harm, and no danger in doing this, and in sinning as much as ever we can, to full measure, as our blessed Saviour says, filled up, and pressed down, and running over, we have the express guarantee of God himself, who, by his holy prophet Isaiah, assures us, that 'though your sins be as scarlet they shall be whiter than snow, though they be red like crimson they shall be as wool:' or, as the Psalmist has it, still more beautifully : 'Though ye have lain among the pots, yet shall ye be as the wings of a dove (that is), covered with silver wings, and her feathers like gold.' (lviii. 13.) O what a beautiful system of morality it is, my brethren : no wonder, then, that all the contention among sincere Christians who of them would be the greater rogue? they'd all be the chief of sinners if they could; and instead of concealing their sins from Almighty God, or wishing to hush the matter up, as any thief who had a sense of shame left in him would do, they actually put forth their confessions; and '*Mea culpa! mea culpa! mea culpa!*' cries the Catholic : 'My fault! my fault! my fault!' 'Ah,' but cries the Methodist, 'I'm a wonder to myself that I'm out of Hell; I have sinned in thought, word, and deed; every imagination of the thoughts of my heart has been only evil continually. Behold I was shaken in iniquity, and in sin did my mother conceive me. I blasphemed my Maker before I was a quarter of an hour old : and I was born so bad, that I feel that if I'm not born again I'll be damned.' Ah well a day! then, would an honest man say to 'em. But is it for such brands plucked out of Hell fire? Is't for such thieves, for such rogues as you acknowledge yourselves to be, to take upon ye to preach in the highway, and to make the little boys and girls, at your Sunday-schools, promise that they won't go to Bartlemy-fair for fear they should spoil their morals by looking at the PUPPET SHOWS! Cannot ye be content, ye Hell rakes, with your good luck in having slipt through the fingers of justice, and had the punishment due to your offences laid on the shoulders of the innocent : but you

—you must set up for guardians of the public morals: you must warn the world of the immoral tendency of Infidelity.

The philosophers of old, also, were always for giving their moral instructions to those who did not want them, and confined their friendship to honest men: but our blessed Saviour was the friend of sinners, and so passionately fond of bad company, that even in the last hour of his life, when he had all the world to choose out of, who should be with him in paradise, he chose a thief. 'This day (said he) shalt thou be with me in Paradise.' 'He came not to call the righteous, but sinners.' His favourite examples of character and conduct are such as prodigal sons who squander their fathers' property, and then come blubbering home to ask for slavery, and broken victuals; secretaries of state, that rob the treasury; bankers, that lend money for cent. per cent. interest; parsons, that claim a day's wages for an hour's work i'th' vineyard; tax-gatherers, who cry 'God be merciful,' with reason enough to cry so: and beggars in Abraham's bosom, that would not give a poor man a drop of water, though they saw him in the flames of Hell.

But that we may never confound our Saviour's notions of justice, with the notions which uninspired and unsanctified philosophers would give us. We have one other parable, which I might lose my opportunity of noting, if I omitted here: 'tis that in which our blessed Saviour describes to us the arrangements, economy, principles, and results of that divine banquet, that marriage feast of the King's son, which is the type of Heaven itself.

Where the guests, you see, instead of being any persons of respectability in life, any persons who were worth a piece of land, or five yoke of oxen, or even able to keep a wife, —all of that stamp, with one consent, began to make excuse; they knew enough of the entertainment they might expect, to send their compliments to his majesty, and they'd rather not, if he pleased, and I cannot come, am engaged in looking after my new estate, and I go to prove my oxen at a ploughing match, and I am married, and I cannot cannot come; and I cannot come was the cry throughout the whole circle of 'em.

Ye see, that the gospel was always peculiarly adapted for the poor: it was always the poor that had the gospel preached unto them: it was always a beggarly gospel.

But, better be king of the beggars, you know, than king of nobody. So 'go out quickly into the streets and lanes of the city, and bring in hither the poor and the maimed, and the halt, and the blind: go out into the highway and hedges, and compel them to come in, was the order of the day. Compel them to come in,—never ask their own consent about it—seize 'em, pull 'em,' thrust them, kick 'em in!

Or, as the gospel invitation is beautifully versified by our evangelical poet:

'Come naked! come wounded! come sick! and come bare!
Come tag-rag, and bob-tail, come just as you are!

This being the nature of the invitation; and no time, and and no rhyme, and no season, and no reason, and no excuse, and no refuse in the matter allowed, it couldn't be the most wonderful thing in the world, that some of them should be in their dishabille, and not make quite so handsome an appearance as became the splendor of a royal banquet. So the King, who in this sublime parable is the *type* of God, and whose reasonableness and justice are set before us, as an example of the reasonableness and justice, which is all we have to expect from God, taps me his royal finger on the shoulder of a poor Irishman, who was there like the rest of 'em, against his will,—and comes it—the good-natured and sincere-hearted Quaker, 'Friend, friend, how comest thou in hither, not having on a wedding-garment.' And the man was speechless. He was speechless; and I don't wonder at it! He was dumb-founded.

But, blessed be God, we can guess what he'd a said if he hadn't been speechless,—we can guess it, as I guess that if I had stood bye, I'd a' whispered in his ear, *Friend, this is a gospel morality for you.*' They brought ye here, ye see, against your will. Now they've got you, they don't like you: good bye! good bye! this is their gospel morality: 'Bind him hand and foot, and take him away, and cast him into utter darkness, there shall be weeping and gnashing of teeth' (Mat. xxii. 13), was the command of this righteous King. Ah poor Patrick. It was a very different use of your teeth that you reckoned on, when you were invited to dine with his Majesty. How do ye like a *King*, Paddy. So pressing at first, you see, that there was no staying away, and so pressing at last, that there's no running away.

And, as if of purpose, to bar off all possibility of pretending that this is not the true nature of gospel justice; or that any greater charity than this was ever intended by gospel invitations. Our gospel ministers continue, to this day, to invite us to the gospel feast, and to partake of the holy Sacrament, upon precisely the same bargain.

And this, then, is the morality of the gospel! this is that pure system of ethics, which, though it were founded on fable, ought to have its fabulous character overlooked, and to be kept up still, on account of its beneficial effects on the morals of the people! Good God, the morals of the people! The statute and common law of the land are proud to claim alliance with the additional sanction of the Bible, in order more effectually to guard the morals of the people. 'Set a thief to'—you know the rest on't—' catch a thief.' But I am sure, that were it true that the Bible is part and parcel of the law of the land, and that part and parcel of the law of the land were to be administered, I would defy the ingenuity of the counsel for the Crown to defeat the legal defence, which, upon the ground of that part and parcel of the law, might be set up in justification of any crime, or extent of crime, whatever.

Is one brought to trial for robbing his master? And what's to countervail the evangelical plea. 'He did it wisely.' And will you, my Lord, condemn a man for doing that for which both his Lord and yours would have commended him? Aye, but, brother Brougham, the man shouldn't have understood it in that way. And will you, my Lord, hang the man for the error of his understanding merely?

Comes a heart-broken father to the seat of magistracy to complain of his prodigal son wasting his substance in riotous living? And is't the tread-mill to which the magistrate should send the darling of dissipation. And is't rebuke, or punishment that your justice will award to the man of whom holy writ instructs to 'bring forth the best robe, and put it on him, and put a ring on his finger, and shoes on his feet?'

Is the wicked burglar brought up for trial, who, in midnight darkness, hath broken in on your security, and held the dagger of terror over sleeping innocence? And what's to answer the plea which Christ himself has put into his mouth.

When a strong man armed keepeth his palace, his goods are in peace, but when a stronger than he cometh upon him, and overcometh him, he taketh from him all his armour wherein he trusted, and divideth his spoils.' Luke xi. 21. And that is gospel justice. Or is't the cowardly midnight assassin, who, like Moses, the meekest of men, when he had looked this way, and that way, and saw that there was no man, smote the Egyptian in the back, and buried him in the sand: and that is gospel mercy! And will ye condemn the meekest of men? will ye pass sentence on a man who made the divine law the rule of his actions, and the very model of his imitation? and who, wading through crime and slaughter, to salvation, will lay his bloody hand upon his conscientious heart, and say,

   'This only shall be all my plea,
   Jesus hath lived and died for me.'

What won't one rogue do for another.

And this is the system which the nation is to be drained of its resources—to support. This the morality which is so necessary to keep the lower orders in subjection,—this the gospel, which, among the thousands that live and thrive upon it, finds not one that isn't, in his own heart, right heartily ashamed of it, and afraid, guiltily, wickedly, and cowardly afraid to trust its merits to that open controversy, and fair discussion, to which Infidels challenge them; and none but impostors would decline that challenge.

Delenda est Carthago.

END OF THE DISCOURSE ON THE UNJUST STEWARD.

The Devil's Pulpit.

"AND A BONNIE PULPIT IT IS."—*Allan Cunningham.*

No. 4.—Vol. II.] [Price 2d.

THE DEVIL!—Part I.

A Discourse,

DELIVERED BY THE REV. ROBERT TAYLOR, B.A.
AT THE ROTUNDA, BLACKFRIARS ROAD, JUNE 6, 1830.

'*Be sober, be vigilant, because your adversary, the Devil, as a roaring Lion, walketh about, seeking whom he may devour: whom resist stedfast in the faith, knowing that the same afflictions are accomplished in your brethren that are in the world.*'—1 PETER, v. 8, 9.

HAVING, in the pursuit of this most interesting and truly divine science, brought those who have regularly attended the course of these lectures, acquainted with *the Lord*: and shown them the knowledge of the *Most* HIGH:

The science leads us, in due sequence, to the knowledge of the Most Low: the adversary, or *stander over against*, as he is called, from the Latin word *adversarius*,* the Διαβολος of the Greek text, of the same signification, *the diametrically opposite:* so that a line drawn through the *Lord of the Ascendant*, which ever it might happen to be, would pass through the *Diabolos*, or Lord of the opposite sign: hence the French word, *Le Diable;* and the English of our text, your Adversary, the Devil, who, as a roaring lion, walketh about, or περιπατει, more literally, *walketh round*, seeking whom he may devour, τινα καταπιη, more literally whom he may swallow up or absorb.

For when this roaring Lion walketh round, so as, in his

---

* *Adversarius* (adjective) opposite, the reverse to.

turn, to become Lord of the Ascendant,—so that is, when the Sun is in this sign, all the Stars in that part of the Heavens where he is are absorbed and swallowed up in his effulgence, they become entirely invisible, till their divine master has passed by.

For 'at whose sight all the Stars hide their diminished heads:'

'Or lost dissolved in his superior rays,
One tide of glory—one unclouded blaze
O'erflows his court.'

And as this constellation, the roaring Lion, has his head directed towards the south, and is coming downward: *the firm in the faith*—that is, those who are instructed in the mystery of the Kingdom of Heaven, are admonished to stand, on the opposite side, and to contemplate the Starry Heavens, *ex-adversis*, as if turning their backs on the foul fiend, as the Apostle James has 'it, 'Resist the Devil, and he will flee from you;' though our blessed Saviour delivers an apparently directly contrary injunction, 'but I say unto you, that ye resist not evil.'

A paradox only to be relieved, by faith—that is, not by credulity, or implicit belief, but by the proper understanding of the science of astronomy, which is *faith*, whereby we understand that this *Devil* is not really evil, nor this resistance moral, but physical and scientific merely, which our text virtually asserts in those words: 'whom resist steadfast in the faith, knowing that the same afflictions are accomplished in your brethren that are in the world.' That is, these τα αυτα των παθηματων, these same stories of sufferings, this Lion walking round in the Zodiac, and seeming to swallow up the Stars, or seeking whom he may devour, which are exhibited in the celestial Zodiac, are a type or hieroglyphical picture of the like afflictions which occur to your brethren that are in the world.

But who, then, could be the persons to whom this Epistle (as it is called the first Epistle General, or the first Catholic Epistle of Peter) was addressed? Or who the Peter who thus addressed them? We must dig, as it were, into the earth, and shut our eyes to hide from ourselves the evidence that blazes before us, that this Catholic Epistle is the composition of a Catholic Abbot, or father of a convent of the order of the Vigilant Monks, the Cenobites, or *continual watchers*, who had retired into their monastery, and shut themselves off from all connection with the commerce and business of life.

> 'From the false world in early youth they fled
> By him to mountains, rocks, and deserts led;
> He raised their hallowed walls, the desert smiled,
> And Paradise was opened in the wild.
> No weeping orphan saw his father's stores,
> Their shrines irradiate or emblaze their floors;
> But such plain roofs as piety could raise,
> And only vocal with the Maker's praise.'

The very name of Pope Gregory, as the founder or consecrator of this order of Vigilant Monks, is involved in the Greek of the text, *be vigilant*. Γρηγορησατε, *play Gregory*. And they who, in the teeth of such palpable evidence, would cheat themselves or others into a notion that it was written by a Jew, must make such peace as they *can*, with the author, who expressly declares of himself (and sure, I hope he ought to know best who he was) that he was a Gentile.

And if ye want to know what sort of a Gentile he was, he tells you himself, in the chapter immediately preceding, that he was a lascivious, debauched, drunken, revelling, banqueting and abominably idolatrous Gentile: though he instructs his holy brethren, that as he was now getting an old man, he had had enough of that kind of life, and intended to become a new creature in Christ Jesus, or to put on the new man, which, after God is created in righteousness and true holiness; thus verifying the universal adage, that the greatest sinners make the greatest saints.

But 'tis the other sacred personage with whom we are now to become acquainted, called expressly by St. John, the Divine, that Old Serpent, which is the Devil and Satan.

Now all of the instances that might be adduced of the demoralizing tendency of superstition, and of the necessarily false, deceitful, truckling, and ungrateful character, which it induces, in all men who yield their minds to its bad influence, none is more striking than that of the process of opinion and sentiment with respect to this divine personage.

Would it be believed, if the evidence were not as glaring as the day, that there are those who profess, and call themselves Christians, who hesitate not to deny, or who boldly avow their doubt of the real and substantive existence of the Devil?

And that dread majesty of Hell, whose fearful name stands first in the Christians' baptismal vow. He first, traitor-like, denies to have any existence,—thus treating that sacred vow as a mockery: sworn to renounce the Devil and all his works: and yet coming to a conceit that there is no Devil, and, consequently, no works of the Devil to be renounced.

But if there be no Devil, there is no Saviour. You cannot take away the foundation stone of the great Christian pillar, and leave the abr c standing. So long as Christianity continues to be part and parcel of the law of the land, its ever to be venerated forms will continue to ascribe all evil deeds to the instigation of this mighty spirit. The felon and the criminal only becomes such by the perpetration of such heinous acts as they were led to perpetrate, 'not having the fear of God before their eyes, but being instigated by the Devil.'

And if, indeed, there were no Devil, or if he were a merely imaginary being: a personification of evil, an allegorical figure only,—what is to hinder all the other personages spoken of in the gospel from being merely imaginary beings, and allegorical figures, as well as he? especially when it must be admitted that there is not one of the personages mentioned in the gospel, whether as man, woman, or child, a whit more known to history than he.

You would find as many and as credible witnesses (and, indeed a great many more), who would profess that they had seen the Devil, and conversed with him, as ever professed to have seen and conversed with Christ, or with any of his apostles: and we have pictures and portraits of him, that are quite as good likenesses as the Madona of Titian, or the Christ of Raphael and West.

You will find no language, either of the Old or New Testament, referring to Christ, or his Apostles, or to God himself, implying any more substantive or real existence in him or them, than the language constantly used in reference to the Devil and his Angels.

But what is more, there is no name, attribute, or title of Godhead, Power, Majesty, ascribed to the God and Father of our Lord Jesus Christ, either in the Old or New Testament; but that that same is the name, title, and attribute of Satan.

The character of *the Tempter* is, in sacred theology, rather more appropriate to God than to the Devil. For though the Devil is represented as tempting particular individuals: yet God is the Great Universal Tempter, who has sent all mankind into a state of probation, and whom the whole Christian world have never hesitated to address and worship, as the *Great Tempter*, in that which is called the Lord's Prayer, saying, ' Our Father, which art in Heaven, lead us not into temptation : ' which would be horrid blasphemy, if leading men into temptation, were the exclusive office and business of Satan.

For though St. James says, ' Let no man say when he is tempted, I am tempted of God : for God cannot be tempted with evil, neither tempteth *he* any man : but every man is tempted when he is drawn away of his own lust and enticed; ' which cannot but strike a reflecting man as a very Atheistical account of the matter, a sort of resolving all things into merely natural causes : and, as our evangelical clergy call it, ' shutting God out of his own world.' Yet nothing can be more explicit, than the assurance, that God *did* tempt Abraham : and St. Paul's most full explanation to the Corinthians, that God is not merely the *Tempter* of all men, but takes a particular delight in this sort of business,—as he tells them, ' there hath no temptation taken you, but such as is common to man : But God is faithful, who will not suffer you to be tempted above that ye are able, but will with the temptation, also make a way to escape, that ye may be able to bear it.' 1 Corinth. x. 13.

The character of an ACCUSER is alone distinctively peculiar to Satan. But though he is called *an Accuser*, even ' the accuser of our brethren, which accused them before God, day and night: ' yet to an innocent man, an accuser was never yet an enemy. None but the wicked, none but the guilty, can have cause to fear or to dislike an accuser. The innocent man may make his confident appeal either to God or Devil, like *King Lear*, in the storm :

> ' Tremble, thou wretch,
> Thou hast within thee undivulged crimes
> Unwhipped of justice; hide thee, thou bloody hand,
> Thou perjured, and thou simular man of virtue,

> That under covert and convenient seeming,
> Hast practised on man's life! close pent up guilts,
> Rive your concealing continents and cry,
> This dread accuser, *grace:* I am a man
> More sinned against than sinning.'

Satan, though called an accuser, is never said to be a false accuser: and in the discharge of this office, day and night, before God, there is at least implied his abhorrence and detestation of iniquity, transgression, and sin. It is Christ who is the friend of sinners: but the Devil is no friend of theirs, nor they of his: and for no better reason than because he *is* their accuser,—and where was the rogue or thief in the world who could be reconciled to the counsel for the Crown, the Attorney-General of the universe. For such is Satan, 'the Government is upon his shoulder, and his name shall be called Wonderful Counsellor, the Mighty God, the Everlasting Father, the Prince of Peace.' Such are the titles and epithets of Satan, in the sacred text. And till they can rail the text from off the book, they but offend their lungs who rail on Satan.

But the most important of all things to be observed is, that though Satan is pre-eminently called an adversary, and the *adversary:* in the strictly geometrically significancy of that word, as that side of the Areopagus is adverse or the diametrically opposite to *this;* and a diameter drawn from any one of these signs of the Zodiac, would pass into its adversary; and any two persons standing opposite to each other, are *adversarii,* in relation to their respective positions, —he is never called Hostis, Inimicus, nor by any other name which would signify a moral hostility or unfriendliness. For opposition is not hostility; and an adversary, therefore, not a term of a moral, but of an astronomical significancy, which significancy will be found as the basis of every one of the names given to Satan; and is the key that unlocks the whole mystery.

For as the Sun passes successively through every degree of these twelve signs of the Zodiac,—the sign in which the Sun, at any given time, is found to be, is for *that* season or time, the Supreme God: and the directly opposite sign is the *accuser,* the adversary, or the *Devil:* so that they are each of them both God and Devil in their turns.

All the titles and names of the Devil found in Scripture,

not excepting one, are the common names of the Supreme God: yet all of them, not excepting one, are directly indicative of the annual phenomena of the Sun's apparent progress through the twelve months of the year.

Nor is there a single allusion to the character of Satan, either in the Old or New Testament, but what bears an astronomical sense, and will bear no other.

The Prince of Darkness is, of course, the adversary of the Prince of Light, and constantly persecutes or follows after him, as the night must follow the day, and the cold and cheerless reign of winter succeeds the summer. As the Earth presents its whole surface successively to the Sun; the illuminated half was the Kingdom of Heaven: while the dark side, being adverse to the Sun, even diabolically adverse, was symbolically represented as the kingdom of the powers of darkness, and literally called *Hades*, or the Invisible World, or Hell, or *Bottomless Pit;* which, indeed, most literally *is* bottomless, there being no bottom nor conceivable limit to the extent of infinite space, towards which the Earth presents its adverse or diabolical surface: and it is none other than the language of the Sun eclipsed by the Earth, which we read in the allegorical complaint of Jonah, when swallowed up by the Cœtus, or Fish of winter. I went down into the belly of Hell,—the Earth, with her bars, was about me for ever.

It is the angel of the bottomless pit, of whom St. John, in the 9th of the Revelation, tells us, that he was king over the scorpions, or angels that were like scorpions, and that had tails like unto scorpions, and there were stings in their tails, and their power was to hurt men five months.

Now *there* is the scorpion, in the gates of Hell,—*that* is, the Genius of October. Count, if you please, the five that are under him, or over which he reigns, October, November, December, January, February; and there, in March, 'Behold the Lamb of God, that taketh away the sin of the world.'

But observe, I pray, the words of John the Baptist, who came baptising, and there he *is, Aquarius,* January, *Janus, Jonas,* Ιωαννης, John, the forerunner of Christ,—have no reference whatever to such an idea as that of sin, or as the taking away of sin,—ιδε ο Αμνος του θεου, ο αιρων την αμαρτιαν του κοσμου—is, 'Behold the Lamb of God,' or the Celestial

Ram, who taketh up, or rectifieth the aberration of the Mundane System.

But that we may not think the worse of our God, the Sun, for putting on this diabolical character, or think him less worthy of our devotion in his state of humiliation than in his glory, when he descended into Hell, than when he rose again from the dead, and ascended into Heaven: the sacred mystagogue tells us explicity, that the name of their king, this Baalzebub, or Belzebub, Lord of Flies, or Lord of the Scorpion, is, in the Hebrew tongue, Abaddon; but in the Greek tongue he hath his name Απολλων.

Now the Hebrew word Abaddon is compounded of the two words, *Abba*, Father, and *Don*, Lord: whereby all good Christians may know who it is that they address, when God doth send the spirit of his son into their hearts, whereby they cry, *Abba*, Father: and we perceive that it was no breach of Christian charity, but a most correct application of the strictly scientific language, when our blessed Saviour told the Jews, 'Ye are of your Father, the Devil.'

The Greek name of the Devil, Απολλων, is the same as the Latin Apollo, the well-known and universal name of the Sun. As in the medals of Nero, this God is represented crowned with laurels, having his quiver upon his shoulder, and the Star of Phœbus by his side, with the Greek words, Απολλων Σωτηρ—*i.e.*, Apollo, the *Saviour*.

That the same king of locusts, Beelzebub Appollyn, should be the *destroyer* as well as the Saviour, is but one among the thousand proofs that I could bring that *the Saviour* and *the Destroyer* are, and ever meant, but one and the self-same being. Jehovah, the Yahouh, invariably challenging to himself the attribute of *Destroyer*, as well as Creator. As in that well-known version of the 100th Psalm:

> 'Before Jehovah's awful throne.
> Ye nations bow with sacred joy;
> Know that the Lord is God alone,
> He can create, and he destroy.'

It is the same eternal Sun, who appears as God the Creator, in that Lamb of God who openeth the Kingdom of Heaven to all believers, who appearing in the adverse sign, the Diabolus, or Devil in the worm that never dieth, who, standing *there*, in October, the gates of Hell, is still the Fire that never shall be quenched. And this is the solution of that enigmatical language of St. Paul, whose purport is to show that Jesus Christ and the Devil are really but one and the self-same God, under different manifestations. The Devil becoming Christ, when at the Vernal Equinox, he ascends into Heaven, and Christ, in turn becoming the Devil, when he descended into Hell, the proper seat and kingdom of Satan. 'Now that he ascended,' says the apostle, 'what is it, but that he also descended first into the lower parts of the earth. He that descended is the same also that ascended, far above all heavens, that he might fill all things'—that is, that he might pass through every one of the signs of the Zodiac, as he does every year, thus accomplishing his annual ministry : of which he speaks in his hieroglyphic character, to the Doctors in the Temple.

'The spirit of the Lord is upon me : because he has Christed me to preach deliverance to the captives, and recovering of sight to the blind (that is, to give the day in due succession to our antipodes, who, of course, are in the dark when we are in the light, it being night with them when it is day with us), and to preach the acceptable year of the Lord.' Language, than which astronomy itself could not be more astronomical.

But take all the names of the Devil which occur in Scripture, and all the attributes ascribed to him, they will be found to be the common names and attributes of the Supreme God.

'I appeared unto Abraham, to Isaac, and to Jacob,' saith he, in the 6th of Exodus, ' by my name.'

    Baal Shadai, God Almighty.
בל-איתן Bel-Aitan, the Mighty Lord.
בל-נה Bel-Geh, the Lord of Health.
בליעל Bel Ial (Belial) Lord of the Opposite.
    Baal-Zebub, Lord of the Scorpion,
    Baal Berith, Lord of the Covenant.
    Baal Peor, Lord of the Opening.
    Baal Perazina, Lord of the Divisions.
    Baal Zephon, Lord of the North.
    Baal-Samen, Lord of Heaven.
    Adoni Bezeck, Lord of Glory.
    Moloch Zedeck, King of Righteousness.

Lucipher, Son of the Morning ; or, as it is rendered in the

margin (Isaiah xiv. 12), *Day Star*, the very name of Jesus Christ in the New Testament. The Day Star from on high, that visited and redeemed his people,—or in his own express challenge of that name, and in the 22nd of the Apocalypse:—I, Jesus, am the bright and Morning Star, than which he could not have said in plainer words, I Jesus am Lucifer—that is, I am the Devil, and Satan. 'And no marvel,' says the apostle, 'for Satan himself is transformed into an angel of light.'

And most literally indeed might he say, *no marvel!* For 'tis no marvel these transformations of Christ into the Devil, and of the Devil back again into Christ, being as regular as the succession of day and night.

All these, and innumerable others of like effect, are names of Satan in the Old Testament, as we find the same divine personage expressly called God in the New Testament, 'the God of this world,' by St. Paul.

'The Prince of this world,' by Christ himself. The Chaldean word for the Hebrew word בעל, *Bole*, or Baal, is בל, *Bel:* and hence Bel and the Dragon are but one and the same Deity, who was worshipped by the Phœnicians and Canaanites under the name of Dagon: which is compounded of the two words דג Dag, *the Fish*, and ע, *the Sun*—that is, the Sun in the constellation of the fish—that is, when the great whale of the northern constellations is Lord of the Ascendant, and seems for the three days and three nights the 22nd, 23rd, and 24th of December, to have swallowed up the Sun. So said the Hierophant of the spell, 'an evil and adulterous generation seeketh after a sign, and there shall no sign be given it but the sign of the prophet Jonah. 'For as Jonas was three days and three nights in the whale's belly, so shall the Son of Man be three days and three nights in the heart of the Earth.' It being exactly three days and three nights cut off from the life or reign of our old friend Jonas, Janus, or January, falling about a week or ten days earlier than in *our* reckoning, which are every year swallowed up in the cold watery Fish.

Milton, who was too good a scholar not to know that the Hebrew name, שטן, *Shethen, Satan*, signified opposition, but not enmity, makes Satan himself give us its etymological signification,

'I Satan, and I glory in the name,
Antagonist of Heaven's Almighty King.'

But we shall not wonder that the characters of Christ and the Devil should prove so much alike in every other respect, that the Devil only could tell where was the difference, when we find the Christ of the New Testament so emphatically declaring that it was none other than himself, who was typified by that same Old Serpent, who, as being indeed the God of this world, has been worshipped by every nation, kindred, tongue, and people under Heaven: and in every age and time in which the world has existed. 'For as Moses lifted up the Serpent in the Wilderness: even so must the Son of Man be lifted up.' Ophiolatry, or Serpent-worship, was the most extensive and universal religion that ever existed.

The Serpent was the universal type and emblem of the Supreme God.

In the ancient ritual of Zoroaster, the great expanse of the Heavens, and even nature itself, was described under the symbol of a Serpent.

Serpents were worshipped in Persia, and throughout the East, and had temples built to their honour, under the express titles of θεους τους μεγιστους, και αρχηγους των ολων, the greatest of all Gods, and the superintendent of the whole world.

By their truly magnificent and silent motion in progression, they represented the elliptical orbits of the planets: and their bright scales, the countless millions of Stars, revolving orbit within orbit, yet never clashing; and advancing, as our whole solar system has, by the only late discoveries of Halley, Lemonnier, Cassini, and Herschel, been ascertained to be advancing the whole together through infinite space towards the constellation Hercules.*

Yet all guided by one purpose, all with one life instinctive.

Their motion without the aid of limb, or any splitting or division of the body into parts, presented the most lively type of the unity of the Godhead, his independence of all foreign support or assistance, his strength and life being in himself.

By putting his tail in his mouth the Serpent is the well-known emblem of eternity.

By shedding its skin, as it does four times a year. It is

---

* Or, more accurately, to a point in the Heavens whose right ascension is 250° 52' 30", and whose north polar distance is 40° 22'.

an emblem of immortality, so curiously and enigmatically described by St. Paul,—'not that we would be unclothed, but clothed upon.'

By its hissing noise it represented the voice of God, which was never distinctly articulate, but always very terrible, as Isaiah assures us, 'that the Lord will hiss unto them from the end of the Earth; and he will *hiss* for the fly of Egypt.' The *fly of Egypt* being the Cock Chafer, or Hercules Scarabœus, one of the names of Jesus Christ, which I explained in a former lecture.

But, above all, its sanative or healing powers rendered the Serpent, the universal emblem of health and salvation, and the invariably attendant symbol of the Gods called *Saviours*. Hercules, Apollo, Æsculapius, Bacchus, Mercury, Adonis, all are characterised and known as Saviours, by the accompanying symbolic Serpent.

The Serpent was worshipped as the Areph, or Serapis of Egypt, as the Agatho-Demon, or Creator of the world of India, the Good Genius of Persia, as the Person of Vichenu himself, in Hindostan, as Vitzepuptzli, the Supreme God of the Mexicans.

Surely, of all ways that ever could have been devised to restrain the Israelites from idolatry (could we for one moment imagine that there had been a word of truth in any part of their history), the most monstrous is that recorded in the 21st of Numbers, 'that the Lord sent fiery serpents among the people, and they bit the people, and much people of Israel died. And the Lord said unto Moses, Make thee a fiery serpent, and set it upon a pole: and it shall come to pass, that every one that is bitten, when he looketh upon it shall live.' Which is none other than a version of his own words, in the 45th of Isaiah, 'Look unto me, and be ye saved, all ye ends of the Earth, for I am God alone, and besides me there is no Saviour.'

And here, indeed, almost from the ends of the Earth, our altar-piece presents you the self-same snaky or serpentine Saviour.

In this emblem, brought from the ruins of the Temple of Mithra, at Naki-Rustan, the ancient Persepolis,—a *Sun*, with wings, and in those wings, as you see, supported that *Old Serpent*, the universal emblem of stealing, the very picture to the words of the prophet Micah

'Unto you that fear my name, shall the Sun of Righteousness arise, with healing in his wings.'

Well, then, might St. John call the Serpent that Old Serpent, the Devil. For the worship of that Old Serpent can be shown, by astronomical monuments, to have been established in the world more than fifteen thousand years ago.

Never was the age or time in which the celestial constellations presented not the wintry serpent pursuing, immediately upon the heels of the woman, who was clothed with the Sun, seeking to devour her man-child. The most incontestable monuments have proved that this system of the signs of the Zodiac, as it is now received, was fully established, when, according to it, Libra, the Scales of September, was the sign of the Vernal, and Aries, of the Autumnal Equinox—that is, that the precession of the Equinoxes has produced a change of more than seven signs.

Now the most learned Bernard has shown, that the ancient Egyptian priests calculated this motion of precession, or precession of the Equinoxes, as it is called, with the most perfect accuracy, as we do at this day, at fifty seconds, nine-thirds, and three-fourths of a third of a degree in a year; in consequence of which, an entire degree is lost, or displaced in seventy-one years, eight or nine months, and an entire sign in 2152, or 53 years.

Now it being known, as it is, to all astronomers, that the Equinoxial point of Spring was in the first degree of Aries, in the year 388 before our present era, it follows that it had left Taurus 2153 years before that time, and had entered it about 4692 years before Jesus Christ,—thus, ascending from sign to sign, the first degree of Libra was the Autumnal Equinoctial point 12,912 years before 388 before Christ. Add that 388 years before Christ with our 1830 years to the present time, and the amount is 15,130 years.

To which accurately established period you must again throw in the allowance of the length of ages that it would take before the Egyptian priests themselves could have arrived at so wonderfully accurate a science of astronomical calculations, in which they have not been surpassed by the Cassinis, Halleys, Newtons, and Herschels of our Christian yesterday.

Thus precisely the same theological confusion and contradiction, upon the same basis of real astronomical science, demonstrates the absolute identity of what is called the Christian Dispensation, and the Pagan Mythology.

Once possessed of the key, the difficulty vanishes. The Holy Ghost is God in the Spring, Jesus Christ is God in the Summer, Jehovah is God in the Autumn, and the Devil is God in the Winter. According to that famous verse of the Orphic Song:

>Εις Ζευς, εις Αιδης, εις Ηλιος, εις Διονυσος,
>Εις θεος εν παντεσσι :

That is, one Jupiter, one Pluto, one Apollo, one Bacchus. It is but one God in them all. Or as, perhaps, I shall more easily find forgiveness, for quoting a Christian plagiarism of the same great truth.

>'These as they change, Almighty Father, these,
>Are but the varied God ; the rolling year
>Is full of thee ; forth in the pleasing *Spring*
>Thy beauty walks, thy tenderness and love.
>Then comes thy glory in the *Summer* months,
>With light and heat refulgent.
>Thy bounty shines in *Autumn*, unconfined,
>And spreads a common feast for all that live.
>In *Winter*, awful thou, with clouds and storms,
>Riding sublime, thou bidst the world adore,
>And humblest nature with thy northern blast.'

END OF THE FIRST DISCOURSE ON THE DEVIL.

The Devil's Pulpit.

"AND A BONNIE PULPIT IT IS."—*Allan Cunningham.*

No. 5.—Vol. II.]   [Price 2*d.*

THE DEVIL!—Part II.

A Discourse,

DELIVERED BY THE Rev. ROBERT TAYLOR, B.A.

AT THE ROTUNDA, BLACKFRIARS ROAD, JUNE 13, 1830.

1 Job—איוב

[After repeating the whole of the chapter, as a specimen of declamatory narrative, the Rev. Gentleman proceeded]:—

MEN and BRETHREN,—I found it impossible, within the compass of any one lecture, to do justice to the infinitely interesting subject on which I entered in my last. In spite of all the disadvantage to the understanding of those who come new and strange to this sublime science, and can consequently have little or no idea of the argumentative process through which we have advanced, I must now resume the glorious science,—beseeching only the candour—nay, the common honesty and justice of that fair allowance, which all honest and sensible men would feel themselves bound to make in every other case, where they had happened to come in, for the first time, upon the far advanced stage of a course of scientific demonstrations; and not knowing the premises on which the reasonings had been founded, nor the proofs by which previous conclusions had been established, should find themselves, as it might be, in a new world of thought, and things entirely wondrous and strange to their apprehension, treated of as familiar and evident to the understandings of those who had the happiness to be before them in the pursuit of knowledge and learning.

For surely *not* to make such allowance, to stumble in, merely upon the middle of a course of science, or upon the middle of a single lecture of that course, and upon the first thing that he might hear, not having heard what had gone before, nor what was to follow, that had struck him as strange and extraordinary to assume a right to judge, or to suppose himself competent to form a judgment, were no more justice, nor no more reason, than that of the fool in the Apologue, who, having a house to sell, presented one of the bricks of which it was built as a specimen of the *whole* edifice: without any more formality of deprecations and apologies, then, I recur at once to the subject of my last discourse, to our old acquaintance, to *Satan*, that old Serpent, as he is called by St. John, the divine, 'that old Serpent, which is called the Devil, and Satan, the great Red Dragon, with seven heads and ten horns, and a tail which drew the third part of the Stars of Heaven, and cast them to the Earth.'

I have repeated to you the whole of the first chapter of the first book (and, as some think, the oldest book in the world) in which first the name of Satan occurs, and where it occurs, together with as grand and sublime an exhibition of the part and character he bears in the sacred drama as was ever conveyed in language.

I have repeated the whole of it, not merely to do what justice I could to a scene that is second in grandeur, in pathos, or in sentiment, to no passage of the ancient Greek tragedians, nor even of our British Shakspeare; and the due reading of which, as it might and ought to be read, would add laurels to the brow of a Kemble or a Siddons: but also, from that principle of critical fidelity which I have ever steadfastly observed, and will never fail to observe, as the grand ruling axiom of these demonstrations, never for any consideration whatever to garble the sacred text, or to quote any passage of it, in such a way as to make it seem to bear a sense which would not be its proper and apparent sense, in the whole context and purport of the book from which I quote it.

This Book of Job, in the English version of the Polyglott Bible, printed page by page opposite the Latin of the Vulgate of Pope Sextus V. and Pope Clement VIII. presents, in its margin, the words, 'Moses is thought to have written this Book of Job, whilst among the Midianites,' B.C. 1520.

It it were so, the book was written before the Exodus of the Children of Israel out of Egypt, before the call of Moses to be their deliverer, before the five books of the Pentateuch; and, consequently, in Christian admission, it stands admitted to be the oldest of all books which either the Jewish or the Christian world have received as of divine inspiration, and therefore, the oldest book in the world.

While its internal evidence supplies a proof demonstrative, which no Christian who knew what a critical demonstration means, could resist, of the absolute truth, and indenegandible certainty of the principles on which our science has proceeded from stage to stage, from step to step, in enucleating the latent sense, and unravelling the clue of the whole 'mystery of God, and of the Father, and of Christ.'

I have shown you, in my last lecture, that the priests of Egypt, of whom Moses, or whoever was the author of the books ascribed to Moses, was one, and which Egyptian priests are the undoubted compilers, both of our Old and of our New Testament, had cultivated the science of astronomy, and attained a perfection of knowledge in that science, which has not been surpassed, even by the last and most refined demonstrations of our own Sir Isaac Newton, Lemonnier, Cassini, Halley, and Herschel. So that many of the great truths which our vanity has ascribed to modern discoveries in astronomy, are found to be nothing more than recoveries, disclosures, and bringings to light of that occult science, which lay hid under the thick veil, and palpable obscure, of a mystical theology.

Thus the great secret of the properties of the magnetic needle, the mariner's compass, which, we are told, was first discovered by the Venetian Marco Paulo, in the year 1260, only 570 years ago, had been known to the priests for ages before that time, had subserved their purposes, extended their power, and directed their voyages, while it was entirely concealed from the knowledge of the vulgar, under the veil of precisely such allegories as these of our sacred Scriptures are found to be.

The priests of Jupiter Ammon carried the magnet with

them, in a compass box, as the Ark of the Covenent of their God, which it was death for the unsanctified to look into.

It was enough that the brute uncurious people could be put off with a miracle. They were told that Hercules had sailed across the ocean in a vase, directed by the arrow of Apollo. It was gospel, and they suspected no other meaning than the grossest and most literal one, Hercules was God, and nothing was impossible to God.

The poet Homer, 900 years before the Christian era, and 2160 years before the pretended discovery of Marco Paulo, had given a yet plainer hint of the possession of the great secret by the priests, for perhaps as many thousand years before his time. The priests of Phæacia had ships that were inspired: and in the 8th Odyssey of Homer they are thus described:

> 'No pilot's aid Phœacian vessels need,
> Themselves instinct with life, securely speed,
> Endued with wond'rous skill, untaught they share
> The purpose and the will of them they bear.
> To fertile realms and distant climates go,
> And where each realm and city lies, they know,
> Swiftly they fly, and through the pathless sea,
> Tho' wrapt in clouds and darkness find their way.'

You see the Devil was in the ships, the sailors were all conjurors, and *Alcinöus*, their great high priest, by these apparently supernatural means, presented on his table the fruits of every point of latitude on the terraqueous globe, in every month of the year. His 'commerce collected the riches of all climates, and the purple of Tyre was exchanged for the precious thread of Serica; the soft tissues of Kachemire for the sumptuous tapestry of Lydia; the amber of the Baltic, for the pearls and perfumes of Arabia; the gold of Ophir, for the tin of Thule.' But it was all by witchcraft.

In like manner the *telescope*, ascribed, as a modern invention, to Galileo Galilæi, about the year of our era 1640, had been known to the colleges of the priests for countless ages before that time; and was concealed from the curiosity of the credulous multitude, under the allegorical miracle, that Pythagoras could read inscriptions on the Moon.

Near the city of Benares, in India, are the astronomical instruments which, at a period of incalculably remote antiquity, had been used for making solar and lunar observations, cut out of the solid rock of a mountain And

Diogenes Laertius, a Greek historian of the first century, assures us, on the authority of an Egyptian priest, that from the reign of Vulcan, or Ptha, son of Nilus, until the arrival of Alexander, there had been observed in Egypt 372 eclipses of the Sun, coincidently with 832 eclipses of the Moon.

It is madness only, or extreme ignorance, that would talk of such accuracies and precision of calculation being imaginary. The exhibition of those hieroglyphical symbols and diagrams in the monstrous shapes of bulls, rams, crabs, lions, virgins, in the architectural structure of the porches of their temples, which amused and deceived the vulgar, contained the clue to the esoteric or interior doctrine, which consisted of the purest and most accurate principles of astronomical science. In the Peristyle of the ancient Temple of Esneh, the ancient Latopolis, in Upper Egypt, its ruins still remaining, though much sunk below the present level of the Earth, even in our own times, has been found a construction of the signs of the Zodiac, precisely such as is received at this day: by the most indubitable of all evidence of date, showing the date of the building of that edifice to have been 6430 years ago, which is 596 older than our Bible date of the creation of the world.

Of which great astronomical principles, the universally established worship of that old Serpent, the Devil, as an emblem and type of the great expanse of the visible heavens, is really magnificent evidence. As, among the many other reasons which I adduced, so very especially for the deep science of the reason of its grand and silent motion, representing the elliptical orbits of the planets: and its bright scales, in the healthy state of the animal, studded with gold 'sky-tinctured grain and colours dipt in Heaven,' representing the countless myriads of Suns, revolving orbit within orbit, yet never clashing: while its progression, or motion in advance, exhibited at the same time the only lately recovered truth of the similar advance of our whole solar system.

Planets, Suns, and adamantine spheres, wheeling unshaken through the vast immense, towards the constellation Hercules, and yielding their place in infinite space, to a succession of system beyond system, universe beyond universe, till the tired thought sinks under the immensity of its own conception. The SERPENT, therefore, of all things else in nature, was the last that could have been the symbol of an *ignorant* idolatry.

It could not have been what a fool might have guessed at, that was all that was meant by the worship of that old Serpent, when we have ascertained that among its worshippers, the priests of Egypt were so accurately acquainted with the whole theory of the universe, as to have calculated the motion of the precession of the equinoxes, to the nicety of establishing that motion to be fifty seconds, nine thirds, and three fourths of a third of a degree in a year: by which the Sun fails of coming up to precisely the same point, in the same given time of his annual course: and thus an entire degree is lost in seventy-one years eight or nine months, and an entire sign in 2152 or 53 years.

Whereby, if the Sun sets out from any Star or other fixed point in the Heavens, the moment when he is departing from the Equinoctial, he will come to the same Equinox twenty minutes, seventeen and half seconds of time before he completes his course, so as to arrive at the same star or point from whence he set out. So that the solar year is twenty minutes, seventeen seconds and a half short of the sydereal year. The Greek *Aristarchus*, of Samos, 264 before Christ, had announced that the Earth is but a point in the universe: that it is spherical: that it turns round on its own axis, moving in the oblique circle of the Zodiac, while the heavens are at rest: that the Sun is a fixed Star, and the fixed Stars are Suns.

The ancient Chaldeans are admitted, by all the learned in these subjects, to have been so much beforehand in astronomical science as to have calculated the length of the solar year, to the mathematical precision of determining its length to be 365 days, 5 hours, 49 minutes, and 30 seconds.

Astronomers so absolutely accurate, as that the nicety of their calculations, even to a moment, remains unshaken by the severest criticism of modern science: assuring us as they do, that since the system of the signs of the Zodiac had been universally received, the point of the Vernal Equinox had been in the first degree of *Libra;* establishes the fact on the most simple principles of arithmetic, even to the nicety of the setting of a chronometer, that that time must have been the 1st September 15,129 years, 5 months, 13 days,—and, if it be at this moment nine o'clock, twenty-one hours ago.

While, by a more than curious coincidence, the English of the Polyglott version of the Bible, assigns the 1st of September, 4004 years before Christ, as the Epocha of the creation of the world; and the learned Dr. Lightfoot instructs us, that Adam was created on a Friday morning, September the 1st, at nine o'clock: that he ate the forbidden fruit about one; and that Christ was promised about three o'clock in the afternoon. (Diegesis, 425.)

But, perhaps, even the dunce who would quarrel with the multiplication table, and whose dulness would be inaccessible to a mathematical demonstration, may at least respect the authority of his own book. And even in his own book, which he admits to be the oldest book in the world, he will find the Egyptian system of astronomy to have been entirely in vogue when that book was written, and the names of some of the constellations the very same as they are received among us to this day.

It is represented as the language of God himself, and in no part of Scripture besides is there any language to be found so worthy of a God.

Where wast thou when I laid the foundations of the Earth? When the morning stars sang together, and all the Sons of God shouted for joy?

Canst thou bind the sweet influences of the Pleiades, or loose the bands of Orion? Canst thou bring forth Mazzaroth* in his season? or canst thou guide Arcturus with his sons? Knowest thou the ordinances of Heaven? Canst thou set the dominion thereof in the Earth?

Here, then, have we the key to the great mystery: the Sons of God are the Stars; the ordinances of Heaven are the principles of Astronomy; the Pleiades are the seven beautiful Stars, in the forehead of the Bull; Orion is that most beautiful of all the constellations which you may see this evening, the most glorious ornament of our nocturnal hemisphere; the Mazzaroth are the twelve signs of the Zodiac; Arcturus is that great fixed Star of the first magnitude in the constellation Bootes, near the Bear's tail; and the Sons of that distinguished Star are the Stars of

---

* מַזָּרוֹת.

inferior magnitude that make up the whole sixty-four of that glorious constellation. Knowing, then, who the Sons of God are, we know who Satan was: for when the Sons of God came to present themselves before the Lord, Satan came also among them: Satan, then, was one of the Sons of God, and Brother of our Lord Jesus Christ: with this only distinction, that *he* was the favourite, and his advice and counsel consulted by God, who suffered his Son, Jesus Christ, to be crucified and slain, but never suffered the Devil to get into any trouble whatever.

Nor does Satan, in this interview with the Almighty, exhibit an unjust character. The worst of him was, that his opinions were of an evangelical turn; he had taken up the notion of the general corruption of human nature, and thought that even the piety of Job himself might be attributable to sordid and selfish motives: but whether right or wrong in his judgment, his guiding principle was, his abhorrence of hypocrisy and priestcraft: he loved righteousness, and hated iniquity.

The character in which Satan is presented in this sacred book, however it be understood, is a character of superior wisdom. His wisdom is represented as directing the providence of God: and no other, or no better reason have our divines for identifying him with the Serpent that beguiled Eve by his subtlety, than that assigned by the sacred text, which everybody knows, but nobody understands: 'Now the Serpent was more subtle than any beast of the field which the Lord God had made.'

From the fact of the Serpent representing in hieroglyph all the great theories of astronomical science, the infinite number of the fixed Stars, by its shining scales, the elliptical orbits of the planets by its undulating folds: the progress of the whole system, throughout infinite space, by its motion in progression. The unity of the great directing mind, by its independence of 'member, joint, or limb' (in so peculiar a manner having life within itself), the eternity of God, and of the universe by its easy junction of head and tail forming a perfect circle; the immortality of the soul, by its shedding of its skin, and bursting again and again into renovated life and youth, and the moral regeneration of putting off the old man with his deeds, and putting on the new man, which, *after God*—that is, after the example or emblem of God, the

Serpent, is created unto righteousness and true holiness these accordances and resemblances, which no creature nor object else in nature presented, by the natural and unavoidable metaphor of language, rendered the Serpent the type of wisdom and learning.

The Serpent itself was imagined to be conscious of all the sublime ideas which its physical characteristics typified: by a bold metaphor, it was *wisdom* itself personified:

1. It was the Agathodœmon or good Serpent, encircling the Mundane Egg of the most ancient theology of Persia.

2. It was, again, the Serpent, ANANDA, on whose mysterious folds the Creator of the world had slept upon the bosom of the ocean during the calm, or period of 100,000 years of the Pouranas of India.

3. It was the Spirit of God that moved upon the face of the waters in the cosmogony of Moses.

4. It was the WISDOM which was with God, as one brought up with him, and which was daily his delight, whom the Lord possessed in the beginning of his way, before the works of old, of the sublime theology of Solomon.

5. It was the Genius of Virtue (of the not less sublime song of Prodicus), addressing her favoured Hercules:

> 'But with the Gods and God-like men I dwell;
> Me, his Supreme delight, th' Almighty Sire
> Regards well pleased, whatever works excel
> All, or divine or human, I inspire.'

6. It was the Logos, or 'word of God, that was in the beginning with God, and which was God, by whom all things were made, and without whom was not anything made that was made,' of St. John's gospel.

7. It was the Holy Ghost, with its never-to-be-mistaken cloven-tongue of fire, that sat upon the heads of the apostles: of which the apostle James explains, the tongue is a fire, a world of iniquity that setteth on fire the course of nature, and is set on fire of Hell.

It being remembered, as I hope it is, that I have shown Hell fire, and the Devil, have no such meaning as the ignorance of believers, and the craft of preachers have attached to them.

A cloven tongue, the most significant emblem of a double sense, and of there being two ways of telling a story, would, one might think, be as little to be mistaken as a cloven foot,

The Ophite priests, who held up the Serpent to the adoration of the wonder-loving world, as they were the most learned of mankind, were said and believed to have received their learning from Serpents.

It is most apparently, from this phenomenon of the Serpent shedding its skin, that Job, who was an Ophite priest, and whose name itself signifies a Serpent, אִיּוֹב, *Aiub*, deduced his hope of immortality in that sublime, but never understood apostrophe, 'I know that my Redeemer liveth, and that he shall stand at the latter day upon the earth. And though after my skin worms destroy this body, yet in my flesh shall I see God.' Job xix. 25.

So the name of Eve, which Adam gave to his wife, 'because she was the mother of all living,' in the judgment of the most learned authorities I could quote, the celebrated Bryant, and as quoted by him, in the judgment of Clemens Alexandrinus, signified a Serpent. So that if we had the true reading of the story of the fall of our first parents, it might turn out that instead of its having been the Devil who tempted the woman, it was the woman who tempted the Devil,—an insinuation almost more than insinuated in that severe objurgation which Milton represents his Adam, as addressing to her after her *faux-pas*.

> 'Out of my sight, thou Serpent! that name best
> Befits thee, with him leagued thyself as false
> And hateful; nothing wants but that thy shape,
> Like his, and colour serpentine, might show
> Thy inward fraud to warn all creatures from thee
> Henceforth, lest that too heavenly form pretended
> To hellish falsehood snare him. But for thee
> I had persisted happy, had not thy pride
> And wand'ring vanity, when least was fit,
> Rejected my forewarning, and disdained
> Not to be trusted, longing to be seen;
> Though by the Devil himself, him overweening
> To overreach. O, why did God,
> Creator wise, that peopled highest Heaven,
> With spirits masculine, create at last
> This novelty on Earth, this fair defect
> Of nature?'

We find the Christ of the gospels, not only exhorting his disciples to 'be wise as Serpents,' but expressly claiming the Serpent, which Moses lifted up in the wilderness, as a type and symbol of himself. And the very earliest sect of Christians were designated by the name of Ophites, or Ophiani, on account of their paying divine honours to the Serpent.

In Egypt (never forgetting that Moses was learned in all the wisdom of the Egyptians), was a Serpent named Thermuthis, which was looked upon as sacred, which the Egyptians are said to have made use of a royal Tiara, with which they ornamented the Statues of the Goddess Isis. But that very name, *Thermuthis*, happens to be none other than the name which Josephus gives us, as the name of Pharaoh's daughter, the foster-mother of Moses.

And surely imagination could not conceive a more express and formal institution of Ophiolatry or Serpent-worship, than that of setting up a Serpent upon a pole, endowed with power, or believed to be endowed with power, of healing the diseases of all that looked to it for health and salvation. For the sacred text is even so; 'The Lord sent Fiery Serpents among the people, and they bit the people, and much people of Israel died. And Moses made a Serpent of brass, and put it upon a pole; and it came to pass, that if a Serpent had bitten any man, when he beheld the Serpent of brass he lived.'

What were the poor people to do? Here was their God, in one fit, actually biting and stinging them into the worship of a brazen Serpent; and in another, in thunder and lightning, proclaiming, 'Thou shalt not make unto thyself any graven image, nor the likeness of any thing that is in Heaven above, or in the Earth beneath, nor in the Water under the Earth.'

So that the poor snake-bitten Israelite had not an alternative, as to whether or not he would become an idolator. He would die if he *didn't*, and he would be damned if he *did*.

'Happy art thou, O Israel! who is like unto thee, O people saved of the Lord!' Only which would they like best, God who stung them, or the Devil who healed them!

But what meant the sarcastic chief of sinners, when in the third of his second Epistle to the Corinthians, he exclaimed, 'Even to this day, when Moses is read, the veil is upon their hearts, which veil is done away in Christ:' but the thick cloak and deep disguising mantle of a barbarous and obsolete language, in the ignorance of which, the Greek and Roman people, as well as the great bulk of the religious communities of Christendom have been hindered from detecting the true origin of the superstition that has subdued their reason. Or it would have been discovered, that these same *fiery* Serpents are in the original text הנחשים־השרפים, *he-nachesim, he Seraphim;* and the Serpent made of brass—שרף, Serap, the very name of the Egyptian God, Serapis, whose bishops were known and recognised under the name of Bishops of Christ, which really *does* do away the veil in Christ, by discovering to us, that Serapis and Christ are one and the self-same Egyptian Idol.

As the name of Moses is precisely the same, consisting of the self-same consonant letters as משה, Mesheh, the Egyptian name of Bacchus, in whose mystical worship the most peculiar feature was, the extraordinary homage and respect paid to Serpents. The frantic women, running about with Serpents in their hands, putting them into their bosoms, twisting them in their hair, and a thousand times repeating the mystic word: even none other than that very word which, to this day, you see written upon your Christian altar-pieces, the I.H.S. most falsely interpreted, *Jesus Hominum Salvator,* Jesus, the Saviour of men, but which really was YHΣ, Hues, the favourite and most sacred name of Bacchus, the God of wine.

In like manner have the letters AD, put before the date of the year, been monstrously read as an abbreviation of the Latin words Anno Domini, in *the year of our Lord:* whereas, the real meaning is, the whole, undivided, and unabbreviated, name of AD, the SUN, who really is the Lord of the year, as that name expressly signified, the *one* and *only God:* and that God was none other than the Jupiter Sabazius, or Lord of Sabaoth, the Dios Νους—that is, the λογος, word, or wisdom of God, which was expressed in the Syriac and Babylonian word, *Aith*-AIN, which is Sathan, or Satan, which was typified under the form of a Serpent or Fiery Dragon, and addressed by his worshippers in the mystic words Io Nissi. 'O Lord, be thou my guide.'.

And there, Sirs, to this very day, in the arms of the City of London, have you a couple of devils supporting the shield, in their own proper shape of fiery flying dragons, and the old Babylonish form of prayer, Io Nissi, 'O Lord, be thou my guide,' translated in the Monkish Latin, Domine Dirige Nos, 'O Lord direct us.'

The City of London being, from time before all records,

under the guardian providence of the God Satan, typified by those fiery flying Dragons: as the city of Paris, to this day, is denominated, from the Goddess Isis, παρα-Ισις—that is, under the protection of *Isis*, by the title of *Notre-dame— Our Lady:* and, as the city of Ephesus was dedicated to the same divine Lady, under her Grecian name of Diana. 'For what man is there that knoweth not that the city of the Ephesians is a worshipper of the great Goddess Diana, and of the image which fell down from Jupiter?'

It has been merely the substitution of one set of names for another: the universally obtaining practice of conducting religious worship, in languages and words not understood by the people: the universal witnesses of the people themselves, to be ignorant of the origin and meaning of the words they used. And the trick of the Latin Monks, in giving Latin interpretations to words of which they themselves knew not the meaning that have caused an appearance of infinite difference, where, in reality, there was none at all, and made Paganism and Christianity, which are in reality one and the same religion, and Father, Son, and Holy Ghost, which are as really one and the same God, to be two religions and three Gods: there was never much to be feared from the criticism of people who were willing to be deceived. So the Monks, wholly ignorant that the name AD was the ancient Ammonian title of the Sun, when they couldn't tell what the word meant, could find out a meaning for the letters, and A stood as well for *Anno* as it would have stood for anything else, and D for Domini.

Just as scholars, quite as clever as they, upon finding the word *Finis* at the end of a book, and making dead sure that there could be no meaning in Finis, found out that F. I. N. I. S. could mean nothing else than *Five Jews Nailed Jesus's Side*, as you may read it back again, *Six Jews Nailed Jesus's Feet*.

They found the name of ΥΗΣ, in Greek letters, the caballistical name of the God Bacchus, set upon his altar in letters of gold, surrounded with golden rays, and as they looked more like the roman letters IHS than a bull's foot, they concluded that J. stood for Jesus, H. for Hominum, and S. for Salvator, *Jesus the Saviour of Men:* while they who had heard the name Hues, pronounced I-ES, clapt the

Latin termination *us* to it: and I-ES, the name of Bacchus, became *I,esus*.

So, again, they found the name of the God Jupiter-Ammon, uttered in low murmurs at the conclusion of every prayer in every form of Heliolatry, or Sun-worship, used throughout the Pagan world, as Lucan assures us:

'Quamvis Æthiopum populis Arabumque beatis,
Gentibus atque India, unus sit Jupiter Ammon.'

Æthiopians, Arabs, Indians, from Mount Atlas to the Ganges, worshipped a common Jupiter Ammon. The mystic name of their God AM-ON, *the Everlasting Fire, the Sun*, was uttered or placed at the beginning, sometimes, but always at the end of all their works, begun, continued, and ended in *him*, in all the varieties of expression and intonation, which the utterance of so many people, nations, and languages, could give it. It was Ammon, Aumen, Armen, Awmen, Omen. But not being able to find the meaning of this, the Monks contrived to give us the word without any meaning at all, except such as is generally sufficient to satisfy the curiosity of the faithful. And Ammon, you know, means Ammon; or, as you have it in the catechism for parish apprentices, 'Verily, I say, Amen, so be it,' than which nothing in the world could be further off the meaning.

So the same one eternal and only God, considered only in his attribute of infinite wisdom, and his all-seeing providence; and as to *that* attribute, typified as a Serpent, the most subtle of all creatures, and denominated Aith-Ain,—השחן, he Sheth-Ain, *Satan, the fountain of wisdom*, has been mo t monstrously taken to be a wholly different and distinct being, as if it had not been the same God who made the day who also made the night.

But the Hebrew word נחש *Nachesh*, and the Greek for both a *Dragon* and a *Serpent*, are each derived from words which signify *the Eye*, and refer to a peculiar perfection of sight. And in all the languages of Asia, the same word expresses the *Eye*, and the *Sun*, as Milton's Adam addresses the Sun, "thou Sun of this great world—both *Eye* and Soul." And if it should startle us from the ordinary state of orthodox stagnation, to discover that God and the Devil are better friends than we took them to be and that Satan and the Holy Ghost are but one and the self-same being; our second thoughts, and the best feelings of rational piety, will, I am sure, admonish us—how much more worthy of God it is to be persuaded (if we be persuaded that there is a God at all), that he exists *in*, and through all things; that he never had, nor can have, an enemy, either as an opponent of his will, or a rival of his power.

But that all the names that have been given to him, are but names and personification of his different supposed attributes, as lovely in Spring, powerful in Summer, beneficent in Autumn, and terrible in Winter.

Which is no more than what the more intelligent of the Pagan world confessed to be the great secret truth, at the bottom of all their Pagan rites.

Εις Ζευς, εις Αιδης, εις Ηλιος, εις Διονυσος,
Εις θεος εν παντεσσι:

One Jupiter, one Pluto, one Sun, one Dionysius. It is but one and the self-same God in them all. So that whatever be the name, God or Devil, Christ or Belial, Satan or Holy Ghost, Demon or Angel, Saint or Fiend: 'be it a Spirit of Health, or Goblin damned,—bring with it airs from Heaven, or blasts from Hell; be its intents wicked or charitable,'—all are but the varied God: they are one and the self-same God, who is above all, and through all, and in us all.

And this is no less than the Christians themselves (when they would own the truth) have owned, by their adoption of that Pagan sentiment: 'Whither shall I go from my spirit, or whither shall I flee from thy presence. If I ascend up into Heaven, thou art there: if I go down into Hell, thou art there also.'

We shall no longer wonder that upon that thorough understanding of the original meaning and derivative sense of words, which it is my object in these lectures to adduce, that God and the Devil should prove to be but one and the self-same being—that is, the same conceit expressed in different words: when we find that the words which we have translated, Hell and Hell-fire, and the worm that never dieth, and the fire that never shall be quenched, are, in the original, nothing more than names and titles of the Supreme God, wrested from their original significancy for the convenient purpose of terrifying weak minds, which, being but once primed with that most wicked sentiment that ever was in the world—namely, that there is no harm in believing—would believe—the gospel.

The Devil's Pulpit.

"AND A BONNIE PULPIT IT IS."—*Allan Cunningham.*

No. 6.—Vol. II.] [Price 2d.

THE RICH MAN AND LAZARUS:

A Discourse,

DELIVERED BY THE REV. ROBERT TAYLOR, B.A.

AT HIS CHAPEL IN FLEET STREET.

There was a certain rich man, which was clothed in purple and fine linen, and fared sumptuously every day.'—LUKE xvi. 19.

THE passage which I have repeated out of God's holy word is, in the running titles, set at the top of our English New Testaments, entitled the parable of the Rich Man and Lazarus. It is frequently referred to, and quoted under the title of the parable of Dives and Lazarus; *Dives* being the mere Latin word for a rich man, and this Latin adjective being naturalized into English, supplies us with a convenient name for the rich man, balancing with the name of the beggar Lazarus, which literally signifies, *the help of God*, or God help him! the natural explanation of pity and compassion which we utter on beholding such a miserable and desolate being as Lazarus is described to have been

It is much to be regretted that the Bible Society, and the Society for Promoting Christian Knowledge, of whose uprightness of intention and sincerity of heart, no enlightened Christian can entertain a doubt, when they professed to circulate the holy Scriptures, without note or comment, should have overlooked the consideration, that those running titles, as well as those little lists of the contents, which stand at the head of each particular chapter are themselves notes and comments, which, though convenient enough as an index to the reader, to show the subject-matter therein contained, may have afforded a no less very dangerous and suspicious convenience to the editor to obtrude his own impertinence, to forestall the judgment of the reader, and to bespeak a character and sense for the matter referred to, which the matter itself would never have suggested, which is not according to the mind of the spirit, but according only to the weak, fallible, and probably mistaken, mind of that unknown and anonymous editor.

A false gloss may be given, and the old sacred text misrepresented, and set aside from its purpose in an inscription, a running title, or a single word, as in ten thousand.

Thus the unknown editor, publisher, or printer of the New Testament, who has affixed over this portion of it the title of the parable of the Rich Man and Lazarus, has taken a liberty which he had no right to take. The passage itself is nowhere called a parable, it has no appearance of being one, but contrariwise it has all the solemnity, importance, and directness of sense and meaning which characterises the most serious and formal history. The presumption, then, which has dared to affix over this lesson the title of the parable of the Rich Man and Lazarus, might as well have entitled the sacred themes which follow it, the parable of the Crucifixion of Christ, or the fable of the tragedy, or the comedy, or the farce, of the Resurrection.

If any one fallible man hath a right to represent any portion of God's word as more sacred and solemn than it really is, any other man may with as good a right represent it as less so. And thus it will turn out in a thousand instances, that it is not the word of God that our good Christians are concerned to propagate, but their own word all the while,—not that we should submit our understanding to the revealed mind and will of God, but that we should submit to their minds, that we should understand just as they understand, that we should think as they think, and not presume to exercise a faculty of criticism, inquiry, or curiosity on our own account.

Take the passage before us as it stands in the sacred text, and no part of that text can be further from any appearance of parable or allegory.

It is as moral, as probable in all its circumstances, and in every iota as true as the gospel, and as certainly delivered as truth by Christ himself.

For though a sceptical mind may raise objections, and conjure up a thousand imaginary difficulties, and inconsistencies, and contradictions; yet a Christian being once entirely persuaded that nothing is impossible to God, confessing with his mouth the Lord Jesus Christ, and believing, in his heart, that God raised him from the dead, should believe everything—that is, everything which he is required to believe.

It is only to bring our reason into due subordination and submission to the great author of our reason, and to read the gospel with that child-like simplicity, and that adoring humility, which saith unto God, 'What I know not, that teach thou me,' and all its apparent difficulties vanish, all becomes intelligible, harmonious, beautiful,—the rough places become smooth, and the desert rejoices and blossoms like the rose, and we are enabled to exclaim with the poet:

> 'Here I am taught how Christ has died,
> To save my soul from Hell;
> Not all the books on earth beside
> Such heavenly wonders tell.'

And of these wonders, none are more wonderful than that awful scene, though not more awful than real, which our blessed Saviour has set before us, in the real and true history of the rich man and Lazarus: There is no part of the gospel more instructive, as to the nature and character of the divine revelation, and more congenial to the dispositions and tempers which genuine Christianity inspires. A good Christian, as the Rev. Mr. Simeon, of Cambridge, says, would not be without the fear of hell if he might. It is a wholesome fear, it is a salutary fear, calculated to prevent their backsliding, and to make them press forward with the more earnestness and zeal in their progress towards Sion, with their faces thitherward.

And even when, through the consolations of God's Holy Spirit, Christians sometimes rise superior to this fear for themselves, there is still a peculiar pleasure and unspeakable gratification in contemplating the just judgment of God as still impending over the children of disobedience; and thus, by faith, sharing or anticipating that heavenly joy which Lazarus must have felt, when

> 'From floods of tears to hills of joy,
> The Lord has set him free;
> And crowned him with eternal bliss—
> A happy change for he."

And to find that heavenly bliss enhanced and heightened, as it must have been to his amiable and feeling disposition, by being permitted to see it set in so strong a contrast with the state of his once neighbour and acquaintance, the rich man, and enabled with those delightful feelings, which none but a Christian can feel, to gratulate his good heart, and to chuckle to himself, 'He in his lifetime had his good things, and I was a beggar; but now I am comforted, and he is tormented.'

Not that these dispositions are incompatible with Christian charity, or at all contrary to that meek and forgiving temper which Christianity inspires in all its humble followers. God forbid that we should think so. 'Tis the very essence of Christian charity. For though Christians are commanded to love their enemies, to bless them that curse, and to pray for them which despitefully use them and persecute them; yet they are not to pray them out of Hell, they are not to contravene the justice of the Almighty. But rather, when they shall see their former oppressors and persecutors brought into the deepest affliction and distress, when they shall see them, as one day they shall do in the flames of Hell, lifting up their eyes in everlasting torment, and calling for so much mercy as a drop of water to cool their burning tongue, but calling in vain; then shall the church triumphers in Heaven strike up the louder Hallelujahs, to the praise and glory of God, and say, 'We thank thee, O Lord, that thou hast judged thus.'

Hence have we the true meaning of that advice of the holy apostle, 'If thine enemy hunger, feed him; if he thirst, give him drink,—for in so doing thou shalt heap coals of fire on his head.'

But let us confine our meditation to the subject in hand. It is a gospel truth—that is, it is as true as the gospel, that there certainly was this same certain rich man, who was 'clothed in purple and fine linen, and fared sumptuously every day.'

And for this offence of being rich, wearing a blue coat, and a clean shirt, and eating and drinking as everybody would do that could get anything to eat and drink, he died, and damnation seized him, body and soul too. We should lose the most important part of the lesson intended to ourselves, as well as be committing an intolerable piece of presumption, should we lay such a flattering unction to our souls, as to suppose that this man must have been peculiarly wicked. Rather let us take in good part the warning which our Saviour has expressly given upon a similar case: 'Think ye that this man was a sinner above all others? I tell ye nay; but except ye repent, ye shall all likewise perish.'

The great and general scope of God's word is, never to show us for how great, how capital, how enormous crimes a man may lose his soul, but for how very trifling, how small, how little—nay, for how altogether unintended an offence, a righteous God will destroy both body and soul in Hell.

For but one hasty word! he that in the irritation of his temper shall but have said to his brother, 'thou fool, shall be in danger of Hell fire.' Nay, for but a mistake in an opinion, where it is absolutely impossible but that human fallibility should be liable to mistake, 'He that shall speak a word against the Holy Ghost!' So comfortable is the Holy Ghost, the comforter, so forgiving is that heavenly dove, that he hath never forgiveness either in this world or in that which is to come, which gives us all the reason which we have to say, with our holy church:

> 'Come Holy Ghost, Eternal God,
> Proceeding from above,
> Both from the Father and the Son,
> The God of peace and love.'

'Tis the peculiar nature of the lambs and doves of the gospel, to be a very particular sort of lambs and doves, that if a man were not obliged to call them lambs and doves, he'd be in great danger of taking them for wolves and vultures.

So the bird that descended from Heaven to comfort

Prometheus upon Caucasus, was a dove. I've no doubt that it was a dove, it must have been a dove, but it ate his liver out.

That the rich man, then, had been in any sense a bad one, is not only not asserted in the sacred text, but not implied. He had only been a rich man, and lived, in consequence, as rich men live,—the very 'head and front of his offending had this extent'—no more.

That he had not even neglected any positive duties of charity or loving kindness to his fellow-men, that he had not even been indifferent to the distress of the beggar Lazarus, who had been laid at his gate full of sores, and desiring to be fed with the crumbs which fell from his table, is implied in the curious incident which could not otherwise have fallen within the analogy, that he knew Lazarus personally, that he knew him in a moment, even *afar off*, that he recognised him by name, that he recognised him, notwithstanding the wonderful improvement in his appearance, after his sore legs were, I hope, got well, and he was dressed like a gentleman, and that he, in a moment, fixed on Lazarus, out of all the company of Heaven, as the idvividual that could least refuse the attention that he required.

'Send Lazarus, that he may dip the tip of his finger in water, and cool my tongue.'

What could it mean: if it meant less than Lazarus is my old acquaintance, I know Lazarus: Lazarus will not forget the kindness he received from me, or send him to my father's house, my brothers, my whole family will remember Lazarus, —we never neglected him.

Now of all the beggars that will go to Heaven when they die, and of all the proud and haughty lords, aristocrats, and rich men that will go to the other place, how many will there be able to lift up their eyes, and recognise the person, or remember the name of a beggar, or be able to look a poor man in the face, and say, *now do me a service*, Christian?

Lay a beggar at a rich man's gate, and how long will he be allowed to lie there? and how long will it be ere the rich man will know the beggar's name, and know him so well as to know him anywhere?

'Moreover the dogs came and licked his sores.' And what o' that! Why, i' the name of God, it is excellent surgery: but when the rich men's dogs find beggars at their master's gates, among ourselves, the dogs bite the beggars, and if the beggars hadn't sore legs before they rang at the gate, the dogs will take care that they shall be sore enough before they get away.

At least, Sirs, nobody can say that the rich man's dogs that licked the beggar's sores were dainty dogs: their master, therefore, must stand acquitted of that title to damnation which Heaven might have written to his account, could it have been written that the rich man's dogs had been better fed than the poor man's children.

But there is a most curious and important ambiguity in the word which our translation has rendered dogs; for in both the Hebrew and Greek, the word for dog means a priest or parson: the priests and parsons, in all ages and countries of the world, having always been peculiarly dogmatical, and always on the look out to bark poor beggars into Abraham's bosom, always retainers about the great man's house, lending him the use of their evangelical bow-wow to keep the beggars at their distance, and make them order themselves lowly and reverently to all their betters.

We know, indeed, that St. Paul, in his Epistle to the Phillippians, calls all the other apostles *dogs*: and, God forbid that I should dispute the authority of St. Paul; no, doubt they were dogs, and sad dogs, only one could have wished to know how those apostolic dogs would have returned the compliment to the apostolic chief of sinners. But it is not literally, but metaphorically only that priests have such a wonderful resemblance to dogs.

Christ himself is the great shepherd of the sheep, and unless the parsons mean to put themselves on a footing with Christ, they must be content to be reckoned as shepherd's dogs, and, like shepherd's dogs, they always take care to catch hold of the sheep by the ear: lend 'em your ear, and they'll be sure to drag you to the slaughter-house. Moreover,

The bite of a mad dog, we all know; is a very frightful thing; but God knows that the bite of a mad parson is the worse bite of the two: in the one case you die of hydrophobia, or dread of water; in the other you die of pyrophobia, or the dread of fire. While all the symptoms of this pyrophobia, by a dreadful analogy, bear the closest resemblance to those of hydrophobia. When the unhappy patient has been *priest-bitten*, though the wound at first may be very slight, and easily healed, yet in longer or shorter time afterwards he loses all relish for cheerful company and innocent pleasures, he falls into the greatest dejection of spirits: he rambles from one kennel of priestcraft to another, as if he wished to get more and more bitten. Hell fire is continually before his apprehension; he smells brimstone in a playhouse, and damnation in the smoke of a cigar. At last he begins to foam at the mouth, and to bark himself, exactly like the dog that first gave him the disease, and dies raving.

But I am the more inclined to think that the word translated dogs, and leading to so unaccountable a sense as that the dogs came and licked his sores, should have been rendered the parsons, inasmuch as we find that they came about him, beggar as he was, for nothing but what they could get of him,—all the charity they had to show was with their tongues, they lickt the wounds they never cared to heal, and never was there in the world the nobleman's chaplain, who would attend to the poor man's grief, where there was nothing to be suckt out of it—that is, if not out of the poor man directly, yet out of the rich, by persuading them how wonderfully charitable they are: and that the poor need no further attentions than such as they receive through their ministry.

'The poor have the gospel preached unto them.' Spiritual food will do for the poor. And when this noble Lord, noble in nature and disposition, as well as in wealth and title, on the first rumour of the distress of the people that had reached him, following the dictate of his noble heart, would have exclaimed, 'What, the people starving, say ye! good God! open my larder to 'em, throw down my park wall, give 'em the bullocks, the sheep, the pigs, the fowls, build them cottages all over my ground, cut it out among them in equal portions.'

But what is the argument of the fawning sycophants of aristocracy. O no, my Lord; leave us to be the ministers of your bounty: we'll attend to the poor for you, and do't at a hundredth part of the expense: we'll go from house to house: we'll give 'em Bibles and religious tracts, and make 'em so contented, and so humble, and so setting their affections on things above, that you cannot think, my Lord, how calmly they'll submit to the dispensations of divine providence, how meekly they'll lie down like rats in ditches, and how happy they'll die. Give us the money, my Lord, and we'll give them the gospel. It's none but infidels that ever intermeddle with politics; let us be-gospel them enough, and then the lily-livered idiots will bear starvation patiently, and they'll die. Ah, my Lord, you cannot think how happy they'll die.

Thus it may seem remarkable, that the gospel dogs should have paid such peculiar attention to the beggar's sore legs: but it is not more remarkable than the fact, that the gospel dogs among ourselves would have nothing to do with their tongues, if it were not for the weaknesses in poor people's understandings.

But we come to the character of the rich man, whose utmost extent of crime,—and let it, if you please, seem to be a crime,—was, that he did by deputy what he should have done himself, and left his knowledge of the state of the poor to be conveyed to him by the reports and representations of those reverend dogs, who betray the rich and the great into an indifference and neglect of their fellow-creatures, of which they never would be guilty, by preaching gospel and patience to the starving people.

But this neglect overlooked, there is no evidence of a cruel or malicious disposition, nor of any fault that could have deserved condemnation in this unfortunate aristocrat. That he had really not been an uncharitable man on earth is evinced by the presumption, *à fortiori*, from the benevolence and goodness of heart which he retained, even in Hell: which induced him to pray for the conversion of his five brethren, and so earnestly to entreat, that even a miracle might be wrought, though not to give a drop of water to himself, yet to save and rescue them.

Now, Sirs, we are either to have ideas on the matter set before us, or 'tis no matter, the thing that will bear to be believed, will bear to be imagined.

Look, priests, at the picture ye have set before us. Look at this grand display of the divine justice. Behold the man whom an Almighty God has endued with an eternal existence to undergo eternal misery.

'For though,' said he, 'I am tormented in this flame,

though all I asked was but the mitigation of a drop of water,

> And none of you will bid the Winter come,
> To thrust his icy fingers in my maw;
> Nor let my kingdom's rivers take their course
> Through my burned bosom; nor entreat the north
> To make his bleak winds kiss my parched lips,
> And comfort me with cold,—

Yet—yet be merciful, where yet thou mayst be mercifu for I have five brethren. Though not to me, be mercifu to them, and send Lazarus to my father's house, that he may testify unto them, lest they also come into this place of torment. They have Moses and the prophets, said the inexorable tyrant,—let them hear them. Thus, with fiend-like malignity, pleased to keep up a religion, whose evidence had been actually proved to be defective, and which was incapable of carrying conviction to the mind, for the purpose of getting an excuse to condemn them. 'Nay, father Abraham,' said he, 'but if one went unto them from the dead, they would repent.'

How earnest is his entreaty, how irrefutable his remonstance; and this, to obtain a benefit for others, from which no possible advantage could accrue to himself, an infinite benefit, for which the party served would never know to whom they were indebted for the service, which their thanks would never acknowledge, their gratitude never repay: pitying others, though he unpitied, and in an intensity of pain and anguish, the remembrance of one hour's endurance of which, even by his deadliest enemy, would pluck commiseration of his state

> From brassy bosoms and rough hearts of steel,
> From stubborn Turks, and Tartars never trained
> To offices of gentle courtesy.

Engaged in meditations of benevolence, in purposes of charity and love, hoping still, when all other hope was gone; yet—yet to serve mankind! And this man damned! Eternal God, didst thou ever create a better man?

But Christian malignity, the most damnable of all malignity, must have its hellish gratification.

The poet Young, the celebrated author of the 'Night Thoughts,' thoughts dark as night, as indeed they are, has lent the powers of his poetic talent to realize this frightful picture to our imaginations, and given us the very words in which he supposes this soul in Hell, would put up its petition to the Almighty:

> 'Grant me, great God, at least,
> This one, this simple, almost no request,
> When I have wept a thousand lives away,
> When torment has grown weary of its prey,
> When I have raved ten thousand years in fire,
> Ten thousand thousands, let me then expire.'

But even that relief, like the drop of water to cool his tongue, was more than the affordings of infinite goodness and mercy!

And the setters up of a tale like this talk of blasphemy! These men call me a blasphemer! These men cast me into a dungeon, imprisoned me in the gaols of felony and crime, and bound me in penalties beyond my utmost means of payment, that I should not blaspheme: These men who have represented the character of God as that of so great a monster of iniquity and cruelty, so foul a fiend of mischief and malignity, that at the bare imagining, the cheek of man doth blanch to chalky whiteness, and the seated heart knocks at the ribs against the use of nature.

These men talk of blasphemy; these men who, if such a crime could possibly exist, are themselves the most wicked blasphemers, and the most impious of the whole human race: these men would be guardians of the morals of the people.

And mark their honesty,—they preach to the people what they don't believe themselves, and we have the express counsel of Bishop Burnet, in his Latin treatise, 'De Statu Mortuorum,' addressed to all the inferior clergy, to advise and command them to preach the doctrine of the eternity of Hell torments: though they knew it to be a lie, because the people must be frightened; because it was the principle of fear alone that could tame the people into submission, and make them the slaves and cowards, that 'tis most convenient to their betters that they should be.

And what's the political gist on't, Sirs?

You'd have reform in parliament, would you? you'd ha liberty; you'd have equal right between man and man you'd have your property to be your own; you'd have something like justice upon earth.

And you'd get the beggar Lazarus to help you to it. You hope his distress, his hunger, his wounds, would sting him into action, and that he'd have one struggle for existence ere he died. Then you must drive away the dogs which the rich man sends to dress his wounds with their tongues, to palaver, and coax, and lick him into patience.

Can we wonder that Christians should have been as they at this day are, and in all ages of the world ever have been, the most wicked, fraudulent, barbarous, and cruel of all that were ever in the world, when we see in their very gospel itself the doctrines, the examples, the precepts, that could have no other possible tendency than to make them such.

Look at the Christian description of God! and imagine for us, if ye could, a more sanguinary tyrant, a more ferocious villian. Your priests have set up a monster, compared with whom Moloch, Juggernaut, and the Devil himself, was innocent; and then talked of his infinite goodness and mercy.

Look at your gospel rich men, betrayed by the dogs that fed upon their bounty, into an oversight of the duties that man owes to man, taught that faith will do instead of charity for the rich, and crucified lamb better than roast mutton for the poor.

And look at your poor, your be-gospelled poor,—your beggarly Lazarus, faint and wounded, sick and sore, contented to have their grievances licked over by the tongues of the curs and puppies of salvation, content to lie down and die, because it'd be a sin ' to covet and desire other men's goods.'

And, instead of meeting their enemies in the gate, with the generous indignation, as far from malice as from fear, that would say, ' *D'ye think we'll starve and die to please you, we'll see you d—d first.*' They put one the cart before the horse, and seem to say, ' O no, we'll starve and die first; and then, through God-a'-mighty's mercy, we shall see them damned afterwards.'

Pretty amiable babes of grace and sucklings of the gospel; they'll never resist the powers that be; they'll keep out of broils on earth, the broils they long for is an everlasting broil. They wouldn't say to the rich man, *let us live as well as you: give us but fair play, and we are friends.* But they prefer to rot on dunghills, festering in malignity, and glutting the cookings of a cowardly revenge by meditating how eternally cruel, and how everlastingly spiteful they can be: and all this, and all the vices besides which afflict society, are owing solely to the clergy: and to that horrible madness with which the clergy, for their aggrandisement, have bitten the people. Lend me your aid, Sirs, in this glorious war in which we are engaged, to drive away the *dogs of Hell*, and we shall have no more beggars lying down and dying at rich men's gates, and no more rich men indifferent to the griefs and sufferings of the poor. We shall hear no more of an imaginary Hell in another world, and have no more of a real Hell in this.

But good feeling, kind-heartedness, and mutual respect of man for man, of the very highest for the very lowest, will prevail over all the world,—the true millenium of universal brotherhood among men will arrive,—and we—we alone, who shall have treated the Christian religion, and everything which bears the name of religion, with the contempt and hatred that it merits, shall have hastened the arrival of that millenium.

Delenda est Carthago.

The Devil's Pulpit.

"AND A BONNIE PULPIT IT IS."—*Allan Cunningham.*

No. 7.—Vol. II.]   [Price 2*d.*

THE DAY OF TEMPTATION IN THE WILDERNESS:

A Discourse,

DELIVERED BY THE REV. ROBERT TAYLOR, B.A. AT THE ROTUNDA, BLACKFRIARS ROAD, SEPT. 5, 1830.

'*Forty years long was I grieved with this generation, and said: It is a people that do err in their hearts, for they have not known my ways,—unto whom I sware in my wrath that they should not enter into my rest.*'—PSALM xcv. 10.

If ever one were disposed to deny that men are rational beings, and to think with the melancholy *Jacques*, that asses, dogs, and mules, are their superiors : it is, when one reflects, that in a hundred thousand churches and chapels, there are millions of these self-called *rational* beings, who will be muttering this sort of language, and think that they are paying the highest homage to God by doing so.

For what poor Devil d'ye suppose they could mean was it who was in the fret for forty years, and who swore, 'and swore in his wrath?' Ask them: you have their answer, 'He is the Lord our God, and we are the people of his pasture, the sheep of his hands.' Sheep, indeed! No! They are no sheep, it is a slander on the brute creation to call them sheep,—no sheep on earth were ever half so sheepish,—no creatures that ever God created did ever so abuse the powers and faculties he gave them, as the things who have imagined a Deity, as if for the sake of insulting him, and imagined him to be such as the meanest of themselves would be ashamed of being; ascribing to *his* glory and honour a character that would disgrace a scarecrow in a garden.

'Tis of their God, of him that made them, that they tell us, that ' Forty years long was he grieved with that generation,' and *said:*

Nor was saying enough for him, but he swore, of which swearing the apostle tells us, that because he could swear by no greater, he swore by himself; and so God swore by God, that they should never enter into his rest. And 'tis on this text that the Holy Father, Origen, with an amiable inconsistency, builds his doctrine of the non-eternity, or only temporary continuance of the torments of the damned : his argument being, that inasmuch as God swore in his wrath, that they should never enter into his rest,—that very swearing is a proof that they most certainly *shall* enter into his rest : because, when he swore that they should not, that was in his rage; and 'tis not to be expected that he should stand to it in his cooler moments. And these men call us blasphemers.

I would relieve them of this mystery of iniquity : I would disembarrass them of this reproach on human understanding. I would point out a latent significancy, where none of their preachers have been able to do so, which shall rescue the character of the Psalmograph from the opprobrium of ever having intended such idiotcy as the literal sense presents, and prove to you that there was no such forty years grieving, no wrath, no swearing, no angry God, and no rebellious people, and no occurrence or existence of any such events or circumstances as ignorance has persuaded itself, and priestly pride and cunning would persuade others, had existed.

The solution of this problem will bring us to the conclusion of our analysis of the subject matter of the five books, called the Pentateuch—*i.e.*, Genesis, Exodus, Leviticus, Numbers, Deuteronomy.

Genesis, referring to a cosmogony, or imaginary creation of the world.

Exodus, to an equally imaginary coming up of the Stars from below the horizon, their house of bondage, into the regions of the milky way, the land flowing with milk and honey.

Leviticus, the book of priestcraft, or directions to the priests for the conducting of the mysteries, rites, and ceremonies, necessary to overawe and overreach the understandings of the bearded and whiskered babes and sucklings of salvation.

Numbers, the book of allegorical arithmetic.

Deuteronomy, so called from δευτερος Νομος. second sense, the book of double entendre, in which one thing is said and another intended: and it is not the first, but the second,— a deep and hidden sense, which the wise are to look for in this enigmatical treatise.

It being the principle on which all these books have been written, that 'none of the wicked shall understand, but the wise shall understand.'

'And 'tis a more than curious analogy, which will strike the observers of the latent science contained in these five sacred books, how curiously they answer in character to the five first rules of arithmetic.

Genesis, is Addition, a mere adding together of a succession of stories, which lose nothing in the telling.

Exodus, is Subtraction, a drawing out or taking away of the chosen people from the remainder.

Leviticus, is Multiplication, of which all the benefit goes to the clergy.

Numbers, is Division, the whole book presenting no other reason for having that title, than as detailing the divisions of the tribes of Israel.

Deuteronomy, is Reduction, in which the human understanding, following the letter, is reduced to the lowest degree of degradation and ignorance, or perceiving the mystic sense and significancy, is brought back to the first principles of astronomical science.

It is certain, however, absolutely certain: and in this respect we indulge no conjecture, and stand on no ground less firm and sure than that, than which, there is no ground of truth more firm and sure to man.

That there is no evidence to make out the shadow of a title of any particular nation, race, or people, to any particular property, or peculiar relationship to the subjects or heroes of these sacred books.

They are not Jewish books: the people called Jews among ourselves, and pretending to be descendants of the race of

Israel, have no more to do with these books, have no more part nor lot in the matter, and are no more descended from the entities of which these books treat, than they are from the inhabitants of the Moon.

While there *is* evidence, and it is certain, that among every nation, language, people, and race of men upon earth, that ever possessed, or pretended to possess, religious legends of any sort,—those religious legends were precisely of the same sort as these, told precisely the same sort of a story, with the same views and ends.

Every nation upon earth has had its Book of Genesis, or fabulous creation of the world, created, as we may be sure their priests would persuade them, with a peculiar view to give origination, consequence, and dignity, to no nation but themselves. So that it was no peculiar bit of Jewish impudence, which we meet with in that humble prayer of their prophet Esdras: 'O Lord God of Abraham, of Isaac, and of Jacob, thou madest the world for our sakes only; but as for all other people which sprang from Adam, thou hast said that they are nothing, and hast likened them unto spittle, and to a drop which falleth from a bucket.'

Every nation upon earth had, in like manner, its Book of Exodus, or fabulous legend, which supplied the place of a history of the supposed origination of their line of ancestry. The Odyssey of Homer, the Æneis of Virgil, are each of them Books of Exoduses, detailing the supposed wanderings and sufferings, bondages and comings out of bondage, of the imaginary founders or fathers of the Greek and Roman nations,—with the only difference, that *they* are better Exoduses, more congruous with themselves, more within the limits of poetical probability, though not more true than the Mosaic Exodus.

Thus that of Greece begins:—

> 'Tho' man for wisdom's various arts renowned,
> Long exercised in woes : O muse resound,
> Who, when his arms had wrought the destined fall
> Of sacred Troy, and raised her Heaven-built wall,
> Thro' various climes, with ceaseless ardour strayed,
> Their manners noted, and their realms surveyed.'

But the whole argument of the Æneis may be read as a poetical version of the contents of the Books of Exodus, Leviticus, Numbers, and Deuteronomy.

'Arms, and the man I sing, who forced by fate,
And haughty Pharaoh's unrelenting hate,
Expelled and excited, left the Egyptian shore,
Long labours both by sea and land he bore;
And in the doubtful war, before he won
The promised land, and built the destined town,
His banished Gods restored to rites divine,
And settled sure succession in his line,
From whence the race of Alban fathers come,
And the long glories of majestic Rome.'

No man, whose understanding were two degrees above idiotcy, would for a moment think that there was a word of truth in either of these Exoduses, or that they were ever intended to pass for truth.

The Exoduses, of more barbarous nations, are precisely of the same character, less artful and poetical, but not on that account more probable or more respectable.

Nor would a sensible man for a moment think of ascribing the wonderful resemblance of the general character of these Exoduses, to so childish a conceit as the supposition, that the very silliest of them had a foundation in fact and real history, and that all the rest were plagiarisms, and borrowed from that original.

It is not the sameness of character and closeness of resemblance of the pretended histories and derivations of nations, which presents any difficulty of solution to the reflecting mind: a moment's reflection admonishing us, that all men having the same physical organization, and receiving ideas only from the same sort of impressions on their five senses, the difficulty would have been to imagine how there might or possibly could have been any material difference in their religious fables.

The tales of the nursery, the lullabies that put children to sleep, and the wonderments that frighten them into good behaviour, are the same from China to Peru; because man's childish nature is the same.

The same love of the marvellous, the same desire and wish to be imposed on, and the same intolerant pride and vanity which makes a fool ready to murder a man rather than have the pretty tale which he once took to be true, shown to be a fable, or explained to some sense in which he had not been able to understand it, accounts for the sameness of the superstitions of human animals, from the

Ganges to the Thames, from the squeeling savages of the woods to the Psalm-smitting ourang-outangs of the cities.

Nothing could be too wonderful to be true, and 'nothing was impossible to God,' were sufficient apologies for the grossest sense which the ignorant could attach to the allegories under which the learned were driven to protect the feebleness of infant science.

Thus the first men of mind, the first who rose to an intellectual ascendancy over the barbarous herds, were driven into priestcraft by a necessity of self-preservation. The lie was demanded from them, whether they would or not. They were called on to give an account to the savages of their ancestry and history, where no vestige, no memorial, had marked a trace of the wanderings and starvations, wars and victories of generations that had gone by, as traceless as the pathway of the keel through the waves.

But the savages must be satisfied,—and the tomahawk and the scalping knife would have avenged the disappointment of their vanity. Had the truth been told them, or anything like the truth, they could not have stood it, they could not have borne it,—they must have a history, the more marvellous and impossible, the more evangelical. And all the poor priest, who wished to live, had to provide for, was to lay it on thick enough. And hence arose each particular nation's Exodus, or book of marvellous history, in which their priests resolved the natural curiosty which would ask the question :

Where did we all come from ? with such an answer, when no other could be given, as ' O you all came from a great way off, somewhere beyond the sea.'

Aye, but how did we get over the sea ?

Oh, why the sea dried up, and let you through. Ye see, that was a very particular sort of sea: it was a red sea.

But when we were come over, how did we get any victuals ?

Victuals ? Oh, why it rained victuals. The nicest apple-dumplings and roast mutton you ever ate in your life.

What did you call it ?

Yes, that was what we called it. *What d'ye call it* was the very name of it, *Manna!*—they called it *What d'ye call it*. It was angel's food.

And how did we do for clothes ?

Oh, the clothes that you came out of Egypt with were a sort of clothes that never wore out.

But what did the people say when we came and drove them out of their land, and took possession of it for ourselves?

O, you cut their throats, and then, you know, they said nothing.

But what right had we to do so?

Ah! but such religious people as you have no occasion to inquire about right,—God Almighty gave you a right.

And where was God Almighty all the while?

Why, you carried him along with you in a box, made of shittim wood.

Such, Sirs, even such, is the natural genealogy of an Exodus.

To which the Exodus of the people of Mexico is so wonderfully similar, that if you had not previously suspected me of drawing from some other picture, you would have felt, assuredly, that it was none other than the Exodus of the Mexicans, that had been the original.

It will not be pretended, I hope, that the inhabitants of Mexico, who, before their invasion by the Spaniards, Pizarro and Cortes, had not heard of the existence of either Jew or Christian, could have borrowed their theology from our Hebrew Pentateuch.

Yet is their *Mexi*, the founder of their race, the perfect counterpart of the Hebrew Moses, and their Supreme God, the adorable Vitziputzli, the very *fac-simile* of Jehovah.

Vitziputzli, the chief Deity of the Mexicans, was made of a very precious wood,—he was represented under the human shape, with a forehead of a blue colour, and a blue streak across his nose, extending from ear to ear: thus presenting that darling and never omitted emblem of all the superstitions upon earth, *the sign of the cross;* and accounting for that peculiar physical fact, that from one end of the world to the other you shall know a believer in the doctrine of the cross, by his looking so blue at you, as if his face were the very reflection of the blue nosed Vitziputzli.

Vitziputzli was seated in a chair of sky-coloured blue, and supported by a litter, with four serpents' heads at the four corners; under his feet was an azure globe, representing the heavens: in his right hand he held a snake, the universal emblem of salvation; and in his left, a buckler, covered with five white feathers, set in the form of a cross. The Mexicans, to this day, ascribe their settlement in that country to the direction of Vitziputzli. The Aborigines, the Canaanites, or first inhabitants of that country, were believed to have been a set of savages, who had no knowledge of the true God, Vitzipultzli, and these, therefore, were subdued by the Mexicans, under the command of Mexi, their captain and lawgiver. Their expeditition was undertaken at the command of their God, who promised them success. Mexi marched at their head, while four priests carried Vitziputzli in a trunk, or chest, made of reeds. Whenever they encamped, they erected a tabernacle in the midst of the camp, and placed the ark upon an altar. They never marched nor encamped without first consulting his blue-nosed Godhead, and implicitly conforming to his directions. Being at last arrived at the promised land, he appeared to a priest in a dream, and commanded the Mexicans to settle in that part of the land, where an eagle should be found sitting on a fig tree, growing out of a rock. The priest related his vision, and the place being found by the signs pre-appointed: they *there* laid the foundations of Mexico. This celebrated city was divided into four quarters or districts, and in the middle was placed the tabernacle of Vitziputzli, till a proper temple should be built to receive him.

In the meanwhile the divine Vitziputzli was content to sit upon his blue *mercy seat*, and to hide his blue forehead and blue nose behind a blue curtain.

And is there not criticism enough in man's nature to urge him to demand why and wherefore 'tis, that in like manner, even the God of Israel, should discover such an extraordinary attachment to the blue colour: that in the furniture of his Holy of Holies, and the garments of his priests,—we have still such a predominance of the blue colour, that he has his blue curtains, blue ribbons, blue robes, blue carpets,—aye, and blue bonnets.

And the Lord spake unto Moses as a boarding-school Miss would give orders to a man-milliner. "And the Lord commanded Moses, and he made the robe of the Ephod all of blue." Exod. xxxix. 22. And they cut the gold into wires to work it into the blue,—and the veil itself of the Holy of

Holy was a veil of blue, and purple, and scarlet of cunning work, with cherubims upon it, and see, said God, 'See that thou make all things according to the pattern.' Heb. viii. 5. And according to what pattern? according to the pattern of things showed thee in the Mount, according to the pattern of things in the heavens, are the answers to that question.

And thus have we a blue curtain, hung upon four pillars, overlaid with gold, and presenting the figures of cherubims of cunning work, according to the pattern of things in the heavens.

And are we to be so stone blind, are we so to renounce all faculties of reason which constitute our rational nature, as to oblige our preachers of the gospel, by not discovering that this blue curtain, with cherubims upon it, was and could have been nothing else than an astronomical eidouranion, an Orrery, or picture exhibiting the relations of the heavenly bodies, precisely of the same nature as Walker's Orrery, which you may see every year, and anywhere, where astronomical lectures are given, with the advantage of a suitable astronomical apparatus.

And here have we the reasons and proprieties of that prevalence of the blue colour, the colour of the canopy of Heaven, and scarlet, and gold, the colours of the planets, and constellations, enwrought, embossed, and set upon that blue, not only in the veil of the Holy of Holies, and in all the furniture of the tabernacle, but in the dresses of the priests, 'who ministered in holy things, and served unto the likeness of things in Heaven. That is, the priests dressed themselves up in the imaginary characters of the constellations, and planets,—and one personated the planet Mercury, another Jupiter, another the Sun, or the Moon, others the twelve signs of the Zodiac, others the constellations without the Zodiac; exhibiting in their dresses, by the golden spangles set upon a blue ground, the exact positions of the Stars in the constellations, which each in his particular function severally represented.

And the Lord God himself, who made heaven and earth, the sea, and all that in them *is*, even God Almighty, the God of Israel was none other than the master of the show, who always acted himself the part of the leader of the band, or leading constellation: and whose language that of our text is:

'Forty years long was I grieved with this generation, and said: It is a people that do err in their hearts, for they have not known my ways,'—and of which the whole and only meaning is:

Forty years have I been manager of this company of strolling players, and have travelled up and down the country with them, with our portable theatre, and yet are they not perfect in their characters. They err in their un-understandings, for they have not known my ways,—they do not understand the science, and are therefore continually crossing the orbits, and making eclipses, occultations, and turning day into night, and night into day, *for they have not known my ways*—that is, my courses and passages through the signs of the Zodiac:

And, therefore, the testy manager relieves his spleen by swearing at them. He swore in his wrath, that they should never enter into his rest—that is, when the performance was over, he should keep up no acquaintance with them in their individual capacity. He would continue to perform with them before the public; but he swore he'd never entertain them at his own private lodgings.

But this curious allegorical rebuke of the chief performer or manager of the itinerant company, for 'erring in their hearts, because they had not known his ways:' is in most curious apposition with a precisely similar allegorical rebuke, which the manager of the New Testament company gives to his comedians for committing precisely the same astronomical mistake, for those players 'also had erred in their hearts for *they* had not known his ways'—that is, they had not known which were respectively the twelve signs of the Zodiac, which they themselves were engaged to personate.

Hence, in the 16th of Matthew's gospel, when they tempted him, desiring him that he would show them a sign from heaven: Of the whole meaning of which, your preachers of the gospel, are as ignorant as they are of Arabic.

The manager answers them: *O ye hypocrites*—that is, O ye players! for the word hypocrites is not originally of a bad sense, but literally means, theatrical performers, 'Ye can discern the face of the sky, and can ye not discern the signs of the times.'

To prevent which mistake, on the part of those who enter this sanctuary, I have ordered *the signs of the times* to be written under the signs of heaven, in order that when you want to see a sign from Heaven, you may at the same glance see the signs of the times, to which the signs from heaven respectively answer, the Lamb for March, the Bull for April, the Twins for May, and so on.

And here have we the clear solution of the riddle that tells, that when Jesus Christ was upon the cross, he bowed his head and said, 'It is finished,' and immediately the veil of the temple was rent in twain—*i.e.*, he made a bow to the audience, he told 'em the performance was all over; and immediately they tore down the scenery, and put out the lamps. But a day or two after the performance (as St. Luke informs us) the manager met two of the company strolling into the country, and called them a set of fools and stupid fellows for not understanding the piece, 'Ought not Christ, said he, to have suffered these things, and to enter into his glory. And beginning at Moses, and all the prophets, he expounded unto them in all the Scriptures the things concerning himself—*i.e.*, the character he was to act, the tricks or miracles that he was to perform, the speeches he was to deliver, and how he was to go through the dying scene, and then to be pulled up into glory, amidst a grand discharge of sky-rockets.

And this explanation, you will observe, he gives them, after he was *theatrically* dead and buried, an absolute demonstration that the whole gospel was a theatrical performance from first to last. For sure, Sirs, we must have put the nightcap on our wits, could we dream that there had been any real and right earnest death, and *bonâ fide* dying in the matter, when the dead man, the corpse that should have been, meets us in the street, we stare like Hamlet at his father's Ghost, and he cries, 'O ye fools! fools! fools!"

But when the *hypocrites*—that is, the players—desired of the manager that he would show them a sign from heaven, they are said to have tempted him. Good God, what sort of temptation was it, merely to ask him to show them one of the signs of the Zodiac!

'As their fathers tempted him, proved him, and saw his works.' And all this 'tempting him,' 'proving him,' and 'seeing his works,' was 'in the day of temptation, in the wilderness.

Now, Sirs, what is the meaning of all this? Can your priests or preachers tell you? No! should you put the inquiry to them, would they answer you? No! they would treat you as a blasphemer and an infidel for presuming to ask them. And e'en the greatest fool and dunce that relieves his idleness by sleeping in a gospel shop, will give himself airs of superiority over you, and treat you as an impious wretch for presuming to think, that ' God cannot be tempted of any man,' and that this cursing, swearing, fretful Yahou, who swore in his wrath, speaks a little bit more in the character of a testy mountebank scolding his vagabond company in a country barn, than in such a character as a wise and good man would venture to imagine of any one whom it was his duty to respect.

But what is the day of *temptation*, and of provocation? The literality of the words themselves will guide us to the interpretation: it is the day of performance of the astronomical pantomime, the time of making astronomical observations, and of *provoking* provocation, or rather convocation or calling up, and grouping together of the stars which spangle the blue arch at night.

And the *wilderness*, literally is, and never was, and never meant any other, than that wild and confused jumble of the stars, of which you can make neither head nor tail, till you have learned to *convoke*, or call them together, and group them into their respective constellations.

And then you will understand that the בני ישרל, *Benui Yesreile*, or *Children of Israel, literally*, really, and from the first use of that term in the ancient Phœnician language, meant the Stars of Heaven, *Yesreile*, being the Phœnician name of the planet Saturn, of whom all the celestial bodies within the range of his immense orbit are the children.

And among these children of Israel, the Lord, or the Lord God of Israel, is the leading constellation, or *that* which brings them up out of the land of Egypt, out of the house of bondage—that is, not out of any real land of Egypt, or house of bondage, but from below the horizon.

In the new allegory, this leading constellation is the Lamb; and, consequently, Jesus Christ, who is the Lord God of the New Israel, is uniformly called the Lamb of God.

But in the old allegory there was no small difficulty in the reckoning, whether it was the Ram or the Bull that should be *considered* as the leading constellation, and therefore entitled to be called 'the Lord God of Israel.'

But whether it were the one or the other, the grand, the all essential predication and definition of 'the Lord God of Israel,' was, that it must be he that was the first or leading constellation,—and he, and he alone, to whom must appertain the exclusive honour of bringing up the children of Israel out of the land of Egypt, out of the house of bondage.

Hence the name and title of the Lord God of Israel, in all its formal annunciations, is continually accompanied with this astronomical explanation:

'I am the Lord thy God, which brought thee out of the land of Egypt—out of the house of bondage.'

So when Aaron set up his calf in Horeb, the formal proclamation of the Godhead of that calf was, 'These are thy Gods, O Israel, which brought thee up out of the land of Egypt.' So when Jeroboam set up his calf in Bethel, the proclamation of its divinity was, 'Behold thy Gods, O Israel, which brought thee up out of the land of Egypt.' The name of God, which brought the children of Israel out of Egypt, always being plural (*Elohim*), and spoken of in the plural pronoun, *these* אלה אלהי־ישראל־אלה, 'these are thy Gods, O Israel,' as referring to the considerable number of stars which make up the whole group or constellation, whether it was the Bull or the Ram that stood at the point where the Ecliptic crosses the Equator; and which, consequently, *does* bring up the children of Israel out of Egypt, and therefore *is* the Lord their God, whose office and character was personated by a priest, dressed in a large wig of white wool, to represent the Lamb; and a mask, with fiery eyes, to represent the Sun shining in his strength; and a golden girdle to represent the Zodiac; and seven candlesticks to represent the seven planets, and twelve stones set upon the girdle, to represent the twelve signs of the Zodiac; and his boots or shoes like unto fine brass, as if they burned in a furnace, to represent the heat produced by the Sun's march through the Heavens. While the dresses of the inferior performers are described as suited to their respective astronomical characters by the holy prophet Isaiah, with a ridiculous minuteness, 'the bravery of their tinkling ornaments, their cauls, and round tires like the Moon, the chains, and the bracelets, and the mufflers, the rings, and the nose jewels, and the mantles, and the wimples, and the crisping pins.' And, on some occasions, when the performance was very badly got up, we find the manager not merely swearing in his wrath, that 'they should not enter into his rest,' but declaring, that 'then shall the Moon be confounded, and the Sun ashamed' —that is, 'the Moon would forget her part, and the Sun would get hissed off the stage,' which, if it be not the true and only meaning of this holy gibberish, I am sure that there is not a clergyman on earth that can tell what the meaning is, or would attempt to do so, to any man that might put him to the question. And as for the scenery of these astronomical pantomimes, which we may guess rarely equalled that of Richardson's booth at Bartholomew Fair,— it was generally painted by the manager himself. So that, 'the side scenes declared the glory of God, and the firmament showed his handywork.'

But that the אֶרֶץ-מִצְרַיִם, *Aretz Metzrim*, scene, which we absurdly take to be the real country known by the name of *Egypt*, on this terraqueous globe, never meant anything of the kind, but referred only to that portion of the heavens which is below the horizon, and therefore in a state of darkness and shadow.

And that the children of Israel are the stars in the eternal game of *follow-my-leader*, brought up out of that dark region, when they rise in the East, and going down again into that Egypt when they set in the West, is betrayed in the fact, which a very ordinary degree of criticism, applied to this mystical language will observe. For the *children of Israel*, and *Israel*, and the *Stars*, and the Heavens, are used as perfectly synonymous and interchangeable terms; and *the Israel of God*, the people of God, and *the children of light*,—aye and the Father of lights (which our brains would be of no use to us could they possibly mean anything else than the Sun and Stars), are exegetical of each other.

So that either Moses or Isaiah, or any one of the performers in the astronomical allegory, meaning to say, *Hear, O Israel*, would say, *Hear, O Heaven;* and for *Sing, O Israel*, would say, *Sing, O Heavens*. And 'there shall come a Star out of Jacob, and a Sceptre shall rise out of Israel,' for a

Star shall appear in the heavens, and the constellation called the *Sceptre* (as there actually is the Sceptre, and the Crown too, among those constellations) shall rise up, at its proper latitude of rising in the visible heavens.

No such persons, as of Israel and Jacob, nor of any descendants of such persons ever having existed upon earth, but owing the supposition of their existence only to that impatient ignorance which would never suffer its first impressions to be corrected, however foolish and erroneous they might be; but would take it to be piety, and virtue, and religion, and goodness, to believe in a wrathful, lying, cursing, swearing, and perjuring deity; and would say of a creature, who really appears on the *literal* showing of their Bible itself to have been nothing else but a mountebank, travelling about the country with a puppet-show, which he called Heaven and Earth. 'He is the Lord our God, and we are the people of his pasture, and the sheep of his hands.'

And all this, rather than exercise so much reason as to perceive what a rational child might perceive, that wherever the name *God*, or *Lord*, or *Lord God*, or the Almighty occurs, either in the Old or New Testament, from beginning to end,—it is the person of the astronomic priest himself that is alone intended.

And if you would take your Bibles, and with your pen erase the word *God*, or *Lord*, whenever they occur, and write *priest*, or bishop, instead, and read it with *that clue*, you would discover what otherwise you must be for ever ignorant of— *its true meaning.*

END OF THE DISCOURSE ON THE DAY OF TEMPTATION
IN THE WILDERNESS.

The Devil's Pulpit.

"AND A BONNIE PULPIT IT IS."—*Allan Cunningham.*

No. 8.—Vol. II.]   [Price 2*d*.

AHAB, OR THE LYING SPIRIT:

A Discourse,

DELIVERED BY THE REV. ROBERT TAYLOR, B.A.

AT THE ROTUNDA, BLACKFRIARS ROAD, OCT. 17, 1830.

' *And he said, Hear thou, therefore, the word of the Lord: I saw the Lord sitting on his throne, and all the host of heaven standing by him, on his right hand and on his left. And the Lord said, Who shall persuade Ahab, that he may go up and fall at Ramoth Gilead? And one said on this manner, and another said on that manner. And there came forth a spirit, and stood before the Lord, and said, I will persuade him. And the Lord said unto him, Wherewith? And he said, I will go forth, and I will be a lying spirit in the mouth of all his prophets. And he said, Thou shalt persuade him, and prevail also: go forth, and do so.*'
—1 KINGS, xxii. 19-22.

THERE'S a lesson of moral virtue for us, my brethren. Now! mark the sincerity of the Christian character, and see if they're not frightened at the text of their own book, before they've heard a word more than the text itself. God is graciously pleased to instruct us in the various duties of life, not merely by precept, but by example also. So that a man has only to make the Bible the rule of his actions, and to conform his whole life and conduct to that perfection which shines forth in every page of this blessed book, and he will be sure to acquire that high sense of justice, and that sincere regard to truth, which is invariably found to characterise a Christian.

But all I want to know is, what that wicked man, King

Ahab, thought of such divine truth, and of the truth-speaking God, the covenant-keeping God, the faithful God, and of his holy prophets, and of his holy spirit, which inspired his holy prophets; and set them lying at such a rate, that Hell and the Devil found themselves outdone at their own game?

What would I have given to have exchanged a word with this sincere believer in the interval of his receiving his death's wound, and his death on the day, when relying on the truth of God, as delivered to him in his holy word, and vouched by the concurrent testimony of his holy prophets (there were four hundred of them), all of whom, in the plenitude of divine inspiration, had sworn to him, by God, that his safety was guaranteed by the promise of that God, who is not a man that he should lie, nor the son of man, that he should repent; and that God had said, 'Go up to Ramoth Gilead, for thou shalt prosper: the Lord of Hosts is with thee, the God of Jacob is thy refuge,—the Lord shall deliver Ramoth Gilead into thy hands, and bring thee back a glorious conqueror.'

But how was that promise fulfilled, when 'a certain man drew a bow at a venture, and smote the King of Israel between the joints of the harness, and the blood ran out of the wound into the midst of the chariot, and he said to the driver of his chariot, 'Turn thine hand and carry me out of the field, for I am wounded.'

'The fainting soul stood ready winged for flight,
And o'er his eyeballs swam the shades of night.'

So—so keeps God his promise of salvation. So—so, in that deathful moment, might one have addressed him in the language of St. Paul to Agrippa, 'King Ahab, believest thou the prophets? I know that thou believest.' As Ahab could not but have answered, 'Ah, had I not been a believer, I had not been betrayed to this destruction, I relied upon the word of God, and thus—thus!' Hold there, King Ahab, hold! none of your blasphemies, I know what you would say: but they won't stay here to hear it: the Lord is righteous in all his ways and holy in all his works.

So he died! he died! at even, and one washed his chariot in the pool of Samaria, and the dogs licked up his blood; and the blessed Scripture says that that was 'According to the word of the Lord.' But our imaginations are left to supply the essential sequel of the scene, when the lying spirit returned back again to the Court of Heaven to give an account of the success of his divine mission. ' Halloo! Yahou, we've done for Ahab, we've gospelled him, we've made dog's meat of him, the Devil's got him. But had ye, God, seen how the parsons lied for't, how devilishly they lied, how natural it came to 'em, I'd only to hitch 'em off the spring, and their clackers ran till their weights were down.'

' Say ye so '—say ye so, said God Almighty, ' then well done, thou good and faithful servant, enter thou into the joy of thy Lord.'

But let me not seem to be profane! no sensible man on earth is intentionally further than I am from being so. The only liberty I take is that which a necessity of my understanding forces upon me. I have ideas; I am troubled with thick forthcoming fancies; I have an imagination, and cannot therefore read my Bible, as good Christians can, without having ideas. I know that it would be all right enough, if one could lay one's ideas aside, and not think at all on what one reads; but thinking, and imagining, and criticising, step following step, and thought succeeding thought, plays the Devil with believing.

I have no doubt, God-a'-mighty knows that I have no doubt, that King Ahab was a very wicked man, and richly deserved the punishment he merited. But how could he be other than a very wicked man? He was a king, and the best man on earth would be spoiled if you made a king of him Moreover he kept four hundred regular clergy to take care of his royal conscience. No wonder, then, if his conscience should get into a very royal condition: at last,— ' *too many cooks*,' you know, and here were enough, not merely to damn his Majesty, but to damn the whole nation. He kept 'em, as all other parsons are kept, at the nation's expense; not quite, though, to the expense of £9,920.000 a year, because that nation was not quite so religious as the clergy could wish. Besides, they had only the Old Testament to keep up, whereas *Goramity* has given us a couple of his divine Revelations,—and we have got to support the Old Testament, and the New, too. One more of his divine Revelations, and we should go to Heaven at such a rate, that there'd be no living upon Earth.

King Ahab kept four hundred parsons to perform divine service round his royal person. Yes! he did; and a pretty service they served him at last. They brought his soul into a state of grace, I'll answer for't. They got him ripe for glory. They dished his immortal part for the angels, but they dished his body for dog's meat: they dished him most completely,—they saved his soul—that is, I hope they saved it, but damned his blood.

But the most curious feature of character in these holy men of God, who spake as they were moved by the Holy Ghost, is, that they were all of the evangelical order: they preached extempore: they were peculiarly spiritual, they dealt out the effusions of the Holy Ghost, neat as imported: but, like all the rest of their order, they would never suffer themselves to be questioned: they were accounted ministers of peace—yet urged they men on to feuds and battle,— their words were smoother than butter, yet they were very swords: they spake of comfort, joy, and glory, only to bring the fool that heeded them to the dogs.

But let me not seem to cast a shade on this sacred subject, which belongs not to it! I could not darken it if I would,— I would not, for the world. My only and most solemn protest is solely directed against those wicked and deceitful preachers of the gospel, who, when they meet with a difficult and perplexing passage, either skip it over entirely, and so contrive to keep people in ignorance of what the true character of the Bible is, or invent hypotheses, and pretend figurative or parobolical senses, to apologise, and screen, and protect their word of God from the judgment which the text itself, in its naked deformity, would inevitably incur.

They would get the Almighty out of the scrape, if they could; and so, if they dared to preach out at all, their hearers must patiently endure the old song.—[Sermon:]

'This, my Christian brethren, must be understood metaphorically. It was an illustration by way of vision, condescendingly afforded to the mind of the true prophet, the more strikingly to exhibit the strong delusion which God, in his righteous dispensation, had allowed to possess the minds of the false prophets of Ahab to lead him to the temporal death which his enormous offences had merited. It was a parable, or rather a dream.'

But hold, there! If it were so, then, so is the whole

gospel a dream from beginning to end. For not a word about parable, or metaphor, or metaphorical sense, occurs in any relation to this frightful story. It is as solemn, as didactic, as positive of term, as plain of sense, as probable in itself, and in every iota of it, as likely to have really occurred as the resurrection of our Lord Jesus Christ. To believe *that*, in the literal sense, and not to believe *this* quite as literally, is but to make a nose of wax of your own word of God, and mould it to the fashion of your fancy.

It is the subversion of all principles of criticism, and all logical equity, if once we are to assume that, because a passage may present us with a few difficulties, or apparent absurdities, it is to be disposed of at once, by a sweeping surrender and conveyance to the province of allegory, vision, or metaphor. It is not more improbable in itself, nor more revolting to reason, that God, for his just and righteous purposes, should condescend to employ the services of a lying Spirit in Heaven, than that he should with equal condescension engage his ministers and preachers of the gospel, in precisely similar services upon earth. And as for what a sceptical mind might insinuate, that '*it will not stand to reason:*' If you are to argue in that way, I should like to know how much of your divine revelation would stand to reason?

Reason is a besom, that will not merely sweep the dust out of your house upon the rock, but 'twill sweep away house, and rock, and all.

A Christian has no right, no security, no safety in reasoning.

When once a Christian begins to reason, he's like a beggar on horseback,—you may guess where he'll ride to. He'll put his precious soul into pawn, and, what's worse than all, he'll never pay the parsons another ha'penny to get it out again.

The deceit (the *apparent* deceit, I should say) practised by the four hundred priests of Ahab, considering that they had the divine authority for what they did, was not in nature and character at all different from that which priests, in all ages, and even the Protestant priests to this day among ourselves, continue to practise upon the babes and sucklings of the gospel.

Allow me but your recognition of that most just principle,

that everything *is* what it is, in relation to the mind, and to the mind's appreciation of it: that if a man's mind were weak and feeble, he ought to have it comforted and strengthened, not insulted, trifled with, and trodden on: and that it would become the wisdom of the wisest man that ever breathed, if he saw a child terrified at the cackling of a goose, to drive the goose away and to protect the child. Say ye, then, what should be said to those cackling tormenters who, in every country parish in the kingdom, invite the Johnny Raws and Bumpkins, from the plow tail to the most comfortable sacrament of the body and blood of Christ, to trap em in for't at last, to the terror of an imaginary chance, that by eating and drinking unworthily, they may have eaten and drank damnation to themselves.

Was Ahab practised on by a grosser or more cruel deceit than this: 'Tis not what the reason of a sensible man might admonish him of that we should look to, or what the knowing ones know of their *damnation-sacrament;* but 'tis what the poor booby suffers, who goes into their wolf's glen, takes them at their word, who trembles at the thunder of their magic, and shrivels at the casting of their seventh bullet.

'Dearly beloved,' say they.

'Dearly beloved, on Sunday next I purpose, through God's assistance, to administer to all such as shall be religiously and devoutly disposed, the most comfortable sacraments of the body and blood of Christ, unto which, in God's behalf, I bid you all that are here present, and do beseech you for the Lord Jesus Christ's sake, that ye will not refuse to come thereto, being so lovingly called, and bidden by God.'

'Well,' says Johnny Raw, to his own raw understanding, and 'By God, that's very loving indeed; and since you're so very pressing, and it's to be so very comfortable, I'll pay my shilling, and I'll take my breakfast of the Lord's supper.'

Let him do so! and let your sympathy perpend the workings of his innocent mind, through the process and catastrophe of that feast of blood, that supper of Thyestes.

'*That feast of blood, that supper of Thyestes,*' where the principal dish is the master himself at supper—where?

Not where he eats, but where he's being eaten.

Where so rich is the preparation made for that spiritual feast, that when you're come to't, our bountiful Lord addresses ye with his ' *Welcome, my hungry guests, to the marriage supper of the Lamb. But if you get anything to eat, you must eat me.*'

Where all is conundrum, quirk, quiddity, and riddle-mere, beyond the faculty of human wit to unriddle,—where, but to come within a guess of what they're driving at, you must evitate the sonorous catachresis of metonymous periphrases, no less than the cabalistical dogmatism of anagogical ratiocination; or otherwise you must immolate the apothegmatical aufractuosity of idiopathic sentiment to the supervacaneous ponderosity of cacophonous periods, polyphonous rhetoricisms, and syncategorimatical collocation, and conturbabantur Constantinopolitani, immumerabilibus solicitudenibus.

And then, perhaps, you'll begin to understand how you show your love to your Saviour, by being so glad that he was hanged: by clasping the darling gallows that he was gibbetted on to your heart, by imagining that you see him spreading out his blood vessels, like the anatomy at the doctor's shop, and by imagining, that if the Jews had left a bit of him, no bigger than the tip of your finger, you yourself would have a bite at him. For lack of which, he takes the will for the deed, you do by faith what you cannot do in reality. So you eat the bread, and smell the cheese: and then you're to say:

'My God, and is thy table spread.
And doth thy cup with love o'erflow:
' Thither be all thy children led,
And let them all thy sweetness know.'

That table is a snare, that cup is poison, that bread is deadly aconite. Ah, poor fool! thou didst take the sacrament to save thee from damnation, and thou art damned for taking it.

Thou hast eaten and drank unworthily, thou art guilty of the body and blood of the Lord Jesus Christ, thou hast kindled God's wrath against thee, thou hast provoked him to plague thee with divers diseases, and sundry kinds of death, in the beautiful language of Watts' hymn:

'He seals the curse on his own head,
And makes his own damnation sure.'

There's a comfortable sacrament for you! There's glad tidings of great joy! What does not the Theophagist owe to his spiritual pastor and master, who has dished him up such a bit of heavenly lamb, with such hellish sauce to it. But, Oh!

> 'Farewell, the tranquil mind, farewell!
> The pride of innocence, the confidence of virtue,—
> All cheerful looks, all joy of heart, all peace, all hope, farewell!'

But could none but the weakest of minds, none but the illiterate and incapable boor, be thus terribly impressed. Alas! the great mind of the poet Cowper sank under this master-stroke of priestly villany. The great philosopher, Robert Boyle, sank under it. I myself have witnessed, in communicants who have received the sacrament from my own hands, these effects of it upon them.

And now, forsooth, our holy men of God, full of the spirit from on high, which inspired the four hundred prophets of Ahab, the goodly fellowship of the prophets, you know, have found out for us, that we may go up to their spiritual Ramoth Gilead with perfect safety; and that there's no such danger of eating and drinking unworthily, as weak minds misunderstanding some of the expressions used in those holy mysteries, have been needlessly alarmed at.

'But well,' says Johnny Raw, not quite so raw as he was before there was so much talk in the world about these here Atheists, and Deists, and Infidels,—'Well, but we'll keep o' the safe side of the hedge, at any rate.'

May be we shall we damned if we don't go to the sacrament, but certainly we'll be damned if we do.

And so at last 't has come to't in this Christian land, that while at the Lord Mayor's feast, Guildhall gates are not large enough to let through all the company. All the company at the Lord God's feast may go through the keyhole.

The Lord Mayor had the king, and the queen, and the court, and the nobles, and the ambassadors, and the plenipotentiaries, and the plenty of all of 'em to breakfast with him; but the Lord God may pick his teeth with the beggar Lazarus.

The character of God, as exhibited in the fate of Ahab, is precisely that of the God and Father of our Lord Jesus Christ, as set forth in the gospel, only with the difference in the gospel God, of an aggravated majesty of horror, en-hanced malignity, and coronary deceit.

Did God lead Ahab, under the influence of a strong delusion, of which himself was the cause, to battle and to death? And sticks that gnat in the gullet, that mere trifle of injustice, that little bit of a lark, with the man whose blood can flow unfrozen in his veins, whose fell of hair can keep its smoothness, while he reads the eleventh verse of the second chapter of the second epistle of the apostolic chief of sinners to the church of the Thessalonians, which was in God the Father and in the Lord Jesus Christ.

Where it is written, 'And for this cause God shall send them strong delusion, that they should believe a lie, that t ey all might be damned.'

There's comfort for you, good Christians, there's joy and peace in believing. Have I forged this? ' Can I put a gloss on't that belongs not to't? Can your lying prophets say *it is not there*, in characters which the wickedest man that ever breathed should shudder at the thought of? You are firmly persuaded that the gospel is from Heaven? What of that! the more likely 'tis to be from that lying spirit, which spake by the prophets. Your faith is strong? What of that—the stronger your delusion.

It hath God for its author? What of that! Your faith itself may probably be the effect of God's curse upon ye. And what should God see in you, that he should be the author of a true revelation to you, who admits himself to be the author of strong delusion to others. But those others, say ye, had pleasure in unrighteousness, and therefore were delivered over by the just judgment of God to believe in strong delusion. But what was it that the converted sinner had pleasure in, ere he was given over to believe the strong delusion which he calls gospel.

Now, Sirs, considering the danger of this strong delusion! How much obliged ought we to be to those good-natured holy men of God, the Methodists, and Christian instruction and religious tract societies, who, though we can never prevail on them to relieve our anxiety, by coming publicly to the *scratch*, and comparing notes in free and open discussion, to prove who are in strong delusion, will yet clap me their pretty bits of paper in our hand, and then skulk off like thieves into their gospel shops, for fear they should hear, what in the gospel-shop they know they are safe from hearing, the language of reason, of truth, and honesty.

Here have we their TESTIMONIES RESPECTING THE BIBLE, to tell us what pretty things the clever fellows that lived a long while ago said of this Bible, in direct contradiction to what this Bible says of itself, telling us that that is fair and right which we see with our own eyes to be most foul and wicked: that that is pure and holy, which modesty dare not glance at: that that is true, which bears the lie upon the face of it, in characters as big as London Monument: that that is honourable to God, which would be disgraceful to the Devil himself.

O, how much obliged are we to these good, clever men, for rectifying our poor fallible judgments, and setting our reason the other side upwards.

We have the great names of Lord Bacon, Selden, Milton, Sir Matthew Hale, Boyle, Locke, and Sir William Jones, telling us what they thought of the Bible, at a time when, to have published a word against the Bible, was death by law, death at the gallows, or at the stake,—perpetual imprisonment, the pillory, the rack, the wheel, when they cut a man's ears off, split his nostrils, tore his eyes out, only for writing against the jure-divino ship of the *bishops:* and, with these intended favours in hand, these loving kindnesses and tender mercies to second their desires, our pretty lambkins of the gospel, our Jesus's blood-hounds, have been collecting testimonies in favour of the Bible. And d'ye think they haven't got testimonies enough? The thief, the murderer holds me his threatening dagger to my throat, and cries, 'Now, Sir, what do you think of me.' I answer, ' O God, Sir, I think what that pointed suggestion of yours makes me think. I think you a gentleman every inch. I think that you have God for your inspirer, salvation for your intention, and truth, without any mixture of error, for your argument.'

Away goes cut-throat to the gospel-shop, and publishes his religious tract, to tell the world what an honourable testimony was borne to his character.

And such, and none other than such, is the predicament of all the testimonies which they can produce in favour of their Bible.

A testimony to be honourable should be free; it should

be unbribed by prospects of reward, unawed by liabilities to punishment: above all, it should be borne where it may be examined, where it may be disputed, where it may be resisted, or the pretence to such a thing is a complete swindle.

Can they, then, produce a single clever man in all the world, who would bear a favourable testimony to the Bible, of whom it could be said, that that man was perfectly free?

Or is the Sun more glaring, at noon-day, than the fact, that in proportion as men become free, intelligent, and virtuous: as the thrones of tyrants begin to discover symptoms of the dry rot, the altar and the pulpit catch the disease, and the Bible, with the crown and sceptre upon it, becomes an idiot's bauble, more to be looked at than to be looked into: and its advocates are driven back into the dark, and the dark ages, to drag forth the testimonies which have been borne to the Bible by men who wrote under terror of penal statutes, or of such wiseacres as Sir Matthew Hale, who burnt the witches; as Dictionary Johnson, who believed in the Cock-lane ghost; and those other ornaments of human nature, who were afraid of going to hell for biting their nails of a Sunday.

Where are the testimonies that should be borne to the Bible, by the great men *of our own times?* What say the Parisians, and the Belgians? What say the Lafayette, and the De Potter, of the Bible? What keeps them in the Universities of Cambridge and Oxford, as snug as rats in the granary, as silent as a jack-ass in a clover-field, about the Bible? Why is it that not a man of science, of superior learning, or of transcendent talent in the world, but who is anxious to be innocent of the Bible? Why is the universal cry, 'Send it to lazar-houses, gaols, hospitals, to parish apprentices, to beggars, slaves, and savages, while learning casts it from her, like something hateful, that her nature's chilled at.

Is it virtue, is it honour, is it honesty, that will struggle still to keep up, in sanctity and reverence, a system of iniquity, deceit, and crime, which its own advocates dared not undertake to defend, where a man might have liberty to show them how iniquitous, how deceitful, and how wicked it is?

Was ever greater outrage offered to human understanding? Was ever every sentiment that is noble, honourable ingenuous, and just among men, more cruelly oppressed, than that we should be forced to pay an exterior respect to a book that, in its mis-translations, sets before us a God, who is blasphemously made to appear the greatest monster of iniquity, that iniquity itself could have imagined, when it strove to be transcendently iniquitous, a lying God, who avails himself of his attribute of infinite wisdom, to overreach the credulity of his creatures, sends them strong delusion, that they should believe a lie, and then damns them for believing it.

And *we* must be regarded as *immoral* men, and bound in penalties, and immured in prisons, for want of any better argument to answer OURS: that a book which represents God as a tyrant, is a book only fit for slaves: that a book which represents him as a liar, is a lying book: and that a book which requires more explanation than it has ever yet had to explain away these representations, had better be done away with, and done with for ever.

And it would be so, Sirs! it would be, but for the secret of it, that 'tis by this wicked craft, and by the very wickedness of it, that bishops, priests, and preachers, have their wealth, and roll in saucy pomp, over the crushed necks of the mentally degraded, and therefore politically oppressed people. Never will tyrants and oppressors be got rid of, till Bibles are got rid of. Μεγα βιβλιον, μεγα κακον is the proverb, the great book is the great evil. Had the pretended revelation of God been worthy of a God, it would never have been done. Had its simple, but holy purport been, 'All mankind are brethren, all are alike the children of one common nature: let them make themselves happy—that is wisdom: let them labour to promote the happiness of others —that, that alone, is virtue.

The tale would have been told too soon,—there would have been nothing in't by which one man could overreach the understanding of another.

There would have been no lies to be made to look like truth, no injustice to be made to appear just, no impossibilities to be made to appear possible, no hell, no devil, no rawhead and bloody bones, that wouldn't stay dead when he was dead, no damnation, and so no clergy.

'No more should nation against nation rise,
Nor ardent warriors meet with hateful eyes,
Nor fields with glittering steel be covered o'er,
The brazen trumpets kindle war no more.

All crimes should cease, and ancient fraud should fail,
Returning Justice lift aloft her scale;
Peace o'er the world, her olive wand extend,
And man to man for ever be a friend.'

Delenda est Carthago.

END OF THE DISCOURSE ON AHAB, OR THE LYING SPIRIT.

The Devil's Pulpit.

"AND A BONNIE PULPIT IT IS."—*Allan Cunningham.*

THE FALL OF MAN:

A Discourse,

DELIVERED BY THE REV. ROBERT TAYLOR, B.A.
AT THE ROTUNDA, BLACKFRIARS ROAD, JUNE 20, 1830.

> '*In the sweat of thy face shalt thou eat bread, till thou return unto the ground; for out of it wast thou taken: for dust thou art, and unto dust shalt thou return.*'—GENESIS iii., 19.

MEN AND BRETHREN,—It has been shown, I hope, to the perfect satisfaction and conviction of all who have attended the analysis of sacred history in the lectures hitherto delivered by me, that *whether the supposed Supernatural Being be good or evil,—whether he be called God or Devil, Christ or Belial, Holy Ghost or Satan;* 'be he a spirit of health, or goblin damned; bring with him airs from heaven, or blasts from hell; be his intents wicked or charitable,'— all, 'are but the Varied God,'—all are but different supposed manifestations of the attributes of One and the self-same physical agency.

We pass now from this analysis of the higher order of abstractions—that is, from the Gods, Devils, Christs, Lords, Angels, and Holy and Unholy Ghosts; all of which are only so many personifications of the Sun of our system to the study of the no less entirely astronomical nature, and mythological history, of the demigods: and heroes, such as Adam and Eve, and Moses and Aaron, and Abraham, Isaac, and Jacob, which are the stars of inferior magnitude, the בני־ישראל *Beny Yesraile*, as they are called the children of Israel—that is, *the sons of* the planet Saturn, Israel being the ancient Phœnician name of the planet Saturn, who, as being the most remote of all the planetary bodies then observed, was considered as the *Father of Heaven*, and acquired the name of אברהם *avro-hom*, or Abo-ram—that is, Father of Elevation.

That this secondary order of personages never had a real existence, any more than the primary ones, is not only expressly asserted, in the text itself, of those words of the apostolic chief of sinners, 'which things are an allegory:' but 'tis the very doctrine of the mystagogue, our Lord and Saviour Jesus Christ, who himself hath said, that 'they shall come from the east, and from the west, and from the north, and from the south, and shall sit down with Abraham, Isaac, and Jacob, in the kingdom of God.' And surely that kingdom is a kingdom not of this world, it is the kingdom of Heaven, even none other than that vaulty arch so high above our heads: as the apostle instructs us, 'if we wish to understand the mysteries of the kingdom of Heaven, we must set our affections on things above, not on things on earth.' 'For our conversation,' says he to his brother Timothy, 'is in Heaven,' than which, we could not have been told in plainer language, that their conversation, all they were talking about, all they said, and all they meant, was the science of astronomy.

To this secondary order of astronomical personages, we are introduced, in an entirely anonymous work, called *the Book of Genesis;* but in the Hebrew text, having no title at all, but an enlarged writing of the first word, בראשית, *'eryshith,—in the beginning.*

In some of the early Greek versions it is called Γενεσιο ...σμου, or cosmogony, or world-making, or birth of the world, or begetting, or *coming to be* of the astronomical arrangement; all which, or any other rendering as a title, or character of the book, will be found to be as decidedly expressive of a fabulous character, as if it had been called a fable.

The whole story of Genesis is so egregiously and manifestly a fable, that *they* have, in all ages, been considered as enemies both of the Christian and the Jewish faith who have ever pretended to consider it as a fact.

Origen, in his celebrated answer to Celsus, upraids that sarcastic infidel with his total want of candour, in treating this story as if it had been delivered as history, and hiding what he ought to have known—*i.e.*, that all this was to be understood in a figurative sense. Celsus, not giving his readers the words which would have convinced them that they were spoken allegorically (Contra. Cels. lib. 4); and 'It is not reasonable,' he says, ' to deny to Moses the possession of truth, under the veil of allegory, which was then the practice of all eastern nations.

It is admitted, then, that this is no true account of the origin of the human race. It is not true, it is not pretended to be so. It is not the doctrine of Scripture (an' ascribe to Scripture whatever authority you please) that Adam and Eve were the first of the human species, or that the human species had any such origination as has been pretended. And Cain, therefore, their first-born son, might have gone and married a wife in the land of Nod, without any inconsistency to the general scope of the allegory.

But the inconsistency is, that a *doctrine* represented to be *true*, should be founded on a basis admitted to be false; and that the whole scheme of salvation should be thought to be *not* an allegory; just, ye see, for no other reason than because of its being founded on the most egregious and manifest allegory that ever was in the world. So that the Christian system, Christians themselves defining it, is from first to last a jumble of contradictions, a collection of quirks, catches, and double-entendres, a play at cross purposes, an exercise to try the sharpness of our wit. Thus the doctrine of the immortality of the soul, is to be inferred from the most emphatic declaration that could be couched in words: that we have no souls, and that we are *not* immortal, that being the Christian way of interpreting the word of God.

And the whole theory of human redemption is gravely deduced as an inference from the very silliest riddle-me-riddle-me-re that ever disgraced the tenant of a cradle.

'And I will put enmity between thee and the woman, and between thy posterity and her posterity; he shall bruise thy head, and thou shalt bruise his heel.'

Of which I shall give no further comment, than that of the most learned and truly pious Christian commentator and translator of this sacred book, Dr. Geddes: 'Whosoever thou beest who understandest the first elements of the Hebrew dialect, and the first elements of logic,—say if thou findest in it any vestige of a seducing Devil, or a redeeming Saviour, thou mayest then turn to Calmet's commentary, or any other commentary of the same bran, and keep thyself from laughing if thou canst.' And at the conclusion of his commentary, on this chapter, the same most learned and Christian Hebraist concludes: 'We have now got to the end of the Mythos (*i.e.*, the fable) of Moses, or whoever else was the author of the wonderful production. I trust I have done something like justice to its beauties; and that it will appear, on the whole, to be a well devised, well delineated, well executed piece—nay, that it has not its equal in all the mythology of antiquity: I mean, if it be considered not as a real history, nor as a mere mystical allegory, —but as a most charming political fiction, dressed up for excellent purposes in the garb of history, and adapted to the gross conceptions and limited capacity of a rude, sensual, unlearned, and credulous people.'

Well then, Sirs, it is admitted by the most learned of the Christian world, that the story of the fall of man is altogether a mythos, a fable, a political fiction, the most charming fiction in the world, if you please,—but yet no more than a fiction. No such persons as Adam and Eve ever existed, no such creation of the world in such a way, and no such fall of man, as has been pretended, ever took place. And there being no reality in the first Adam, there can be none in the second: no fall, no redemption, no betrayer of our race into transgression, no Saviour, and no need of one; and the whole story,

> 'Of man's first disobedience, and the fruit
> Of that forbidden tree, whose mortal tase
> Brought death into the world, and all our woe,
> With loss of Eden, till one greater man,
> Restore us, and regain the blissful seat,'

Is a poem, a fiction, a fable, as far from the sober realities of history and truth as the tissue of a drunkard's dream.

The adversaries of Christianity are justly charged by its advocates with want of candour, in not giving the literal meaning of the words and names of sacred theology, which, on being understood, would themselves have shown, that nothing like historical truth was ever so much as pretended.

These literal meanings, then, of the principal names and terms, I shall proceed to give. I shall show you the Pagan and idolatrous origination of the story of salvation. Its existence in ages long anterior to any age that has ever been assigned as the age of Moses, even admitting that such a person as Moses ever existed; and, lastly, the real significancy and meaning of it.

Now, observe ye, Sirs! all these scenes of the creation, temptation, and fall of man, whether understood literally or figuratively, whether as fable or fact, as false or true, is said to have occurred in *Paradise.*

And is not that word Paradise, one of the words of which the infidel Celsus, uncandidly kept back the true meaning from the knowledge of his hearers, as well knowing that the meaning of that word, being once understood, none but a stark staring fool would ever have dreamed of the story being meant to pass for truth.

It was in Paradise! Now, in the name of God, where is Paradise? It is the place where so much of a man will go to, as remains of him after the worms have done dinner.

It is the 'country from whose bourne no traveller returns,' and where no traveller goes that can stay on *terra firma* any longer.

It is in *terra del Fuego*. It is the country that lies on the other side of the grave when the gallows stands on this. You must cross the line to it. As our blessed Saviour said to the evangelical thief, when the thief was in no hurry, 'this day shalt thou be with me in Paradise.' It was the third heaven, the place where St. Paul says 'he was caught up into, when he could not tell whether he was in his body or out of his body, and where he heard unspeakable words, which it is not lawful for a man to utter.' Corinth. ii 12.

The word Paradise, adopted into the English, and other European languages, without being translated, from the Greek, παρα δεισος, which is the Septuagint rendering of בן-בעדן-מקדם, *Gan-de-eden me kay-dem,* 'a garden in Eden eastward,' divides itself into its compounds Παρα-diis, which is literally among the *Stars.*

The very first noun, and first verb which follows it,

of the very first sentence ascribed to divine revelation, בראשית ברא אלהים את השמים ואת הארץ,* has no such sense as that put on the words, 'in the beginning God created the heavens and the earth,' the reference being, not to an original creation, but to a *renewal* and *renovation* of the face and appearances of the heavens and the earth: not to anything imagined to have taken place then for the first time, and not of a nature to be repeated, but referring to the annual and diurnal phænomena of the visible heavens and earth, which take place every year, and every day of our lives. The heavens and the earth according to the doctrine, of the most ancient Jewish Rabbins, following that of the Pythagorician, and elder Platonists, being co-eternal with God, as the Sun's rays are co-eval with the Sun.

And there, in the garden of God, looking eastward among those flowers of the sky, which adorn the beautiful bosom of the night, will be seen depicted in the groups of Stars the whole drama of Paradise.

The constellation, or group of Stars, represented as falling within the imaginary outline of a Serpent rising in the east, and followed by the woman, whom he may therefore, in the most literal sense, be said to seduce, *seducere*, to lead on, as the woman with extended hand, holding a branch of fruit in her hand, is said to seduce, or lead on her husband, the celestial herdsman, Bootes: till, at the moment when the Virgin and the Herdsman, having run after the Devil through the whole garden, are seen to set on the western horizon, which is literally the fall of man, and at the moment of their setting on the western side, the constellation Perseus, the cherubim with the flaming sword will be seen to rise on the opposite side (the east of the Garden of Eden), and so to drive them out, with his flaming sword, which turned every way to keep the way of the tree of life.

The representation of this astronomical phænomenon, as if it had been a real scene, and the Paradise as some place on earth, which might be ascertained by geographical description, by the courses of a river which watered the garden, and from thence was parted, and became into four heads, the Pison, which Josephus says is the Ganges; the Gihon,

---

* Be-ry-sheeth Bo-ro-E-lo-him eith Hash-sho-má-yim ve-eith Ho-o-retz.

which is the Nile; the Hiddekel, which is the Tygris; and the Euphrates, which is as well known as the River Thames, is a grand specimen of the art which runs through both the Old and New Testament—*i. e.*, the art of dressing up fiction into an appearance of history, which has served so effectually to employ the idleness of learning, and to deceive the simplicity of ignorance.

Critics and philologists have fatigued the faculty of invention, in their game of *scratch-cradle*, and the association of the most egregious fables, with so much chronology as *once upon a time:* or, *it came to pass in those days*, and the mixing up of some names of places, and of persons known or spoken of in real history, has served to produce that glorious confusion, and that sublime bringing of heaven and earth together, which so well subserves the purpose of darkening counsel, by words without knowledge. Thus there certainly are such rivers as the Nile and the Ganges, the Tygris and the Euphrates in the world; but if you were to travel by the course of either of those rivers, till you should arrive at the side of the Garden of Eden, you should wish your friends good bye before you set out.

So, were a man to write a romance, and intend to make it as romantic as possible, he would find he could not help associating his reveries with some circumstances of real life, and relieving the rack of his invention by borrowing from his memory. And not more than such evident borrowings of exhausted fiction from natural and probable fact, will be found in any part of sacred theology.

The whole story of the creation of the world, and the allegorical life, character, death, and resurrection of Christ, was acted as a play, or holy pantomime, in the ancient mysteries of Mithra and of Bacchus, from which every doctrine which we now call Christian, is entirely derived; and in the study of which we discover, in a thousand instances, the meaning and reference of passages, which to the Christian ear have no sort of sense at all.

Indeed, the gospels are the books, or compilations more or less spurious, of the Mythriacs of Persia, as the Christians were a sect, and Christianity nothing more than a sectarianism of that infinitely ancient idolatry.

The books were called *sacred*, as signifying *secret*, hidden and set apart from the understanding of the uninitiated

And that appearance of natural dialogue, and real character of speeches and answers, which runs through the four gospels, results from the fact of their being the speeches set down to be spoken by the persons who enacted the characters. The persons being as real as the Keans, Kembles, Youngs, and Wards of the modern drama: but the characters being altogether as imaginary as the Vampires, Fiends, Gods, or Devils, which they represent so ingeniously.

The character, when highly wrought, would often cause the fiction to be overlooked, and the player himself to be mistaken for the character he represented.

As I witnessed myself, on Tuesday evening last, at Coventgarden theatre, in the case of a lady who sat in the same box with me, observing the well-exhibited follies of the Baron Pumpolino, in Cinderella,—till she was so entranced in the cunning of the scene, that, entirely forgetting that it was only a scene, she cried out, '*what a silly old man that is.*'

The historian, Gibbon, relates a story more honourable to the feelings than to the understanding of a Gothic King, who, hearing a preacher of the gospel tell the frightful tale —how God had suffered his only Son, by wicked hands, to be crucified and slain, leaped from his seat, and grasped his spear with a noble oath to the effect:

'If I and my Franks had been there, it should not have happened.'

Thus, in the factitious caves of Mithra, which priests everywhere constructed, and from the ruins of one of which, at Naki Rustan, this hieroglyph of 'the Sun of Righteousness, with healing in his wings,' is derived, they celebrated mysteries which consisted in imitating the motion of the stars, the planets, and the heavens. The initiated took the names of the constellations, and assumed the figures of animals;—one was a lion, another a raven, and a third a ram: and hence arose the use of masks in the first representations of the drama.

In the mysteries of Ceres, the chief in the possession was called the CREATOR; the torchbearer was called the SUN; the person nearest the altar, the MOON; the herald, or messenger, Mercury; and so on.

The proper signification of the word *Creator*, translated from *Tsour*, is a name of the Egyptian God, *Osiris*, signifying, to *give forms*—that is, rather to join and put together than to create. In which, the Creator, of the Old Testament, appears again as the Joseph the carpenter, or joiner of the New.

The name *Joseph*, formed from the Egyptian word Sar Osiph, signifying the Lord Joseph.

But, as if no possibility should be left to hang a doubt on that the personages or personifications of the gospel are the very same as those of the Pagan mythology, and that no such persons ever existed, but in imagination and scenic exhibition only, the gospel opens, with a description of the costume itself, as supplied from the theatrical wardrobe. The order and furniture of the procession in the mystical sanctities of Bacchus and of Christ are precisely the same.

Never was the tragedy of *Macbeth*, as acted at Coventgarden, more like the same tragedy as acted at Drury-lane, than the mysteries of Bacchus and of Jesus, the very name of mystery derived from the Egyptian word Mistor, a *veil*, proves the common Egyptian origin.

In the *ancient* orgies of Bacchus, the doctrine of the purification of souls was represented by a procession of priests, habited in character, and carrying each the emblematical implement of the modes of purification, by the several elements of water, air, earth, and fire. The first in the habit of penitence and abstinence, having his raiment of camels' hair, &c., carried a vase of water in his hand, and 'came baptising with water unto repentance,' announcing a second, who came with a fan in his hand, and a sieve, representing the winnowing of corn,—he baptised with air, the use of the fan being to create that rushing mighty wind, which is the Holy Ghost, or more efficient purifier of souls, 'whose fan is in his hand, and he will thoroughly purge his floor:' a third carried a lighted torch, to burn up the chaff which the motion of the fan blew out of the sieve, with unquenchable fire: a fourth carried the implements of purification by earth, a pruning hook, or adze, 'to be laid at the root of the trees, that every useless branch might be cut off and cast into the fire.' This officer was the husbandman, whose hieroglyphic baptism was by earth, his mode of purification being, 'that every branch that bore not fruit he cut off, and cast into the fire; but every branch that beareth fruit he purgeth it, that it might bring forth more fruit.' John xv. 2.

Eternal God! With evidence in our hands of these ceremonies and processions, having constituted the orgies of Bacchus, and admitted to have done so, by the earliest Christian writers themselves, for countless ages before the Christian era, is it possible to doubt that Christianity and Paganism are as essentially the same, as the natural fruits of the earth of any one year, or country, are of the same nature as those of another. As men and women now are of the same species as the men and women of ten thousand years ago.

'All these religious tragedies,' says Clemens Alexandrinus, 'had a common foundation, only differently set off, and that foundation was the fictitious death and resurrection of the Sun, the soul of the world, the principle of life and motion.

I have explained in previous lectures, how every one of those signs of the Zodiac has, in turn, been the emblem of the supreme God, has been worshipped as such, and has supplied from its physical analogies, all the attributes, characters, and titles which we find ascribed to God, both in the Old and New Testament. The most orthodox Christians are not startled nor offended, when they are told that their Jesus Christ is the Lamb of God, that openeth the kingdom of heaven in March: nor have they any objection to recognise him as the Lion of that tribe of Judah in July. Nor do they blush to own, that when he took upon him to deliver man, he did not abhor the Virgin of August. Though they suspect the orthodoxy of St. Augustin, in addressing his prayers to Jesus Christ, as his good Scarabæus, or Scorpion of October. But though Jesus Christ be admitted to be the Creator, as well as the Saviour of the world, they will hardly forgive their Bible itself, for discovering to them, that the Creator of the world was a GOAT, PAN, even none other than the Capricornus of the Zodiac, which stands there, immediately upon the point when the new year begins, the Sun beginning to ascend, and the days to lengthen as the Goat skips up the mountains.

In reference to which, by an ordinary metonymy of language, the Psalmist represents the mountains, as skipping up the Goats. He only takes the stable for the horse, in exclaiming 'Why hop ye so, ye high hills?' for it was not the hills that hopt upon the goats, but the goats that hopt upon the hills,—' this is God's Goat, in which it hath pleased him to dwell; yea, the Lord upholdeth the same for ever.'

And, as the Sun first begins to renew the world, in entering upon the sign of the Goat, which is the first of the ascending signs, the Goat was called the Creator of the world.

And the original Samaritan Hebrew text of the Samaritan Pentateuch of the first verse of the first chapter of Genesis, was, ' In the beginning the *Goat* created the heavens and the earth.' *

The Sun, taking his name from the Goat, as the first of the ascending constellations, had his whole annual history exhibited in theatrical pantomimes, as the mystical life, death, and resurrection of the Goat. And our word tragedy, always signifying a performance in which there must be a *death*, or something very sanguinary and cruel, is derived to us from the Greek word τραγωδια, which is composed of τραγου ωδη—*i.e.*, the ode or opera of the Goat; and they were performed in honour of the God Bacchus—that is, the Sun who commences his annual career in the sign of the Goat.

The first tragedians upon earth were the priests of Bacchus; the first tragedy was the gospel. And from the first verse of Genesis to the last of the Revelation, we have but varied and diversified scenes and acts of that deep tragedy, which, with reference to the Sun in the Vernal Equinox, is called the *Song of the Lamb*, or the New Song; but which, with reference to Sun in his first degree of ascension, was called the Tragedy, or Song of the Goat, which was the Old Song.

So the sacrifice of Abel, the very first to which God had respect, was a Goat. The 'Scape Goat, that ran away with the sins of the Jews between his horns, was the first type of salvation. ' And the Lamb of God, that taketh away the sins of the Gentiles,' was the second. And it was only to prevent the Rams and the Goats from butting at each other, that Jesus Christ set the *Day of Judgment* sheep on his right hand, and the goats on his left, as we read in the 34th of Ezekiel, ' Thus saith the Lord God, I judge between the Rams and the He-goats.'

* Dupuis, Vol. III., p. 54.

It is admitted and well known by the learned in Biblical criticism, that it has been chiefly the authority of the Jew Rabbi, Moses Maimonides, who lived in the twelfth century, the middle of the dark ages, that the first chapter, or first verse of the first chapter of Genesis, came first to be taken to refer to a real creation of the world.

But how deceitful this old Rabbi was, needs but a knowledge of what himself hath written, under the veil of a language not understood by the people as a word to the wise, —his words, being translated, are:

'We are not to understand, nor take what is written in the book, about the creation, according to the letter, nor to have any such notions of it, as the common people have,— for otherwise our ancient sages would not have recommended us, with so much anxiety to conceal the sense, and not to lift up the allegorical veil, which hides the truths which it contains. This book of Genesis, taken according to the letter, gives the most absurd and extravagant notions of the Deity. Whosoever, then, shall perceive the true meaning, ought to take care not to divulge it.' It is a maxim which all our wise men repeat to us. 'It is difficult for any one, either from the text itself, or from lights elsewhere afforded, not to keep off from a good guess at what it means; but then he ought to say nothing about it: or, if he speak on the subject, he ought to do so only by obscure hints and insinuations, and in an enigmatical way, as I do myself, leaving the rest to be found out, by those who can understand me.' *

This is Jewish honesty! And shall we wonder that the Jewish Rabbis should alter the text, from the original Samaritan reading, 'In the beginning the Goat created the heavens and the earth,' into, 'In the beginning God created the heavens and the earth,' substituting the word אלהים, Elohim, for היזים, hee-zim. When we find our English translation, changing the earlier rendering, 'Abel brought the firstling of the Goats' into 'Abel brought the firstling of his flock,' From the same apparent intention of concealing the part which the astronomical Goat sustains, not only as the first creator, but as the first sacrifice, and first type of the redeemer of the world, and making over his

---

* I Translate this from Dupuis, Vol. III., p. 9.

honour to the sheep: who, in the 3rd of Revelation, calls himself Amon, the beginning of the creation of God, and in the 13th is called 'the Lamb slain from the foundation of the world:'

When it is so evident that the first beast that was slain at the foundation of the world was a Goat, and that the Goat was the beginning of the creation of God—that is, as you see its place in the Zodiac, the beginning of the Sun's ascension in his annual progress through the signs which follow.

END OF THE DISCOURSE ON THE FALL OF MAN.

The Devil's Pulpit.

"AND A BONNIE PULPIT IT IS."—*Allan Cunningham.*

No. 10.—Vol. II.]　　　　　　　　　　　　[Price 2*d.*

NOAH:

A Discourse,

DELIVERED BY THE REV. ROBERT TAYLOR, B.A.
AT THE ROTUNDA, BLACKFRIARS ROAD, JULY 4, 1830.

'And it repented the Lord that he had made man on the earth, and it grieved him at his heart. And the Lord said, I will destroy man whom I have created, from the face of the earth, both man and beast, and the creeping thing, and the fowls of the air: for it repenteth me that I have made them. But Noah found grace in the eyes of the Lord.'—GENESIS vi., 6—8.

WHERE is the wit of man, or where the piety and conscience, that could treat the subject, which now in consecutive series of the great science we are entered on, it becomes our duty to investigate, with solemnity, with seriousness, with sober criticism, with calm and manly reasoning, beyond the measure in which we purpose to do so?

Here is the great cataclysis, the flood, the universal deluge, the whole world drowned, except Noah and his family, and a menagerie ' of every living thing, of all flesh, of fowls after their kind, of cattle after their kind, and of every creeping thing of the earth after his kind—two of every sort, male and female; but of every clean beast, seven of a sort, the male and his female.' So that there must have been an odd one, an old bachelor beast, or an old maid beast of all the clean species. 'These all went in two and two unto Noah into the ark, and the Lord *shut them in.* And the waters prevailed exceedingly upon the earth, and all the high hills that were under the whole heaven were covered. Fifteen cubits upward did the waters prevail, and the mountains were covered. And all flesh died that moved upon the earth, both of fowl and of cattle, and of every creeping thing that creepeth upon the earth, and every man. All in whose nostrils was the breath of life, of all that was in the dry land, died. And every living substance was destroyed. And Noah only remained alive, and they that were with him in the ark. And the waters prevailed upon the earth an hundred and fifty days.'

Though, by an awkward oversight of the divine historian, it appears from the Septuagint that Methusaleh, Noah's grandfather, who was not in the ark, contrived to swim a hore, and lived fourteen years after the flood.

And all this was because God saw that the wickedness of man was great in the earth, and that every imagination of the thoughts of his heart was only evil continually.

And it repented the Lord that he had made man on earth, and it grieved him at his heart.' ויתעצב אל לבו—*Ve Yetobzebhel Lebo*—' And it grieved him at his heart.' The phrase is peculiarly pathetic.

What blasphemy! thus to represent the Creator of the world. Omnipotence repenting that he had made man, sitting upon a stone, and crying like a child, wringing his hands, tearing his hair, calling himself all the fools and idiots he could think of, stamping his foot, cursing, swearing, and vowing vengeance, that he would not leave a dog nor a rat alive. We should yet have but a faint idea of the exceeding sinfulness of sin, and how poor and impotent language of any kind must be, to convey to us the emotions of that infinite wisdom and inconceivable benevolence which repented that he had made man, and grieved that man was no better than he had made him.

There can be no doubt at all that such language as this, when used in relation to the Supreme Being, is used only in gracious condescension to our ignorance, and in accommodation to the dulness and stupidity of our powers of conception, which require to be stimulated and excited by strong and impassioned figures of speech, ere they can be led to form any idea at all, on sacred subjects.

In the Church of England Collect *for fair weather*, the General Deluge is alluded to with equal sublimity and simplicity in those words : ' O Almighty Lord God, who, for the sins of man didst once drown all the world, except eight persons, and afterward of thy great mercy, didst promise *never to do so again.*' Another dish of Christian blasphemy! He promised not to do so any more ! But even that promise is evasive—for though he is made to say he won't drown the world any more, St. Peter tells us that he means to *burn* it one of those days.

The most magnificent poems have been written, the noblest paintings ever produced by the hand of man, have been dedicated to the labor of realising to the imagination the scene of the universal deluge. The Tower of Babel, the Pyramids of Egypt, have been raised in commemoration of this physically impossible event. Not a nation upon earth has existed, whose records have not supplied some attestation to the general belief of the world having been once destroyed by waters. The very form and arrangement of our hills and valleys over the whole earth's surface, is adduced as demonstration to the eye of scepticism itself, that such an event must have taken place. The libraries of the world groan under the weight of millions of folios, written in corroboration of this physically, morally, and absolutely impossible event, which not only never did, but never could have been brought to pass: no, not by the Almighty power of God himself, nor be conceived to have been brought to pass, unless we are to take leave of our rational faculties, and believe that God could commit suicide upon himself, or make a thing to be, and not to be, at the same time.

The passage, as it stands in the Hebrew text of Genesis, may be justly called the *opprobrium doctorum*. For the better skilled in the Hebrew tongue, the more learned, the more shrewdly acute, the more deeply critical, our commentators are, the further off they are from any sort of agreement among themselves, as to the meaning of any one verb or noun of that very sacred text.

What are we to do, gentlemen, when the doctors and rabbis differ so widely in their different translations, as upon a comparison of them, to leave it infinitely problematical, whether we are in possession of any translation at all, or whether the scope and intent of the original text be not a hundred thousand miles off the meaning of any meaning that they have put upon it.

Never forgetting this grand truth, that the oldest Hebrew texts which the doctors and rabbis can pretend to, are themselves not originals, but translations from a language, in all probability as much older than the Hebrew, as the Hebrew is than the modern Italian. Our pretended original is itself a translation.

There was never an author or divine yet, who attempted

to explain the doctrine of the universal deluge, but an observer of his explanation might discover that the water had set his head a swimming.

I shall adduce only a few of the translations that have been given by equally learned and profound Hebrew scholars, of what might pass for as easy and simple a text as could occur in the whole narrative. Our English Bibles have it, 'And God said unto Noah, Make thee an ark of gopher wood: rooms shalt thou make in the ark, and shalt pitch it within and without with pitch.'

The learned and evangelical Hebraist, Bellamy, who smells out evangelical meanings, where no man on earth but himself had ever dreamed of them, assures us, that, this verse ought to have been rendered, 'Make for thee an ark of the wood of gopher: for thou shalt expiate in it, even a house also, with an outer room for atonement.'

Eternal God! let us throw words together with a shovel, we should have as good a chance for finding meaning in them.

'Light and darkness,' says this great Hebraist, 'cannot differ more than Hebrew differs from the English.' And we shall find, that instead of Noah being informed that he was to pitch the ark within and without with pitch, God commands him to build apartments in the ark for sacrifice and atonement.

So that, notwithstanding the space that would be occupied in the ark, by two of every species of unclean, and seven of every species of clean animals, and provender for them for two years; there was room enough to spare for a church and churchyard aboard the ship.

The transition of idea from pitch to cobler's wax (which is made of pitch) is not more apparent in the judgment of this learned Hebraist, than is his influence, that God could not have given any orders about pitching the ark with pitch, without intending some provision to be made for the *sole*. He is sure that the word which our English Bibles have rendered *pitch*, ought to have been rendered *atonement*: as I might be sure that the word cobler's wax is synonymous with the word salvation, because when a man comes to the *last*, he will find salvation as precious to the *sole* as atonement is to the upper leather.

Only, how comfortably sure we may make on't, that our

English Bibles are faithfully translated, when the most learned of the learned world assure us, that the difference between our translations, and the original Hebrew, is only as different as light and darkness.

The real waggery is, in the contradiction of the ideas themselves, that God should employ almighty power and infinite wisdom to save a ship from foundering, and yet hit on no better way than having it well caulked. It would have sunk if it hadn't been made of gopher wood. It would have sprung a leak if it hadn't been pitched with atonement wax.

And what was gopher wood? Hear the wise rabbis and most learned commentators: 'It was cedar,' says the Targum of Onkilos: 'It was juniper,' says Castellus: 'It was boxwood,' say the Arabic commentators: 'It was pine-tree wood,' say the Persic: 'It was ebony wood,' says Bochart: 'It was no sort of wood at all,' say the no less learned Dawson and Geddes: 'It was made of wicker-work,' says Geddes: 'It was made of bulrushes daubed over with slime,' says Dawson: Go it, my boys! Go it! I warrant ye it was made of some wood: Was it not made of *false-wood*?

But the most plausible interpretation of all, and infinitely nearer the sense of the original is, that it was made of barley-sugar for the children of Israel to suck: of which the great Hebraist gives us a hint in a very shrewd note at the bottom of his page, where, in an explanation of the text, 'Fifteen cubits upward did the waters prevail, and the mountains were covered:' he admonishes us that, 'It is not at all necessary to suppose that the Antediluvian mountains were as high as those of the present earth, they may have been of a very different form and size, and composed of other materials."

Indeed it is almost impossible to tell when the learned, and most learned and grave authors, are serious with us on this subject. For notwithstanding an infinity of research, and immense literature expended, it is impossible for anybody but a fool not to suspect them, *ever and anon*, of that mode of sarcasm, called the *Diasurmus*, or what, in the vulgar phrase, is called 'Coming it' upon us—that is, trying how far we may be led by the nose, and how much we will swallow.

But can we blame them for deceiving us? Or have we

any right to expect that they should tell us the truth: or to
imagine that it is the truth which they are telling us, when,
if they discover to us that they are wiser than we are, we
kill them, or cut them off from social existence: and the
man of learning who had only ventured to speak the convictions of his heart, is dealt on worse than the house-breaker
or common thief: and honest learning bears the lash of vice.

There are no two authors in the world who have
attempted to treat the story of the deluge as an historical
fact; and Noah, as the person who had a real existence,
who have not differed from each other, in their interpretations, as widely as it was possible to differ. Each successive
interpreter emerging only to oppose and overthrow the
interpretation which his predecessors had given.

Thus the learned Faber cites proof from the Etymologi-
con Magnum, that the word תבה, *Thebah!* which we render
ark, signifies, in Syriac, a cow. So that the command of
God to Noah, to make an ark of gopher wood, should mean
only that he was to make a wooden cow, as we have a
curiously coincident passage in Diodorus.

'Some say that when Osiris was killed by Typhon, Isis
having collected his scattered limbs, put them into a wooden
cow, covered over with cambric or lawn: and hence the
town was called *Busiris:* and hence, too, our bishops, to
this day, continue to wear lawn sleeves.'

As the word which we translate an *ark*, so certainly
signifies a cow, we shall not wonder that NOAH might be
saved from drowning in a wooden cow: when we have such
good reason to suspect that the whale which swallowed
Jonah might have been a wooden whale.

And as salvation was always a wooden affair, we have a
clear analogy, for the office and character which the
carpenter bears in it. The ark could not have been built,
unless Noah had been a carpenter; nor could God have
instructed him how to put it together, unless God had
possessed considerable skill in carpentry: the cross could
not have been constructed without a carpenter. So that the
very scribes and pharisees could not make the matter plainer,
that Jesus was come to be the Saviour of the world, than by
their unanswerable question, 'Is not this the carpenter's son?'

The natural and almost inevitable transition of human
ideas, from the supposed *cause* of salvation, to the means

and instrument of it, and the transfer of feelings of gratitude, for being saved: into a peculiar respect for the particular matter instrumentally employed in their salvation accounts for the wooden ark, and the wooden cross, leading men on to the worship of wooden gods.

The natural succession of human ideas, their origin in the impressions of matter upon the five senses, and their combinations in the sensorium of a similarly constructed brain, accounts at once for the uniformity and similarity of all the great archetypes of religious terror in all parts of the world, and among all generations of the human species. It could not possibly have been that creatures, often destroyed by floods, and always liable to drowning, should be without that natural exaggeration which ignorance and terror must suggest, of the drowning of the old world.

And hence no nation, or race of men, has existed, or ever could exist, without its imaginations and fables of miraculous deluges, and miraculous escapes from drowning, and the story of Noah and his ark is found with only immaterial variations in the legends of Prometheus, Deucalion, Atlas, Theuth, Zeuth, Zeus, Xisuthros, Inachus, Osiris, Helius, which is the Sun, *Meen* or *Man*, which is the Moon: from which Egyptian word, our Teutonic name of our own species, *Man* and *Men* is derived, as Noah was believed to be the first of the present race of men.

The crescent and gibbous forms of the moon, presenting the shape of a *boat*, seeming to sail without oars or masts in the waters which are above the firmament, over the tops of the highest mountains: the physically apparent influence of the moon upon the tides of the sea, and the inundations of rivers; and the irresistible association of ideas which could not by any possibility shut out the conceit of there being *a man in the moon*, a directing mens, a good and just man be sure on't, guiding its navigation through the trackless ocean, and preserved in its concave from the desolation of all sublunary things, presents a demonstration, not indeed that the world could ever have been drowned, but that there never could have been a nation or people in the world, who must not by the necessary actions of the human mind, and the immutable laws of nature, have stumbled on some such conceit.

The man in the moon, then, is Noah in the ark, and this

so literally, that the very names, Egyptian, Chaldean, Hebrew, Greek, Latin, German, Saxon, French, English, betray the identity Μην, Μαν, Μον, Μοον, Men, Mens, the mind, all of the same family, all bearing the same likeness.

In the Hebrew word נח Noach, which we translate Noah, consisting only of the two consonants, N and Ch, or X, to be supplied by vowels, *ad-libitum*, we have Ia Nach, the root of the name Inachus, Noux, and Nox, the night, Noos, or Νους, the mind, and Ναυς or Νävς, a ship, Hebrew, Anceyah: All referable to the boat-like form of the *moon*, sailing without chart or mast upon the ocean of the *night*, and bearing and guided by the divine mind for the preservation of animal existence.

We are constantly reading in the ancient mythology of the Θεοι ναυτιλλοντες, or sailing gods. Porphyry assures us that the ancients described the Sun himself in the character of a man sailing on a float,—and Plutarch observes that they did not represent the Sun and Moon in chariots, but as wafted about in floating machines, a sort of motion more homogene to that which we see the motion of the heavenly bodies to be.

And, notwithstanding the intolerant insolence with which heaven and earth have been brought together; the bowels of the earth been ransacked, and all heart and nature, science and learning, laid under levy to make the story of the deluge in the grossest sense of it, appear a real fact, on the supposition that the credit of what is called divine revelation, could only be maintained as that fact should be shown to be incontrovertible; it happens that that divine revelation expressly instructs us, that the story of the deluge is not a literal fact, nor so to be understood, but a figure only. As in 1 Peter, iii. 19—21 are spoken of, ' the spirits in prison, which sometime were disobedient, when once the long suffering of God waited in the days of Noah, while the ark was a preparing, wherein few—that is, eight souls were saved by water, the like figure whereunto even baptism doth now save us.'

A sufficient intimation, one would think, for stupidity itself to have noticed, that the whole affair of Noah, and his watery salvation, was a figure of speech, as our salvation by the water of baptism is but a like figure.

But it happens that the whole history of Noah is entirely

a Chaldean fable; and the 6th, 7th, 8th, 9th, 10th, and 11th chapters of Genesis are a mere episode and interpolation, plagiarized out of the sacred legends of the Chaldean priests, and inserted into the book Genesis. As an attentive reader of the Bible, will observe, throughout the whole Bible history (if it were a history), that the supposed descendants of Abraham, Isaac, and Jacob, had never heard of their descent from the old drunkard Noah. Nor is his name mentioned, nor his history glanced at, till after the period of their supposed Babylonish captivity in Chaldea, from whence the silly legend was derived.

The Books of Psalms, Proverbs, Chronicles, Judges, Kings, amidst innumerable references to Patriarchs, to Moses and Aaron, and the manifestations of God's power and goodness, in the most contemptible and ridiculous miracles, the covenant which he made with Abraham, and the oath which he sware unto Jacob, and his drowning Pharaoh and his host in the Red Sea, never once allude to the prettiest miracle of 'em all, his drowning the whole world at once.

What other supposable cause of the omission can be assigned, than the evident one, that it had not at that time been introduced into their book?

Their historian, Josephus, however, found it in the text of Genesis, in his time, and in his defence of the Jewish people against the attacks of Apion, justifies the account of the deluge, given in the Book of Genesis, on the sole ground of its perfect agreement with the account to be found of it in the ancient Chaldean legends. After having collated the testimonies scattered in the writings of various nations, 'Now,' says he, 'I shall interrogate the monuments of the Chaldeans; and my witness shall be Berosus, born himself a Chaldean, a man known to all the Greeks, who cultivate letters, on account of the works he published in Greek concerning the astronomy and philosophy of the Chaldeans.

'Berosus then, after having compiled and copied the most ancient histories, gives the same accounts as Moses of the deluge, of the destruction of men by the waters, and of the ark in which Noux* was saved, and which stopped on the mountains of Armenia.'

Josephus continues, 'Hierome, the Egyptian, who wrote upon Phœnician antiquities, also speaks of it, as does Mnaseas, and several others.'

Thus we see that Josephus is so far from looking upon Berosus, and the other historians, as having derived their stories of the deluge from the Book of Genesis, that his whole argument is in challenge of respect for the Book of Genesis, solely on account of its having been derived from them; and he invokes the Chaldean, Armenian, and Phœnician monuments, as the first and original witnesses, of which the Book of Genesis is only an emanation.

A proof external, which I undertake to support by innumerable internal proofs that our Genesis and other sacred books in the Hebrew and Greek tongues, were not originals, but translations from some infinitely remote original, of which no vestige remains.

But the most particular history of the deluge, and the nearest of any to the account given in the Book of Genesis, is to be found in Lucian's treatise of the Syrian goddess,[*] who describes Noah under the name of Deucalian, as does the poet Ovid; and his account is so entirely coincident with that of Genesis, as to leave no possibility of doubt, that they were both derived from the same original.

A similar story is found in the Bhagavat Pourana, the sacred *Bible* of the Hindoos, which contains also the substantive story of Jesus Christ; thus proving the derivation of both the Old and New Testaments from the same sources: the words of that divine poem are thus given by Sir William Jones:—

'The demon Hayagriva having purloined the Vedas from the custody of Brahma, while he was reposing at the close of the 6th *Manwantara*, the whole race of men became corrupt, except the seven *Rishis*, and *Satyavrata*. This Prince was performing his ablutions in the river *Critamala*, when Vishnu appeared to him in the shape of a small fish; and after several augmentations of bulk in different waters, was placed by Satyavrata in the ocean, when he thus addressed his amazed votary. In seven days all creatures who have offended me shall be destroyed by a deluge, but thou shalt be secured in a capacious vessel miraculously formed. Take, therefore, all kinds of medicinal herbs and grain for food, and together with the seven holy men, your respective wives, and pairs of all animals, enter the ark without fear, then

---

[*] Bryant's Analysis, Vol. III., p. 28.

shalt thou know God face to face, and all thy questions shall be answered. Saying this he disappeared; and after seven days the ocean began to flow, the coasts, and the earth to be flooded by constant showers: when Satyavrata, meditating on the Deity, saw a large vessel moving on the waters, he entered it, having in all respects conformed to the instructions of Vishnu, who, in the form of a vast fish, suffered the vessel to be tied with a great sea serpent as with a cable to his measureless horn. When the deluge had ceased, Vishnu slew the demon, and recovered the Vedas, instructed Satyavrata in divine knowledge, and appointed him the 7th Menu, by the name of Vaivaswata.'

The expression, ELOHIM, *the Gods*, so often and almost exclusively found in the Book of Genesis, from which our Hutchinsonian divines so ingeniously argue the existence of a trinity of divine persons in the Godhead; because God said, 'Let us make man in *our* image after our likeness,' is but another demonstration of the Chaldean origin of the whole system; because, in the Chaldean, and in almost all the Asiatic theologies, It is not a single God who created; but they were the Gods, his ministers, his angels, and especially the deacons and genii of the twelve months who created each his part of the world—that is, the circle of the year.

And thus have we a reasonable and philosophical explanation, of that apparently most monstrous absurdity, which I explained in a discourse, on the first verse of the first chapter of Genesis; that that verse in the Samaritan Pentateuch, originally was: ברא העו את השמים ואת הארץ בראשית 'In the beginning the Goat created the heavens and the earth.' The word ברא, *Boro*, conveying no such idea as that of a creation out of nothing, but a renewal only. And in the annual renewal of the circle of the heavens and the earth, which commences from the winter solstice, immediately after the shortest day, the 21st of December, or when first the Sun appears to have gained the first degree of ascension, which is on the 25th of December, our Christmas-day. You see the Sun is in Capricornus, the Goat, who is therefore the Creator—that is, the renewer or first opener of the annually repeated Genesis, or creation of the heavens and the earth.* As in the sign which imme-

---

* About the 'goat created the heavens and the earth,' my authority

diately follows, you see the Genius of the waters, Aquarius, January, Noah, the Nile, Reuben, Inachus, St. Peter, St. Mark, St. Januarius, Bishop of Benevento, pouring out his urn of water upon the world. He is the just man, in whom the system, after the deluge, is again renewed. And though, in the beginning, it was the Goat, the emblem of wickedness and of wicked people, who created the heavens and the earth, the year has since been reckoned to begin in January, that just and righteous man, who, you see, has turned his back upon the wicked generation of the Goat; and succeeded to all the titles, names, and attributes of Supreme Deity; which we find in turn given to every one of these signs of the Zodiac, as the Sun in succession seems to pass through them; and was worshipped as being *in* them.

Thus all the deluges mentioned by Jews, Chaldeans, Indians, Greeks, or Romans, as having destroyed the world, under Ogyges, Noah, Inachus, Xisuthrus, Satavrata, or Deucalion, are one and the same physico-astronomical event, all the marvellousness of which has arisen from the metaphorical language employed to express it, and that foolish love of wonderment and absurdity, which makes men who have once taken up a conceit, how gross or irrational soever it may be, impatient of that further instruction and better information which would rectify their mistakes, and rob them of their faith in the gods and *godlings* of the babyhouse.

If we dissipate their delusion, and spoil the amusement which the children of Israel find in so pretty a toy as Noah's ark, with all the pretty little lions, and tigers, and elephants, and cats, and dogs, and rats, and birds, and snakes, marching into it, two and two, like a regiment of soldiers: not only shall we lose all favour with the six-foot-high babies themselves, who will be sure to cry out, 'if you rob us of Noah's ark, what other ark will you give us in it its stead?' but their papas and mammas will swell the hubbub against us, and become our enemies, on the score, as they will say, that '*the children must have their Noah's ark.* It's

---

for this curious criticism is the great Dupuis, Vol. III., p. 84. 'C'est donc par elle que l'on pourra expliquer l'expression singulière, dont se sert La Genèse des Samaritains, pour désigner le Dieu-Créateur. On y lisoit ces mots : Au commencement, le Dove créa le ciel et la terre.'

perfectly innocent, it's politically useful. It serves to keep 'em out of mischief; and suppose 'it is a delusion, what harm is there in it? What would they gain by discovering that it was a delusion?'

But enough of this. Its answer is at once: Is it better to be a dunce and an idiot than to be rational? is folly better than wisdom? Is God's best gift of reason so vile in our esteem, that we should think man the better for being without it? If not so, then, the irrational only will be unwilling to correct those errors of language, and vagaries of conceit, which have held the human mind so long in the swathing bands of a perpetuated infancy.

From the primordial imperfection of language, no other word was found to express the great circle of the heavens, than such as the Greek Κοσμος, which signifies the arrangement, the Latin Mundus, of precisely the same signification, the Hebrew תבל. *Tycel*, of the same signification, and our English WORLD, derived by the same analogy from the *whirl*, or circular ring of the revolving Zodiac. The revolution of this circle by the Sun, comprising the year of twelve months, was called *Orbis*, the world, the celestial circle; consequently every twelve months the world ended, and the world began again, the world was destroyed or expired, and the world was renewed. And at whatever point of this circle, or in which ever of these signs, the *whirl'd*, or the *go-round* was reckoned to begin, *that* sign was deemed the *beginner*, or creator of the world.

Now, of course, the epoch or point of beginning in the reckoning of this annual whirl varied considerably, according as different people or countries reckoned their year to begin, as they might reckon it to begin, on any day, or in any month they pleased. There being, however, but four distinctly marked points in the circle, which would be convenient for accurate reckoning. These are the two points in the year when, once in Spring, as the days lengthen, about the 25th of March; and once again in Autumn, as the days shorten, about the 21st of September, the days and nights are exactly of the same length; and these are called the Vernal and Autumnal Equinoxes—that is, *equal nights*. And when the Sun is at its highest point of ascension, and the days are consequently the longest, which is about the 21st of June, and when again the Sun is at its lowest point of declension, and the days are the shortest, which is about the 21st of December,—where you see the Goat, in which the Sun begins immediately to re-ascend: thus supplying us with a clear and philosophical sense for the most literal rendering of the 1st of Genesis, 'In the beginning the Goat created the heavens and the earth;' and enabling us to trace that very curious association of idea, which led the wisest and most philosophical nations of the earth to worship the Supreme Being, the Great First Cause of the universe, under the name of PAN, and under the imagined form of half a man and half a Goat. The Creator, or annual beginner of the whirl, having his lower or Decembral part in Capricornus, and his upper part in the good and just man of Aquarius.

But among those nations which reckoned the annual whirl, or circuit of the Sun through the heavens, to begin from the Vernal Equinox—that is, when the Sun was in the Lamb of the Zodiac, the Lamb was considered as the Creator of the *whirl*. And as you see that the Lamb or Ram of God has his position in the Zodiac, precisely at the point where the Ecliptic crosses the Equator: the Lamb and the cross became essentially and inseparately associated ideas; the Lamb was said to be crucified; and you arrive at the meaning of that passage of St. John, in which Jesus Christ—that is, the SUN, is spoken of as crucified from the beginning of the world—that is, he is crucified or crosses the Equator every spring, immediately at the beginning of the annual circle.

But this is but half the coincidence of the language of science and theology. For look to your New Testament, and you will find that your Jesus Christ is positively declared to have been crucified twice. Because the Sun, having crossed the Equatorial line, at the Equinoctial point in Spring, when he ascended into heaven, must cross it again, at the Equinoctial point in Autumn, when he descended into Hell. As in Revelations xi., 8, the same St. John, who had taught that Christ was crucified on Mount Calvary, in Judea, as positively asserts, that he was also crucified in Egypt in those words, 'and Egypt, where also our Lord was crucified.'

And so St. Paul, preaching Jesus Christ, and him crucified, when he tells us that he humbled himself, and became obedient unto death, explains himself by adding to those words, 'obedient unto death,' *even the death of the cross—* that is, you see, no death at all; only such a mystical and metaphysical sort of death as the Sun dies, when he crosses the Equator. For had it been in right earnest,—had there been any real, downright dying and *going dead* in the matter, there would have been a dead end both of our blessed Saviour and our blessed Salvation too, and we should never have seen the Sun again.

But in Egypt they reckoned their year from the summer solstice, when the sun has reached his highest point of elevation, which is the 21st of June. The Hebrew or Egyptian name of which month is THAMMUZ, which is absolutely none other than *Thomas*, the disciple of Christ, who, in the moral representation, had half a mind to go back again, as in the physical one, his sign in the Zodiac is Cancer, the Crab. As the allegorists have given him a crabbed moral character in the gospel. And just at this season of the year it is, that the river Nile begins to show the first indications of the approaching inundation, according to which physical phænomenon, you will find, in your Prayer Books and Almanack, that the 24th of June is assigned as the day of the nativity of John the Baptist, and in forty days from that time the annual deluge is found to cover all the land of Egypt, to an average depth of fifteen cubits, while a hundred and fifty days (the term during which the flood is said to be upon the earth,) added to the 24th of June, the beginning of the inundation brings us to the exact place of Noah, the Aquarius of the celestial whirl, who is again John the Baptist come in the wilderness baptizing with water to repentance.

And it is this double way of reckoning,—the one considering the time of the increase which was forty days, and the other the whole term of the inundation, and the mixing up of the times of the inundations of the Tigris, the Euphrates, and the Ganges (which exhibit the same annual phænomena), which has occasioned the egregious apparent contradiction in the story of Genesis, which twice asserts that the waters were on the earth forty days, and yet so emphatically concludes that the waters prevailed 150 days.

And thus has an entirely natural and annually recurring event, by the common metaphor and exaggeration of language, been conjured into the most monstrous and idiotish conceit that ever frenzy dreamed or folly credited.

And we have only to learn the humiliating lessons, how dreadful an insanity religion is, what desparate havoc it makes in the brains, even of the wisest and cleverest men in all other respects; and, how entirely and for ever we must say good night to reason, to sobriety, to truth, and honesty, or to any expectation of them from any man when once that cruel disease has seized on him.

For look ye, Sirs, we have the long succession of Christian fathers, even into the fourth and fifth centuries, solemnly appealing to the fact of the existence of the remains of Noah's ark, upon the mountains of Armenia, in their own times.

And the learned Bryant, than whom a more learned man could not exist within fifty years of our own, exhausting his vast stores of learning, to vindicate the authenticity of his Apamean Medal, struck, you may suppose, on board the ark itself, exhibiting the head of Philip of Macedon on the one side, and Noah, Shem, Ham, and Japheth on the other.

And you have all the religion in the world, and all the religious men in the world, engaged in maintaining and giving an air of respectability and seriousness to a conceit so monstrous, that the story of the cow that jumpt over the moon is sobriety itself compared to it.

Extensive and desolating inundations, irruptions of the sea upon the land, and tremendous bursts of cataracts, and water spouts, have undoubtedly taken place, in all parts of the globe, and in all ages of the world. Nor is there, perhaps, a spot on the whole earth's surface, that has not been, and may not be again, a part of the bed of the ocean.

But that the waters should have ever covered the whole globe at once, is an absurd chimera in physics,—impossible in nature, and inconceivable in reason.

No such person, then, as Noah, or as any of the persons who are said to have been with him in the ark ever existed: no such an event as the deluge ever did or ever could have happened. And we can only take this story as an admonition to us, through our future investigations, of what we are to think, and how we are to understand all the other sacred personages, and sacred histories of sacred scripture.

END OF THE DISCOURSE ON NOAH.

The Devil's Pulpit.

"AND A BONNIE PULPIT IT IS."—*Allan Cunningham.*

No. 11.—Vol. II.]   Price 2*d*.

ABRAHAM:

A Discourse,

DELIVERED BY THE REV. ROBERT TAYLOR, B.A.
AT THE ROTUNDA, BLACKFRIARS ROAD, JULY 21, 1830.

'*After these things the word of the Lord came unto Abram, in a vision, saying, Fear not, Abram: I am thy shield and thy exceeding great reward. And Abram said, Lord God, what wilt thou give me?*'—
GENESIS, xv., 1.

THERE is a very curious, but most essentially important variation of the *name* of this most extraordinary personage, with whom I am now to bring you acquainted.

From the eleventh chapter of this ancient Chaldean Mythos, called the book of Genesis, in which he is *first* mentioned as *Abram*, the Son of Terah, in the land of his nativity in Ur of the Chaldees (which demonstrates the Chaldee origin of his whole story), he is called אברם Ab-Ram. But in the 17th chapter God changes his name from אברם into אברהם, *Ouvroime*, assigning that never-to-be-forgotten reason for that change, 'Neither shall thy name any more be called Abram, but thy name shall be Abraham, for a father of many nations have I made thee.'

This passage alone is fatal to the pretence of the people called Jews, or of any other particular nation, to be called the descendants or children of Abraham; since he was not to be the founder of a nation, or any peculiar people,—but 'a father of many nations,' the common progenitor of all the families of the earth.

A similar change of name, and for a similar reason, is announced with respect to Sarah, the wife of Abraham, in the 15th of this chapter:

'And God said unto Abraham, as for—שרי—thy wife, thou shalt not call her name שרי, but שרה shall her name be: and she shall be a mother of nations, kings of people shall be of her.'

The name Sair, afterwards ill pronounced and ill written Shari or Shira, was the name which the ancient Arabians originally gave to the Star *Sirius*,* and literally rendered, signifies a STAR.

If, then, we chose to suppose the highest respect to be due to this Book of Genesis, it is an evident outrage against it, and an egregious vanity and impotence, either to pretend or to admit the pretention of any particular nation or people upon earth to be peculiarly, or in any exclusive or distinguished sense, the descendants or race of this Universal Father and Universal Mother of mankind.

Nor is there a single passage of either the Old or the New Testament, that recognises or countenances a national or political claim of any race or community of men, that ever were upon earth, to be related to these entities, any more or any nearer than any other people. But contrariwise, the relation to Abraham and Sarah is, in every instance in which it is alluded to, spoken of exclusively as a *moral*, and not as a national, political, or hereditary relationship.

There are no people on earth,—there never was a single individual of the human race, in any *literal* sense, descended from Abraham and Sarah, any more than there were never any literal children of the Devil, or sons of Belial.

There never was any idiom of speech in the world, so common and universal, as *that* by which, in the Hebrew and all oriental languages, anything which bore a resemblance to some other thing, or stood in some close association of comparison with it, was called the *son* of that thing, or its *daughter*. These languages had no adjectives, and were therefore driven on a necessity of expressing the qualities of nouns, by the use of other nouns, supposed to bear a relation to them : and hence, they could not designate a righteous man, but as the son of something or somebody that had been supposed to possess a character similar to that which they would ascribe to him.

The 'generation of the faithful,' and the 'children of the wicked one,' were the necessary periphrases to express the characters of persons who were themselves *faithful* or *wicked;* but not at all implying the real existence of the

---

* Sir William Drummond's Or'ginos, Vol. III., p. 460.

faithful and the *wicked*, whose generation or children they were said to be.

Thus we read continually such figures as 'the Sons of Eli, were Sons of Belial'—that is, they were bad men: not literally *Sons* of Belial, nor had any such person as Belial really existed. They were only *like* to what was *adverse* or *opposed*. So, when Saul would call his son perverse and rebellious, he could find no other phrase for that sense, than " Thou son of the perverse rebellious woman,' nothing being further from the meaning than any idea of his really being the son of any such a woman, or any woman of such a character having a real existence.

Nor is any real existence implied, in the abstractions which are hieroglyphed under the names of Abraham and Sarah; nor any real physical descent or continuation implied in that orientalism of speech, whereby good and virtuous persons are called the children, or sons and daughters of Abraham and Sarah.

The relationship is always moral,—never national or personal. It was those only who resembled the character attributed to Abraham, or who studied and understood the astronomical science, veiled under the names and allegorical histories of Abraham and Sarah, who were the children of Abraham, as in that noble challenge of the evangelical prophet, 'Harken to me ye that follow after righteousness, ye that seek the Lord, look unto the rock whence ye are hewn, and to the hole of the pit whence ye are digged. Look unto Abraham, your father, and unto Sarah, that bare you.'

As St. Paul, in his Epistle to the Romans (who certainly were not Jews nor of Jewish extraction), emphatically calls Abraham, 'the Father of us all,' grounding his argument on the text, 'as it is written, I have made thee a father of many nations.' Romans, iv., 17. And in his Epistle to the Greeks of Galatia, he as expressly designates Sarah, the wife of Abraham, 'the mother of us all.'

I shall have the happiness of introducing you to a better acquaintance with our Mother Sarah in a future lecture; I must confine the present to the business of cultivating a due intimacy with the great universal Patriarch, our Father Abraham.

The claim of the Jews, among ourselves, to be in an

exclusive sense, the race of Abraham, can be founded on no other, and no better argument, than that of their resemblance to what appears a considerable defect in the imaginary character of this prosopon,—and that is, his extraordinary avarice. For the moment the Lord God had said to him, 'Fear not Abram, I am thy shield and thy exceeding great reward,' Abram immediately replied, 'Lord God, what wilt thou give me?' Nor are we to think this a disrespectful or too familiar sort of language for Abraham to use towards the Almighty. But far from it, since we read, that when the Lord spake unto Abram about his wife, 'he fell upon his face and laughed.'

And, indeed, this Jewish characteristic of keeping an eye to the main chance, seems to have run in Abram's family.—as we find his grandson Jacob, in the very fervours of devotion and piety, not forgetting that those fervours would not keep the pot boiling,—he therefore intimates that godliness would never do for him, unless godliness should be profitable for the life which now is, as well as for that which is to come: he therefore puts up, in the 28th of Genesis, that truly sublime and most rational form of prayer that ever was in the world: 'If thou, Lord, wilt keep me in this way that I go, and wilt give me food to eat, and raiment to put on, so that I come again to my father's house in peace: then shall the Lord be my God, and of all that thou shalt give unto me, I will surely give the tenth unto thee.'

A thrifty bargain, you see. God was to give him a suit of livery, and allow him board-wages; and then, he would allow God ten per cent. out of the profits of all his swindling and tricky trade. As his very name Jacob signified that he knew how to get his mutton without saying a word to the butcher about it.

But our more immediate business is with his grandfather, Abraham. Our inquiry is, *Who was Abraham?* And it is of singular importance to observe, that he is designated the Son of *Terah*,* (Terra), and of Ur of the Chaldees.† His story, then, is not Jewish, not Hebrew, not of Palestine, of Judea, or of Egypt, but of Chaldea,—not possibly, therefore, of the composition of any such person, as the supposed Moses must be supposed to be,—not possibly original in any

---

* תרח.   † באור כשדים.

Hebrew exhibition of it, but necessarily derived to the Hebrew, Syriac, Phœnician, or Greek versions, from its native Chaldea.

To Chaldea, then, and Chaldaic records, we must necessarily turn for the solution of our inquiries, as to the first types of this Chaldaic person, or personification of Abram, the son of Terah, of Ur of the Chaldees.

Of the Chaldaic history, our knowledge is derived mainly from such fragments as the Greek writers have preserved to us, of the writings of Atydenus, Apollodorus, Alexander Polyhistor, and Berosus, of Babylon, the capital of the Chaldean empire, a priest of the God Belus, who was contemporary with Alexander the Great, of Macedon—that is, about 330 years before Christ. These all concur in representing the existence of political government, learning, and science, as of infinite antiquity in that country.

As Atydenus and Berosus speak of regularly reigning sovereigns, through a period of ten sari, which is 36,000 years, and Apollodorus, of dynasties continued through four times that period, which is 144,000 years: It never being to be forgotten, that whatever we may think of such dates, resting on such authorities, compared to our Mosaic accounts, which reckon the world but as 6,000 years old, the ancient Chaldee astronomers are proved to have been acquainted with the very highest discoveries of astronomical science, and to have calculated the measure of time, to the precision of the setting of a chronometer; while the whole world besides were as ignorant as religious people in all the world have ever been.

The prophet Isaiah speaks of 'Babylon, the glory of kingdoms, the beauty of the Chaldean excellence.' Nor was it till after the return of the Jewish people from their Babylonish captivity, that the name of Abraham, or any portion of the Chaldaic story, was found in books that claimed a Jewish origin. The demonstration, then, is complete: it is a plagiarism. They stole it from their masters, the Chaldeans; and, without caring to acquaint themselves with the astronomical significancy, they adopted the veil of an occult science, as a tissue of real history, and pretended that that history was peculiarly their own.

But as Abraham, in the very significancy of the name, ignifies *a Father*, or the Father *superlatively exalted:* and by inference, 'the father of many nations,' reason and common sense would dictate, that we must look for the bearings, gist, and purpose of his history in some sense that shall be common to the understanding of many nations.

And such a sense will be found only in restoring him to his proper place and relations 'in the kingdom of heaven.'

The Chaldeans, the most skilful in astronomy of all nations, delighted to veil their astronomical science under the types of imagined histories.

It would be seen, however, at once, by any attentive reader of the New Testament, that it could never have been intended that Abraham should be taken for a real personage, who had existed in any bye-gone era of the world; in, that he is spoken of in the New Testament, as being as much in existence at the time of the writers or speakers in the New Testament, as he had *ever* been. He is addressed by the rich man in Hell, who lifteth up his eyes, and seeth Abraham afar off, and Lazarus in his bosom. Where the story is not said to be a parable, and has not the appearance of being so, than many of the details of his parabolical history, in the Book of Genesis. And St. Paul, in his Epistle to the Galatians, refers even the most probable and apparently historical features of the detail, to an allegorical significancy. For, 'it is written,' says he, 'that Abraham had two sons, the one by a bond-maid, the other by a free-woman, which things are an allegory'—that is, *a fiction*, indicating no such thing, nor the like of any such thing as appears in the literal text of what is written;'

And sure, if his having two sons was a fiction, clothing some other and more exalted meaning, it is madness or wickedness to suppose that there could be anything more than fiction in his setting about to murder one of his sons, and then seizing a ram caught by the horns in a thicket (just as the Ram of the Zodiac is caught by the horns in the thicket made by the crossing of the Equator by the Ecliptic at the Vernal Equinox), and sacrificing that ram in his stead.

Assuming, as I must, for brevity sake, that your memories will supply what the Scriptures of the Old and New Testament deliver, touching the person and character of Abraham, I proceed now to the demonstration of the important fact, that no such person as Abraham ever existed; that this character and actions are altogether a fiction, and that that fiction was a part of the sublime system of occult science, which is traceable throughout all the mythology of the Pagan world.

1st. Then, you have the admission in the sacred text that Abram was the son of Terah, a native of Ur of the Chaldees.

His is therefore a Chaldean story.

The Chaldeans are admitted on all hands to have carried the science of astronomy to the highest pitch of perfection, and to have veiled their astronomical science under precisely such allegorical personifications and fabulous histories as this of Abraham appears to be.

The name of Abram, itself, is absolutely an astronomical term, composed of the two syllables, Ab and Ram, signifying *Father of Elevation*, which is the astronomical characteristic of the planet Saturn, the highest, and most devious of course of all the heavenly bodies.

But not only is the name of AB-RAM most literally an astronomical term, so clearly indicating that no such person as Abraham ever existed, any more than as we know that no such persons as Orion, Beltigeour, Arcturus, Aldebaran, or any other of the Stars, ever existed as real persons; but the name of the place of his nativity, *Ur of the Chaldees*, is also strictly astronomical, indicating that no such *place* ever existed,—the original text, אור כשדים, signifying *the light of the Chasdim*.

'The Chasdim, translated, the Chaldees, not being a national name, but a professional one, signifying the same as the magicians, the astrologers, the soothsayers, with which synonymous terms it is continually associated. And thus the phrase, 'I am the Lord, who brought thee out of Ur of the Chaldees,' when divested of its enigmatical character, resolves itself into the language of an astronomical priest, meaning to say, 'I, the Master, evolved and laid down this allegorical picture of the phænomena of the planet Saturn, out of the light (or theory of the heavenly bodies) of the college of astronomers.'

With which understanding, quadrates every phrase of our text, 'The word of the Lord came unto Abram, in a vision.' *The word*, that is, the Logos, discourse, science, understanding of the Lord—that is, of the Sun, came unto Abram, in a vision—that is, in a solar observation, taken by a quadrant at twelve o'clock.

The word בַּמַּחֲזֶה, *Bamechezeh*, does not mean *in a vision*, in any notion of a dream, or supernatural revelation, but is literally in *a sight*, in such a view as may be taken through a telescope; which is the way in which all the דְּבַר יְהוָֹה, or science of the heavenly bodies has been acquired by men: so that we must actually go out of the way, and pervert and alter the meaning of words, and dig for folly and foolery, to evade the clear and obvious astronomical significancy. As if we would have wonder, mystery, and nonsense, and would quarrel with God himself, if he would not give 'em nonsense, absurdity, and folly enough. As I have heard of the most sincere Christians, who, upon being told how the whale swallowed Jonah, have seriously declared that they would have liked the story the better, if Jonah had swallowed the whale. A priest could never *outlie* a fool's appetite for lying.

But if we seek truth and reason, we may thus arrive at what we seek.

Uniting the mythological history, the hieroglyphical character, and the astronomical phænomena of the planet Saturn, we shall achieve a clear unravelling of ever iota of the story of Abraham. When God changed the name of Ab-Ram, or *Father of Height*, or *Elevation*, the natural oriental superlative for *Father of Heaven*, or *supremely exalted Father*, into Abraham: the addition is only by that of a letter, the Hebrew *He!* which makes a part of the divine name, 'which means,' says Bellamy, 'the ESSE of the Deity:' and was a direct authentication of the divine honours paid to this *exalted Father*.

But the name of Sarai, his wife, is also astronomical, and literally signifies a *Star*, to which the addition of the same part of the divine name, by the change into *Sarah*, in like manner, authenticates the divine honours paid to that Star.

We cannot wonder, then, that in the gospel itself, we should find divine honours paid, and prayer expressly addressed to Abraham: as in that fervent aspiration of the rich man in hell, 'Father Abraham have mercy on me,' without any intimation on the part of the person who speaks of the prayer, as having been said by another, that it was in any sense improper or heterodox. And, indeed, what is called *the Lord's Prayer*, is addressed to Abraham, and not to God: inasmuch, as though Abraham's name be not expressly used, his distinctive astronomical attribute is used instead; and that, in most marked contradistinction and opposition to any name or attribute that could possibly apply to God. The faithful were therefore taught to say, ' Our Father which art in Heaven :' because they believed that Abraham was their Father, and that that Father was in Heaven, whereas God, I hope, is everywhere present. And they prayed 'thy kingdom come,' because the planet Saturn, being the most remote of all the planetary bodies, *his* kingdom was the furthest off, and the longest in coming round: whereas the kingdom of God is *not* a kingdom to come, nor an infinitely remote *millenium* or *golden age*, as that of Saturn was supposed to be,—but is, and ever was, present in all places, and existing through all ages.

And they further prayed to Saturn, ' Give us this day our daily bread.' Because the very name of *Saturn* was derived from the word *Satu*, to sow, as corn is sown in the earth, and Sator, the sower: and Saturn it was, who was believed in that happy *golden age*, to have taught mankind the arts of agriculture, and to raise their bread out of the earth, agreeably to which conceit, they represented him with his cycle or sythe in his hand, wherewith to cut down the corn, and piously pledged themselves to desire from him no more than that vegetable diet, that simple bread, with which the happy denizens of the golden age had been entirely content. And it was to be in a particular sense *quotidian* or *daily* bread, as being the especial gift of Saturn, the 7th of the planets, the 7th of the days of the week, and the genius or demon of TIME.

And, as the planet Saturn was the Deity addressed in that prayer, called *the Lord's Prayer*, though neither the name of *Lord* or *God* occurs once in that prayer: so his worshippers, in all ages and countries of the world, have steadily continued to keep their weekly Sabbath, on the day over which the planet Saturn astrologically presides, which is Saturday. And also, they have never ceased to inflict on their own persons a cruel commemorative exhibition of the fabulous suicide of Saturn, in the mythology, and of the real phænomenon of Saturn's belt, the starry ring which appears *cut off* from the body of that planet in the visible heavens.*

The apostatizing chief of sinners, who forsook the faith of his ancestors, upon passing over from Judaism to Christianity—that is, from the worship of the planet Saturn to the worship of the Sun, exclaims: 'from henceforth let no man trouble me, for I bear in my body the marks of the Lord Jesus.' What those marks are, deponents depose not, —but what the marks of the planet Saturn are, you will best learn by going to church, on the first day of January, —that is, the day of Janus, who is the same as Saturn, the demon or genius of TIME, whose festival is analogically fixed to mark the 'first day of the year, and called the CIRCUMCISION!

But as Abraham is especially called, *the father of many nations:* we cannot wonder to find his characteristic sacrament observed among many nations: and his name itself, with very little variation, retained in the religions of all nations.

He is the original *Abram Esrael*, or Angel of Death, of the Chaldeans. He is the *Israel* of the ancient Phœnecians, as the only Phœnecian historian, Sanchoniathon, who wrote 1300 years before our era, and whose text is preserved to us by Philo Biblius, of the first century, expressly assures us that the Phœnecian name of the planet Saturn is *Israel*. And Israel and Abraham are names constantly confounded, and used as perfectly synonymous with each other, throughout Old and New Testament. The God of Israel, and the God of Abraham, the children of Israel, and the children of the stock of Abraham, are but poetical variations of one and the self-same sense. So he is the same *Abraham* in the *Brahma* (which is but Abram, with the first letter put last) of the Hindoos, and the *Ibrahim*, which is Abraham, more delicately uttered, of the Arabs, the Abraïn Zerouan of the Magi, the Abram Zarman of the Persians, the *Kronos* of the Greeks, the planet Saturn of Astronomy, the God *Saturnus* of the whole Pagan world, and the personified genius of Old Time, whom you shall see to this day, retained

---

* Thus you see the astronomical phænomena of the planet Saturn, the mythological story of the God Saturnus, and the sacred history of the Patriarch Abraham, run in every respect, in every circumstance, in every iota, text for text, and line for line together!

in our Christian idolatory, even in our Christian temples, sitting in all the accompaniments and emblems of his everlasting Godhead upon our clocks, and pointing to the dial plates, in indication that whatever other Gods we may please to address, it is he, and he alone, who shall reign for ever and ever. And to *his* honour is that anthem constantly reiterated, ' As it was in the beginning, is now, and ever shall be, world without end.'

But if our dulness can possibly mistake the hieroglyphical identity of ABRAHAM, offering up his only legitimate Son, with TIME, who offers up all his children to heaven, who puts to death all whom he brings into life, and before the sweep of whose awful scythe, ' all flesh is as grass,' how can we misunderstand the written word of this God, who points with his finger to the legend, ' Verbum Domini manet in Æternum,' ' the word of the Lord remaineth for ever.' Or how not understand that he is the very *Esrael*, the Angel of Death, who points to our observance the dreadful admonition, ' Memento Mori,' ' remember to die ; ' or warn us, ' Fugiunt at Imputantur,' ' they fly, but are imputed ; ' ' Ex hoc momento pendet Æternitas,' ' on this moment hangs eternity ; ' or ' Qua redit nescitis horam,' ' ye know not the hour of his return ; ' or, as on the dial that fronts our highest court of justice, ' Discite Justitiam Monite,' ' Learn righteousness, being admonished ? '

But not only is the identity of the planet Saturn, with the Patriarch Abraham, established in the physical significancy of the name *Abraham*, or *Father of Elevation ;* * but the name of *God*, in relation to whom Abraham acquires the honour of being called *the friend of God*, that famous plural word Ελωειμ,† on which our orthodox divines infer their doctrine a of plurality of persons in the Godhead, is none other than the very Chaldaic astronomical name of the five satellites of the planet Saturn, the *Cronians* or *Cronies* of Saturn, who, in the 1st of Genesis, say among themselves, ' Let us make man in our image, after our likeness : ' and

---

* And in the identity of the name, *Remphan*, which is the Arabico-Persic name of the planet Saturn, whom St. Stephen, in the Acts, expressly accuses the Jews of having continually worshipped, ' Ye took up the tabernacle of Moloch '—that is, the planet Mars, and the Star of your god, Remphan—that is, the planet Saturn.'

† אלהים

who, in the 18th, after having eaten up a whole calf, tender and good, served up with butter and milk, say to themselves, 'Shall I hide from Abraham that thing which I do, seeing that Abraham shall surely become a great and mighty nation?' Where, then, shall we find the difference between the Patriarch Abraham and the god Saturn. Saturn was the son of Terra, and Abraham was the son of Terah.

Saturn married his own sister, who was a Star; Abraham married his own sister, whose name signifies *a Star*. The name of the planet Saturn is by the Phœnecians called Israel: the name of the Patriarch Abraham is synonymous with the name of Israel: Saturn had a great many sons, and yet had one particular son called *Jeoud*,* which signifies his *only* son. Abraham had a great many sons, both by his maid Agar, and his Keturah, as Ishmael, and Zimran, and Joksham, and Midian, and Medan, and *Ishbag*, and *Shoebag*, and yet had only one son, Isaac, whom he loved. Saturn offered up his only son *Jeoud* as a burnt offering. Abraham was about to offer up his only son, Isaac, as a burnt offering.

Alas, you shall look for an essential difference between the two stories, but in vain: they are but two editions of one and the self-same fable.

The planet Saturn being the highest and most remote of all the planetary bodies, and measuring time by the highest career and slowest motion,—his mean distance from the Sun being 906,000,000 of miles, would justly be entitled to the distinction of being called the *Father of Heaven*, and we have a literal and physical exactitude in the oath of God to him, 'I will multiply thy seed as the Stars of heaven.'

The *Stars of Heaven* being not merely a figurative comparison, but the literal sense of the terms, the *Seed of Abra-*

---

* And Jeoud is likelier than any other name in the world to have been the real origin of the name JEWS. For the accusative case of the name Jeoud, is literally, in every letter or point by which it can be written Jeudem, the very same as the nominative plural *Jeudem*, which we translate *the Jews*. Now, let the reader but observe what emphasis is laid on that distinction, both in the Old and New Testament. 'In Isaac shall thy seed be called.' And remember that no seed or race of men in the world were ever called in Isaac, or derived their name from any name like that. But the name יהודים, the Jews, is a direct and immediate derivative from Jeud the son of Saturn, in the Phœnician fable of Sanchoniathon.

ham. And thus the rich man in AD-EES, in the fire of the Sun, or Hell fire, looking up, would, with astronomical accuracy, see Abraham, with his shivering Lazarus, in his cold bosom, afar off—that is, exactly 900,000,000 miles off.

The *Ben Ouvroime*, sons of Abraham, and *Benui Yesroile*, children of Israel, are nowhere spoken of in the Old Testament in any way that can connect them with any particular nation or people upon earth: that phrase being, in the Old Testament, perfectly synonymous with its rendering in the New, 'children of light'—that is, the Stars, which shall shine in the kingdom of their Father.

And thus, throughout the *New* Testament, which is but a new version of the Pagan mythology, Abraham is precisely the same hieroglyph for TIME, which Saturn was in the *old* system.

Its metaphor for eternal duration is the phrase, 'Abraham and his seed for ever.' To express an eternity gone by, or eternity, *a-parte-post*, the phrase is 'before Abraham was'— that is, before *time* was.

For an eternity, *a-parte ante*, the phrase is, ' when time shall be no more'—that is, when Abraham shall be no more.

The heiroglyphical office of Abraham, as of the planet Saturn, to measure time, and to observe the day and the hour, is so emphatically marked, that not only have we the account of his execution of that chronometrical office, in the words, '' your Father Abraham rejoiced to see my day, and he saw it and was glad.'

But all interference of any other Deity, even of Christ, or his apostles, with that peculiar office. is excluded: ' It is not for you to know the times, or the seasons, which the Father hath put in his own power.' Acts i. 7.

And ' of that day and that hour, knoweth no man, no not the angels which are in heaven, neither the Son, but the Father.' Mark xiii. 32.

And 'tis a more than curious analogy, that our English word FATHER, derived from none of the classical languages, but directly from the language of Egypt, the great cradle of astronomical science, and of all the religions that grew upon astronomical observations, retains to this day its affinity to *remoteness of space, distance of situation*, and being the *further* or *farther* off ; which is the definition of the planet Saturn, in relation to all the celestial bodies, as the male is the father, or more distant relation to the offspring of animals: and the mother only immediately the parent! while the Hebrew and Chaldean אב, and Abba, Father, the essential root and etymon of the name Ab-Ram, or *Father of Elevation*, has passed through all the languages of Greece and Rome, in all the combinations of their prepositions, Aπo, *Ab*, and ABS. retaining still the leading idea of distance, remoteness of situation, and lying without or beyond the orbits of all other bodies, which is still the astronomical identification of the planet Saturn. Nay, the Greek and Latin words Πατηρ and *Pater*, from whence, in all the languages of the earth, derived from those languages, are derived all words expressive of paternity, *patrician, paternal, patrimony, patriotic*, and every word ever uttered by the tongue of civilized man, whose leading idea was borrowed from the idea of a *father*, was the distinctive and peculiar epitheton and title of the planet Saturn, as in that choriambic distich preserved by Bryant.

Jane Pater, Jane Tuens, Dive Biceps, biformis, O Cate rerum, SATOR, O Principium Deorum! O Father Janus, protecting Janus, two-headed, double-formed Saint! O wise sower of things! O Prince of Gods!

Now, let any man look heedfully into the precise language of the sacred Scriptures (which I regret to know is what no Christian will be found to do), and see if he will not find a divine personage continually referred to as the FATHER, or the *Father of Heaven*, or the Heavenly Father, where it is certainly neither God, nor Jesus Christ, nor the Holy Ghost, that is meant, but one wholly distinct and infinitely superior to the whole Trinity, the Father of God himself, and the *grandfather* of Jesus Christ? whose names, attributes, and offices, are precisely those of Father Abraham, of the planet Saturn, and of the personified genius of *Time*, of whom the apostle has those very words: 'He exalteth himself above all that is called God:' doubtless, leaving that inferior title to the vanity of the three persons of the Trinity, from whom he is contradistinguished by the exclusive style of the planet Saturn, the FATHER, to whom the apostle alludes (Coloss. ii. 2), in insisting on the importance of acknowledging the mystery of God, and of the *Father*, and of Christ, and in innumerable other passages in which, in like manner, the *Father* is distinguished from God, as a wholly distinct and infinitely superior personage.

And it is never enough to be observed, that Jesus Christ, who is expressly called the Son of Abraham, and the *Son of the Father*, that is unquestionably of Father Abraham, never prayed himself, nor ever taught or authorized anybody else to pray to God, but always to Abraham: never once is there such a prayer, from beginning to end, as should begin with an *O God*, or *O Jesus*, or *O Holy Ghost*: nor did Jesus Christ ever once utter such a word as *O God!* But his forms of prayer always were, 'O Righteous Father!' and 'O Father Abraham!' Of which the Holy Ghost himself is also witness, in that express assurance, that when the spirit of grace and supplications is poured into our hearts, it does not set a man, like *Sir John Falstaff* in the comedy, crying God! God! God! but thereby we cry Aby! Aby! Aby! that is, Abba, Abraham, Father! and the man who cries anything else, has certainly got no grace in him.

And that we may not mistake who this Abba or Abraham is, to whom alone our prayers are to be addressed, nor ever lose sight of his identity with the planet Saturn, as the genius or great measurer of *time*,—not only are we bound to say our prayers with the regularity of clock-work, and to mark our days and nights by crying Aby! or saying, 'Our Father which art in heaven,' the *first* thing at getting up in the morning, and the last on going to bed at night, 'with groanings,' as the apostle says, 'which cannot be uttered:'

But the prophet Daniel has given us his title of *the Ancient of Days*, and described his hieroglyphic attributes.

'His garment was white as *snow*, his throne was like the fiery flame, and his wheels as burning fire.'

Is it possible that a man can be such a dunce as ever to have put his eye to a telescope, and to mistake that double wheel of burning fire, which surrounds the cold body of the planet Saturn?

'Thousand thousands ministered unto him, and ten thousand times ten thousand stood before him:' numbers, whose astronomical accuracy may be ascertained by reference to the minutiæ of astronomical calculations, beyond the scope of a general and popular discourse.

The absolute identity, then, of the planet Saturn, with the

Patriarch Abraham; and the certainty, that all that is related of Abraham in the sacred Scriptures, is allegorical, and consequently that no such persons ever existed, and no such events ever occurred, is established beyond all controversy.

Among all the oriental nations, from whom this collection of oriental fables, which constitutes the two *Eidouranions*, or Orreries, which we call the Old and New Testament, is derived, fiction was the organ of philosophy.

The astronomic priests, the Chaldeans, the astrologers, and the soothsayers, the magicians, and the wise men, as they are called, delighted in veiling their science of the phænomena of the universe, and their astronomical observation, under the guise of fictitious histories, imaginary personages, and marvellous adventures: and when national curiosity or vanity called on them, as the persons most likely to know, to give some account of the early history of their country; finding, that if they spoke the truth, they must not only disappoint public expectation, but confess their ignorance, they substituted fables for facts; while under the veil of allegory, they conveyed lessons of instruction to those who would care to unravel the clue of their metaphorical language.

And this duplicity, once given into, the mischief was done that could never be repaired. The priests who had once deceived, were never able again (had they been willing) to undeceive the people, or to rectify the erroneous impression which the first and gross metaphors of language had produced on their understandings. The fable that was once got up was obliged to be kept up; inasmuch as the knave who could tell it with the greatest gravity, and put the longest face on't, was sure to make his fortune; but of the good and honest man who loved the truth, and sought and wished to communicate it, no man cried *God bless him!*

END OF THE DISCOURSE ON ABRAHAM.

The Devil's Pulpit.

"AND A BONNIE PULPIT IT IS."—*Allan Cunningham.*

No. 12.—Vol. II.] [Price 2d.

SARAH:

A Discourse,

DELIVERED BY THE REV. ROBERT TAYLOR, B.A.

AT THE ROTUNDA, BLACKFRIARS ROAD, JULY 24, 1830.

'And the Lord said unto Abraham, Wherefore did Sarah laugh? Then Sarah denied, saying, I laughed not,—for she was afraid. And he said, Nay; but thou didst laugh.'—GENESIS, xviii. 13, 15.

AND is there among men the man alive who would expect to be accounted a rational being, who could say that he believed in his heart that it was really the Almighty Lord and Everlasting God of the whole universe, ' whom no man hath seen or can see,' who thus suffered himself to be laughed at, and contradicted : or that such a scene ever did or ever could have happened, or so much as be conceived to have happened? There *is not.* It will not, it cannot be maintained: it is an outrage against the faculty of thought to think it.

And the sincerest and most passionate asserter of the divinity of the sacred Scriptures is absolutely obliged and compelled to admit that something very different indeed from what appears in the gross letter of the text, must be intended, or it is sheer madness.

But this admission once made, the rubicon is passed, and

the inviolability of holy ground exists no longer. We are authorised and necessitated to call in the aid of critical learning, and to solve the enigma of language which cannot be denied to be enigmatical; by bringing in the lights of science and philology to shine upon it.

The great certainty of the case *is*, that no such scene as is here described, ever really occurred. And of that certainty, the great corollary and consequence is, that no such persons ever existed.

They are personifications of abstract principles, as the virtues, the graces, the fates, the loves, the furies of the ancient mythologies were, and all the events in which they are spoken of, as concerned, are emblematical pictures of the phænomena of the universe.

We treat the Scriptures with respect and reverence,—when with the clue thus put into our hands, we endeavour to wind the maze of their occult significancy.

In every matter of inquisitive disquisition among men, it is held as an axiom of indisputable certainty, that *that* hypothesis which solves the phænomena, must be received as valid, and must as necessarily set aside and supersede every other hypothesis.

Such a key does the astronomical reference which I have thus far induced apply to the wards of theology. In every point of contact have we found the one coinciding with the other: and the bolt obeying the direction of the key. What can science do more?

In an algebraic equation, how difficult soever, the premises of the reasoning are still but these, 'Given the equality of unknown quantities, to find the quantity which shall make them known.'

And precisely such a problem, is the whole text of sacred theology, which presenting in its letter the most apparently monstrous combinations and egregious contradictions, demands from us that calm and patient sitting down to it, and that diligent bringing to bear of every possible turn and direction that our thoughts can take,—whereby, and whereby alone we may approach to the solution of the difficulty, and happily find what was so wild, and so disordered, falling into astonishing method, arrangement, and order.

' So the pure limpid stream, when foul with stains,
 Of rushing torents, and descending rains,

Works itself clear, and as it runs refines;
Till, by degrees, the floating mirror shines,
Reflects each flower that on its margin grows,
And a new heaven in its clear bosom shows.'

Be patient, then! ye who love and seek the truth, of the discipline of heart and mind, which truth enjoins upon her votaries,—and let not the strangeness of a new idea startle you into offence, or into an apprehension that that idea, how strange soever it may seem to you, may not be the very unknown quantity itself, which the solution of the problem calls for, and which shall be capable in its application of answering all the requisitions of your data.

It has done so, through all the difficulties of the creation, the histories of Adam and Eve, of Noah, and the Deluge, and of Abraham.

We come now to its application to the character of the first distinctly marked and materially important heroine or feminine personification of sacred theology, Sarah the wife of Abraham.

The business of our inquiry, then, on this occasion, is to determine who or what was Sarah!

Now, Sirs, let us arrange the absolute *data*, supplied by the sacred text itself, to assist our inquiry.

It is with reference to Sarah, most especially, and with reference to what appears in her history most historical, most probable, most likely to have really occurred, that the apostle, in his Epistle to the Galatians, pledges the authority of his inspiration (to those who may believe him to have been inspired), that it was *not* historical, that it never *did* occur, that something wholly different from what appears in the letter of the story, was intended, and that it was *not* intended that the story itself should, in any part or any sense of it, be taken as a real history.

' For it is written that Abraham had two sons; the one by a bond-maid, the other by a free-woman. But he who was of the bond-woman was born after the flesh; but he of the free-woman was by promise,—which things are an allegory. For these are the two covenants, the one from Mount Sinai, which gendereth to bondage, which is Agar. For this Agar is Mount Sinai in Arabia, and answereth to Jerusalem, which now *is*, and is in bondage with her children. But Jerusalem, which is above, is free, which is the mother of us all.' Galatians 4.

As far, then, as we have the guidance of Scripture itself, the reality of the person of Sarah, as also of her handmaid Agar, is entirely given up: and we are referred to some far higher and sublimer sense, than any that appears in the mere shell and husk of the apparent history.

Sarah is Jerusalem, a city; but not a city built by human hands,—not that Jerusalem which is in Palestine, or anywhere on this terraqueous globe. But *Jerusalem which is above*, and which the apostle tells his Galatian converts (who were not Jews, nor ever would have admitted their descent from Jewish ancestors) is 'the mother of us all.'

If, then, there were no personal reality in the character of this 'mother of us all,' can we, without the grossest impiety and the maddest folly, imagine that there was any personal reality in the character of the LORD, or any historical occurrence of such a scene as that of the Lord suffering himself to be laughed at, and bandying the lie with an old woman: and he said, 'You did;' and she said, 'I didn't;' where infancy itself must blush at it!

But observe now, I pray, the process of our demonstration, and reject the whole, I beseech ye, as folly and impotence, if anywhere ye detect but the shadow of a defect of proof,—or if it be possible, with intelligence and candour to say, that there ever was a matter of like antiquity, that ever passed for truth among men, whose truth was more clearly established, or whose demonstration was more complete, than this.

The apostle assures you, that the main circumstances related of Abraham and Sarah are allegorical.

You cannot take the circumstances detailed in the text, otherwise than as containing some hidden and allegorical significancy, e'en an' you were to try to do so.

Now! you read that these personages or personifications, or whatsoever or whosoever they were, this Abraham and Sarah, and their story, be it what it may, was of Chaldaic origin: their very definition, in the sacred text itself, is Abraham and Sarah, or Ur of the Chaldees.

Follow, then, the clue thus put into your hands, and you arrive at the admission, that the—

1. People of Chaldea, the first and deepest skilled in astronomical science of all people, professed and delighted in veiling their astronomical science, under precisely such

allegorical histories as this of Abraham and Sarah appears to be.

2. That they were followed in the rage for doing this, by the astronomical priests of India, of Phœnicia, Egypt, Greece, and Italy.

3. That their first draughts and sketches of these imaginary histories were plagiarised and carried over from one nation and language to another, even when the sense and significancy was entirely lost: and thus have we, *in* the book *Genesis* (which is a hasty and careless compilation of several versions), those ridiculous repetitions, which betray that the compiler himself did not even cast his eyes back to observe what he had written, nor reck his own read.

He tells his tales twice over, and you have two editions of all the leading features of his story.

His Abraham, in the 12th chapter, sells his wife to Pharaoh, King of Egypt, and the Lord plagued Pharaoh: and in the 20th he sells her again to Abimelech, King of Gerar, and the Lord again plagued Abimelech. In the chapter immediately preceding our text, it was Abraham who laughed at God, and laughed till he could not stand, at precisely the same spurcity, while in our text, it is Sarah who laughed at it, and incurred the ridiculous rebuke of Omnipotence.

The Princess Sarah, then, in the most respectful understanding of this *laughter*, which must be understood allegorically, and form the name of Isaac her miraculously born son, which literally signifies *laughter*, cannot but recal to every classical mind both the epithet and character of *the Queen of Smiles*.

And assuming now, as I must, the completeness of the demonstration, which proved the identity of the Patriarch Abraham, with the God Saturnus, of the Pagan mythology, and the planet Saturn, of the visible heavens:

Our problem now, is to wind through the analagous relations of the theological Sarah to the theological Abraham as answering to their great archetypes in the Pagan mythos and their primary suggestion in the visible phænomena of nature.

And here, Sirs, observe ye, that it is of the very first importance in this great science, to guard the mind from the mistake of supposing, that a difference of names, or a very considerable difference in the incidents of the allegory, or even a wholly different allegorical delineation, doth imply or suppose any difference at all in the archetypes or original substantive science, so variously delineated.

The same planet, viewed in different aspects, or presenting varied phænomena, or understood with more or less correct astronomical science, must necessarily originate as many varied forms of the allegorical veil thrown over it.

And as that allegorical veil were more or less delicately constructed, according to the different degrees of refinement, or policy of the allegorists, would its drapery nicely fit in, and transparently exhibit the beautiful form of the truth which it invested, or coarsely and loosely hide and bury it from the dull eye of popular superstition.

Hence we find an infinite variety of names and epithets, where it is still but one and the self-same physical phænomenon, which is and ever was the unaltered and unalterable basis and type of the allegorical delineation. We meet with infinite repetitions and revivals, under immaterial variations, of the same kind of a story: in which, however, multiform and heterogeneous the mode of exhibition, our criticism detects, and can demonstrate, the identity of the one great leading idea, which, like the deity that changes through all, was yet in all the same.

There have been a thousand versions of the story of Orestes, and Orestes, it may be, has been honoured under a thousand names, and under it many varied ways of narrating his tale of sorrows.

So have there been ten thousand varied stories of creations, destructions, and restorations of the world,—and ten thousand Adams and Eves, Noahs, Abrahams, and Sarahs: as Universal Fathers and Universal Mothers of the human race, according to the varied fashions of human vanity and folly, and as the arrogance of human ignorance supplied from the fancifully exhibited phænomena of the starry heavens, the total want of records, or traces of the fate of their ancestors upon earth, which must have obtained before the art of writing, or any other mode of perpetuating the memory of what was passed, had become common among men.

Hence, as we have a father of the human race in Adam, who is the constellation Bootes, we have the same imaginary character revived, in a second Adam, whose astronomical identity is expressed in his epithet, ' the second Adam is the Lord from Heaven'—that is, the SUN, the name AD-HAM, literally signifying, *the Lord, the Everlasting Fire*—that is *the Sun.*

Thus have we seen the *Abram*, another *Universal Father*, whose name, compounded of the Hebrew and Syriac words, *Ab* and *Ram, Father of Elevation*, is the astronomical characteristic of the planet *Saturn;* whose name, again, derived from *Satu* to sow, and Satur the *sower*, expresses what Abraham was, ' the sower that went forth to sow his seed,' and whose Phœnician name was literally *Israel*, actually renewed again in the character of Israel, as if Israel had been another and distinct personage.

And precisely thus, have we the twelve signs of the Zodiac, allegorized in the twelve Patriarchs, or sons of Saturn—that is, of Israel, as the inferior and infrajacent Stars of our system, would necessarily be called. And these, again, re-edited in the twelve Great Gods, or *Dii-Consentes*, Jupiter, Apollo, Mars, Mercury, Neptune, and Vulcan, Juno, Minerva, Venus, Diana, Ceres, and Vesta, of the Pagan mythos. And these, again, in the twelve apostles of the gospel; in the twelve gates of the Apocalyptic city; in the twelve Stars of the celestial crown; in the twelve fruits of the tree of life; in the twelve legions of angels; the twelve foundations, twelve pearls, twelve stones, twelve altars, and eternally-recurring astronomical number twelve, or multiplies of twelve, in every relation, and reference *to the* mysteries of the kingdom of heaven: thus proving, with the certainty of arithmetical induction, that it was never any other than the visible astronomical heaven, that was to be understood by that kingdom, and never any other than the phænomena of the heavenly bodies, that was intended, in the imagined histories, and imaginary persons, set before us, alike in the Christian and Pagan mythology.

Thus the name itself of *Sarah*, literally signifies a *Star*, and is the basis of that self-same *Astarte*, or Ashtoreth, the Goddess of the Zidonians, sometimes singular, sometimes plural, according as it is a single planet, or a whole constellation, that is to be designated by that name: just as the name of God is plural, with a singular signification, or singular with a plural significancy, according as it is, a particular Star, or the constellation, or group of Stars, the *Sun*, or the planet, with his attendant satellites inclusive, which is meant under that name.

Thus, the perfect equality of character, and similarity of nature, between Sarah and the Lord, supplies us with an apology for Sarah laughing at the Lord, as Venus laughs at Jupiter, in the Pagan mythos; and the morning Star may be said to smile at the promises of the dawning day, in the real phænomena of the visible heavens.

The principal source of difficulty to the unskilled in this great science, is, that as the planet *Venus* is sometimes the morning, and sometimes the evening star, and is alternately seen under different aspects,—so we are continually encountered with different names, and varied allegorical representations, — where no essential difference really exists.

And one and the self-same planet will be really intended under different names, and diversified allegorical exhibitions, as *that* planet is considered in its state of occultation or emergence, as sinking below the horizon in the west, and consequently a suffering and crucified Saviour, or rising again in the east, and becoming, in turn, a glorified and triumphant Redeemer.

So it is, the self-same 'Mother of us all,' in the Eve of Paradise, who is revived again, in the same conceit remodelled, in *Sarah*, the Princess of Smiles, and mother of the miraculously born *Isaac*, whose very name is retained in the Astarte of the Zidonians, the *Sarah Apis*, or Serapis of Egypt,—and whose very attribute of that eternal laughter was sculptured in the exquisite Venus Urania, or Heavenly Venus of Praxiteles, with the mouth a little open, and the lip so nicely turned, as if so archly smiling she would fain deny that she had smiled at all, and as if the very allegorical dialogue were going on while you gazed on her trancendant beauty, and she were retorting her pretty *fib*, 'I laughed not,' to her entranced admirer, who couldn't but say, 'Nay, but thou didst laugh.!'

For the scriptural allegory has called our observance to note that Sarah was very fair, and very *young*; and what is very chiefly to be noted, none the less fair, nor the less young, when she was ninety years old. But even then, like the personified virtue of Proclus:

'August she trod, yet modest was her air,
    Serene her eye, yet darting heavenly fire,
Still she drew near, and nearer still more fair,
    More mild appeared: yet such as might inspire
Pleasure corrected with an awful fear,
Majestically sweet, and amiably severe.'

The scriptural allegorist is so evidently pleased with this personified Universal Mother, who is the Cybele, or Mother of the Gods of the mythology, the Virgin Deipara, or God-bearer of the Zodiac, the Virgin Mary, or Christ-bearer of the gospel, and the Wonder, or Woman in Heaven of the Apocalypse,—that having allegorically buried her in the allegorical cave of Machpelah, he revives the self-same character again in the person of Rebekah, to be the wife of Isaac, with the self-same story of her being his sister, as well as his wife, and her being exceeding handsome as Sarah had been, and Isaac selling her again to Abimelech, King of Gerah, just as Abraham had sold his Sarah to the same Abimelech, King of Gerah.

And having done with her, in the character of Rebekah, the wife of Isaac,—he actually brings her on the stage again, the third time, in the character of Rachael, the wife of Jacob, who is the same goddess of beauty and of smiles, and makes precisely the same covenant with her maid, Billah, which Sarah had made with her maid, Hagar.

Thus proving to demonstration, that no real personages or real history was ever intended, that Sarah, Rebekah, Rachael, like Abraham, Isaac, and Jacob, are but one and the self-same personification of the imaginary genii of the Stars; that not one of them ever existed as real personages upon earth, nor was it ever intended that these charades and riddles, that veiled the detail of astronomical science, should ever have been taken for historical facts. There is not a vestige, not a feature of historical fact, in any part of sacred theology.

As that very word, *theology*, itself might have admonished us. The word $\theta\epsilon o\varsigma$, which we translate God, being literally a planet, as $\alpha\sigma\tau\eta\rho$ is a star: so theology and astrology are perfectly synonymous terms: and the Divine Mother, from the first heroine in the Book of Genesis, to the last heroine of the Book of Revelation.

The woman clothed with the Sun, and having the Moon under her feet, as to whom stupidity itself must actually take pains to be so stupid as to avoid seeing the astronomical significancy, has never been any other than that self-same *Seclenidos de Darzama*,* the August Virgin of the Zodiac, who, whether as Sarah, Rebekah, or Rachael, whether as the wife of the Goldsmith Abraham, the Blacksmith Vulcan, or the Carpenter Io Sæpe, the laughing Sarah, or the smiling Venus,—whether as the Genius of the Old Paradise of Genesis, or of the New Jerusalem of the Revelation, the Cybele of Greece,† the Isis Omina of India, the Sarah Apis of the Egyptians, or the Seraphim of the Hebrews, is, and never was other, than a variously exhibited personification of the maternal principle of vitality or *life*, expressed in the name itself of Eve, the 'Mother of us all, and *in* and by whom we and all things live, and move, and breathe, and have our being.

That the Hebrew Sarah really was none other than the Goddess Isis, the Great and Supreme Maternal Deity of Egypt, is demonstrable, not merely in the perfect resemblance of attributes and character, but in the identity of the derivation of the names.

The promise to Abraham, so remarkable, repeated, that, 'in Isaac should his seed be called: in Isaac, whom Sarah should bear to him,' could have been fulfilled in no race of people: but such as should bear a name derived from Isaac.

So did not Hebrews, Israelites, or Jews: but so *did* the children or worshippers of Isis, whose religious rites celebrated through a thousand ages, were known under the name of the *Isiac* rites, and whose *self-supposed* descendants were scattered through every country of the earth, and recognised as the *Gens Isacida;* or the Isakian race. The Mother Sarah, by the most natural and obvious mutation, deriving her name *Isis*, from her distinguished honour in being the Mother of Isaac. And as 'in Isaac should her seed be called,' Isis, rather than Sarah, would be her favourite and prevailing name.

Apuleius introduces Isis, giving this account of herself: 'I am Nature, the mother of all things, mistress of the elements, the beginning of ages, the sovereign of gods. My divinity alone, though multiform, is honoured with different

---

* Adrenedeſa. Arabice; θεοτοκος, Græcò; Deipara, Latin.
† The Venus Genetrix of Rome.

ceremonies and under different names. The Phrygians call me the Pessinuntian Mother of the Gods; the Athenians, the Cecropian Mother; the Cyprians, the Paphian Venus; the Cretans, the Diana Dictynna; the Sicilians, the Stygian Proserpine; the Eleusinians, the Old Goddess Ceres; some Juno, some Bellona; but the Oriental Ethiopians, and Egyptians, honour me with peculiar ceremonies, and call me by my true name, Isis.'

In her temple at Sais, was the famous inscription, 'I am whatsoever was, is, and shall be: no mortal has yet drawn aside my veil; and the fruit which I brought forth is the SUN.'

There is another inscription still extant on a very ancient column, 'I am Isis, Queen of Egypt; I first invented the use of corn; I am the mother of King Horus,—I shine in the Dog Star.' *Horus*, again, being the Egyptian name of the Sun.

Her statues represents Isis with the turrets of a city upon her head, thus identifying her with what Sarah is, in the apostolical solution of the hieroglyph declared to have been New Jerusalem. And that she is the same, and still worshipped under the same name, passed on into the type of the Virgin Mary, is manifest in the noble edifice, the church of Notre Dame, in the city of Paris, that city to this day being a worshipper of the Great Goddess, *Isis*, and taking its name itself, of Paris, from a clipping of the Greek name, Παρα Ισις, which literally signifies under the protection of *Isis*, into *Far ise.*

It is impossible, it is inconceivable, that such innumerable points of undesigned and unpremeditated coincidence, could have obtained between the Jewish, the Pagan, and the Christian systems: and *that* two, in countries the widest apart, in ages far removed from each other, and in languages that were to each other mutually unknown, unless all had been derived from some type common to all, and that type presents itself nowhere but in the inscriptions of that vaulty arch, so high above our heads,—wherein, as we more and more contemplate the phænomena presented to our eye, and compare therewith the allegorical language, both of sacred and profane theology, do we more clearly perceive, and more convincingly understand, that the one is derived from the other, and detect thereby the fallacy and folly of any pretended historical basis for any religion whatever

Mathematical demonstration itself knows no argument stronger than the argument of coincidence. When two triangles coincide with each other in every point of the three lines which constitute them, and occupy precisely the same space,—those two triangles are said, in mathematical language, to be equal to each other, and to be virtually one and the same triangle.

And to such a coincidence, such an entire setting of the one upon the other, between the Jewish, Pagan, and Christian mythologies, and their common astronomical archetypes,—approach we nearer and nearer, at every stage of our advance in these delightful studies.

I must not now recal the demonstrations which have evinced the identity of Abraham with the planet Saturn, but have to add only the coincidences of the allegorical picture of Sarah, the wife of Abraham, in the Genesis, with Vesta, the wife of Saturn, in the Mythos.

The name Vesta is a derivative of the radical Ast, Asta, Esta, and Hestia, all of them signifying Fire,—as the name Sarah signifies a *Star* (Sirius); Vesta was married to her brother Saturn, as Sarah was married to her brother Abraham; and Isis was married to her brother Osiris.

Vesta, the celestial fire, appears again under the names of Ops and Rhea, which signify *wealth* and *means*, the characteristics of the wife of the wealthy Abraham.

Vesta bears to Saturn the Twins Jupiter and Juno, as Sarah, in her secondary character of Rebekah, bears to Isaac the Twins Esau and Jacob.

Vesta, as Astarte, the Queen of Heaven, was believed to have taught mankind the arts of architecture, and her images exhibited her as wearing a crown composed of the battlements or turrets of a fortified city : but Sarah, even in the apostolical interpretation of the allegory, is expressly declared to be the City Jerusalem ; not a Jerusalem which now is, and is in bondage with her children, but Jerusalem which is *above*, which is the mother of us all.

So that as we are commanded, in the Old Testament, to seek *the Lord*, so we are enjoined in the New to seek *the Lady*—that is, the Lamb's wife, 'the holy city, New Jerusalem, coming down from God out of Heaven, prepared as a bride adorned for her husband.' Rev. xxi., 3. And we have the assurance of the apostle to the Hebrews, that when Abraham was paying his addresses to Sarah, he was looking for a city, 'which had foundations, whose builder and maker is God.'

And all the faithful, who are said to have died in faith —that is, in a proper understanding of the science of astronomy, or as they are expressly defined, *they who say such things*—that is, who talk in this enigmatical and hieroglyphical way, 'declare plainly that they seek a city.'

And here have we all possible and conceivable identifications of that castle, or turret-crowned Mother of the twelve Great Gods, as Sarah was the Great Mother of the twelve Patriarchs, and as the Heavenly Jerusalem, which was Sarah herself, was built on the foundations. And as we, the Church of God, are built upon the foundation of the twelve prophets, and twelve apostles. Jesus Christ himself being the chief corner stone—that is, the capital of the pillar, of which the heathen idolatry was the shaft, and astronomical science the base.

END OF THE DISCOURSE ON SARAH.

The Devil's Pulpit.

"AND A BONNIE PULPIT IT IS."—*Allan Cunningham.*

No. 13.—Vol. II.]   Price 2*d*.

MELCHISEDEC:
A Discourse,
DELIVERED BY THE REV. ROBERT TAYLOR, B.A.

AT HIS CHAPEL IN FLEET STREET.

'*The Lord hath sworn, and he will not repent: Thou art a priest for ever after the order of Melchisedec.*'—PSALM 110:4; Heb 7:21

MELCHISEDEC! *Who or what was he?* I shall show you now, in the solution of this curious question, which no Christian commentators have ever yet had courage or honesty fairly to grapple with, a resulting demonstration which shall bring forth a certain knowledge of something worth knowing, which was not known before.

Melchisedec! appear! Melchisedec, mysterious entity! I summon thee, by thy great name מלכי צדיק *Molochi Tseduk,* King of Righteousness. By thy high title, כהן־אל־עליון *Cohen-El-Elion,*[*] priest of the most high God. Βασιλευ Ειρηνης, *King of Peace!* απατωρ αμητωρ, αγενεαλογητος, without father, without mother, without descent, having neither beginning of days, nor end of life, but made like unto the Son of God, 'a priest to perpetuity!'

'I adjure thee, by the living God, that thou tell us whether thou be the Christ, the Son of God?'

Thus, every phrase and form of expression found in either the Old or New Testament, tends to exalt our ideas of this mysterious character, and to impress upon our minds

---

[*] El Eon—God, the Being, or Eon: hence *Lion.* Cohen: hence the Greeks made κυων *Dog.*

that something more, far more than would strike us on a cursory reading, is intended and conveyed under these images. The poetry of the language is exquisite,—the sublimity of idea of the very highest order of didactic grandeur : so that one knows not whether more to admire the insensibility of the Christian community to the graces and beauties of the composition, or the stupidity and moral wickedness of their patient willingness to be ignorant, and unwillingness to discover its real significancy.

I wish it were not true that there are no persons on earth, so ignorant of the contents and purport of the Scriptures, as those who profess the most devoted faith in them. They who have continually in their mouths the text, ' Search the Scriptures,' are themselves the most careless, negligent, and inobservant readers that any Scriptures in the world ever had.

And in the teeth of the solemn entreaty of the apostle, touching the character and person of Melchisedec : ' Now consider how great this man was :' you'll not find a Christian upon earth that ever set himself to consider how great this man was, or who he was, or whether he was a man at all.

I propose, however, to consider this matter at all hazards, and by unravelling the clue through the only three passages of the Scriptures, in which it is referred to (the 14th of the Book of Genesis, the 110th Psalm, and the 7th of the Epistle to the Hebrews), with such aids of extraneous elucidation as my research has supplied, to lay before your conviction the most ample and irrefutable demonstration of a *truth*, which thus discovered, like the discovery of the hidden quantity in an equation, will solve all the difficulties of the problem, and bear on all the relations on which the mind can wish for satisfaction, or be capable of certainty in these interesting studies.

Of all certainties, nothing can be more certain than that whatever respect be due to the authority of the Book of Genesis (which is a subsequent consideration), this Melchisedec is, in the 14th chapter of that book, introduced as as real a personage as Abraham. The author of that book supposes him to be a personage with whom his readers could hardly be acquainted, and of whom it was enough to say that he was King of Salem, that he brought forth bread and wine; and he was priest of the Most High God. And he blessed Abraham, and said, Blessed be Abraham of the Most High God.

Who then is the Most High God?

In pursuing studies of this curious speculation, and unspeakably delightful entertainment, we must have no, prejudices, no prepossessions, no theories to support, no systems to subserve, but should follow through all issues, as evidence conducts, to whatever conclusion truth may establish: we are to derive our knowledge from our authorities, not to bring it to them. (An anticipation of the result is treason against the inquiry.)

That extraordinary epithet, *the Most High God*, first occurs in this enigmatical passage, as also the term PRIEST, and again occurs, not till, in like manner, it is found in the mouth of an alien, a stranger, and even an enemy to the race of Israel. 'Balaam, the son of Beor, hath said, and the man whose eyes are open, hath said, *He* hath said, which heard the words of God, and knew the knowledge of the Most High, I shall see him, but not now; I shall behold him, but not nigh: there shall come a Star out of Jacob, and a Sceptre shall rise out of Israel, which shall smite the corners of Moab.'

Nothing can more necessarily lead to infinite mistakes and endless confusion, than the folly and unreasonableness of carrying back *our* ideas of particular terms, as interpreters of the terms of ages and nations, which certainly attached no such ideas to those terms, and had no such notions (and could by no possibility have had them), as our improved science, and consequently enlarged range of thought, has familiarized to us.

In the curious fragment of Sanchoniathon, a Phœnician historian, who flourished before the Trojan war, or at least 1,800 years before our era whose text has been translated out of the Phœnician into Greek, by Philo Biblius, and preserved by Eusebius, we learn that this *Elion*, this Hypsistos, the Most High God, was a certain man, who, with his wife, BEROUTH, dwelt near Buibel, Byblos, in Phœnicia, and begat a son named Adam, because he was formed out of the earth, and that *this father of Adam*, this Most High God, was killed by wild beasts. This hieroglyphical language evidently points to the Phœnician astrology, in which the Sun, literally the Most High, is allegorized under the image of a man, and the wild beasts which slay him are the Zodiacal animals, more especially the wild boar, under whose ascendancy the Sun seems annually to expire in the Winter, as he revives in the Spring. And 'the knowledge of the Most High, which formed the great matter of boast to the prophet Balaam, and gained him the credit of supernatural wisdom, was nothing more than his skill in the science of astronomy, and of the laws by which the highest of the heavenly bodies regulates the succession of the seasons, and the motions of the whole planetary system.

But whatever sense be given to that manifestly astronomical term, *the Most High God*, nothing is more obvious than that this Melchisedec, priest of the Most High God, appears as a sort of personage for whom the author of the Book of Genesis challenges far higher respect than for the Patriarch Abraham, and assumes that his readers could have no need of more particular information.

A similar abruptness characterises the introduction of this mysterious personage in the 110th Psalm: 'The Lord said unto my Lord (or Jehovah said unto Adonis), Sit thou on my right hand until I make thine enemies thy footstool.' On which mysterious passage, the Jesus of Matthew xxii., 42, assuming that Adonis and Christ were one and the same person, enigmatically proves that Christ was *not*, and could not have been in any sense, the son of David. 'Thou Lord said unto my Lord,' had been the words of David. 'If David then call him Lord, how is he his son?' is the challenge of the speaker in the gospel, upon those words: 'And no man was able to answer him a word, neither durst any man from that day forth ask him any more questions.'

'The Lord shall send the rod of thy strength out of Zion. Rule thou in the midst of thine enemies.'—*Bible Version.*

'In the day of thy power shall the people offer the free-will offerings with an holy worship. The dew of thy birth is of the womb of the mornng. The Lord sware and will not repent. Thou art a priest for ever, after the order of Melchisedec.'—*Prayer Book Version.*

Who does not see that this Melchisedec, this 'King of Righteousness,' thus spoken of as much higher in dignity, than that Lord to whom the Lord sware, and on whom he could confer no higher dignity than an eternal priesthood, secondary, and according to his order, could have been none of woman born?

As is expressly asserted in the whole argument of the Epistle to the Hebrews, 'without father, without mother, without descent, having neither beginning of days, nor end of life.'

To evade this evidence, the Unitarian editors of the New Testament have inserted in italics, the word '*recorded*' before father and mother; so that in *their* translation, the text stands, 'without *recorded* father, without *recorded* mother, without pedigree;' and they have excused their interpolation, with a note explanatory, 'of whose father, mother, pedigree, birth, and death we have no account.' 'WAKEFIELD,' they say, 'prefers this intelligible, through *free* translation of the original, to what must appear a strange paradoxical account to common readers.'

Thus, we see, what shuffling evasive tricks, divines will have recourse to, and how they will *dig*, as it were, into the earth, and run away, and falsify the text of their own Scriptures, to hide themselves from the danger of letting in too much light on the dark archives of a barbarous antiquity.

In order to support their Unitarian scheme of reducing their Son of God to a mere man, and feigning an historical existence for a being which certainly never did exist, they have found it necessary to reduce their Melchisedec also to the same level : to avoid the paradox of his being without father, without mother, and without descent;' they have found no paradox in supposing the apostle to argue against his own argument, and to have laboured to show us how distinguished a being this Melchisedec was, by showing us that he had no distinction at all : and a moment's fair dealing with the text of Scripture, will most convincingly solve the whole problem.

No words in which ideas of any sort could be conveyed, could be more explicit than those in which the apostle assures us that this Melchisedec had 'no father, no mother, no descent,' was never born, had never died—that is, indeed, that he was not a human being. Had he been a man, who, in any era of time, and in any country of the world, had lived and died, as all men live and die, the whole argument of the apostle to prove the superior dignity of Christ in being a priest after the order of Melchisedec, and not after the order of Aaron, would be absolute idiotcy and mere jargon, unpregnant of a meaning.

But that he was *not* a man, in no sense a man, and had no substantive existence, is the essential onus of the whole conundrum: 'He of whom these things are spoken,' says the apostle, 'pertaineth to a tribe of which NO MAN gave attendance at the altar' (Heb. vii., 13).: and in the 8th, 'Here men that die (mortal men) receive tithes: but there he, of whom 'it is witnessed that he liveth'—that is, assuredly, that he was not a mortal man, but that he was a being still existing. Again, in the 28th verse: 'The law maketh *men* high priests which have infirmity:' and in the 23rd: 'And they truly were many priests, because they were not suffered to continue by reason of death, but this (man), because he continueth, ever hath an unchangeable priesthood.' In the original text, the word for *man* nowhere occurs in connection with the name Melchisedec; he is nowhere called a man. Every term, every idea, every epithet, not excepting one, associated with the part *he* bears in sacred writ, is purely astronomical.

We are commanded to *consider*, that is according to the derivative sense of our English word, *to put the Stars together*. Θεωρειτε δε πηλικια ουτος, and *see behold*; not *think* merely, but *look up* upon the vaulty bosom of the night, and see how great *this*: not *this man*, but this heavenly being, this constellation, was unto whom even the Patriarch Abraham gave the tenths (the *decimals*, the *decades* of the highest tops, the astronomical divisions). And to what sense can the κατα την ταξιν, *according to the order* of Melchisedec, be interpreted; but according to the astronomical arrangement, or disposition of the heavenly bodies, by *him* 'who telleth the number of the Stars, and calleth them all by their names?' Psalm 147. And wherefore is it, that the secondary personage, in being made a priest, or holy one, or set in the heavens after the order or astronomical arrangement of Melchisedec, derives his assurance of his permanency in that high office, inasmuch as *not without an oath*, is he made a priest, ου χωρις ορκομοσιας—that is, not without an appeal to HELL—a consultation and consent of that bottomless pit of infinite space, out of whose dominion the orbit and kingdom of the new created Star must necessarily be apportioned? And what sense shall we find for those sublime images, 'the day of thy power:' 'the dew of thy birth is of the womb of the morning:' if we are to withhold our conviction from the clear and literal astronomical sense, which, in not one or two, but in innumerable passages, discovers to us, that all the persons of sacred poesy are purely astronomical figments. Thus the priest, after the order of Melchisedec, is nothing more nor other than a Star in the Melchisedekian projection of the planetary system: and you have the literal and unsophisticated avowal of the sacred text, as to *who*, and *which*, that particular Star was (in Rev. xxii., 16). 'I Jesus am the bright and morning Star—the Star which has its *birth*, or period of rising, just as the dews of the morning begin to fall,—which gives us a rational meaning, where none other such can be conceived, of those words: 'The dew of thy birth is of the womb of the morning.'

'Fairest of Stars, last in the train of night,
If better thou belong not to the dawn,
Sure pledge of day that crown'st the smiling morn
With the bright circlet.'

As the same Jesus is expressly called by St. Peter, the DAY STAR. 2 Peter i., 19.

While Melchisedec himself, from all the analogies of his mystical character, presents us with no closer an approximation to identity than to the Pole Star, to whose astronomical affinities and relations, all the forms of speech occurring in Scripture with respect to Melchisedec, will be found most scientifically applicable. Every genius of a Star being a *King*, gives us his title Moloka, and the whole heavens turning round on him, as on their pivot, gives us his name of Zedek, or the Just One, who regulates, or rectifies the order of the whole: and his character of Hierophant, or priest, as showing the law of heaven to all the celestial hosts.

But as the personified genius of a planet, or constellation, a mere abstraction of the mind, cannot be supposed to have held dialogues, and transacted business with any real and corporeal beings: it will follow, that if Melchisedec were not a real personage, who blessed Abraham, neither could

Abraham have been a real personage, who received the blessing: nor could there have been any reality in the transaction represented to have happened between them.

Nor was there! The discovery may startle us at first, and break in upon the stagnation of our established modes of thinking, or rather of contriving not to think. But a little inquiry and research will satisfy us, that Abraham, as well as Melchisedec, was 'without father, without mother, without descent'—that is, that he is a fictitious personage altogether; that he never had any real existence, but is the personified genius of a planet; and all the actions and circumstances of his allegorical life, a mere poetical paraphrase of physical phænomena. 'Such is the case with a crowd of pretended kings, princes, and patriarchs of the ancient traditions of the east. From the moment that by the natural metaphor of their languages they began to personify the celestial bodies;' astronomy became religion; the forms and figures of speech intended only for illustration, were taken as literalities. The names given to particular stars, were taken for names of real personages: and the vanity and ignorance of whole nations led them to claim relationship and family affinity to these exalted abstractions.

Thus the name which the Chaldean astronomers had given to the planet *Saturn*, in signification of its distinctive phænomena in the planetary system, as the most remote, most elevated, and most devious, of course, of all the then known planetary bodies, *Father of Deviation:* AB-RAM, presented at once the name of Abram: and Abram, both in the Arabic and in the Hebrew (which is but a dialect of the Arabic), is none other than the name of the planet Saturn.

This same planet Saturn, in the language of the Phœnicians, a people much more ancient than the Hebrews, was called *Israel.** So that Abram is the Arabic, and Israel the Phœnician name of the planet *Saturn.* From the never-failing course, and punctual return of the seasons of this remotest of the planetary bodies, his physical character became the most expressive emblem of moral fidelity, and his name of *Abram*, Father of Elevation, acquired the epithet of *Father of the Faithful.*

---

* Κρuνος τοινυν, ον οι Φοινικες Ισραηλ προσαγευ ευυσι προσαγορευουσι. Saturnus igitur, quem Phœnices Israelem nominant—Sanchon: apud Euseb: ita redit Franciscus Vigerus Rothomagensis, p. 40.

The planet Saturn, measuring time by the longest career, and the slowest motion of all the planets, was personified as the genius of TIME. The Arabians and Persians call him ESRAEL, or *Angel of Death*, and represented him with a scythe in his hand, in signification that it is *he* who mows down all creatures, that he devours his own children, and puts to death all that he gives life to.

All idolatrous nations have had a *Saturn* of their own: and of all their Saturns, the main and characteristic notions are precisely the same: and so little are *we* removed from the practices and conceits of idolatrous nations, that we have *our* Saturn too; and set him, even to this day, in the very temples and sanctuaries of the Star of our God, Ιησους,— where we shall see the old enemy carved in *gold*, with the very characteristic scythe in his hand, sitting upon the clock, and pointing to its dial plate, in indication of his eternal power and Godhead, and that it is *he* alone who shall reign for ever and ever. And that *that* indication, may not possibly be mistaken, a legend is often subscribed to convey the same sense, as if the demon spoke to us from his oracle. 'Go about your business!' '*Memento Mori:*' 'Remember to die.' '*Verbum Domini manet in eternum:*' 'The word of the Lord remaineth for ever.' '*Fugiunt at imputantur:*' 'They fly, but are imputed.'

The Hebrews invariably associate their notion of great length of time, of perpetuity of succession, and of infinite generations, with their hieroglyph for TIME, their patriarch or old father, Abraham, whose 'seed is as the sand on the sea shore.' Their metaphor for eternal duration is, 'Abraham and his seed for ever.'

Would the Egyptian monks put into the mouth of their hero, a metaphor to express an infinitely remote antiquity, an eternity, *a part post?* it is, 'Before Abraham was'—that is, before time was; for an eternity, *a parte ante*. It is, when time shall be no more—that is, when Abraham shall be no more. So the boast of the speakers in the New Testament, 'We have Abraham to our father,' was nothing more than a figurative form of pretending an infinitely remote antiquity. The hieroglyphical office of Abraham, and of the planet Saturn, to mark and measure time, is precisely the same: 'Your father Abraham rejoiced to see my day, and he saw it and was glad.'

While this distinction of regulating TIME is so peculiarly and exclusively challenged as the sole prerogative of Father Abraham—that is, pre-eminently the FATHER: that the JUST ONE, or *Tsedec* of the New Testament tells his satellites, 'It is not for you to know the times and seasons, which the father hath put in his own power.' Acts i., 7. 'Nay more,' he adds, 'of that day and that hour, knoweth no man, no, not the angels which are in heaven. Neither the Son, but the Father.' Mark xiii., 32. None but Old Father Abraham having anything to do with TIME.

The relative astronomical distances of Abraham, in the Evangelical Ephemeris, and of the planet Saturn, in the solar system, are also precisely the same. The rich man tormented in that flame, lifteth up his eyes, and seeth Abraham afar off, and Lazarus in his bosom: which is just as the planet Saturn is seen, with his cold shivering and beggarly satellites in relation to the central fire,—the Sun, *our God,* 'for our God is a consuming fire.' Heb. xii., 29.

The notion of an historical and personal existence of these astronomical figments, is not merely discountenanced, but explicitly opposed and denied, by the only sense that can possibly be found for the whole argument of the Christ of the New Testament against the Jews. 'Abraham is dead, and the prophets are dead,' had been the Jewish argument: and dead enough, in God's name, they must have been, had they been persons who had had a real existence, so many hundred years before. But the argument of Christ was, that they were *not* dead, but beings still in existence,— in that God had said, 'I am the God of Abraham, the God of Isaac, and the God of Jacob,—and God is *not* the God of the dead, but of the living.' Therefore (Matthew xxii., 32.), certainly they were not men, as dead they must have been, had they been so, or had ever lived in any sense of a life subject to death.

The language which runs through both the Old and New Testament, in relation to these personifications, presents a most manifest impropriety, and a glaring absurdity: if we take them to be *mortal* men, and are to suppose that the eternal God should derive to himself titles and honours from sinful flesh and blood. But these titles fall into keeping: they harmonize with the laws of the drama, and are indeed magnificent hyperboles in the proper oriental style, when we understand the God of Abraham, of Isaac, and of Jacob, as a periphrasis; for the God of heaven, the God of the bright squadrons of the twinkling night.

> 'Ten thousand marshalled stars, a silver zone,
> Effuse their blended radiance round his throne.'

As no Christian doubts, or *can* doubt, that by that sublime title, *the Lord of Hosts*, the *Ye heevah Shabba-yut*, is meant pre-eminently the Lord of the Hosts of Heaven, and certainly no mere captain or general of armies marching to battle: connected as that title is, with the name of Jacob, and of Israel, as exegetical or explanatory of it, as the Lord of Hosts, the God of Israel, the Lord of Hosts, the God of Jacob: there can be no doubt, that Abraham, Isaac, and Jacob, are to be understood as the names of planets, the most distinguished members of the Hosts of Heaven. And *Saturn*, the most remote of all the planets, whose Arabic name is AB-RAM, whose Phœnician name is Israel, and whose Chaldaic name is REMPHAN, is with striking propriety specified under that name, where the title is rhetorically abbreviated, 'The God of Israel,' being nothing else but a regular sycopation of the title, the God of the planet Saturn—that is, the *eternal* God, the God whose power reaches over all TIME. SOL, the Sun, the Eternal One, whose influence extends even to the planet Saturn, as the utmost measure of the mind's power to form a conception of duration, and of distance. So the title of FATHER, and *the Father*, and God the Father of Heaven, and our Heavenly Father, were but abbreviations of the name Abraham. And it was Abraham, and Abraham only, as the genius of their tutelary planet *Saturn*, whom the Jews were taught to address in that self-condemning prayer to the unforgiving, 'Our Father, which art in Heaven.'

And thus, in that sublime Chaldean melo-drama, the Book of Job: the 'God who is in the height of heaven, makes it the distinguishing challenge of his pre-eminence.' 'Canst thou bind the sweet influences of the Pleiades, or loose the bands of Orion? Canst thou bring forth Mazzaroth in his season? or canst thou guide Arcturus with his sons? Where wast thou when I laid the foundations of the earth, when the morning stars sang together, and all the sons of God shouted for joy.'

Here, the very astronomical names of the constellations and stars which obtain in use, to this day, are substituted in the place of those Hebrew names for the *same*, or different constellations and stars, which our ignorance has mistaken for real personages.

We have *Mazzaroth*, the twelve signs of the Zodiac, for the twelve Patriarchs; and *Arcturus*, that beautiful Star of the first magnitude in the knee of Bootes or Adam, Arcturus and his sons, instead of Israel and his sons. The difference of the one set of names from the other, being *all* the difference. *Those* were the Chaldean names, *these* were Hebrew. But the essence and meaning of both are purely astronomical, and all their singings and shoutings, their wanderings and returnings, their sufferings and victories, and all other adventures and actions ascribed to them, are merely a metaphorical history of the phænomena of the visible heavens.

So early as 100 years before the vulgar era, Alexander Polyhistor assures us that the ancient annals of the Babylonians are filled with allegories, descriptive of physical phænomena. His words are: 'But this they say allegorically, as discoursing of natural phænomena:' which is nothing more that St. Paul has owned, of the whole history of Abraham and his sons: 'which things are an allegory.'

It is certain that no record or vestige whatever of such beings as Abraham, Isaac, and Jacob, or of a people who believed, or pretended to be descended from them, can be traced higher than the period of the emergence of this people from their Babylonish captivity: from which captivity, or rather from which their native origination, they derived that allegorical and strongly figurative idiom of language, which has caused astronomical terms to be taken for historical ones.

Their very name itself, of *Children of Israel*, was derived to them from the Phœnicians, on the showing of their own historian Josephus: *Israel* being the Phœnician name of the planet Saturn, of the same signification as the Chaldean word Abraham, and identically synonymous with the Star of their God, *Remphan*.

END OF THE DISCOURSE ON MELCHISEDEC.

The Devil's Pulpit.

"DELENDA EST CARTHAGO."

No. 14.—Vol. II.] [Price 2d.

THE LORD:

Ο Κυριος OF THE OLD TESTAMENT.—Part 1.

A Discourse,

DELIVERED BY THE REV. ROBERT TAYLOR, B.A.

AT THE ROTUNDA, BLACKFRIARS ROAD, JULY 24, 1830.

'*And the apostles said unto the Lord, Increase our faith. And the Lord said, If ye had faith as a grain of mustard-seed, ye might say to this sycamore-tree, Be thou plucked up by the root, and be thou planted in the sea; and it should obey you.*'—LUKE xvii., 5, 6.

THE greatest error ever committed in the world was the suffering the sacred scriptures to come into the hands of the common people. The greatest crime ever committed by man against the peace and happiness of society, as well as against the Holy Majesty of Heaven, was the act of translating these sacred records into the vulgar tongues of the different nations of Christendom, and thereby putting barbarian vanity and savage fanaticism into a mad conceit, that they could judge as well of the nature of the 'deep things of God,' as his own holy priests, who, by his express appointment, were to be 'the ministers of Christ, and stewards of the mysteries of God:' from whose oral instructions alone, the people were to receive the measure of divine truth, apportioned to their capacity, and of whom God hath said, 'The priest's lips shall keep knowledge: the people shall hear the word of the Lord at their mouth, and by their word shall every controversy and every stroke be tried.'

But how lay-people, the unlearned, and unskilled in sacred science, were like to get a chance of coming any nearer the sense of the original, by means of the vulgar translation, may be inferred, from the confessed ignorance and infinite discrepancies, and differences of understanding, which obtain, even among the most learned of Protestant divines and scholars, and the universally admitted defects and errors of that translation.

It amazes me,' says the great critic, and most learned Protestant theologue, Dr. Markland, in his letter to the learned Bowyer, 'It amazes me, when I consider what strange oversights have been made in the New Testament, by men of the greatest learning and sagacity, in a book that has been read more than any book in the world. What can be the reason of it? They would not have done so in any other author. Reverence, perhaps, has got the better of common sense. I could send you instances that would astonish you.'

And if learned men have made such monstrous blunders, and fallen into such egregious mistakes,—as they never would have fallen into in the understanding of any other book,—what must we think would be likely to be the misconceptions and misapprehensions of the unlearned and unstable,—but that they should wrest the scriptures, as indeed they do,—to their own destruction.

Or where need we seek further for the reason of all this, than *that* reason, which the scriptures themselves assign, that, 'Even to this day, when the scriptures are read, the veil is upon their heart. According as it is written, God hath given them the spirit of slumber, eyes that they should not see, and ears that they should not hear, unto this day.'

And is it not so, Sirs! that 'the spirit of slumber,' a lazy, drunken drowsiness of mind, and a palsy of the very faculty of curiosity and inquiry, seizes the rational nature of man the moment he hears or reads the violated text of God's word?

Nor is it unintelligent and exceedingly weak-minded men, who are alone visited by this palsy of the mental faculties, upon any approach to the mysteries of our most holy faith. The shrewdest, the quickest, the cleverest in every other respect: *men* who, in the reading of an ordinary lease or title-deed, or *will*, that might affect their claim to temporal property, would not let a word, nor a syllable, nor a dot, nor a comma, escape their criticism, who would sift and resift, weigh and weigh again, every possible sense that every noun, pronoun, verb, participle, adverb, conjunction, preposition, or interjection of such a document would bear, will read their Bibles with their eyes shut,—and any meaning will do for *that*, that any man may put on't,—so that they be but sufficiently sure that he'll not say anything to shake their faith, or put 'em to the mortification of discovering that the scriptures, which are able to make them wise unto salvation, through faith, which is in Jesus Christ, have made no conjurors of 'em, for all that.

What man, upon reading the words,—' And the apostles said unto the Lord, And the Lord said unto the apostles,' would in any other respect have been so measurelessly stupid, and so drivellingly idiotish, as to let such words pass in at one ear, and out of the other, without stopping them by the way to certify what weight of mettle they carry with them, and whence they bought, or brought, or found, or stole it. Who would not ask? Who is this O Κυριος, the Lord? And these, οι Αποστολοι, the apostles?

What greater proof, then, can be imagined, that God indeed hath visited the Christian community with 'the spirit of slumber' than the fact, that of the millions, to whom the words, 'the Lord,' and 'the Apostles,' as rendered into their own tongue, are as familiar as their teeth,—not one in a million hath any more idea of what those words really mean, than he has of the Abracadabra, or Shem Hemephoresh, or magical incantations.

Why, to be sure, do they not mean our blessed Saviour, Jesus of Nazareth, and his twelve disciples, Andrew, Thomas, Peter, James, John, and the rest of them? No! they do not.

The Tower of Babel, and the twelve stones that Joshua threw into the River Jordan, is a better guess at it.

Well, then, if men may be so monstrously deceived as *thus*: it may be asked, how can moral certainty, or any knowledge of the past, be ensured to man: how can it be possible to arrive at any truth whatever?

Why *thus* it may—by setting out in the pursuit of it in a different direction, and on other principles than those on which you have hitherto acted, even by that patience to hear arguments, the like of which you had never heard before; that diligence to inquire, and that candour to compare the merits of what may be new and strange to you, which is included in that sacred precept: 'Prove all things, hold fast that which is good.' But never think of holding fast till you have proved.

And on this principle of *proving*, as you would be ashamed not to apply it, in the ordinary business of life, a sensible man would pause first, and insist on receiving a perfect satisfaction as to what such words as *the Lord*, and *the Apostles* respectively mean: and from what sources and authorities their meaning is derived: and how it has come to pass, that in these mystical and double-meaning books, called spells or charms of God, or God's spells, these technical terms, the LORD, and the APOSTLES, are played off upon us with such a flinging familiarity, as if it were a thing to be taken for granted that everybody must know who *Lords* and Apostles were?

And of this familiarity in the use of these terms, without any further exposition of them, the resulting proof is, as that proof would be received in a court of justice, with respect to the authenticity of any other writings in the world, that these writings could not possibly have been written before the notion of *the Lord* and *the Apostles* was fully up, and universally established in the world.

Neither, then, could this gospel *according* to St. Luke— that is, not by St. Luke, but according to St. Luke, as God only knows who he was, have been written as the basis of Christianity: inasmuch as there is not a single sentence in it but what supposes the whole mysterious system, already fully established, and entirely prevalent, before this gospel was written, even to such an universality as that its most isoteric and peculiar terms and phrases might be used, without any apprehension, on the part of the writer, that his readers would want to know to whom they referred.

Assume any terms of art, to be used with great familiarity in any treatise whatever, and you have in the familiar use of those terms, a chronological demonstration, that *that* treatise could not have been written before the general understanding of mankind was fully possessed of the significancy of those terms, and the art to which they belonged sufficiently apprehended and understood.

So the style of the blessed gospels throughout, in every term which they contain, involves the proof and demonstration that they were not, and absolutely could not have been written, till long, very long, many hundred, and I believe in my heart thousands of years after the general and universal prevalence of the notions which they detail.

They are not the rule of what the faith should be, but exhibitions only of what it was: Christianity is not founded upon them, but they are founded upon Christianity: they derive their authority *from* the church, and not the church from them.

Any other records whatever, which the church had adopted, would have been as sacred and as holy as these holy writings by virtue of that adoption. And I'll answer for it, that good Christian people would have found them quite as comfortable to their soul, and as answerable to the spiritual cravings of the inner man. For blessed be God! the spiritual appetite of our immortal souls was never very delicate in its choice of what it fed on.

The term the LORD, even in the plain English ear (if that ear hold any communication with a mind within), in its most ordinary acceptation, leading the idea, as it does to its great reference to the *Lord God*,—the Jehovah God of the Old Testament,—must assure us that it could not have appertained nor meant to designate any human being whatever.

But the term *apostles*, is a Greek word adopted or naturalised, without translation, into our English language : in which, unless we refer it to its derivative significany in the language from which it has been been borrowed, it has absolutely no meaning at all,—the only clue afforded to the mere English reader is, that there is certainly some very particular and essential relation between the Lord and the Apostles, they are correlative and inseparable notions. And the company always consists of thirteen : there in *one* Lord, —and never be it forgotten, his name ONE: but there are always twelve apostles, neither more nor fewer: but so necessarily and essentially twelve, that when one (as good as any of the rest of 'em) hanged himself, another was immediately put into his place to keep up the exact number twelve.

The words of the original Greek text are: Καί ειπον ο

Αποστολοι τω Κυριω, ειπε δε ο Κυριος. Why, then, was not the term, ε Κυριος, naturalized into *the Curios*, as well as the οι Αποστολοι into *the apostles?* It would have sounded as well in the brute ear of uninquisitive credulity.

But the meaning of the word, ο Κυριος, which we have translated, *the Lord*, demands, and would demand, from any man who sincerely loved and sought the truth, the severest sifting, and the most unflinching and uncompromising criticism of which his mind is capable. If it were possible that any man on earth could better know what that word meant, whence it was derived, and to what it tended, he would bargain that Omnipotence to forfeit his salvation. 'Were it in heaven above, or in the earth beneath, or in the waters under the earth,' thence would he drag it forth; nor live nor die till he had known the Lord; nor would he suffer that *word* to be uttered in his ear, by one of woman born, who knew *the Lord* better than himself. Ο Κυριος, in our Greek Testament, is an adjective ungrammatically used as a substantive: ο Κυριος should signify *of* or *pertaining to* that which is ο Κυρος. And Κυρος, we shall find to be a God who was worshipped under that name by the ancient Persians. And that God, so worshipped under that name, Κυρος, which is the theme and root of the Greek name, ο Κυριος, which our translators have rendered *the Lord*, was the Sun.

'For the Persians,' says Plutarch, in his Artaxerxes, call *the Sun* Κυρος. Κυρον γαρ καλειν Περσας τον Ηλιον. And Ctesias, the ancient historian of Persia, informs us that Cyrus, the Mede, who is expressly designated by Jehovah, in the 45th of Isaiah, by the titles given to Christ in the New Testament, received that name of Κυρος (*Cyrus*), as derived from the name of the Sun.

Και τιθεται το ονομα αυτου, απο του Ηλιου.

'Thus saith the Lord to his anointed, to Cyrus, whose right hand I have holden to subdue nations before him:' which is but a repetition of the similar idea of the 110th Psalm.

Yahouh said unto Adonis, which our translation renders, 'the Lord said unto my Lord,' sit thou on my right hand until I make thine enemies thy footstool.' Though we sometimes find this infinitely important word Κυρος written Κυρις; but still with reference to the Sun, the Adonis of the

East, as Hesychius, the great critic of the third century expressly states, Κυρις ο Αδωνις—that is, Κυρις is Adonis, as that *Adonis* was the Sun, the name Adonis being compounded of the two words Ad and On, being the title of the Supreme Being, the πρωτος των πρωτων, first of the first, or the Most High, and ON, the Egyptian name of the Sun.

Among the Eastern nations, AD was a peculiar title, always signifying and referring to the Sun: as being pre-eminently the One, or the Alone, and this is the derivative sense of that word HOLY, and of those phrases, Holiness to the Lord, the קדש of the Hebrew, the Αγιος of the Greek, the Sanctus of the Sabines, and ultimately the Solus or Sol of the Latins,—all these words signify the Oneness or Unity of the Godhead.

Hence the Apollo, literally signified the one, apart and separate from *the many*.

The Syrian, Chaldean and Egyptian nations, for the greater reverence, doubled the word Ad, which was their way of forming the superlative degree, and made *Adad*,—the ONE the ONE. And you find that very name ascribed by the Moses of the Old Testament, and the Christ of the New to the Supreme Jehovah, שמע ישראל יהוה אלהינו יהוה אחד. 'Hear, O Israel, Yahouh, our Alehim, is Yahouh Achad.

But the Greeks and Romans, not content with doubling the word that expressed *the One*, from still greater reverence tripled it, and sung to the tune—the One, the One, the One, —Holy, Holy, Holy, is the Lord, while by the three ones, they still meant only the One One: and thus made a Trinity in Unity, and a Unity in Trinity, without intending it: both Father, Son, and Holy Ghost, never having meant more than one God, and one Lord, and that Lord God was the Sun.

Thoth or Theuth, the Egyptian name for the Sun, was the root of the Greek word Θεος—God.

And Κυρος, or Cyrus, the Persic name for the Sun, was the root of the Greek word Κυριος—the Lord.

And the God Apollo was actually worshipped in his Holy Temple at Phocis, under that epithet Κυρραιος—Apollo, (Bryant, Vol. I. p. 101)—the Lord of Glory.

Nor is the meaning even of our English word, *the Lord*, as the translation of the Greek (ο Κυριος), so entirely disguised, but that a man who would attend to the *meaning* of words, might find out what Deity *is*, that is worshipped under the name of *the Lord*, even in the Collects of our own Common Prayer Book,—as in that of St. John the Evangelist: 'Merciful Lord, we beseech thee to cast thy bright beams of light upon thy church, that it being enlightened by the doctrine of thy blessed Apostle and Evangelist, St. John, may so walk in the light of thy truth, that it may at length attain to the light of everlasting life, through Jesus Christ our Lord Amen'—that is, our Lord Jupiter Ammon.

That mystically muttered word AUMON, through all the variety of intonations and cadences that can possibly be given to it, *Ah-men*, *Aumen*, *Amen*, *Omen*, never having meant anything else than *Jupiter Ammon*, the Egyptian name for the SUN, retained, at this day, at the end of every creed, of every prayer, of every devotional form whatever; to intimate, that by whatever other names *the Lord* may be addressed, they are all included and summed up in the name AMON—that is, the SUN, even 'the Father of lights, with whom is no variableness, nor shadow of turning. JESUS CHRIST, the same yesterday, to-day, and for ever.' Whose sacred emblem, you see here on our holy altar, sketched from an entablature found in the ruins of *Naki Rustan*, near the temple of the God *Mithra*, in Persia, the Sun with wings: and the uplifted Serpent, that mystic hieroglyph, which spake to the worshippers of the Sun of a thousand years before our Christian era, none other than the purport of our sacred scriptures. both of the Old and New Covenant,

וזרחה לכם יראי שמי שמש צדקה ומרפא בכנפיה.

Ve zercheh lekem yerai shemi, Chemosh Tzedequeh ve Merpa bekenpihog. 'Unto you that fear my name shall the Sun of Righteousness arise, with healing in his wings.' Malachi 4.

Και καθ.ως Μωσης υψωσε τον οφιν εν τη ερημω, ουτως υψσωθηναι δει τον υιον του Ανθρωπου.

'And as Moses lifted up the Serpent in the wilderness, even so must the Son of Man be lifted up.' John iii., 14.

Under which you read the appropriate legend, which it would have been impious to translate from the ancient Orphic hymns:

Παντοφυης γενετωρ παντων, πολυωνυμε Δαιμον.

'Of all natures, parent of all things, demon of many names.'

Which Pope has versified in that truly Catholic stanza:

> 'Father of all, in every age,
> In every clime adored;
> By saint, by savage, and by sage,
> Jehovah, Jove, or Lord.'

And understanding now, who the Lord is, the unknown quantity is found, and the equation is solved.

You can be no longer at a loss to tell why there should be just twelve apostles, through whom the great physician of our souls should diffuse his healing influences through the world: and that each of their mystical characters should answer, as they do, with an astonishing minuteness to the respective physical phænomena of the twelve months of the year, and the twelve signs of the Zodiac.

Now it is of infinite importance, to have it deeply impressed on our minds, that of all religious customs and usages, that have ever obtained among men (it would be a sarcasm to say rational men), none besides was ever so universal, so invariable, as that of priests assuming to themselves the characters, taking the names and titles, and speaking and acting as in the person of the God, whose priests they affected to be. A priest of Jupiter would be content with nothing short of the honour of being addressed as Jupiter himself.

Chreses, the priest of Apollo, hesitates not to challenge from the Kings of Greece the reverence due to Apollo. Αζομενοι Διος υιον εκη βολον Απολλωνα τα δ' αποινα·δεγεσθε. And take the gifts in reverence of the Son of God, the far shooting Apollo.

'I am the Lord thy God, thou shalt have none other Gods but me,' was a bit of impudence, that the modesty of a priest would never bogle at, an' let the gulled people *stare.*

One would say, 'I am the Lord's:' and another would subscribe himself by the name of the Mighty God of Jacob; till at last, Lords were so cheap, and there were such a many 'mighty Gods of Jacob,' that the poet said—No; I'll not tell you what the poet said. But, with this understanding, we have light enough in our hands to advance upon the last argument of our text, 'The Apostle said unto the Lord, Increase our faith.'

Now whatever that principle of faith was, it seems that the apostolic stock of it ran very low,—they had not so much as the size of a grain of mustard-seed among the twelve of 'em. The great question is,—what *was* or *is* that principle of faith? It was evidently the principle necessary to the right understanding of everything said, or done, or enjoined throughout the whole system of divine revelation.

'For without faith it is impossible to please God,' which is the way the priests quote the text (Hebrews, xi., 6). Though, if a man brews for himself, he'll see not a word in the text itself about pleasing God. It is only 'without faith it is impossible to please.'

Χωρις δε πιστεως αδυνατον ευαρεστησαι—that is, it is impossible to please your teachers, spiritual pastors and masters: and to order yourself lowly and reverently to all your betters.

For among all the forms and follies of Pagan piety or impiety, I defy imagination to conceive, that the human mind ever sunk, or could sink into a depth of folly and madness, second to that of imagining that the Almighty should want a man to believe something to be true, which, in the natural exercise of his rational faculties, he could not help suspecting to be no better than a lie.

But all the mistake, so far as it has not been wilful, has originated in the confusion caused in the resemblance of the word faith to that faithfulness, by which, in ordinary parlance, we mean integrity and truth, and should call a man faithless who broke his promises, and deceived us, and went from his engagements with us.

But no true words ever used by man were ever of more diametrically opposite and contradictory signification. Faith in the gospel so far from meaning *taking it to be literally true*, means, *taking it as it was intended to be taken;* and, *believing it*, means understanding it. So that a true faith is a mountain-removing and sycamore-transplanting principle.

As when you know that an allegory is only the vehicle of some great moral truth, you don't stand higgling with its dead letter, the mere shells and husks on which the swine do feed, as contra-distinguished from that spiritual sense, that bread of life which is the children's food: of which our blessed Saviour so emphatically speaks, 'It is not meet to take that which is holy, and give it to the dogs.'

But dogs and swine in understanding are they, who take

the gospel to be literally true, and 'stumble at the word, being disobedient whereunto also they were appointed.'

Wherefore saith Christ our Lord to his disciples, 'Unto you it is given to know the mysteries of the kingdom of heaven, but unto them that are without all these things are done in parables, that seeing, they may see and not perceive, and hearing, they may hear and not understand.'

'Neither,' said he, 'cast ye your pearls before swine, lest they turn again and rend you.' As in all ages of the world, the swinish multitude, gospel-crammed fools, that feed upon the *letter*, and rest only in the first sense of things, do gnash their teeth, and are ready to turn and rend the man, whom they behold, 'full of the Holy Ghost, and of faith,' and from that fulness of the Holy Ghost and faith, able to show them that 'there are more things in heaven and earth than have been dreamed of in their philosophy.'

'For God hath made us,' what the ministers, which better please the multitude, are not. 'God hath made us able ministers of the New Testament, not of the letter, but of the spirit, for the letter killeth,' said the holy apostle— that is, there is not a word of truth in the letter of the New Testament: it was never intended to *pass* for true, and none but the swine who feed on husks would have ever taken it for truth. 'But the spirit giveth life:' thus *faith*, which is an entirely technical term, and peculiar to the language of theology, is theologically defined as 'a right understanding in all things,' it is to understand a Παροιμια, a משל, 'and interpretation thereof, the words of the wise and their dark sayings.'

Or, as the apostle to the Hebrews laboriously defines it, with a precision which one might have thought it impossible to misunderstand. It is, ελπιζομενων υποστασις, Ου βλεπομενων ελεγχος—that is, the imagination of things which have no reality: the seeing of things which nobody ever saw.

And then follows the application of this realising view of divine things, to all the allegories of the Old Testament, which the ignorant have so absurdly taken for real histories. It is *by faith* that we understand how the world was made. And how Abel, 'being dead, yet speaketh.' As in God's name, what should hinder a dead man from speaking,—*by faith*. 'By faith the walls of Jericho fell down,' as by faith, if occasion had called for it, they'd have got up again.

'By faith, the children of Israel went through the Red Sea, as on dry land,' as any other children in the world might have done—*by faith*. As said our Saviour Christ, 'If ye had faith as a grain of mustard-seed, ye might say to this sycamore-tree, Be thou plucked up by the roots, and be thou planted in the sea, and it should obey you:' or as he saith in further exposition of this saying, 'If thou canst believe all things are possible to him that believeth.' There's no difficulty, then, in the matter—that is, make believe, imagine, fancy that it was all *so:* work up your humour to the conceit of the thing, and *then* look at the sycamore-tree, and the mountains.

> 'And then see lofty Lebanon his head advance,
> See nodding forests on the mountains dance;
> The Saviour comes, by ancient bards foretold,
> Hear him, ye deaf, and all ye blind, behold.'

Then shall triumphant faith drive out rebellious reason, then 'all things are yours, and ye are Christ's, and Christ is God's.' (1 Corinth. iii., 23.) Then issue your command, and Omnipotence shall obey you: then 'whosoever shall say unto this mountain, Be thou removed, and be thou cast into the sea: and shall not doubt in his heart, but shall believe that those things which he saith shall come to pass: he shall have, whatsoever he saith:' as much as to say,— the fool shall have the moon to play with; he shall direct the counsels of infinite wisdom; he shall be regent of the universe, and in his brain sick vanity shall imagine the Almighty to obey his bidding.

Can we wonder, that amid language so evidently ironical, so severely sarcastic, as the language ascribed to Christ, is so continually found to be,—we should every now and then stumble upon the *key* to the whole mystery,—*the word to the wise:* the word of faith, which unlocks the whole mysterious jargon, of which it is written, 'None of the wicked shall understand, but the wise shall understand.'

And what is that word of faith? Will ye hear it from the Apostolic James? this it is: 'My brethren have not the faith of our Lord Jesus Christ—the Lord of Glory with respect of persons'—that is, no such a person (*as a person*) ever existed.

Hear it from the Apostolic Paul! *this* it is 'There is no

respect of persons with God.' God knows that no such a person ever existed.

Hear it in the words set down in the text, and spoken in the character itself: 'Doth this offend you? What and if ye shall see the Son of Man ascend up where he was before? It is the spirit that quickeneth, the flesh profiteth nothing: the words that I speak unto you, they are spirit and they are life' (John 6), that is (than which no hint could be broader) this whole doctrine of Christ, and of the Christian scriptures, is (as I shall in these lectures abundantly convince ye) millions of miles off any such a sense as Christian folly, fraud, and falsehood have put on it.

Hear, then, the voice of wisdom, ye that desire to attain unto true counsel. 'For the merchandise of it is better than the merchandise of silver, and the gain thereof than fine gold. She is more precious than rubies, and all the things thou canst desire, are not to be compared unto her. Her ways are ways of pleasantness, and all her paths are peace.'

Delenda est Carthago.

END OF PART I. Ο Κυριος OF THE OLD TESTAMENT.

NOTICE.

Mr. Crone, of '50, New Bond Street' will perceive that his polite request, on the behalf of Mr. Allan Cunningham, is complied with: an example, we submit, of the superiority of civility over menace. The Attorney-General might have threatened us in vain. But why Mr. Allan Cunningham's native modesty should have taken alarm at the situation given to his Anglo-Scotch expression, after such a lapse of time, seems, at first sight, extraordinary. No one thinks Shakspere is identified with the works that borrow his lines—But, we forget, 'A living dog is better than a dead lion.' We *mean* nothing more by the expression than the metaphor itself warrants (though a one-eyed, unimaginative judge and jury would, perhaps, construe it as did those who tried Mr. Taylor—literally.) We never thought the motto graced our front, nor had we, in truth, more than the Rev. Mr. Taylor, to do with the selection of it, or title of the work. And further, truth to tell, both were suggested by a literary facetious friend and countryman of Mr. Allan Cunningham himself, who perhaps thought to give Mr. C. a longer literary existence than his own merits as an author entitled him.

Be that as it may, whatever other motive was intended, we are sure it was not an ill-intentioned one. We cannot but think, if the objection be on the score of morals, it is rather of the *Mother Cole* School—scruples of the Laureate—the *penitent* author of 'Wat Tyler.' Of a verity, we suspect the motives to be near akin. The 'wild oats' apology cannot be accepted after the age of maturity. What you have begotten you should not disown. Southey's bantling of liberty will long survive his legitimate, consumptive offspring; and we suspect the best things produced by Allan Cunningham have been supplied by Auld Nickie, when the pulse beat high, though he appears now to be ashamed of his backer.

We are not disposed to be testy, or say we think that the gloomy month of November has caused this much-ado-about-nothing alarm, or that Mr. Allan Cunningham is putting his 'house in order,' lest he should be visited by the cholera; but we will say that we are benefitted by his request,—inasmuch as we shall substitute a sentence expressive of the wish of the persecuted author, as of every honest man,—for the downfall of evil.

We have said enough, we hope, to convince Mr. Allan Cunningham that his words were not chosen by Mr. Taylor, and if the choice had been left to him, never would have been. The Bird of the Sun would not be encumbered with a peacock's train,—and we are quite sure that Mr. Taylor, could Mr. C.'s request be communicated to him in his dungeon, would be most earnest to grant his emancipation from unpleasant (though not unlawful) purgatory, from a feeling of disinclination to give unnecessary pain or uneasiness to any one. Would that his enemies were endowed with similar feelings!

We have said that Mr. Taylor was as innocent of giving the title to the work as of extracting the motto for it. We repeat the assertion; though Thesiger, the slobberer of the indictment, in his harangue to the jury, declared that Mr. Taylor published a work, which HE ENTITLED 'The Devil's Pulpit' (an assertion as false and wicked as the whole proceedings were unlawful). And we firmly believe that the *enlightened* jury who tried him, but assured of that fact alone, would as readily have found him guilty of dealing with the Devil, had the indictment so charged him, or the chairman so instructed them, as they did of uttering blasphemy.

Had the work been called 'Mr. Taylor's Astronomico-Theological Lectures,' as he himself styles them, we believe its circulation would have been greater even than it is at present.

But dismissing the further consideration of comparative trifles, let us turn to the victim of priestcraft, and reflect how lamentable it is, that the blunderings of fools, and the artfulness of knaves, should so work in unison to destroy an innocent man, who happens to have more learning and more sense than a bigotted court, a venomous clergy, a *Dogberry* magistracy of Surrey, or a few daftie M.P.'s (auditors of the Rev. Edward Irving), whose speeches in Parliament, for any reason to be obtained from them, might, like their ravings in the kirk, as well be in an 'unknown tongue.'

Nov. 16, 1831. THE REPORTER.

The Devil's Pulpit.

"DELENDA EST CARTHAGO."

No. 15.—Vol. II.]   [Price 2d.

THE LORD:

OR יהוה OF THE OLD TESTAMENT.—PART II.

A Discourse,

DELIVERED BY THE REV ROBERT TAYLOR, B.A,
AT THE ROTUNDA, BLACKFRIARS ROAD, MAY 30, 1830.

'Then shall we know if we follow on to know the 'Lord,'—HOSEA vi., 3.

ON this text I addressed a very attentive, and as they were attentive, I hope I may say a much-instructed audience, on a former evening. So that we enter now on the third stage of the most important, the most morally useful, and the most intellectually delightful study to which the inquisitive faculties of man could be directed.

For surely no language, with respect to this sacred subject, in its proper acceptation and understanding, could better become a rational Man than that which authority has put in the mouth of the Patriarch Moses: 'I beseech thee, O Lord, show me thy glory:' or then the still more emphatic exclamation of the constellary Jacob, when he wrestled with God, and said, 'I will not let thee go, unless thou bless me.'

Our application of the text to our immediate purpose: 'Then shall we know if we follow on to know the Lord,' is to impress on our minds its sacred, yet most rational admonition, that knowledge on this subject is not to be acquired without study and diligence, without a pursuit of the science from stage to stage, as it opens before us a willingness to give up the misconceptions and prejudices which grew on our less extended information, and an ardent desire to enlarge our views, to increase our stock of ideas, to extend our range of thought, to add to our faith virtue, and to our virtue knowledge.

And this is none other than the method of study propounded to us, in the mystic allegory, by Wisdom herself personified.

'My son, if thou wilt receive my words, and hide my commandment with thee, so that thou incline thine ear unto wisdom, and apply thine heart unto understanding: yea, if thou criest after knowledge, and liftest up thy voice for understanding: if thou seekest her as silver, and searchest for her as for hid treasures: then shalt thou understand the fear of the Lord, and find the knowledge of God.'

But what pursuit of knowledge, what seeking as for hid treasures, what application of the heart, what fidelity to their own rational faculties, can *they* pretend to have exercised, who would never go to hear, or never stay to hear, anything that might suggest to them a new train of thought, or discover to them that the first impressions made on their childhood may have need to be revised and corrected.

Our only difference with the community of our Christian brethren, is on the ground, that they do *not* observe the admonition I have quoted, and that we *do*: that they do not seek to know the Lord; and to discover the real meaning of 'their own scriptures: but are, on the contrary, afraid of nothing so much as that they should discover it,—and thereby dissipate the delusion of fanaticism, and awaken from the drowsy lethargy of faith to the business, care, and pains of being rational.

'It is a pain,' says Solomon, 'for a fool to get knowledge:' and he looks on anyone who could communicate it to him as an enemy. Hence the eternal war of the dunces and ignoramuses of society against all means and all persons, suspected of competence to disturb the stagnation of popular ignorance: and that peculiar injustice, and indeed wickedness of heart, which a man would be ashamed of in any other respect, and which he would most justly and bitterly complain of, if shown towards himself, which will set such a character, in very malice, to hear only so much as may authorise him to say he *has* heard, and to exhibit his misconception of something of which he has neither trusted himself to know the beginning or the end, the context or the bearing, as a representation of the knowledge which has indeed been too wonderful and excellent for him.

And so much justice was it, that the very prototypes and examples of such characters, the scribes and pharisees of the gospel are represented to have shown to its Jesus Christ, when they went to hear him, with a view and *wish* to find matter of offence in what he should say, He said something about a *Temple*, or he said that St. Paul's Cathedral was built in three days,—or no matter what he said, so he said something to authorise them in saying, 'Away with such a fellow from the earth, for it is not fit that he should live.'

If those who hear me now for the first time, are minded to be more just than thus, they will patiently endure the very succinct recapitulation of what has been proved in the previous discourses, and suppose that they might have been as entirely convinced by the proofs then adduced, as they may be by the further information to which now we tend.

The general object of these discourses is, to exhibit the true meaning and original sense of all the great archetypes and leading ideas of sacred theology,—to set before you the etymons, roots, and derivations of all its mystical prosopopeia, whether taking their rise in Sanscrit, Egyptian, Hebrew, Chaldee, Persic, Arabic, Greek, or Latin originals, —to illustrate its occult and hidden science,—and to present the real and primitive meaning of words, with all the indifference and impartiality with which a dictionary would present them. In doing which, it will always be my method to give you the literal English in so close and easy a way, as to make my hearers imperceptibly become scholars, as they become critics; to make learning delightful, and investigation of sacred theology the vehicle of learning.

In the first of these discourses, we unveiled the mysterious sense and significancy of the word, *the Lord*, as it is predicated of the Lord Jesus Christ, in the New Testament, and is presented to the English reader as a translation of the Greek word ο Κυριος, which Greek word we traced from its Persic original, as identical with the name of Cyrus, King of Persia, a title which that prince held as derived from *the Sun*, which the Persic word Κυρος signifies,

—and whose representatives on earth, the ancient Kings of Persia, affected to be.

We before treated on the mysteries of the name of the LORD, as it is exclusively meant of the Lord of the Old Testament, and presented to the English reader of the Hebrew word יהוה, absurdly pronounced Jehovah, properly pronounced YAHOUH, and synonymous with the very oldest Arabic name of the Supreme Deity, *Yagouth*, who was worshipped under the form of a Lion by the wild Arabs of the desert, who was the Lion of the Zodiac, or the Sun in the burning heat of the month of July. Who was the Lion of the tribe of יהודה (YAHU-DAH!) which we call *Judah*, who was the SING-AVATAR or Man-Lion of the Hindu, represented as bursting from a pillar to destroy a blaspheming Monarch, and who, in the sacred text of Hosea xiii., 8, which is the same picture in words, is represented as speaking in character: 'Therefore will I be unto them as a Lion, as a Leopard by the way will I observe them. I will meet them as a Bear which is bereaved of her whelps,—and I will rend the caul of their heart: and there will I devour them like a Lion.'

The Egyptians, from whom, or unquestionably through whom, both the Jewish and Christian religion are derived to us, were the most refined in their superstitions of all nations, and veiled the whole of their astronomical science under the allegories and emblems of religion. Thus the name of the Lion of the Zodiacal constellations, in passing through the λεων of the Greek, the *Leo* of the Latin, *Le Lion* of the French, and the similarly formed word in all the languages of Asia and of Europe, even to our own word *Lion*, retains in its etymon, the original name of God, EL-EON*—*i.e.*, God, *the living* ONE, or the *living God*.

This peculiar character of *living*, or being the eternal and necessarily existing *one*, is not only found as the basis or radical idea of the name of *Yahouh*, of *Jupiter*, and of the Egyptian *Isis*, but it is found still earlier, as derived to the Egyptians themselves, from the sacred text of the *Bhagavat Pourana*, or Book of God of the Hindus, as constituting the basis of the name of the Supreme God of India, who is thus announcing himself to *Brahma* (whom nobody can doubt to

---

* Bryant's Analysis, Vol. II., p. 18, has suggested this argument.

be the same as Abraham). 'Even I was: even at first not any other thing: that which exists unperceived—supreme: afterwards I am that which is: and he who must remain am I:' so literally translated from the Sanscrit by Sir W. Jones.—*Asiatic Researches*, Vol. I., p. 245.

The happiest rendering of the original word, which our English Bibles call *the Lord*, is that of the French version, which is *L'Eternel*. The *Eternal*, presenting this idea of everlasting and necessary existence, which is the essential basis of the name of Yahouh, so awkwardly paraphrased in the 'I am that I am,' and so entirely lost sight of in our bald English the LORD.

The radical syllable of the word LION—that is, ON-EON, or AON, was the Amonian title of the SUN, and expressed that particular idea of eternal and necessary existence, which all nations attached to their terms for the Supreme Being, and which is traceable in all his names and titles, even to our own English word ONE, the first of numbers, as God is *one*. In the supreme sense the ONE and first of all things.

The synonyme of the name Yahouh is given in that truly sublime poem, called the Blessings of the Twelve Tribes, in the 33rd of Deuteronomy, 'The eternal God is thy refuge, and underneath are the everlasting arms.'

From the original Amonian word ON, the name of the Sun, the Greeks formed their ο Ων, the *Being*, and their adjective forms of that word αιωνιος, which is the word translated *eternal* and *everlasting*.

My English readers will easily remember this derivation, by the substitution of the *aonian* instead of eternal, which they find in the first stanzas of Pope's Messiah:—

> 'Ye nymphs of Solyma, begin the song,
> To heavenly themes, sublimer strains belong;
> The mossy fountains, and the Sylvan shades,
> The dreams of Pindus, and the Aonian maids,
> Delight no more! O thou my voice inspire,
> Who touched Isaiah's hallowed lips with fire.'

The Aonian maids means the *eternal* maids, and this attribute of eternity, the nine muses received from their constant attendance on the Sun, whose Egyptian name was ON, and who was always meant and referred to as the Everlasting God and the Eternal ONE.

The Greek word for ONE, the first of numbers, though not formed, as all our European words for ONE are, from the Egyptian word ON, which means the SUN, is the word εις, which is the Greek pronunciation of the Hebrew word U'N, *the fire*, which is *the Sun*, of which, by a most wondrous assimilation, they formed the feminine in the wholly different word Mια, which is an abbreviation of the word Maria, and the neuter in εν, which is the same as ON. Thus have we, in the first word of the Greek language, as found in the first writer that ever wrote in that language, even in the structure of the language itself, the primordial theme of the Christian Trinity, the *three-in-one*: the εις, masculine ; Mια, feminine ; and εν neuter—that is, the fire, the Virgin Mary, the Sun.

To the Amonian title ON, or EON, was frequently added the universal name of God, *El*, and the compound word El-Eon, signifying *God Eternal*, or the *Eternal God;* and also the name of the noblest of animals, the LION: the Lion was transferred to the highest domicile of the Zodiac, and became the type of the Sun, being then *most high:* the Sun in July, as having attained his highest altitude and splendour. *El-Ion* is the Hebrew for the most high,—and from this word, the Greeks formed their objective case of ηλιος, ηλιον, the Sun. From the domicile of the Sun in the Lion of July, adjoining on that of the Crab of September, when the Sun begins to descend, the claws or arms of the Crab in the Egyptian diagrams of the Zodiac, were represented as spread out or extending below the path of the Lion: and hence affording the idea of support and security from falling, which is the solution of those beautiful figures of the allegory, 'the Eternal God is thy refuge, and underneath are the everlasting arms.' It is none other than the claws of the Crab, which, had they been duly depicted according to their position in the heavens, would have presented to your eye the exact position of *the everlasting arms:* as it is none other than the Lion of the tribe of *I,ou Dah*, who is the literal and ultimate antitype of the Hebrew El-Elion, the Most High God.

As also had the Zodiacal Lion been depicted, as it certainly was in the most ancient Persian and Arabian Zodiacs, with the *Bee* which the Arabs call the honey-fly, flying into his mouth,—I would not have told the fool that couldn't have guessed the meaning of Samson's riddle, 'Out of the eater came forth meat, and out of the strong came forth sweetness.' Judges, xiv., 14.

The LION bears a most prominent part in all the figures of speech of all languages, expressive of strength, power, and magnanimity. The cherubim which shadowed the mercy-seat of Yahouh, had each four faces, the face of a man, and of a calf ; and an eagle, and a lion.

'And every one,' says the holy prophet, ' had four faces, and every one had four wings. And their feet were *straight* feet: and the sole of their feet was like the sole of a calf's foot, and they sparkled like the colour of burning brass.' (1 Ezekiel.) Their wings were joined one to another, they turned not when they went, they went every one straightforward : And they had the hands of a man under their wings : but they had but one leg between the four of 'em. So that, however, they might differ in opinion, there was at least a common understanding between them.

Now look ye, Sirs, at the desperate ignorance and measureless intolerance of your Protestant preachers of the gospel. It is thought no impiety, no profaneness, no approach to a disrespect for the language of holy writ, and no dishonour of the Supreme Being, where the most evangelical and orthodox Parkhurst, adorns his Hebrew and Greek Lexicons, with a picture of these four-fold Siamese youths, and declares in his text that they are the real likeness of God Almighty, even the express image of his person.

So—so! And do fools rush in where angels fear to tread ? Or does that name rather belong to those who receive a book as the word of God, of which they no more know the meaning than the incapable earth on which they tread, or to the man who does know the meaning ?

Can anything be more immoral, more essentially unjust, cruel, and wicked, than the conduct of those barbarous dunces, who, conscious of the deepest ignorance, and of their utter inability to give any sort of explanation of the deep things of God, become the enemies of those who can explain them.

This can I, ישמע חכם יוסיף לקח *Yeshemeng Chequem ve yousip lequech.* ' Let the wise hear, and he shall increase learning.'

Turn we to the mystic text of the New Covenant, and

we shall find these same cherubic monsters which, in the Old Covenant, were represented as the person of Jahouh himself, in the most uneasy state imaginable: 'they were full of eyes within, and they rest not day nor night, saying Holy, Holy, Holy Lord God Almighty, which was, and is, and is to come.'

But you don't know the meaning of all this,—and I am sure that your Christian ministers cannot tell, as I am sure that I can, and that is the ground of all difference between us. Go to your churches and chapels, ye who are content to be ignorant, and wish to know no more: But *here* we follow on to know the Lord. Attend ye, Sirs, and I will teach you the fear of the Lord, and show you the knowledge of the Most High.

Upon the Egyptian radical word, ON, for the Sun, adopted as the participle present, of the Greek verb, ειναι, to BE: and hence, forming the participle noun substantive ο Ων, *the Being*, that which *is*, followed the necessary addition of the two other participles, the ο ην, and the ο' ερχομενος, *which was*, and *which is to come*.

The notion of a trinity, or triple mode of existence, thus grew upon the unity and emphatic oneness of the Supreme Being, growing as naturally out of the three tenses,— *present*, *past*, and *future*, of the participle of the verb *to be*, which expressed being and existence,—as it grew out of the three genders, masculine, feminine, and neuter of the noun substantive ONE. And they who worshipped the Almighty, which *was*, and which *is*, were led by the sound of the word rather than the sense, to imagine a distinction where none was intended, in the ο' ερχομενος, *which is to come*. And hence, the universal expectation originating in an abuse of language, of some divine person that was to come, and even the title itself of the *He that should come*, which opened the door to the infinite superstitions which grew on so ridiculous a mistake.

Hence the allegorical message of John the Baptist to Christ, 'Art thou the ο ερχομενος, *the He that should come*, or do we look for another?"

And that commonly quoted, and as commonly misquoted passage of Suetonius: Percrebuerat Oriente toto, vetus et constans opinio esse in fatis ut eo tempore Judæa profecti rerum potirentur. An ancient and fixed opinion had prevailed throughout the east that it was decreed by the fates that some coming out of Judea, at that time, should obtain the empire of the world.

But it was always from the east, never anywhere but from the east, that this always and *eternally to come* deity, was to be expected: thus identifying him with the ο ην, the *which was*, and the ο Ων, the *which is*—*i.e.*, the ON, which is the direct and literal name, the SUN, which is God Almighty, the eternally existing *one* 'which was, and 'which is, and which is to come?

Who, then, are those, or rather *is*, those four in one Siamese youths, with their Man, Lion, Eagle, and Bull faces, with six wings, and full of eyes within, which address the Triune Yahouh, which was, and which is, and which is to come? Abeste, Abeste, O procul abeste profani. Be far from hence, be far from hence, O be far from hence, ye who are profane,—for it is written, none of the wicked shall understand, but the wise shall understand.

Unto you it shall be given at this moment to understand the mysteries of the kingdom of God, but unto them that are without, all these things are done in parables, &c.

I cut the ligature which ties this Lion, Man, Bull, and Eagle together, and let them betake themselves to whatever point of compass they please.

Now, then, let them tell us who can; and for what other reason, than that which will occur is it, that in all their painted windows and altar-pieces in the most ancient and venerable Christian cathedrals, churches, and temples: the four evangelists *are* (and ever have been) depicted as writing their gospels, with the demon or genius under whose divine inspiration they are believed to have written them, making an essential part of the picture,—so that you distinguish the one from the other, only by their respective genius: that of Matthew is a LION, who sits under the table like a domestic dog, and growls forth inspiration. But there the Lion is the genius of the month July, and of the summer quarter of the year.

But the genius of St. Mark, by a more than extraordinary coincidence of emblem and character, happens to be *a man*, in a stooping attitude, leaning over his shoulder, and whispering to him the dictates of infinite wisdom.

Nor has the church of Christ any better evidence than

this hieroglyph, for the universally received notion, that St. Mark wrote his gospel under the direction and dictation of St. Peter. And *there* he is, the genius of the month of January, and of the winter quarter of the year,—for ye need not wonder, after his cursing and swearing as he did, that he did not know his master, that there should be a little coolness between them: for though he afterwards repented and wept bitterly, yet one cannot look upon his hieroglyph, without something suggesting to us, that water might be cheap enough with him.

As the days, during the winter quarter, are the shortest, so St. Mark's gospel, as written under the inspiration of this genius, is twelve chapters short of the length of St. Matthew's, which is the longest: eight short of that of St. Luke, and five short of St. John, which two are about an equinoctial length.

Of what use would an understanding be to man, if it were possible to mistake, in that same *Aquarius*, the Waterbearer, the genius of the first of the months, the common characters of Reuben, the first of Patriarchs, of whom the dying Jacob prophesied, 'Reuben, thou art my first-born, my might, and the beginning of my strength,—unstable as water, thou shalt not excel.'—Gen. 49. And of whom the living Balaam prophesied, 'He shall pour the water out of his buckets, and his King shall be higher than Agag, and his kingdom shall be exalted.'—Numbers xxiii. 6.

The same Janus Bifrons, or two-faced Janus of mythology that looked both on the old and new year, as the St. Peter looks one way and the St. Mark the other, in the Christian hierogram.

The St. Peter, the chief of the apostles to whom was committed the keys of the Kingdom of Heaven. And the Saint Januarius, Bishop of Benevento, whose blood is kept in a bottle at Naples, and turns to water every year, which is as true as all the rest of it.

But the inspiring genius of St. Luke's spell is always represented as a Bull,—and there he is, the genius of the month April, and of the spring quarter.

The inspiring genius of St. John's spell is an eagle, and there he is *not*: because the eagle, not falling within the breadth of the Zodiac, yields his place to the Scorpion, the genius of October, or the Autumnal quarter; though being nearer to the Sun. As John was the beloved disciple, and leant on his bosom as he sat at meat—that is, the Sun in Autumn. A line drawn through the Scorpion would pass through the eagle, and therefore the eagle is as essentially the genius of October as that hideous animal.

The three months of the year, commencing in October, and introducing the reign of winter, were emphatically called the gates of hell, and the key of hell gates, as being a more important trust, was committed to St. John, who is the angel or demon that had the key of the bottomless pit: while the keys of heaven, a charge of less importance, were committed to St. Peter, with the consolatory assurance, that the gates of hell should not prevail against it.

But I will unlock to you the gates of hell, and what see ye there? even none other than the Scorpion of October, that hideous crawling worm, which our blessed Saviour, three times declares to have its place in that mansion of the damned, 'where their worm dieth not, and where the fire'—that is, the solar heat, notwithstanding its sensible diminution to our perceptions—'is not quenched.'

It is that Scorpion, that immortal worm, 'the worm which never dieth,' which, standing there in the gates of hell, pledgeth to us the consolatory assurance that the Sun—that is, the Supreme God, in descending into that gloomy region, is still immortal,—and as that worm dieth not, so the glory of the Sun is not impaired, and his fire is not quenched.

This Zodiacal worm, like all the rest of the signs of the Zodiac, was, in its turn, worshipped as the Supreme God, and it is none other than the most intelligent fathers of the Christian church, who assure us that it was Jesus Christ himself, who, in the 22nd Psalm, contemplating his descent into the lower regions, spoke in this character: 'But as for me, I am a worm: and no man, a very scorn of men, and the outcast of the people.' Psalm xxii., 6.

Many of our learned translators render the word תולעת, Tulenget,—σκωληξ, or scarabæus, or cockchafer, and one of the titles of Hercules was Scarabæus, or Hercules, the cockchafer.

But it is Christian, and not Pagan piety, to which we owe this sublime interpretation.

It is the learned father Athanasius Kircherius who instructs us, that by that black-beetle, the scarabæus, was signified 'the only begotten Son of God, by whom all things were made, and without whom was not anything made that was made.'

The reasoning, then, of the Christian father, Irenæus, that there were four gospels, because there were four seasons of the year: after all the contempt which those who have invented the absurd conceit of a supposed historical basis of these divine poems would cast on it, is indeed the true and real account of the matter.

The spells themselves *are*, and ever *were*, entirely anonymous compositions: and their descent to us, under the names of Matthew, Mark, Luke, and John, merely signifies that Matthew, Mark, Luke, and John, are the allegorical names of the Genii of Spring, Summer, Autumn, and Winter. As the express term SAINT, added to their names, expressly assures us,—Saints, signifying precisely the same as the Genii of the Arabian Nights' Entertainments, whose bodies were all smoke, and who never had any speculation in those eyes which they did glare withal.

Sanctus was the ancient Sabine name of the Sun, and no word derived from it, or compounded of it, ever had or could have any other signification than of something of, or *pertaining to* the Sun. The spells, therefore, are not said to be written *by* these Solar Genii or Saints, but *according* to them—that is, they are proper to be read as so divided, each spell in each respective quarter of the year, over which the genius or demon, Matthew, Mark, Luke, and John, respectively presided. And in this character these demons of the Good Spell succeeded the Dii Penates, or Household Gods of the ancient Pagans, of whom Dionysius of Halicarnassus instructs us, that we must restrain our curiosity; and, out of respect, abstain from penetrating too far into these mysteries of religion.

We certainly know, however, that these evangelists have been worshipped in the Christian church for ages, under the same secondary or subordinate homage as was paid to the *little gods*, or guardian angels of Pagan, Greece, and Rome.

As in that Christian form of prayer, to be said every night, expressly addressed to them, beginning

'Matthew, Mark, Luke, and John,
Bless the bed that I lie on, &c.'

Or, as in the well-known evening hymn of our Protestant Bishop Kerr:

'May my blest guardian, while I sleep,
Close to my bed his vigil keep:
And in my stead all the night long,
Sing to my God a pretty song.'

Their emblems are the mystic cherubim, distinct in their respective faces, as that of the Lion of Matthew, the Man of Mark, the Bull of Luke, and the Eagle of St. John, as distinctively presiding over the seasons to which they are assigned, yet uniting in object, and standing upon one leg, as common to the four of them, with one instinctive spirit, one common design and purpose, to fulfil their high function as ministers of the Sun, and to proclaim the acceptable year of the Lord.

And 'they were full of eyes within'—that is, innumerable stars of all degrees of magnitude fall within the imaginary monstrous outline of the whole constellation.

And 'they rest not day nor night,' they are in continual motion, moving with a velocity in comparison to which the motion of a cannon-ball, or the swiftest stroke or momentum known to man were tardy as the creeping of a snail,

'So late descried by Herschell's piercing sight,
Hang the bright squadrons of the twinkling light;
Ten thousand marshalled stars a silver zone,
Effuse their blended radiance round her throne;
Suns call to Suns, in lucid orbs conspire,
And light exterior worlds with golden fire.'

'And the sole of their foot was as the sole of a calf's foot.' In this apparently most monstrous and insanely foolish statement, which is, however, the text of sacred scripture, which none of the Christian community understand, and none of their Christian ministers could explain to them, is involved a most curious and inestimably valuable item of chronological knowledge.

Before closing this discourse, I wish it to be remembered, that it is no part of my design to bring the holy scriptures into unmerited contempt, but purely to show what their real and unsophisticated meaning is,—which I am sure the general body of the Christian community are as entirely ignorant of as the general order of Christian preachers are unable to instruct them. However strange, monstrous, and apparently ridiculous many of the great discoveries I shall have to make may seem at first blush as the signs and symbols of every science would to the dunce who had no mind to study them, or to the bad and wicked man who wished to be ignorant of them,—delight, instruction, and the entire conviction of your minds, in the great truths of which these much misunderstood and infinitely perverted allegories are the type, will, I am sure, reward the pains of your ingenuous attention to the following facts:—

Upon our certain knowledge, collected from independent sources, it appears that the priests of Egypt (the religion or astronomical allegory of both the Old and the New Covenant—that is, the Old and New Projections of the planisphere), calculated the procession of the Equinoxes, with absolute accuracy, even to the same fifty seconds, nine-thirds, and three-fourths of a third of a moment, which is the calculation at this day,—we find an entire degree is lost or displaced in seventy-one years, plus eight or nine months; and, consequently, an entire sign is lost in 2,152 years.

Now, it being ascertained as it is, beyond all question, that the Vernal Equinoxial point was in the first degree of Aries, the Ram or Lamb of God, in the year 388 before our vulgar era (as it is now somewhat beyond the second of the Fishes), it results that it was in the first degree of Taurus, the Bull or *Calf* of God, exactly 2,540 years before that time, making 4,370 from the present time, when the Vernal Equinoxial point, or the Sun's position upon entering into his heavenly kingdom, was in the foot of the calf, and inferentially this divine covenant or planisphere of the visible heavens was constructed,* and this is the solution of the sacred enigma, 'the sole of their foot was as the sole of a calf's foot.' Their having but one foot when reckoning two for the eagle, two for the man, and four a-piece for the Lion, and the Bull, there would at least have wanted twelve feet, is further proof that the sole of their foot being as the sole of a calf's foot, is a mystical indication of data or

---

* And, indeed, the bull always represented as couching, turns up his left fore foot, as if to show there the very star which, upon regular principles of science, will show not only the year, but the day of the month.

time, which being fixed and determined, can necessarily be but one.

And as the Lion is the common emblem, both of God and the Devil,—so the cloven foot was common to both those parties, as we find the Devil himself was worshipped by the Syrians, Cretans, and Canaanites, under the title AB EL EON—that is, Abelion—that is, Father, God, the Sun, or 'our Father which art in Heaven'—that is, the angel of the bottomless pit, whose name, in the Hebrew, says St. John, is Abaddon, but in the Greek tongue hath his name Apollo.

Of which the result is, that this whole mystic doctrine of the two principles of good and evil, God and Devil, is an allegorical exhibition of astronomical science, drawn up, by whoever drew it up, when the Vernal Equinoxial point was in the calf's foot—that is, as the calculation proves, 4,870 years ago, which may be safely assigned as the nearest possible data of the gospel of Matthew, Mark, Luke, and John.

END OF PART II. יהוה OF THE OLD TESTAMENT.

The Devil's Pulpit.

"DELENDA EST CARTHAGO."

No. 16.—Vol. II.]   Price 2d.

MOSES:

A Discourse,

DELIVERED BY THE REV. ROBERT TAYLOR, B.A.

AT HIS CHAPEL IN FLEET STREET.

'*But even unto this day, when Moses is read, the veil is upon their heart.*'—2 CORINTHIANS, iii. 15.

THE veil! Gentlemen, O' God's name! *the veil*, what is a *veil?* but something that hides something? a something that sometimes may be very pretty, and sometimes something that we won't say anything about.

And what is a veil upon the heart? but a force of prejudices and prepossessions there, which hinders a man from seeing, what were else plain enough to be seen, and sets him, like the Devil in Chaos, groping his way at noon-day, as if to justify that satire on humanity—

'Sole judge of truth, in endless error hurl'd;
The glory, jest, and riddle of the world.'—POPE.

And what is such *a veil upon the heart*, so particularly hiding and obscuring what else should be sufficiently apparent, 'when Moses is read,' but that egregious vanity and dreaming arrogance which has led men to mistake fictious for facts, allegories for histories, the vehicle that conveyed the instruction *for* the instruction, the shell and husk of knowledge for the kernel, and the gross first sense that first struck their infant stupidity, for the ultimate sense intended.

The mischief of this resting in the first sense that first strikes the mind, is deplored by the apostle, even with respect to the allegories of the New Testament, of which he says, 'the letter killeth;' and than which, in no terms else, more strong and more emphatic could he have said that the taking the New Testament to be a history, or to contain a word of literal truth, is the most murderous mistake and 'damnable heresy' that ever—*No more about that.*

But 'when Moses is read,' there is also *a veil* in the case. We have seen of Abraham, and of his bond-woman, and of his free-woman, and of his two sons: the one by the bond-woman, who was Mount Sinai, in Arabia, and the other by a free-woman, which was Jerusalem in the sky, that these things are an admitted and declared allegory.

It is they, therefore, who impugn the authority of scripture, who, in despite the declared allegorical sense, take upon themselves to burthen the text with a sense which the text itself disclaims,—a sense, or rather nonsense, of their own arbitrary imposition, a sense that outrages reason, and would pawn our full-grown faculties in a subscription to tales so monstrous, as infancy might point the finger at, and cry shame upon manhood!

For where were there ever any tales of the nursery that had more of the character of *lullaby baby* in them, than the egregious literality of Noah's Ark, and Moses in the bulrushes, and the children of Israel in the wilderness, and God with them, and nothing to eat, and 'forty years long was he grieved with that generation, and said'—but saying wasn't the worst on't, he swore, and because he could swear by no greater, he swore by himself, and so *God* swore by *God*,—and after promising them a land flowing with milk and honey, killed them all, and left to their descendants no better land than the best that was to be got, by fighting for it.

But the allegorical sense, which we have followed so distinctly, and I hope convincingly, through the whole detail of the Book of *Genesis*, relieves humanity, relieves our reason, from what the Apostle Peter, with striking propriety, calls a yoke, which neither our fathers nor we ' were able to bear,' and for which the apostle of the Gentiles so tartly rallies his converts of Galatia: 'Are ye so foolish, that having begun in the spirit, ye would now be made perfect in the flesh. Tell me, ye that desire to be under the law,—do ye not hear the law? How turn ye again to those weak and beggarly elements, whereunto ye desire again to be in bondage?'

To the astrological Book of *Genesis* succeeds another entirely anonymous volume, bearing the *Greek* title *Exodus*, a word nowhere occurring in the course of the treatise to which it is affixed, nor in any part of the whole compilation which we designate the Bible, or book.

As I have already shown proofs, I think irrefutable, that the earliest or original text of the whole, or very much of the New Testament, was in the Latin tongue, afterwards rendered into Greek: so I think that it is never for a moment to be admitted, that the Hebrew was the original vehicle of the Books of the Old Testament. The Greek title *Exodus*, like Genesis, which is also Greek, would, in its extraneous sense, evidently bespeak an astronomical technicality. As Genesis refers to the cosmogony or imaginary 'generation of the heavens and all the hosts of them;' so the Exodus, or *coming out* (till other reasons shall seem to challenge a more confined sense of the word), would refer to the coming out or emergence of the Stars, those literal בני ישראל from their house of bondage, or land of darkness, below the visible horizon, into the region of the milky way, the astronomical promised 'land flowing with milk and honey.' Its elementary reference, however, is evidently to the allegorical history which the book details of a set of slaves most absurdly and monstrously supposed to be the direct ancestors of those whom we now call Jews.

But the fact may startle the stagnation of faith itself, that as all nations have had their fabulous Genesis, or cosmogonies, in which they have described an imaginary creation of the world; and created you may be sure, for nobody's convenience but theirs, and that of their immediate pedigree, so even the most barbarous nations have invented their imaginary *Exoduses* too, or fabulous accounts of their emigrations, settlements, and colonizations, of which, the Odyssey of Homer, and the Æneis of Virgil, are direct specimens; and in which respect our Bible story is so far from originality, that we find in it nothing else but a direct plagiarism, how derived we need neither know, nor care; but most certainly it is a plagiarism from the *Exodus* of the God Vitziputzli, the Almighty and Everlasting God, be sure on't, of the Mexicans, who was made of very precious wood,—wood quite as precious (I'll answer for't) as the cedar beams of the temple, or the shittim wood of the covenant box. This God was represented under the human shape, seated in a chair of sky-coloured blue, and supported by a litter, with four serpents' heads at the four corners. He had a *blue* forehead and a blue streak, right across his nose (a sort of sign of the cross, I dare say, extending from ear to ear). So ye see, my brethren, there are such things as blue *Gods*, as well as blue Devils; and, for all I know, this may be the best reason which can be assigned why Godly people, of all denominations, whenever you say anything about their Vitziputzlis, always look *blue* at you.

But this extraordinary attachment to the *blue* colour, which runs through all the multifarious, modifications of human piety, demands from us its physical interpretation.

Whatever beauty there might have been in the blue nose of the God of Mexico, it must be insensibility itself that could resist the blue eyes of the sixteen thousand wives of the God of India. The poetry of their divine book rises into astonishing sublimity in the description.

'The flowers that fell from the bosoms of the Gopias, as they danced round Chrishna, attracted all the bees of heaven. The bird's wing suspended its stroke on the bouyant air, to listen to the tinkling of their feet; and nature panted in sympathetic languishings, while their blue eyes were fixed on Chrishna.'—*Maurice's History of Hindostan.*

So, too, forsooth, the God of Israel must have his blue curtains, blue ribbons, blue robes, blue carpets, and blue bonnets.

'O the blue bonnets are over the border.'

And the Lord spake unto Moses as a boarding-school Miss might to a haberdasher. And the Lord commanded Moses, And he made the robe of the Ephod of woven work, all of *blue.* And they did bind the breast-plate by his rings unto the rings of the Ephod, and they cut the gold into wires to work it into the blue,—and the veil itself, of the Holy of

Holies, was a veil of blue, and purple, and scarlet, of cunning work, with cherubims upon it, ' and thou shalt hang it upon four pillars of shittim wood, overlaid with gold ; and see (said God) that thou make all things according to the pattern.'

Would anything but a severe experience have led us to believe, that it should be those who did not mean to launch the keenest sarcasm against scripture, who would contend for a literal sense, or the existence of an iota of literal truth, in these transactions between God and the milliners and mantua makers in the wilderness, whilst they could dispute the equal respectability, the prior existence, and the identical significancy of the mythology of the blue-nosed Vitziputzli.

With how poignant a significancy might the apostle say, ' Even unto this day, when 'Moses is read, the veil is upon their heart, who see on that blue veil, with its cunning work of cherubims, aught else than an astronomical *Eidouranean*, a picture of the blue arch of night, all of it the workmanship of a cunning workman, who taught astronomy by a mechanical apparatus : and 'spreadeth out the heavens like a curtain.'

Thus the God, Jehovah of the Israelites, is but a version, and evidently a considerably improved version of the blue-nosed Vitziputzli of the Mexicans. A literal rendering of the Hebrew text would, however, present us with stronger features of resemblance, than appear in our *wide-off* European translations.

The Lord is long suffering and full of compassion, is a sublime, but not a faithful rendering of the original text, which is :

The Lord hath a long nose.

Vitziputzli's astronomical character, in common with that of Jehovah, was indicated by an azure globe under his feet, representing the heavens ; and, like Jehovah, he was placed on every high altar,* and surrounded with curtains : in his right hand he held a snake. ' As Moses lifted up the serpent in the wilderness,' the universal emblem of eternal life, and in his left a buckler covered with five white feathers, set

---

* For, ' as the Hill of Basan, so is God's hill, even a high hill, as the Hill of Basan. Why hop ye so, ye high hills ?'

cross-wise. He had also on his head a helmet of feathers, made in the shape of a bird.

I build no argument on what I must, nevertheless, hold to be the only probable significancy of these hieroglyphs: the shield, the natural emblem of a warrior. 'And it is the Lord, who is a man of war, the Lord of Hosts is his name.' The feathers on the head, the emblem of victory; the cross upon the nose, from ear to ear; the cross again, set in feathers upon the shield, indicating a victory or triumph on the cross, or some sort of mystical victory connected with, or resulting from the cross, and the bird upon the head, alike the Eagle of Jupiter, the Peacock of Juno, the Owl of Minerva, the Sparrow of Venus, the Crow of Mithras, the Hawk of Osiris, the Cock of Esculapius, the Kite of Vichenu, the Swan of the nine Muses, the Dove of Jesus Christ, and the Holy Ghost upon the top-knot of God the Father: the never-omitted never-wanting hieroglyph of every form, in which religion of any character, in all ages and nations of the world, hath ever existed among men.

But it is the peculiar theology of the Exodus of this God, which demands our selection of him, out of the millions of chimerical creations, as the evident first sketch of the mythological Exodus of the Bible.

The Mexicans ascribe their settlement in that country to the direction of their blue-nosed deity Vitziputzli. The first inhabitants were a set of savages, not to be compared, I dare say, with the highly civilized worshippers and chosen people of the true God, the blue-nosed Vitziputzli: they were all Canaanites, you know, and Hivites, and Hittites, and Perrizites, and Jebusites, and that was reason enough for their having their throats cut by the command of Vitziputzli, under the direction of the great captain and lawgiver of the Mexicans,—that meekest of men, their General Mexi.

These Mexicans were a northern people, and undertook this expedition at the express command of their God, who promised them success; with this only apparent difference, between his promises and those of the other deity, that blue nose seems to have kept his promise, while long-nose let 'em *know his breach of promise.* 'And ye shall know my breach of promise.' Numbers xiv. 34.

MEXI marched at the head of these adventurers, while

four priests carried Vitziputzli in a trunk or chest made of reeds. But whenever they encamped, they erected a tabernacle in the midst of the camp, and placed their jack-in-the-box, master Vitziputzli, box, and all, upon the altar. They never ventured to proceed in their march, or to encamp without first consulting Vitziputzli, and implicitly received and obeyed his orders. Being at last arrived at *the promised land*, the God appeared to one of their priests in a dream, and commanded them to settle in that part of the lake, where an *Eagle* should be found sitting on a fig-tree, growing out of a rock. The priest related his vision, and the place being found by the signs pre-appointed, they *there* laid the foundations of Mexico. This celebrated city was divided into four quarters, or districts, and in the middle was placed the tabernacle of Vitziputzli, till a proper temple should be built to receive him.

Precisely such an appearance of God in a dream is detailed, as occurring to the priest Nathan (2 Samuel, 7), and in the 132nd Psalm, that beautiful collection of the idolatrous piety of the whole world: we have the impassioned exclamations of their king upon the admonition so conveyed:

'Lord, remember David, and all his trouble. How he sware unto the Lord: and vowed a vow unto the Almighty God of Jacob: I will not come within the tabernacle of my house; nor climb up into my bed. I will not suffer mine eyes to slumber, neither the temples of my head to take any rest, until I find out a place for the temple of the Lord, an habitation for the Mighty God of Jacob. Lo, we heard the same at Ephrata, and found it in the wood. Arise, O Lord, unto thy resting place, thou and the ark of thy strength.' As much as to say, go to bed, Vitziputzli, for I'm sure you must be confoundedly tired, and take your box of shittim wood with you.

But what but an hallucination of mind can it be that makes the words of so flagrant idolatry, so sublime and solemn to our apprehension, just so long and no longer than, as we are ignorant of their meaning.

Or what but the veil upon our hearts, when Moses is read, and the perfect applicability to ourselves of that severe rebuke, 'This people's heart is waxed gross,' has hindered us from seeing that the whole story of the Exodus of the children of Israel, never had a word of truth in it, nor ever was intended to pass for truth.

'For I would not, brethren, have ye ignorant,' says the apostle, now that *all* our fathers were under the *cloud*, and *all* passed through the sea; and were *all* baptized unto Moses, in the cloud and in the sea.

And this, Sirs, is the language of inspiration to a Gentile people, not to Jews; to Greeks, not to Hebrews; to the church of God which was at Corinth, as far off, and as unambitious of any claims of pedigree or descent, in common with those whom we now call *Jews*, as the church of God which is in Jewin-street, or as any church or community of people upon earth.

But it was all our fathers,—the primeval ancestors and aborigines of every nation under heaven, who were all of them under the cloud, and all passed through the sea; and did all eat the same spiritual meat, and did all drink the same spiritual drink—that is to say, ' God only knows what they ate or drink, or who they were, or how they lived, or where they came from.' 'For,' says the Psalmist, 'he rained down Manna upon them for to eat, and gave them food from heaven.' So man did eat angels' food, for he sent 'em meat enough. It was very cheap, and they called it מן הוא Man-hua—that is to say, *What d'ye call it?* Which is as accurate a description as we can reasonably expect of the nature of spiritual food. But by comparing spiritual things with spiritual, we learn that this angels' food was not only very cheap, but it was very nasty: and God not only gave 'em enough of it, but a little more than enough, since they had the impudence to tell Moses that their soul loathed it.

For, notwithstanding its descent from the celestial pantry, it was very apt to offend the nostrils.

The Rabbinical commentary on the Chaldee version of Onkelos, intimates that it was not unlike the scrapings of a wall.

For that they hadn't much reason to say, 'thank God for a good dinner,' after it, is more than intimated in the 78th Psalm, where we are told that, though it rained flesh upon them as thick as dust, and poultry like as the sand of the sea, and they were not disappointed of their lusts, yet while the meat was yet in their mouths, the heavy wrath of God came upon them, and slew the wealthiest of 'em.

Can a literal sense, can any sense whatever approaching to a feature of possible reality be imagined for such words, as that they all drank of the same spiritual drink, for they drank of that spiritual rock that followed them, and that rock was Christ—that was drink that there was no drinking of—Drank of a rock! a spiritual rock, a rock that rocked along with them in their march, a rock that followed them, a rocking rock, a rock that was no rock at all, a rock that was a man! and a man that was no man at all! not in existence till three or four thousand years after the rocking was all over, the spouse of the church, the same, says St. Stephen, that was with the church in the wilderness, a spouse that she could drink—

'Her little husband no bigger than her thumb,
She put him in a pint pot, and there let him drum.'

Thus, Sirs, must we descend to the idea of slobbering infancy, and lock ourselves up in the nursery, to shut out the better information which challenges us in the summons of those words: 'To-day, if ye will hear his voice, harden not your hearts as in the provocation in the day of temptation in the wilderness'—that is, to-day, after so long a time as it is said to-day. In the era of time, if ye will understand the meaning of these things, 'harden not your hearts,' stupify not your own understandings so egregiously as ye have done in the provocation—that is, in the provocation in the allegory, or calling things which be not as though they were, the calling out of a sense utterly distinct from the weak and beggarly elements of the mere words by which the moral history of the dark and ignorant wanderings of the unknown progenitors of the human race, and the physical phænomena of the Beni-Yesroile, or children of Israel, the stars of heaven, were pictured under the hieroglyph of a nation going down into Egypt, and wandering in unknown regions of sandy desolation, and fed there, as of course they would have need to be, with pabulum cœli, food from heaven, the proper food for stars, till their emergence again on the opposite side of the horizon.

And this *provocation*, which is expressly called an allegory, in the Epistle to the Galatians, with reference to the persons of Agar and Sarah, and which, in a former discourse, I so clearly unravelled through its involutions of the no less allegorical or *provoked* personages of the twelve patriarchs, is, in the 4th of the Epistle to the Romans, given as a definition of the *Faith of Abraham*, who is the father of us all—that is, the *theory*, the science, or mystical clue to the right understanding of the Abrahamic allegory.

'As it is written, I have made thee a father of many nations before him *whom he believed*'—that is, whom he understood, whom he was *up to*, was aware what he was driving at, ken'd the clue of his riddle, even God who quickeneth the death, and calleth things which be not, as though they were. For thus, and thus alone, have the inanimate bodies and natural substances and forms of the whole planetary system been vivified into a poetical life, the physical phænomena of the universe, paraphrased into imaginary histories, persons who never existed been represented as having existed, and things which were not, *called* or spoken of as though they were.

Thus the Apostle to the Hebrews, having expressly defined *faith*, or this sublime allegorical science, as 'the substance of things hoped for'—that is, *the supposition of imaginary transactions*, the evidence of things not seen—that is, a sort of second sight, a seeing of what nobody ever saw, a seeing of the things which were invisible, proceeds through all the great figments of the sacred science, to show us that it was *all by faith*, or *through* faith, or in this enigmatical way of seeing the things which were invisible, that we understand that the worlds were framed by the word of God, so that things which are seen were not made of things which do appear (and which God knows there's no other way of understanding.) And so it is *by faith*, that we are to understand how Abel, being dead, yet speaketh, and Enoch never died at all, and Noah prepared an ark, and Abraham, Isaac, and Jacob looked for a city which had foundations, whose builder and maker was God, and Sarah had a child by a husband who was as good as dead. And by faith it was, that *Moses* was such a proper child, by faith they passed through the Red Sea as on dry land,—by faith they blew the walls down with rams' horns.

And Gideon, and Barak, and Samson, and Jephthah, and David, and Samuel, and all the rest of 'em.

By *faith* it was, that they subdued kingdoms, wrought righteousness, obtained promises, stopped the mouths of lions, quenched the violence of fire, escaped the edge of the sword, out of weakness were made strong, came to life again after they were dead, were stoned, were sawn asunder, were tempted, were slain with the sword, and wandered about in sheep skins and goat skins. It was *all* by faith, every word of it *by faith*. There never was an iota of literal truth or real history in any one of their hypostatical matters. Truth was not the thing intended. It was all in the visible and invisible, the substantiated unsubstantialities of allegorical astronomy, that the whole romantic theory was excogitated. In this sense of *faith*, is it to be understood, even where no other sense can be conceived; in this sense, its monstrosities, its absurdities, and contradictions, are innocent of those atrocious and revolting features, which might justly authorise the apostle in saying, whatever is not of *faith* is sin, is hideous, is execrable, not to be borne, not to be endured; but considered *in faith*, viewed only as the vehicles of an ulterior and latitant significancy, the mute symbols and senseless hieroglyphs of the science of the heavens,—they fall like matrices and types into the setting forth of a glorious system,—a system, in the sublime study of which the human faculties can never engage unprofitably,—a system, of which our poets would say—

'In boundless love, and perfect wisdom formed,
And ever rising with the rising mind.'

Thus it proves that that peculiar technical term, FAITH, and those innumerable commendations and recommendations of the principle of *faith*, which occur throughout the whole sacred allegory, instead of being *calls* on our credulity, are checks and notices set up in bar of it, instead of requiring us to believe, are admonitions to us that we should not believe, are deprecations of our criticism, and warnings to our understanding, that the matter offered to us is not in itself true, nor of such a nature as that literal truth should be any part of its intent or purport. And thus our phrase, *sacred history*, is a contradiction in terms, a joining of two predications which are negations of each other. For nothing that is sacred can be *historical*; and nothing that is historical can be *sacred*. If a thing be sacred, it is therefore, and on that account, certainly not history: and if it be history, it is therefore *not* sacred.

Sacred history is as monstrous a contradiction as fabulous truth, or a true romance,—and as gross an absurdity in the conceit of the thing, as if a fool should imagine that the diagrams in Euclid were his science, and the sketches of animals on the celestial sphere had been all the sphere was made for.

No such a term, nor any that could bear a sense of such a term, as history is to be found in any part of the sacred volume.

It has originated mainly in the indolence and apathy of the clergy, and partly perhaps in their own participation in the common ignorance; who, finding how hard it was to beat the vulgar mind out of the first impressions, that the outward vehicles and machinery of instruction made upon them, and to raise their understandings to a comprehension of the sublime but occult meaning, gave way to the humour of the ferocious idiots, and let 'em rest in their first impressions, with a sort of despairing *Devil give 'em good on't.*

And so Abraham, and Isaac, and Jacob, and Moses, and Aaron, and the arks, and the covenants, and the veils, and the altars, and the curtains, and the cherubim, and their ascendings and descendings, and their comings in, and goings out, and their houses of bondage, and their lands of promise, all of them the machinery and figures of astronomy, were mistaken for realities, just as the Orion, Arcturus, Perseus, Andromeda, Bootes; and the arks, ships, fishes, snakes, serpents, dogs, lions, rams, and lambs of the celestial sphere, mere figures to aid the memory, and to assist astronomical description, were mistaken for realities by the vulgar of the Pagan world,—what was all that they could understand, was with them,—all that was to be understood, the figures and epigraphs of science, were science enough for the comprehension of the staring and gaping baboons, who, while they had not wit enough to admit of their being better instructed, had physical force enough to be—better not offended. Such pretty pictures, they thought, could not but belong to as pretty stories, and such pretty stories—Ah! 'a man must know how to get out of a window before he ventured to say that they were not exactly true.

But it will be asked, If it be thus, then, that an historical sense put on what are called the records of the Jewish people, is so egregious an error,—and that no basis of reality or fact ever existed, or was so much as implied or intended in these scriptures, where does the province of reality commence? where does history begin? The answer, in general terms, is obvious,—it begins where the principle of infidelity begins, and where the principle of faith ends,— where men are no longer required to subdue and control their understandings, but allowed and invited to the most unrestrained and fearless exercise of them.

In which unrestrained and delightful freedom, of which the apostle speaks hieroglyphically, as being 'no more entangled in the yoke of bondage,' we arrive through a series of analogies at a discovery of truths which the mind contemplates as calmly and indifferently, but as satisfactorily, as the demonstrations of Euclid.

And of such truths, these (as our investigations have thus far advanced) are emergent.

1st. That the books called Jewish in modern language, are in reality no more Jewish than they are Chinese.

2nd. That the people called Jews, among us, are no nearer related or connected in any sense with the Beni-Yesroile or children of Israel of the Bible, than they are to the Stars of heaven;

3rd. And can no more make out a genealogy or descent from any such persons as Abraham, Isaac, and Jacob, than I from Hercules.

That the Genesis and Exodus of sacred writ, instead of being a national or provincial archive, are the theogony and cosmogony of the universe. 'These are the generations of the heavens and the earth,' the very title of the book itself, where it commences at the 4th verse of the 2nd chapter, after a preface by some other author, and where no other title is pretended.

'These are the generations of the heavens and the earth' —that is, through all that follows the whole five books, absurdly ascribed to one of the principal heroes of the fiction, and probably inclusive of all the books, as far as the devotional Book of Psalms: these are the generations— that is, these are an allegorical panorama of the phænomena of heaven and earth. Of which no nation upon earth, nor any sect of people that ever lived, were ever farther off from the right understanding, or ever had less share or lot in the matter, than those whom we now call Jews.

It could not have been that real history, or any written

notices whatever, should have been made or preserved of the insignificant adventures, and obscure and ever equivocal origination of the uncivilised progenitors of all nations; and in the absence of these, awakening curiosity was *posseted* to sleep again, by a substitution of the allegorised phænomena of the visible heavens.

And thus, as the natural question,—who made us?—God Almighty, would be followed by, and

Where did we all come from: and how came we here?

Those questions found equally sagacious answers in—

Why you all came out of Egypt to be sure, or out of anywhere that was far enough off?

And who brought us out?

Why Yahouh sent Moushah, or Vitziputzli sent Mexi, or Jupiter sent Bacchus, or somebody else sent somebody else, and fetched you out.

But how did he get us over the sea?

Why the sea dried up, to be sure, and ye went over dry shod.

And how did Vitziputzli travel?

They carried him in a box.

But where did we get victuals and drink all the while?

Why it rained victuals and drink.

And what did we do for clothes?

O, the clothes that ye brought with ye out of where you came from, were a sort of clothes that never wore out.

Ah! but what said the Canaanites, and the Hivites, and the Hittites, and the Perizites, and Gergashites, and the Jebusites, whose country we came to take away from them?

Why you cut their throats, and then, you know, they said nothing.

Then why is it that not a single historical vestige exists, and no historian in the world has taken the least notice of these wonderful events?

Why, Sirs, in the name of God, does not Josephus tell you that it was because God Almighty would not let 'em take any notice of them: God, he assures us, punished all foreigners who dared to speak of the Jewish histories. The historian, Theopompus, for only designing to mention them in his work, became deranged for thirty days; and the tragic poet, Theodectes, was struck blind for having introduced the name of the Jews into one of his tragedies.

Such has been the early history, or the earliest account of any sort that could be given of every nation under heaven, in which there is nothing more peculiar to the Jews, or peculiarly Jewish, than their teeth and beards are Jewish.

Every nation that hath ever had priests and religion of any sort, have had their Genesis or fabulous history of their Gods; their Exodus, or fabulous history of their men; and upon those fables, their Leviticus or institutions of priesthood, to hold human curiosity in check, and to supply the place of real knowledge, by perpetuating and consecrating the errors of a barbarous antiquity.

END OF THE DISCOURSE ON MOSES.

The Devil's Pulpit.

"DELENDA EST CARTHAGO."

No. 17.—Vol. II.] Price 2*d*

THE TWELVE PATRIARCHS:
A Discourse,
DELIVERED BY THE REV. ROBERT TAYLOR, B.A.
AT THE ROTUNDA, BLACKFRIARS ROAD.

'*The twelve patriarchs, and the patriarchs moved with envy, sold Joseph into Egypt: but God was with him.*'—ACTS vii., 9.

I WOULD summon only the remembrance of those who are here, perhaps, on the present occasion, for the first time; and who find me far advanced in a science of whose existence they had not heard before, to the great principle on which this science is founded. And that this is a principle which anyone who had not known what the Christian character really is, would have thought that a Christian would never have quarrelled with, even none other than the principle which holds (and no man living holds it more sincerely than I do), that 'All the words of the Lord are pure words, even as the silver, which from the earth is purified and refined in the fire seven times.'

Upon this axiom, we conclude that any words which are not pure are not the words of the Lord, and *may* and ought to be rejected, as spurious and base, wherever found, or under whatever pretences of admitting of explanation, or our not properly understanding them, their apparent impurity may be screened from our criticism, or protected from our disgust.

But all the words of the Lord, being of such essential

holiness and purity, as having undergone, or requiring to undergo, a process of criticism as severe and trying as a seventh passing through the fire: can any absurdity be more monstrous, than that of those who, professing to call the scriptures 'the word of God,' would never subject them to any critical inquiry at all, nor ever allow themselves to revise or to doubt the first impressions which their text had made upon them?

But behold I show unto you a more excellent way: 'The patriarchs moved with envy, sold Joseph into Egypt; but God was with him.'

Would not any man who intended to treat the scripture with the respect which he would show to any other work of high antiquity, ask the emergent questions—

1. What are patriarchs?
2. Why moved with envy? Why sell Joseph into Egypt? And why and how was God with Joseph?

To the first of these questions we may be thus resolved: The word patriarch occurs in no other passage of scripture but this that I have quoted, except once in the singular form, in the 2nd of the Acts of the Apostles, where we have the phrase, *the Patriarch David;* and again in the 7th of the Epistle to the Hebrews, where is the phrase, *the Patriarch Abraham.* It is nowhere found in the gospels, calling in, as we are in reason bound to do, the light afforded to a strict adherence to the original Greek, we find that Πατριαρχαι ζηλωσαντες does not mean *the patriarchs moved with envy,* which is a moral sense, and certainly a bad one; but the twinkling, sparkling, glowing, effervescing, ardent patriarchs, which is a *physical* sense, and therefore neither good nor bad:

But which, if *the patriarchs* should happen to mean anything of a sparkling and twinkling nature, would, without any departure from the most literal sense, present us with a clue to the significancy,—especially if it were absolutely sure (as to those who had regularly attended these lectures, it is sure) that the Patriarch Abraham was and is nothing else but a Star, even the planet *Saturn,* and the Patriarch David, likely hereafter to be proved to be—no more than a Star. And that the word *patriarch* should primarily and originally have reference only to a star or combination of stars.

And then the form of speech, which we have rendered, they 'sold Joseph into Eygpt' απεδοντο, is still more exactly, they 'gave him over,' which, without a metaphor, is such an action as might be ascribed to these sparkling and glowing patriarchs; especially if Joseph were one of their own sparkling, glowing, starry, and patriarchal nature and family, which is more than intimated in the phrase—και ην ο Θεος μετ αυτου—'But God was with him.' God always being believed to be in a very peculiar manner resident in every one of the Stars.

Which probability, as to the real sense, is still further enhanced, from the curious fact, that this account which St. Stephen gives to the Jewish counsel of the history of their supposed ancestors, is very materially different from what appears in the Books of Genesis and Exodus; and that where *those* books seem to speak of *a person*, and were so understood by the Jewish counsel, this explication of the matter makes the person to have been a *Star*, or a tabernacle —that is, a celestial mansion or constellation of Stars. He tells them, 'Yea, ye took up the tabernacle of Moloch, and the Star of your God Remphan.'

The tabernacle of Moloch, being most certainly nothing else than the constellation Ursa Major, the Greater Bear, or the *Ass of Typhon*, as that constellation was anciently called: and Moloch being the North or Pole Star itself, in the tale of that Bear or Ass, round which the whole heavens seem to revolve, as upon their pivot or imaginary axis.

Thus, as the whole heavens seem to ride round upon this Northern Ass, the ancients represented the God Bacchus as riding in triumph upon an Ass, who was their personification of the Sun.

But in the New Covenant, when, about 2,500 years before our era, the solstitial point was in the tribe of Issachar— that is, in the constellation of Cancer: their being in the domicile of that sign the two Stars called the Asses, our Christian allegorists have represented our Bacchus, as riding in triumph upon two asses. Even upon an ass, and a colt, the foal of an ass: they have set him, like Mr Ducrow, at Astley's theatre, astraddle across 'em both, the boys and girls cried out, Hosanna! While Bacchus himself was so much tickled by the drollery of his situation, that he said,

'If these should hold their peace, I tell you that the very stones would cry out.'

But if words may deceive us, actions can hardly do so: and we have happily, in the present case, an account of the action of St. Stephen, in illustration of what his words referred to.

For, all the while that he was delivering this strange rhapsody of a discourse, about patriarchs and tabernacles, and angels, and *God in the bush*, not a word of which, from beginning to end, had the least possible reference to any apparently existing circumstances upon earth,—we are told, that " He being full of the Holy Ghost, looked up steadfastly unto heaven ? "

And what could he be looking there for ? but for his text in that true word of God, spread out to the study of all nations, in the sparkling canopy of the visible heavens : to whose stars and groups of stars he was giving names and titles ; and whose real and visible phænomena of rising and setting, he was describing as a sort of imaginary history : just as you would yourself describe them, and could find no other way of doing so, to the imagination of those whom you were endeavouring to instruct in the first principles of astronomy.

As you would say, ' See there in the east, how yonder group of stars is rising, as it were, out of the sea, that looks so red with the reflection of the Sun's rays, that you may call it the *Red Sea:* and that you may know the group again, mark yon bright Star that seems to lead them, and call him *Moses*. And there is one, not quite so bright, who shall be his brother Aaron ; and there's a sister for them, that beautiful pale-looking Star, that seems to rise out of the froth of the sea, which makes her look so white—that is, *Miriam*, she has got the leprosy,—and is the Venus Anaduomenè of the Pagan, and the Virgin Mary of the Christian fable.

And thus, you see, would the whole hieroglyphical history inevitably follow upon the natural workings of imagination. The vanity and pride of ignorance that had once been so entertained with the illustration, would never brook the being put back to the sober sense of the argument. The story was too pretty not to be true : it would spoil it to suppose that it was not true.'

As no account had been kept, nor could have been kept of the millions of the races of squeeling savages, ourang-outangs and wild men of the woods, who were the ancestors of the human race, these astronomical illustrations supplied the place of history: each individual was believed to have a particular star or group of stars, that had presided over his nativity, and that would continue over him a guardian protection through all his life, and receive him into his own bright sphere of happiness and glory after death.

Hence the notion of guardian angels. The expression, *my stars!* was synonymous with my God! my Father! my Protector!

And Christ promises that to him who overcometh, he will give him the Morning Star—that is, I hope, not merely to scorch his fingers with, by putting it into his pocket, but to become his tutelary or protecting genius.

A feeling of relationship, and a sentiment of gratitude and piety, grew on the pleasing fiction, and it became duty and virtue not to suffer themselves to be disabused of the impressions the fiction had made upon them.

Though there was no confirmatory document, and no history whatever has made the least mention of any of these personages, or their adventures, yet there was no counter or contradictory history,—nobody could prove the *negative.* And as they must have had some ancestors, or been descended from somebody or something, why might not the stars have been their forefathers, or be believed to contain the genii or souls of their fathers? and why might not the curious and entertaining illustrations which the astronomical priests gave of the starry heavens, be the real history (in the absence of all other history) of the progenitors of mankind?

Thus were the stars, their fathers: and thus were the phænomena which the priests described, in relation to the stars, supposed to be the real history of what had occurred to those from whom they believed themselves to have descended. The names which the priests gave to distinguish one star from another, passed for the names of their particular ancestors: while the priests, by their manner of turning their eyes up, and like St. Stephen gazing steadfastly into heaven, all the while that they were discoursing about these imagined fathers of mankind, gave a sufficient hint to those who had wit enough to look to actions rather than words,—as to what the real nature of those fathers was, and where the text of their marvellous history was to be found.

Of which St. Paul, ever and anon, gives us the broadest hints that ever were in the world; and which, if experience had not shown, that the stupidity of the religious world is absolutely infinite, one would have thought that stupidity itself could not have mistaken: as he says, 'Set your affections on things above'—that is, to be sure, upon the stars which you see so high above your heads: and, 'Our conversation is in the heavens,—that is, all that we discourse about, is the science of astronomy: and, 'Moreover, brethren, I would not have you ignorant how that all our fathers were under the cloud.'

Why, to be sure, and O' God's name, *they were under the cloud,*—and of a cloudy night you cannot see any of them.

'And all passed through the sea, and were all baptized unto Moses, in the cloud and in the sea.'

The very phænomena, which we see ourselves, and could hardly describe in any other language as occurring to the stars, which are continually baptised, or dipt, or ducking behind the cloud, as the cloud passes over them, and ducking in right earnest, as we see them set, or go down behind the waves of the western ocean.

And as the stars, in this hieroglyphical language, are so evidently meant—and all that is meant—by our *Fathers* or *Patres*, we have the clue in our hands to lead us to the discovery, as to who were the *Patriarkai,* or pre-eminent and great arch-fathers, or patriarchs in the system, in the never-to-be-forgotten essentiality of the system. that they were exactly twelve of them, nor more nor fewer, answering exactly to the number of the twelve signs of the Zodiac—that is, those twelve groups of stars which lie in the course which the Sun appears to pass through in the heavens in that annual revolution which constitutes the twelve months of the year.

These groups of stars were distinguished from each other, and depicted as supposed to fall within the outline of such imaginary figures, as you see delineated on the concave of this dome. And the figures and names given to them, founded on reasons of some hieroglyphical significancy, o some association of idea, which may perhaps now be entirely lost, has remained the same from before all records of the thoughts or devices of man, there being no language, nor any trace of the existence of men upon earth, among whom this division of the Sun's annual course through these twelve groups of Stars, was not the same as it is with us, and the names and figures of the groups, the same too.

An imaginary character and imaginary history was referred to these groups, analogous to the character and history of nature pending that portion of the year, during which the Sun appears to be in that part of the heavens over which the Stars that make up that group spread themselves.

And the Sun itself, by the ordinary metonymy of language, took the name and character, and was the imagined genius of each of these groups of stars, pending the period of time that he appeared to be passing through it. And as the Sun was always the Supreme God, so each of these signs of the Zodiac were all of them Gods in their turns: so spoken of, so adored and worshipped, and so one or other adopted by different nations, as the Great Father or Patriarch, from which they imagined themselves to be descended.

While the very name of tribes, or twelve tribes, is as technically astronomical a term as the name the *twelve signs of the Zodiac* itself,—the word *tribe* actually meaning, and never having had any other meaning than a path or course, such as that of the Sun through the signs of the Zodiac actually is. So the word Πατηρ, meant not a father or parent. It was a religious term, imported from Egypt, the same as Pator or Patora, the Amonian name of the Sun. whose priests were called Petor or Pator, in honour of the Sun; and in their religious ceremonies they danced round a large fire, in representation of the Sun in the visible heavens.

Hence the name of PETER, the chief of the apostles of Christ, and the name *Patriarchs*. or most distinguished *Peters*, given to the twelve tribes of Israel—that is, the twelve signs of the Zodiac, which really do seem to dance round the Sun in the annual revolution of the heavens.

So the word apostles, αποστολοι, which Greek is a name which never could have been given by any person of Jewish education and habits to persons whom he had sent on an errand or embassy of any character, but is directly the most obvious astronomical term for the twelve months, as *sent forth*, or given to the world, by the Sun in his annual *tribe*, or course through those signs. Hence that great mystagogue, St. Paul, talks so much about the *signs of an apostle*. And the Jesus of the gospel speaks of the time when the Sun shall be darkened, as it is in the dark days of winter,— 'and *then* shall appear the sign of the Son of Man in heaven.' Matthew 24. And there is the sign of the Son of Man in heaven, who is none other than the Aquarius of the Zodiac. But as if this hint as to the astronomical significancy of the whole gospel were not plain enough, the same astronomical priest further explains himself: 'A wicked and adulterous generation seeketh after a sign from heaven, and there shall no sign be given to them, but the sign of the prophet Jonas.' And there is the sign of the prophet Jonas, in that self-same Son of Man, the first sign of the Zodiac, whose very name of Jonas, or Janus, is retained to this day, in our name of the month January.

As if the indignant teacher, disgusted at the egregious stupidity of his audience, had said, or meant to say: An' if ye be so dull as not to understand the sign of the prophet Jonas, the Devil may teach you the eleven other signs.

Now if the names and characters of the twelve tribes of Israel, whom St. Stephen calls the twelve patriarchs, shall actually prove to answer to the physical phænomena of the twelve signs of the Zodiac: the demonstration of their identity will be complete: the proof that the apparent history of the Book of Genesis is an hieroglyphical picture of the phænomena of nature, will be absolute, it will be fatuity and ignorance alone, that will ever more imagine that any such person ever really existed, or that a word of historical reality was ever intended.

To this proof, then, now we tend. See the truly sublime and magnificent passage of the 49th of Genesis: ' Gather yourselves together, and hear, ye sons of Jacob, and hearken unto Israel your father.

1. 'Reuben, thou art my first born, my might, and the beginning of my strength, the excellency of dignity, and the excellency of power: unstable as water, thou shalt not excel.'

Here is Aquarius, with his never-to-be-mistaken monogram, the two zigzag lines which represent the unsteady or wavy surface of water, to which he is compared. He is the first of the four royal signs, the beginning of the Sun's strength, the first month of the year. The Janus of Paganism, the St. Peter of the apostles, the St. Mark of the evangelists, whose gospel is the shortest as the days are short in January.

2. 'Simeon and Levi are brethren, instruments of cruelty are in their habitation.'

These two, you see, are united, as are the two Fishes of the month' February: the instruments of fishing-nets, hooks, spears, and harpoons, are necessarily associated with the business of fishing, and therefore represented in the domicile or part of the heavens, assigned to this constellation.

'But I will divide them in Jacob, and scatter them in Israel,' says the inspired speaker, forgetting that he is speaking in the character of Israel himself.

I beseech ye, Sirs, to cast your eyes on the celestial globe, and see if that is not the precise definition of the Fishes of the Zodiac, which are so scattered that the one, which is a John Dory, reaches the pitcher of Aquarius, and the other a Cod-fish, is on the shoulder of Andromeda.

The twelve Apostles, however, who are but another edition of the twelve Patriarchs, were all of them supposed to be fishermen, and therefore literally have the scaly character of Simeon and Levi scattered and divided among them.

And Peter, the first of the Apostles, that cry, 'I go a fishing,' actually gets the name of *Simeon*, the first of the fish, super-added to his name of Peter, as Levi was another name of the evangelist Matthew. And the twelve signs that make up the whole band of the Zodiac, were called fishermen, because of the natural appearance which they have, of going down or setting in the sea, from which imagination supposed them to derive their nourishment.

3. 'Judah is a Lion's whelp, he stooped down, he couched as a Lion, and as an Old Lion. Who shall rouse him up?'

Here is the undoubted Lion of the tribe of Judah, the name given to Jesus Christ in the Apocalypse, the Leo of the month of July in the Zodiac, and the EL-EON, *God the Sun*, of the Egyptian language, from which our English word Lion is derived, and the Old Lion of the Zodiac was always represented as a Lion *couchant*, or stooping down.

4. Ephraim, omitted in the blessing of Jacob, but supplied in that of Moses, in the 33rd of Deuteronomy: 'His glory is like the firstling of his bullock, and his horns are like the horns of unicorns.' Samaria was the capital of the tribe of Ephraim, and *thy Calf, O Samaria!* is the prophetic designation of the tribe of Ephraim, as that same calf is the *Taurus* of the month of April,—Ephraim literally signifying that which brings forth fruit, or grows, or causes to grow.

5. 'Dan shall be a serpent by the way, an adder in the path that biteth the horses' heels.' This Cerastus, Serpent, or Adder that biteth the horses' heels, is the Scorpion of October, which you see so near the heels of the horse of November, and to which answers the Eagle, or Vulture, which rises at the same moment with the Scorpion, and is therefore called its parouatellon: the Scorpion you see is found as the sign of October, the first of the winter months, in which the Sun sinks below the Equator, and is therefore said to descend into the invisible regions or Hades: this month, then, is the place of the gates of Hell, within which is that Scorpion, the worm which never dieth, as Hades itself, though translated Hell, is literally AD-ES, *the Lord, the Fire*, the Sun itself, the fire which never shall be quenched.

But the Eagle, the Paronatellon of the Scorpion, was, say the ancient astronomers, for mystical reasons, substituted in the place of the Scorpion, in the pavilion of the tribe of Dan, and was the insignia or armorial bearing on the banner of Dan.

Thus the four royal tribes, Reuben, Ephraim, Judah, and Dan are the unquestionable genii of the four seasons of the year, Winter, Spring, Summer, and Autumn. And their insignia or hieroglyphical signs, the Man of Reuben, or Aquarius, the Bull or Bull-calf of Ephraim, the Lion of Judah, and the Eagle of Dan, are to this day the accompanying symbols of the four evangelists, Mark, Matthew, Luke, and John, as you will see them in this same arrangement, on the western pediment of St. Paul's Cathedral, and as they have been presented in all the painted windows and altar-pieces of all the ancient religious edifices in Christendom.

6. 'Zebulon shall dwell at the Haven of the sea, and he shall be for an haven of ships.'

Here is the characteristic of the Capricornus of December, the Goat, who in all the ancient planispheres was represented with the tail of a fish, and, by the ancient astronomers, called the Son of Neptune.

7. Issachar is a strong ass, couching down between two burdens, and in the domicile or department of the heavens, assigned to the cancer, the crab of June, the Hebrew name for which month is Thomas, the very name of that stupid apostle, that had half a mind to go back again, are the two stars called the Asses, even that very ass, and the colt, the foal of an ass, upon which Jesus Christ rode in triumph into Jerusalem.

8. 'Gad, a troop shall overcome him: but he shall overcome at the last.'

Here is Aries, the Ram of March, whose place in the heavens is in the domicile of the planet Mars, the Lord of Hosts, whom the prophecy describes as a warrior, who is first to be conquered, and afterwards to be himself the conqueror, as Jesus Christ, who is the Ram or Lamb of God—that is, the Lamb of Gad, for our English word God is actually derived from Gad, the name of this tribe of Israel, which triumphs on the Cross—that is, by crossing the Equator at the point of the Vernal Equinox. And as the month of March is said to come in like a lion, but to go out like a Lamb, beginning in blustering winds and storms, and ending in the mild and genial zephyrs of the spring.

9. 'And of Asher, he said, Let Asher be blessed with children, let him be acceptable to his brethren, and let him dip his foot in oil.'—Deuteronomy 33.

And there are the brethren, the children, the Twins, the Gemini of May, that delightful month, when the fresh grass so much improves the milk and butter, that the power of poetry could hardly have devised a more characteristic description than that of the sacred song, he shall dip his foot in oil, his bread shall be fat, and he shall yield royal dainties.

10. 'Napthali is a 'hind let loose: he giveth goodly words:' and here have we that deeply couched enigma, of the Virgin of August, whose place in the heavens is in the domicile of the planet Mercury, the God of Eloquence, as

the hand of the Zodiac Virgin was represented as holding the Balance of Justice, in pleading for which the power of eloquence and of goodly words has its most distinguished and peculiar province.

But the blessing of Moses on this tribe, determines its identity with the month of August, beyond all emergence of a doubt. O Napthali, satisfied with favour, and full with the blessing of the Lord.

11. 'JOSEPH is a fruitful bough, the archers have sorely grieved him, and shot at him, and hated him; but his bow abode in strength, and the arms of his hands were made strong by the hands of the mighty God of Jacob.'

Is it possible to mistake the hieroglyph of the month of November, Sagittarius, the Archer, the Genius of the season for hunting, who is flying as if he had been shot, while he is shooting as he flies.

12. 'Benjamin shall raven as a wolf : in the morning he shall devour the prey, and at night he shall divide the spoil.'

The constellation Sagittarius in the Zodiac, immediately precedes the celestial Wolf, which hardly falls within the Zodiac. But the character of ravening as a Wolf, indicates the hungry and bleak character of the deep winter, and the devouring the prey in the morning, and dividing the spoil at night, the extreme shortness of the days at that season of the year.

Jacob, on his death-bed, is represented as having adopted the two sons of Joseph, Ephraim, and Manasseh, and to have made a tribe of each of them, which would have made the number thirteen to the dozen.

But the astronomical error which *this* adoption would have induced, is corrected by Moses throwing out Levi, and putting Manasseh in his place, and giving Levi a place in the priesthood instead :

'Wherefore Levi has no part nor inheritance with his brethren : the Lord is his inheritance.'

And we actually find the same error with respect to the same name, and the same correction of that error in the same way, and for the same reason, in the lists of the names of the twelve apostles, where the *Levi* of the first list is thrown out of the second, and adopted into the priesthood instead : and LEVI is made the same as Matthew, the publican, or public character, and the Genius of the word of God, or gospel, which is said to be according to Saint Matthew.

Thus have we found the twelve patriarchs or tribes of Israel each severally corresponding to its respective type in the twelve signs of the Zodiac: as the twelve great Gods of the Pagan mythology, and the twelve Apostles of the gospel do, in like manner, most wonderfully correspond to the same great Archetypes.

When we look into the derivative meaning of those words, *Patriarchs*, Types, *Apostles*, we find them absolutely to be astronomical terms, and to present none other than an astronomical sense and significancy.

When we look into the derivative or first sense of all the terms, and phrases, and periphrases, by which divine revelation is spoken of, we find that first sense is absolutely an astronomical one, and we are obliged to strain and transpose, and do no small violence to the first principles of language to make them bear any other than an astronomical sense. Why are our holy books called respectively the Old and the New *Covenants*. What are *Covenants* or *putting together*, but puttings together of the stars? Why is the whole system called the Dispensation of the fulness of times, but as being the scientific making up of certain astronomical circles or periods of time? Why is it the wisdom from above? Why is our God a consuming fire? Why is our Christ the Day Star from on high? Why is our Jesus ' the same yesterday, to-day, and for ever,' but that the Sun it is who is 'the same yesterday, to-day, and for ever.'

All who have treated of divine matters, says Clemens Alexandrinus, the barbarous nations, as well as the Greeks, have hid the principles of things, and delivered down the truth enigmatically, by signs, and symbols, and allegories, and metaphors.

Among the arts and mysteries which Philo, the Jew, says Moses learnt from his masters, the Egyptians, was that of philosophy, by symbols, hieroglyphics, and marks of animals.

When we bow with submission, or are pleased to bow to the authority claimed for the sacred text, and take that text as the only source of information and of truth upon the matter, that authority also confirms the same conclusion.

If the children of Israel, the tribes, the patriarchs, the

apostles, were creatures of this earth, what became of them? If they had ever trodden on our globe, why are they off it like the sparks off of burnt tinder?

Or with what right or reason is it, that any one professing to believe the scriptures to be the word of God, and unable from any other source to determine who or what the patriarchs of the Old, or the apostles of the New Testament were, should resist the determination which, if the scriptures be the word of God, God himself has given? 'They serve unto the example and shadow of heavenly things.'— Heb. viii., 5.

And I, Sirs, have shown you what those heavenly things are unto, whose example and shadow they *do* serve, and correspond as exactly as the bright orbs of heaven to their reflected figures upon the glassy bosom of the lake, as the wax to the seal that has been set upon it.

END OF THE DISCOURSE ON THE TWELVE PATRIARCHS.

The Devil's Pulpit.

"DELENDA EST CARTHAGO."

No. 18.—Vol. II.] [Price 2d.

WHO IS THE LORD?—Part I.

A Discourse,

DELIVERED BY THE REV. ROBERT TAYLOR, B.A.

AT THE ROTUNDA, BLACKFRIARS ROAD.

And Pharaoh said, Who is the Lord, that I should obey his voice, to let Israel go? I know not the Lord, neither will I let Israel go!'—Exodus, v. 2.

THERE is something so delightful in the mere sound of thorough good sense, that it gives eloquence to any sort of language in which it may be uttered: it is delightful to the mind, and soothing to the heart, wherever heard. Its refreshing cadence falls on the grateful ear, where we meet it in our Bibles, like the note of a nightingale in an aviary of peacocks, hawks, and vultures.

It is on the evidence of this spontaneous accordance of the mind to the impulse of reason, that we are authorised in concluding that man, though not truly defined as a rational being, is yet a being *capable of becoming rational*. And the apology for the deficiency of intellect in men, which evidence supports, and calm reflection admits, is, that in reality so very little of good sense has ever been set before them.

And those who have possessed this rare commodity, discouraged by the contrast of surrounding imbecility, have been too often disposed to play the monk, to hold their intellectual ascendancy as a monopoly, and rather to thicken the obscurity and fortify the ignorance of their fellow men, than to run a hazard of inconvenience to themselves, by generous exertions to remove it.

There is nothing peculiarly poetical, no grandeur of point, no antithesis, no rhythmus, and rather a startling opposition to all the modes of persuasion, and habits of association, among good Christian people, in this retort of the hard-hearted Pharaoh, to the messengers and ministers of the God of Israel. Yet scarce a Christian could perpend this answer, without feeling an instant consciousness of the majesty of superior good sense, and a disposition to lose his anger in his admiration. Such an answer became *a man:* and we rather envy than deplore the fate of Pharaoh, when we are told that 'the Lord hardened Pharaoh's heart,' and we find him giving so noble a proof that he was indeed not quite so soft as his friends Moses and Aaron wished to have found him.

As far as I shall trouble you with the machinery of the tale, it is enough to recollect, that the *parsons* had been for playing off their old canting everlasting trick of 'Thus saith the Lord,' that mystical talismanic *Abracadabra*, that moulds the shivering fools and slaves of priestcraft to the purposes of whatever knave can say, 'Thus saith the Lord' the loudest, and look the savagest at it. It is that most wicked, most villianous, and most mischievous 'Thus saith the Lord,' to whose accursed incantation may be ascribed, in the sum total, all the miseries and vices, and all the degradation and imbecility of mankind.

The withering fascination poured first upon the ear of unresisting infancy, like the mildewed air, doth blight the germ of reason, and hath inflicted a palsy on the mind, so grievous, so perpetual, as never more to permit the mind to grow up to the acquisition of its natural functions; and thousands and millions of creatures who have been *called* rational, but further off from being so, than dogs and rats, have stolen their way from the cradle to the grave, with the sound of 'Thus saith the Lord' in their ears, without wit enough in their brains, or curiosity enough in their nature, to ask the question 'Who is the Lord?'

The very cadence of such a question in a Christian ear

would sound like blasphemy? Who but an infidel would ever have thought of asking it? Who but an infidel would find courage enough in this respect to say *bo* to a goose, and undertake to answer it?

Yet so essentially connected is the *moral* with the *intellectual* character; so impossible is it that the heart should go wrong, where the understanding has been set right, that could we suppose such a character as Pharaoh to have existed, and such an answer, under such circumstances, to have been given, we should feel in ourselves an incongruity and heterogeneity in the supposition, that the man who gave it could possibly have been a tyrant and oppressor, or in any respect wanting of the virtues which ever wait on reason.

'Who is the Lord, that I should obey his voice, to let Israel go? I know not the Lord, neither will I let Israel go!' There's a sort of fine fellow cadence, 'ith the very cadence of it! The man who could so express himself, wanted not a diadem to make him every inch a king; and even in the squalors of poverty, would have been as intellectually superior to the herd of *say-belief* idiots, as the mighty oak of the forest to the funguses and weeds that fester round its roots.

For what is the perfection of virtue, but the influential governing, and ever present determination of the mind, never to do anything *without a reason?*

What is the perfection of reason, but that manly strength of mind, that will never be put off with anything like a 'Thus saith the Lord' for a reason?

But these perfections are combined in this most admirable apothegm of the great Egyptian, 'Who is the Lord, that I should obey his voice, to let Israel go?' Could that question have been answered the suit had been obtained. But anything but that for the parsons! The ambassadors of Omnipotence could not answer the fair challenge, 'Show me your credentials!' and their embassy, therefore, was abortive.

The conclusion became the evidence, 'I know not the Lord, and you cannot introduce me to him. I have no doubt that he's a gentleman. Good morning to your reverences.'

I have done with the allegorical story, in deriving from it as a mere *motto* to my present purpose, the question, *Who is the Lord?* A question which I propound to sift so entirely, as shall ensure to you a satisfaction worthy of your patience.

Who is the Lord? the LORD? Yahouh, in Hebrew; Eoru, in Persic; Alla, in Arabic; Theuth, in Egyptic; Adod, in Chaldaic; Adad, in Syriac; ο Κυριος, in Greek; *Dominus*, in Latin; *L'Eternel*, in French; *the Lord*, in English; with all its vocabulary of periphrases.

1. The אהיה אשר אהיה, *Aheyhe ashur Aheyho*,* of the Hebrew.

2. Εγω ειμι ο ων, *I am the being*, of the Septuagint Greek.

3. The Εσομαι, Εσομαι, *I will be, I will be*, of the versions of Aquila and Theodotion.

4. The *Sum qui Sum*, I am who I am, of the vulgate Latin.

5. The *Sono colui che sono*, I am that which I am, of the Italian of Diodati.

6. The *Jesus celui qui est*, I am he, who is, of the French of Le Gros.

7. The *Je serais, car Je Serai*, the I shall be, for I shall be, of Le Clerc.

8. The *ego is ero, qui olim futurus sum*, I will be he who hereafter am about to be, of Houbigant.

9. The *Ero qui ero*, I shall be who I shall be, of Rosenmuller.

10. The Great *I am*, of the Protestant Dr. Watts.

11. The no less Great *I am, because I am*, of the Catholic Doctor Geddes.

12. The *I am that I am*, of our common version; and

13. The *Tetragrammaton*, or mystical four letters, set in a triangle, surrounded by a circle of golden rays upon our Christian altar-pieces, but always on the east side of the edifice, and called by the vulgar Jehovah.

It is to be observed, moreover, with respect to the vulgar among ourselves, that the name *the Lord*, is a much greater favourite, and familiar of their utterance, than *God*, or *the Almighty*, or any other supposed synonyme for the same imagination.

It is with the very lowest and meanest of the people (low and mean in understanding, as well as in grade in society, and among the wilder and more ourang-outangish sort of

---

* EIEH.

fanatics), that *the Lord* entirely carries the day against *the God*, and *the Almighty*, of persons of education and good breeding: and of this difference,—all their hymns, prayers, preachings, religious tracts, and published discourses, present unequivocal evidence.

Compare the epithets for Deity, which you should find in a sermon delivered before the *Court*, or either of our Universities, with the slang of a Methodist chapel, and you would find the difference as great as between any two forms of the ancient Pagan idolatry.

Men, indeed, cannot rise above the ideas which their situations force upon them. They can have no other ideas than such as take their type wholly from the impressions which their circumstances make upon them. And hence it is, that the term *the Lord*, inseparably associated as it is with its correlative terms, *servant*, *vassal*, *understrapper*, *hireling*, *beggar*, and *slave*, has a direct homogeneity and correspondence to the ideas of persons of a mean and servile condition.

The saints have knowledge enough of human nature, to be content with sticking their low-life *blessed Lord*, and *O Lord Jesus Christ* collects, in their prayer-books for hospitals, gaols, and charity schools, while they have recourse to their *triangles*, and *doves*, and *golden rays*, to gild the pill for the swallowing of aristocratic piety: and *our Saviour*, and *the Almighty*, is the utmost extent of condescension to be claimed from persons of good breeding, and polite education.

Could *the Society for Promoting Christian Knowledge* have primed Moses and Aaron for their errand to King Pharaoh, they'd have made a better hit of it, than by saying anything *to him* about *the Lord*, and not have subjected themselves to be answered, as they might be sure *a gentleman* would answer them, '*Who is the Lord? I know not the Lord. Go preach to the slaves and idiots who will submit to be* BE-LORDED and be-priested, ye carry no point with me, with your 'Thus saith the Lord.' And, indeed, Pharaoh had more than half-a-dozen bits of very good and wholesome scripture on his side, as he might have quoted either Isaiah, Jeremiah, or Ezekiel. 'For thus saith the Lord, The prophets prophecy falsely, they lie unto thee, they do it to get dishonest gain, and they prophecy unto you a false vision, and a thing of naught, and the deceit of their own heart. And they say, Thus saith the Lord, when the Lord hath not said it.' But so it falls out, that whenever there happens to be a bit of downright good sense and honest truth in their Bibles, you'll always find that those are the passages which Christians never care to remember.

We must be heedful, never to confound *the Lord* with *God*. There is no necessary connection between them.

They are NOT synonymous nor convertible terms,—so that the *one* might be used indifferently for the other. But far from it, very far. The one is *particular*, the other *general*, as WE say with propriety, THE *Lord*, meaning particularly the figment with whom I am now to bring you acquainted,—but could hardly say *the* God. So that the compound epithet, *the Lord-God*, is a syncopation, or abbreviated phrase, of which the filling up is 'The Lord, *who is a* God.' For while all nations had their Gods, individual nations, sects, and clans, have ever had their particular conceits to which they adhered, subordinate to the general notion. So that it seemed but a fair bargain which Jephtha proposed to the King of the children of *Ammon:* 'Wilt not *thou* possess that which Chemosh thy God giveth thee to possess. So whomsoever the Lord *our* God shall drive out from before us, them will we possess.' Judges, xi. 24.

Here we see, that Chemosh—that is, the literal Hebrew for the *Sun*, is synonymous with AMMON, as each nation called themselves the children of the *Planet*, under whose protection they placed themselves: but *God* was the general term.

Indeed the bargain was not unfrequently propounded to the particular conceit or tutelary genius, under whose patronage they put themselves, that he should grant them success in war, and comply with their requests, as the condition of his *being* their God, and under penalty of being turned away. So Jacob made his covenant and agreement upon the specific terms, 'If thou wilt keep me in this way that I go, and wilt give me bread to eat, and raiment to put on, so that I come again to my father's house in peace, then shall the Lord be my God, and of all that thou shalt give me, I will surely give the tenth to thee.' Genesis 28. And there the chapter ends, leaving it to our own imaginations to fill up the evidently implied *alternative* of the covenant,

'But if I get into any bad bread, or have any sort of ill luck under your divine providence, look ye, my Lord God, never trust me if I don't send your Godship packing, and try if I cannot strike a better bargain with the other gentleman.'

Notwithstanding this ridiculous grossness of familiarity with their notion of *the Lord*, which appears in every page of the sacred text, our modern Jews, who claim a peculiar property in the Old Testament (to which they have no right or title at all), would cheat the world into a notion that it is only from excess of reverence, and from an overwhelming awe and veneration to be sure of the divine name, that they substitute the word, אדני, *Adon gnaw-ye*, their utterance of the word *Adonis*, the name of the Pagan God, the Son of Venus. The name *Adon*, or Adoneus, being the same as *Baal*, *Baalsemen*, or *Bel*, and literally signifying *the Lord*, with its pronoun suffix *Adonai*, literally *our Lord*, the name common to Jupiter, Bacchus, Pluto, Apollo, Æsculapius, Hercules, Osiris, and all the grand personifications of *the Son*. Yet the name of *Adonis*, is found in the sacred writings, as distinctly different from that, which our translators have rendered *the Lord:* as in that most marked and memorable passage, the first of the 110th Psalm: 'The Lord said unto my Lord, sit thou on my right hand, until 'I make thine enemies thy footstool.'

נאם יהוה לאדנישב לימיני עד אשית הרם אינד לרוליר

Nam Yahouh Le Adonai Sheb le yemini od ashut aibike hedem le regelike.

Ειπεν ο Κυριος, τω Κυριω μου. lxx.

And the mystical *tetragrammaton*, or name of four letters, or two syllables, *Yahouh*, which we absurdly pronounce *Jehovah*, is found in the 68th Psalm, written but with two letters, and necessarily requiring to be uttered but as one syllable, *Yah*, *Jah*, or *Jack*, where certainly no irreverence is meant by that seemingly strange abbreviation.

'Sing unto God,—sing praises to his name. Extol him that rideth upon the heavens by his name JAH, and rejoice before him.'*

---

* So the Spaniards dropt the first letter or syllable of the Syriac Adon, and formed their word *Don* or *Lord* as a title of nobility; and the English dropt the first of the Chaldee, Adod, and thus formed Don,

The attribute of 'riding upon the heavens,' is so peculiar, so distinctly marked, so incapable of being strained from its one and only apparent significancy, that nothing but that obdurate stupidity which shuts out light, and would say to itself, 'I will not see the Sun,' could cause any man to mistake as to what that significancy must have been.

And this abbreviation of the name of Jehovah, into Jáh, as peculiarly applied to him 'who rideth upon the heavens' —that is, the *Sun*, is precisely the same as the Æolic or Latin abbreviation of the name *Solus*—that is *the Alone*, or *the one by himself*, into Sol—that is, the Sun, abbreviated for the same reason, expressive of the same significancy, and devised to confine the utterance, as well as the thought, to the same strict notion of unity or oneness.

The language of *the Ode* rises into astonishing sublimity in its majesty of emphasis, to exclude all possible idea of Trinitarianism, or plurality of any sort, in its deity.
Deut. vi., 4. שְׁמַע יִשְׂרָאֵל יְהוָה אֱלֹהֵינוּ יְהוָה אֶחָד.
Shemang Yesroile! Adon-gnaw-ye, Alahinu, Adon-gnaw-ye, Achad.

'Hear, O Israel, Adonis our God is Our Adonis. For the Lord is our defence, the Holy ONE of Israel is our King.' Psalm 89.

And that that Holy *One* was none other than the *Sun*, we have again and again impressed, in the repetition of his attribute of 'riding on the heavens.'

'There is none like unto the God of Jeshurun, who rideth upon the heaven in thy help, and in his excellency on the sky The eternal God is thy refuge, and underneath are the everlasting arms.' Deuteronomy 33.

The *everlasting arms* being the claws of the Crab, which lie immediately underneath the Sun's path, as he rides in the heaven, through his highest acme of ascendancy, on the 21st of June.

The name of *God* is merely titular, and an epithet that may or may not be conjoined, to the alone specific and definite idea of THE LORD. But the *Lord* and the *Sun* are perfectly convertible terms, and may be put indifferently the one for the other, in every passage in which either of them occur.

---

which was the old Saxon root of the German GOTT, and of our present English GOD

As in that beautiful astronomical apologue to which I shall hereafter engage your studies, 'Then spake Joshua unto the Lord in that day, and said, Sun, stand thou still upon Gibeon.'

'So the Sun stood still, and there was no day like that before it or after it, that *the Lord* hearkened unto the voice of a man.' Joshua 10.

'God is the Lord, who hath showed us light. Bind the sacrifice with cords, even unto the horns of the altar.'

'For behold darkness shall cover the earth, and gross darkness the people; but the Lord shall arise upon thee, and his brightness shall be seen upon thee.'

'O Lord, the Gentiles shall come to thy light, and Kings to the brightness of thy rising.'

'Heaven and earth are full of the majesty of thy glory.'

Thus may we, through all the modifications of Egyptian, Pagan, and Christian piety, indifferently substitute the name of *the Sun* for that of THE LORD.

They are perfectly synonymous; as to this day among ourselves, the *Lord's-day*, and the Sun's day, means but *one* and the same day:

Lord's-day being the technical or cant phrase for that 'weekly market-day of imposture and priestcraft, when honest folks are obliged to shut up shop, that other folks may have all the custom to themselves, and nothing be bought or sold but gospel.

Our annual festival of *Easter*, when we gratulate the resurrection of *our Lord and Saviour*, from his state of declension and decadency, ' to renew the face of the earth,' was never held at any other season but the spring of the year, and never on any other day than on a Sunday, because it is the *Sun*, and the Sun alone, who *is* our Lord and Saviour.

> 'Et nunc omnis ager nunc omnis parturit arbos,
> Nunc frondent sylvae, nunc formosissimus annus.'

> 'Now every field, now every tree is green,
> Now genial nature's fairest face is seen:'

And

> 'Now is the winter of our discontent
> Made glorious summer, by this holy Lord,
> And all the clouds, that lowered upon our house,
> In the deep bosom of the ocean buried.'

The word *Easter* has been supposed to be derived from a Gaelish or ancient British Goddess, named *Eastré*, and analogous to the Egyptian *Isis*, whose mystical death and resurrection had been celebrated in the spring of every year, by our forefathers, from the days of an infinitely remote antiquity: But the *East* and the *Easter* is so universal a metonymy for the *Sun*, which *rises* in the East: hence called the *Orient* or the *Riser;* that if we are to entertain a doubt as to its being the Sun, and the Sun only, whose *rising* is celebrated on Easter Sunday, the difficulty would be to tell where the doubt is to come from. Our shrewder divines have expressed their vexation, that that awkward word *Easter* should have found its way into the text of our New Testament, 'Herod cast Peter into prison, *intending after Easter to bring him forth to the people.*' Acts 12. But Peter made his escape out of that prison, in such a hurry, as to leave one of his keys behind him.

But as the name of the LORD, in a religious sense, in all interpretations which it hath ever borne, among all people, nations, and languages, and in all ages in which religion of any character hath been known to exist, always referred to THE SUN, so the term *Saviour*, so essentially connected with it, was ever the specific and distinctive epithet of all the personifications of the SUN, and the Saviour, and our Blessed Saviour, and the Lord and Saviour, were the epithets of Apollo, Bacchus, Adonis, Æsculapius, Hercules, Osiris, and all other emblems, whose type and significancy was the Sun: and Σωτηρ, *the Saviour*, separately from any name whatever, never signified anything else but the SUN. No two words ever uttered by the tongue of man were ever more perfectly synonymous than the Sun and the Saviour.

It is but a forlorn and desperate flinging for a desperate cause, to set up a conceit of Pagan, India, Egypt, Greece, and Rome, having possibly derived some of their theological notions and forms of expression from corrupted fragments of primitive tradition, or scattered rags and tatters of salvation, which the wind had blown to them out of *the old clothes bag.*

When we have evidence at hand, absolutely fatal to such a pretence, and must shut up for ever all record, and all means of record of what the world has been before we came into it: if such a pretence is any longer to be pronounced respectable.

In the most extensive numismatic work, the most careful collection of medals in the world, that of Monsieur MIONET, which presents an exhibition of all the most ancient medals and coins which have been preserved to human curiosity, where there are thousands of Greek, Armenian, Persian, Egyptian, and Phœnician medals, going back to a very high antiquity, there is not one among them that appertains to an Israelitish nation, to its theocracy, or to its government,* not one to give a feature of history to their sacred legends, or to make it seem probable that either their altars or their thrones, their priesthood or their kings, their Davids, Solomons, Sauls, Jeroboams, Ahabs, or Hezekiahs, ever existed.

Our good Christian brethren, who can apologise and explain away the apparent spurcities and grossness of their own most holy Bible (and o' God's name let 'em explain it away), while they would never endure nor forgive a wrinkle in the nose at what we know (about what we know) of the mysteries of their own most holy faith, have had no mercy upon the mysteries of the ancient Paganism.

They have revelled in sarcasm, and rioted in scorn and scoffing, at the emblems of a religion as pure, and of mysteries as august, as ever were the vehicles of knowledge to the wise, and the veil of it, from the curiosity of the vulgar.

They have set our modest and holy God, the immortal Bacchus, at whose adorable name 'every knee should bow, of things in heaven and things in earth, and things under the earth,' our great personification of the God of day, and whose moral never spake other admonition to the hearts of men, than they should cast off the works of darkness, and put on the whole armour of light.

They have set him as a drunken boy astraddle across a

---

* Dans l'ouvrage numismatique le plus soigné qu'on connaisse, celui de M. Mionet, où l'on trouve des milliers de medailles qui remontent à une tres haute antiquité, Grecque, Armenienne, Perse, Egyptienne, Phenicienne, il n'y en a pas une seule qui appertienne a la nation Israelitique, a sa theocratie, ou a sa royauté. Rhegellini, *La Maconnerie consideree comme le resultat des Religions*, Egyptienne, Juive, et Chrétienne.—Vol. I., p. 210.

beer-barrel, inviting to licentiousness, and sanctioning inebriation.

Forgetting, in the intensity of their scorn, that it is none other than *He*, whose Phœnician name is written in those three mystical letters, I, H, Σ, upon their altars, and whose Greek name *Dionysius* (as signifying Διος Νους, the Logos, or mind of God), is found in the first verse of the first chapter of St. John's gospel, whom they so impiously dishonour.

They have pourtrayed our mystical PAN, the most august emblem of universal nature, with their own Devil's cloven foot, as half a man and half a goat, in order to carry the votes of the common cry of curs, that never yet gave breath to a cadence of rationality, against a system of physics and morals, as far superior to anything they set in its place, as the harmony of Apollo's lute to the twang-twang of a Jew's harp.

Forgetting the testimony of their own Eusebius, that that PAN was none other than Jesus Christ himself, to whose honour all good Christians eat pancakes on Shrove Tuesday, and hot cross-buns on Good Friday, the pan deriving its name from its resemblance to Jesus Christ, as serving to cook anything, and the cakes from the fools that would take anything for a God.

But 'twas that great personification, an immortal *Pan*, that conveyed and preserved the august truth of the unity of God, his exemption from all the bad and vindictive passions which superstition has ascribed to deity, and his equal benevolence and regard to man and beasts, which Mr. Pope has adorned in that grand apostrophe of *Pantheistical* piety:

> 'All are but parts of one stupendous whole,
> Whose body nature is, and God the soul,
> That changed thro' all, yet still in all the same,
> Great in the stars, as in th' eternal frame.
>
> To him no high, no low, no great, no small,
> He fills, he bounds, connects, and equal all.'

END OF PART I. OF WHO IS THE LORD?

The Devil's Pulpit.

"DELENDA EST CARTHAGO."

No. 19.—Vol. II.] Price 2d.

WHO IS THE LORD?—PART II.
A Discourse,
DELIVERED BY THE REV. ROBERT TAYLOR, B.A.

AT THE ROTUNDA, BLACKFRIARS ROAD.

'And Pharaoh said, Who is the Lord, that I should obey his voice, to let Israel go? I know not the Lord, neither will I let Israel go!'—Exodus, v. 2.

THE philosophers of ancient Greece took the words Εν το παν, the All is One, as the formula of their religious creed: and there is not a philosopher or man of learning, at this day, in Europe, who has in the least degree swerved from that creed. Every physician, anatomist, naturalist, and geologist talks of nature, the works of nature, the *vis medicatrix naturæ*, leaving the cure to nature, and so on, who would justly bear being laughed at, if he spoke of either God or Devil, instead of nature.

It is, then, absolutely not true, to represent the ancient Paganism as a system of Polytheism; or to maintain that the intelligent among the ancient Indian, Phœnician, Egyptian, and Grecian people, really worshipped the various emblems of their sacred science. The very names of many of those emblems contain specific evidence, that they held one God only, and his name to be unutterable, and his nature incomprehensible. It is Christians alone who have been really and truly Idolatrous and Polytheistical.

Thus the very name *Apollo* did literally contain the great truth, and could not be spoken without reminding the speaker of that truth, that there is but *one* God. As *Sol* is literally the *Alone*, the *Only One*, the Chaldeans worshipped the Sun, under the name Adad, or *Adodus*, which is the Chaldee rendering of the Hebrew אחד, emphatically repeated *Ad-Ad*, the One, the One.

The *Isis Omnia* of India and of Egypt, bore in her name itself, and in the sacred inscription that adorned her shrine, a protest against any idolatrous understanding of the homage by which men expressed their conviction of the truth, so symbolized. And it was one of the express laws of Numa Pompilius, 600 years before Christ: Nequis Deum, vel hominis speciem vel animalis alicujus formam habere existimaret.

We see no idolatry in such a mode of expression as that 'the heavens declare the glory of God, and the firmament showeth his handy work:' and none there is, in the supposition that if universal nature, the *Isis Omnia*, the mighty whole, could be supposed to declare its great resulting truth, that truth would *be*, the legend that shone in letters of gold in the temple of Isis. 'I am what *is*, what *shall* be, what *hath* been: my veil hath never been raised, and the fruit which I brought forth is the Sun.'

I find a form of prayer in Danet's Greek and Roman antiquities, addressed to the Goddess Isis, which I translate, as a specimen of the general character of Pagan piety:—*

---

* 'Tu quidem sancta et humani generis Sospitatrix perpetua semper fovendis mortalibus munifica, dulcem matris affectionem, miserorum casibus tribuis, nec dies, nec quies ulla, ac ne momentum quidem tenue, tuis transcurris beneficiis otiosum, qua mari, terraque protegas homines, et depulsis vitæ procellis, salutarem porrigas dextram, qua fatorum etiam inextricabiliter contorta retractas licia, et fortunæ, tempestates mitigas, et stellarum varios meatus cohibes. Te superi colunt, observant inferi, tu rotas orbem, luminas. Solem, regis mundum, calcas Tartarum, tibi respondent sidera, redeunt tempora, gaudent, numina, serviunt, elementa, tuo nutu spirant flamina, nutriunt nubila gemmant semina, crescunt gramina. Tuam majestatem per horrescunt aves cœlo meantes, feræ montibus errantes, serpentes solo latentes, belluæ ponto natantes. At ego referendis laudibus tuis exilis ingenio, et adhibendis sacrificiis tenuis patrimonio. Nec mihi vocis ubertas ad dicenda quæ de tua majestate sentio, sufficit; neu orá nulle, linguæque totidem vel indefessi sermonis æterna series. Ergo quod solum potest religiosus quidem, sed pauper, alioquin efficere curabo, divinos tuos vultus, numenque sanctissimum intra pectoris mei secreta conditum perpetuo custodiens imaginabor.'

'O Holy and Eternal Sospitatrix of the human race, ever munificent in protecting mortals, who showest the sweet affection of a mother to the misfortunes of the miserable. Nor is there day or night, nor the shortest moment which thou passest over, unmarked of thy beneficence, where by sea or by land thou protectest men, and; dispelling the tempests of life, stretching forth thy saving right hand, with which thou unloosest even the inextricably twisted thongs of fate, allayest the storms of fortune, and restrainest the various passages of the stars. Thee, the powers above worship,—thee, the infernals honour,—thou rollest the sphere, givest light to the Sun, rulest the world, treadest on Tartarus. To thee, the planets respond, the seasons return, the Gods rejoice, the elements obey. At thy command the winds arise, the rains descend, the seeds germinate, vegetation flourishes. Thy majesty is felt by the birds that fly in the air, by the beasts that roam the mountains, by the reptiles of the ground, by the monsters of the deep.

'But I, slender of ability to praise thee, and poor in means to sacrifice, have not fluency of utterance to express what I feel of thy majesty, nor would a thousand mouths and as many tongues enable me to do so. What then alone can be, in another way, devout, however poor, shall be my care to do: I will meditate thy divine character, keeping thy most holy deity laid up in the secret recesses of my heart for ever.'

A conceit which our poet Thomson has plagiarized in his hymn:

'But I lose myself in Him, in goodness infinite—
Come thou, expressive silence, muse his praise.'

I am not maintaining that any one form of prayer was ever more rational, or in itself a whit better or worse than any other, yet as far as comfort might be afforded to a sick mind, by prayer of any sort, it would be hard to say how a man might not make as much of it by reposing his sorrows on the imagined sympathy of an Almighty Mother, as in calling himself a miserable sinner, and sinful dust and ashes, and all the dirt he could think of, just to soothe the irritability of an imagined—(Hold, thou accusing Spirit, write not so fast in thy Day of Judgment Book,—I did not say it,—I'm on the salvation side still.)

But it is dulness itself that could miss of being struck

with the perfect identity of character, betrayed by the inscription in the Temple of Isis, 'I am what is, what shall be, what hath been,—my veil hath never been raised:' and the mystical 'I am that I am:' and I shall be what I shall be:' and 'I am he who is:' or, 'I am the necessarily existing being,' which supplies the derivative meaning of the name Jehovah.

While, by a coincidence still more striking, the sacred text of the Bhagavat Pourana, or *Book of God*, of the Hindoos, compiled fourteen hundred years before the Christian era, contains almost the same words as the basis of the name of the *Supreme God* of India. He is represented as thus announcing himself to *Brahma* (whom nobody can doubt to be the same as Abraham):—

'Even I was, even at first, not any other thing, that which exists, unperceived, supreme:' afterwards, 'I am that which is, and He who must remain, am I.'

So literally rendered by Sir William Jones.—*Asiatic Researches*, Vol. I., p. 245.

Now, in the 4th of Exodus occurs that most curious passage, 'And God spake unto Moses, and said, אני יהוה *Ani Yahouh*, I am Yahou.

וארא אל אברהם אל יצחק ואל־יעקב באל שדי
ושמו יהוה לא נידעתי להם.

Yara ol Ouvroime, ol Yetschek veol Yoquove Beal Shadai, ve Shemi Yahouh lo nidoti le hem.

I appeared unto Abraham, to Isaac, and to Jacob, as Baal Shadai; but by my name, *Yahouh*, was I not known unto them, Baal Shadai, our translators have rendered God Almighty: a complete admission that Baal Shadai, Belzebub, and God Almighty, are one and the same deity.

Yet so positive a declaration, notwithstanding,—we find Abraham repeatedly addressing the Lord by his name Yahouh: a contradiction so gross, as clearly to prove that the writer of the Book of Exodus could never have seen the book Genesis.

The name Baal literally signified THE LORD, and by that *Lord*, was never meant any other than the Lord, the *Sun*, as will be seen in all its compounds.

בעל־המון Baal-Ha-mon, the Lord, the Sun.

Baal Berith, Lord of the Covenant.

Baal Peor, Lord of the Opening.
Baal Perazim, Lord of the Divisions.
Baal Zephon, Lord of the North; aye, and
Baal Zebub, Lord of Flies :

Inasmuch as he, being a God kissing carrion, breeds maggots, and thence flies in putrid vegetable and animal substances: and hence

Baal Berith, Lord of Purification, the Sun purifying all things.
Baal Samen, Lord of the Heavens.
Baal Aitun, the Mighty Lord.
Baal Elion, the Lord Most High.

Can we wonder, then, that the ancient religionists should have been perplexed and pestered as they were with eternal feuds and controversies, as to whether the Lord were God, or Baal were God—that is, whether they should say Yahouh Alehim or Baal Alehim, when both names had precisely the same signification, and the same reference—that is, to the Sun; as we find Yahouh complaining of his people, in the 23rd of Jeremiah, that their fathers had forgotten his name in that of Baal. שכחו אבותם את שמי בבעל. *Shekchu abutem at Shemi be Bole.*

While, in the 2nd of *Hosea*—(that is, of Jesus)—v. 16, is the prophecy, ' And it shall be at that day, saith the Lord, that thou shalt call me Ishi (or Itchy), and shalt no more call me Baali.'

And so as if to make sure of accomplishing the prophecy, that they might no more call him *Baal*, their pretended successors, who tell us that the proper utterance of the name of *the Lord* has been irrecoverably forgotten, have taken the *itch* for calling him *Adonis*, which name has the same signification, and the same reference to *the Lord*, the Sun, as Adonibezek, Lord of Splendour; Adonizedek, Lord of Righteousness ; Adonikam, the Rich Lord; Adoniram, the Lord Most High ; Adonijah, Master.

It must never be forgotten that the names Jehovah, Jupiter, Adonis, Ammon, Hercules, Osiris, Dionysius, Æsculapius, Apollo, Phœbus, Bacchus, Pluto, and Baal, Bel, El Belus, and how many others? were not names of different Deities, but different names for one and the same Deity, and that Deity was the *Sun*, as represented under his different manifestations, or phænomena in his daily and annual apparent course in the heavens, worshipped as the Stygian Jupiter, when he descends into the lower parts of the earth; the Olympian Jupiter, when again his rising beams peer over the mountain top; the Jupiter Ammon, when he appears to be hidden or concealed; the Jupiter *Easter*, when he is found again, as rising from the dead, coming forth as a bridegeroom out of his chamber in the east, and rejoicing as a giant to run his course, according to the beautiful verse cited by Macrobius:

Εις Ζευς, εις Αδης, εις Ηλιος, εις Διονυσιος.

'It is one Jupiter, one Pluto, one Sun, one Dionysius.'

The name Jupiter is precisely the same as that which we so egregiously pronounce Jehovah: and the four letters of which it is composed are, J, E, U, E, which, pronounced as one syllable, is Jew, to which the addition of *Pater*, or father, for the greater reverence makes Jupiter, the *Pater* being dropt in all the other cases of the noun. The Jeue, or *Jeve*, uttered in the most solemn manner, became *Jove*.

And accordingly in the liturgical Latin of the Psalms, and in the Latin Bibles of Dathe and Castalio throughout, the word Jove is substituted instead of the *Dominus*, or Lord of the Latin vulgate.

The soft harmonious utterance of the Greeks was abhorrent to the harsh sound of the J, in the Jao, Jove, and Jupiter, and substituted its own more elegant and euphonous Zeta, or letter Z, and thus made Ζευπατερ! and Ζαω, the Greek for 'I live,' as the root or theme for their name of the Supreme Being, expressed precisely the sense of the old 'I am that I am,' or the living God, which was the meaning of the barbarous sounding Jah, or Yahouh.

Though Macrobius pretends that the oracle of Apollo gave this name to the Sun, pronouncing him at the same time the greatest of all the Gods φραζεω των παντων υπατον εμμεν Ιαω. I pronounce Jao to be, of all the Gods, the greatest: and hence those three mystical letters, which you will see to this day inscribed upon the pediments of our Christian churches and on all religious monuments, D. O. M., *Deo Optimo Maximo*. Indeed, you will find them generally printed, by Christians themselves, at the head of Pope's Universal Prayer.

That the ancients referred this title to their God, the Sun

will be found in the context of all the beautiful prayers of Homer, in which that luminary is addressed: nor indeed could any form of devotion surpass the grandeur and sublimity of their addresses:

Ζευ κυδιστε μεγιστε κελαιναφες αιθερι Ναιων.

'O Lord, Most Holy, Most High, compelling all heaven dwelling in æther.'

While, in no part of either of our Old or New Testament is the unity of the Godhead, and his unapproachable holiness of character, insisted on with half the emphasis and dignity of the style of the father of Gods and men.

The Lord of the Ode, indeed, gets upon his Mount Sinai, and storms and thunders about his godhead, and tells us, that he is a jealous God, and that his rage comes up into his face, and that his nostrils smoke, and he hisses, and smites, and kicks, and storms, and raves, and curses, and swears, and damns, and vomits forth his divinity: which, God knows, is condescending enough to our capacities, and thank the parsons for the compliment. But contrast we for one moment the mild majesty of the Olympian Jupiter, as described in the 6th Iliad, not quite so condescending:

'Aurora, now fair daughter of the dawn,
Sprinkled with rosy light the dewy lawn,
When Jove convened the senate of the skies,
Where huge Olympus' clould-capt tops arise.

'The Sire of Gods, the awful silence broke,
The heavens attentive listened as he spoke:
Celestial states! Immortal Gods! give ear,
Hear our decree, and reverence what ye hear.

'Let down our golden everlasting chain,
Whose strong embrace holds heaven, and earth, and main;
Strive all of mortal or immortal birth,
To drag by this the Thunderer down to earth.

'Ye strive in vain; if I but move this hand,
I heave the heavens, the ocean, and the land;
For such I reign unbounded and above,
And such are men, and Gods compared to Jove.'

But of all the manifestations of the Sun, his personification in the character of Jupiter Ammon, was the most extensively prevalent. From that name Ammon, is derived the name of the Ammonites, and the children of Ammon or worshippers of Ammon, with which we are so familiar in the text of our sacred scriptures.

I have shown you, that the meaning of the word sacred is secret—that is, something that covers a concealed and hidden meaning. So, according to Manetho, as quoted by Plutarch, we find the name *Ammon* signifies το κεκρυμενον, και την κρυψιν, the hidden one, or the concealed,—as we find him directly addressed in Isaiah, xlv. 15: 'Verily, thou art a God that hidest thyself: O God of Israel, the Saviour,' whereby he is identified with Osiris, or Adonis; in short, with *the hidden one*, for whom the Egyptians made an annual search. 'Now this *hidden one*, by whatever name invoked, was no other than the SUN.'

The name of ADONIS is substituted by every Jew in the world, in his reading of every text of the Old Testament, which our English renders THE LORD; while the name of AMMON is pronounced in the most solemn manner by every Christian in the world at the end of his creed, and of every prayer which he believes himself to address to the Supreme Being, in express declaration that that Supreme Being is none other than Jupiter Ammon. And hence, in all our Christian temples, churches, and chapels, to this day, has been retained the never-varied, never-suspended Pagan custom of having an officer called the *clerique*, the clarke, or the *learned one*, in a box, under the hierophant, who, at the close of every prayer, and at the conclusion of every ceremony, ducks down his head, or puts his hand before his mouth, and groans, or whispers, or breathes through his nose, in all possible varieties of twang and cadence, the mystical word, *Amen*, *Emen*, *Aumen*, *Hemen* and *Hor-men*, that conveyed the secret to the few who may care to know what the secret is, that it is Ammon to whom their prayers are addressed, as Lucan has said—

'Quamvis Æthiopum populis, Arabumque beatis,
Gentibus atque Indis, unus sit Jupiter Ammon.'

Æthiops, Arabians, Indians, and he might have added Ægyptians, Greeks, Romans, Pagans, Jews, Christians, have but one God, and that *is Ammon*.

The Egyptians, says Herodotus, call the Supreme God Ammon:* while in our book of the Revelation of St. John,

---
* Αμμοῦν γαρ Αιγυπτιοι καλεουσι τον Δια

we find the name *Amen*, assumed by Jesus Christ, together with an exegetical mention of the occultation or circumstance of being hidden, and found again, which the name *Amon* signified: 'I am he that liveth, and was dead, and behold I am alive for evermore, Ammon.' Rev. i. 18. 'And Egypt is declared to be the place where also our Lord was crucified.' Rev. xi. 8. And the whole volume of our *secret* scriptures concludes with the declaration of Christ, and the response of his apostle. 'Surely I come quickly, Ammon. Even so come Lord Jesus.'

But in the 65th of Isaiah, v. 16. is the most unequivocal name Ammon, and his astronomical character of occultation or being hidden, applied to the God Yahouh.

'He who blesseth himself on earth shall bless himself by his God Ammon: and he who sweareth on earth shall swear by the God Ammon, because the former troubles are delivered to oblivion, and because they are hidden from mine eyes, saith the Lord.'

Amoun, or more reverentially, Jupiter Ammon, was the Sun in the sign Aries, and as returning with never failing constancy, into that sign, after having been hidden or occult, during the reign of winter: he acquired the characteristic epithet of 'the faithful and true witness:' as we find him speaking of himself in the Apocalypse. 'These things, saith Ammon, the faithful and true witness.' Rev. iii. 4. And in the 89th Psalm, 'I have sworn by my holiness that I will not lie unto David. His throne shall be as the Sun before me, even as the faithful witness in heaven.'

And the annual Egyptian ceremony of seeking for Ammon, the God that hides himself; the everlasting game of *Hooper's Hide*, or *hide and seek*, is enjoined in a thousand beautiful recitatives of our own *Ammonian*—that is, secret—that is, sacred scriptures. 'My heart hath talked of thee, seek ye my face. Thy face, Lord, will I seek. O hide not thou thy face from me.' Psalm xxvii. 9. 'O God, thou art my God, early will I seek thee.' Psalm lxiii. 1. 'And why standest thou so far off, O Lord, and hidest thy face in the needful time of trouble.' Psalm x. 1. 'Lord, how long wilt thou hide thyself?' Psalm lxxxix. 45. And we find the same old game of blind man's buff announced in the 1st of Isaiah: 'When ye spread forth your hands, I will hide myself from ye: yea, when ye make many prayers, I will not hear you:' as the same game is proposed by the Amen of the spell, 'A little while and ye shall see me; and again a little while and ye sha'n't see me.'

'The difference between the words Aman, Amen, and Amon,' says Sir Wm. Drummond, 'is nothing;' the aspirate was used or dropt, as it is with us, indifferently.

The Egyptians, as well as the Hebrews and Arabs, omitted the vowels entirely, the Greeks supplied either one or other at their fancy.

And thus has the Egyptian Jupiter *Ammon*, the God that hideth himself during the winter, and is found at Easter without so much as an attempted translation of the name, without the variation of an iota of the ceremony of *seeking him*, been adopted into all the languages and all the religions of the earth: and you shall see, to this day, in every church or chapel you may enter, the self-same ceremony of seeking for Ammon, performed in the self-same words, and even with the self-same gesticulations and manœuvres.

The priest, invariably shutting his eyes, and spreading forth his hands, as we do at blind man's buff; and either he or another lured to play a part in the game, crying out *Au-men*, as the boys cry whoop, in the game which is a mockery of the game of *seeking the Lord*.

So as, upon the repetition of Ammon's allegorical history (a most essential part of the ceremony), detailing his passing through the Virgin; his descent into the lower parts of the earth, and his rising again into the heaven: the whole congregation turn to the east, as the place where Ammon may be expected to appear again, and again cry Ammon.

Thus, Sirs, have I given what I am sure you would seek elsewhere in vain,—a fair answer to the question,—Who is the Lord? and shown you the knowledge of the Most High.

A knowledge which I think must establish your conviction of that great truth, that there never was a race of people upon earth so entirely ignorant, and monstrously mistaken, as to the real origin and meaning of their religion, as those who profess and call themselves Christians, and never any men so little able or so little willing to instruct them as their own wonderfully fine men, their reverend and right reverend theologues.

But can it be wondered at that it should be so, when we see the principle of deceiving the people, and of perpetuating ignorance, beyond all example of either barbarous, Pagan, or Popish ages, inculcated and avowed as the very essence of Protestantism: and the multitude are taught to turn from any work or treatise that might make them wiser than they are as from poison, and from the face of a scholar and an honest man as from a serpent.

And of the millions of our fellow creatures who would be ashamed of such ignorance on any other subject, not one would be found who knows, or ever cared to inquire the meaning of the principal word of his own devotion.

The VERILY, and *so be it*, which our catechised school-boys and parish-apprentices are whipt into the saying of, in their *yes, verily, and by God's help, so I will*, is as wild a fling off the mark, as mutton and boiled turnips: as any but a fool, who had made up his mind to see nothing, might see in a moment, by applying that explanation of the Amen, instead of the Amen, wherever it occurs.

The *aussi soit il* of the French, *so let it be;* the *so be it,* of the English; or the fiat, be it so, from whence FATE, of the Latin, is the language of command and authority, which could never have comported with the humility and submission of a prayer, and still less of a confession of sin, which, like every other solemn act, was to begin and end with the name of the Deity to whom it was addressed. As in the ancient form of wills, the worshippers of Ammon always began them with the words, ' In the name of God, AMMON.'

So whatever other epithets of Deity, as Adonis, Osiris, Most High, Most Holy, were introduced in the course of the prayer, the propriety was observed of summing them all up in the name of Him to whom they all referred, in the manner of our '*through Jesus Christ our Lord, Ammon,*' which form rendered most literally, according to the derivation of each particular word, is Bacchus, Apollo, Jupiter, Ammon.

It would seem a profaneness, even to Christian stupidity, to attempt to put their verily, or so be it, in the stead of the word Ammon, where that name is expressly used as the name of God: and so to give 'em, thus saith verily, or thus saith *so be it*, instead of thus saith Ammon, where that adorable name occurs in so many passages, as interchangeable with that of the Lord of Hosts, the God of Israel, and the Moloch, or King of Heaven, the abomination of the children of Ammon, from whom all the Christians of the present day are lineally descended, and from whose worship they have never swerved.

The pretence to an historical foundation of the Christian religion, I have so completely overthrown in my work, 'The Diegesis,' that I may hold it a certainty that no man who has ever read that work will ever attempt to set up that pretence again in any assembly whatever, where he may be liable to meet those who can confute its fallacy and confound its falsehood.

Delenda est Carthago.

END OF PART II. OF WHO IS THE LORD?

The Devil's Pulpit.

"DELENDA EST CARTHAGO."

No. 20.—Vol. II.]   [Price 2d.

EXODUS.—Part I.

A Discourse,

DELIVERED by the Rev. ROBERT TAYLOR, B.A.

AT THE ROTUNDA, BLACKFRIARS ROAD.

> 'And when the Lord saw that he turned aside to see, God called unto him out of the midst of the bush, and said, Moses, Moses; and he said, Here am I! And he said, Draw not nigh hither, put off thy shoes from off thy feet, for the place whereon thou standest is holy ground.'—Exodus, iii. 4.

I am now to introduce you to the critical study of the second of the sacred books, which bears, in our English Bibles, the title, the Second Book of Moses, called Exodus.

This book is, in the Latin vulgate of Pope Sixtus the Fifth, and Pope Clement the Eighth, called merely *Liber Exodus*—that is, *the Book of Exodus*, without any mention of the name Moses.

In the Greek of the Septuagint, it is called only *Exodus*.

In the Hebrew, it is called merely ואלה־שמות, *Veelle Semoth*—that is, '*And these are the names*,' which is nothing more than the first words of the book itself, written a little larger than the rest, to mark the place of beginning, but being no title at all.

So that there is no authority whatever to show who the author of the book was. It really is anonymous, and our

English translators, in taking upon themselves to call it the Book of Moses, have committed an impertinence, and taken a liberty, which they had no right to take, and for which they had no authority of any Latin, Greek, or Hebrew original. They have added to the words of this book, and therefore have shown how little respect they had for that fearful denunciation of the apostle.

'If any man shall add unto these things, God shall add unto him the plagues that are written in this book.'

If they found the book without a title, why did they not leave it so? Why presume to give it a title, and to assign it to an author of their own mere conjecture and guess, in which indeed they have guessed so ill, and conjectured so widely off the mark, as to expose our English translation to the scorn and ridicule of illiterate and uninformed infidels, where certainly the divine original itself would have stood unimpeached, and is, indeed, absolutely unimpeachable.

The silly and malapert objections of our infidel and sceptical writers, and the still more silly and absurd answers of our Christian advocates to those objections, as that Moses has drawn his own character, has called himself the meekest of men, and has described his own death and funeral in these books, and therefore could not possibly have been their author, are dissipated in a moment before the merits of that simple, but certainly first to be answered challenge. Where was it ever pretended that Moses was the author of these books? Or what should render them of less authority, had they been written by the prophet Samuel, or the priest Hilkiah, or by any other holy and inspired personage?

Ere I proceed upon this second stage of the sacred science, in which I am so far advanced, I must again repeat the principle which I at the first laid down, and from which I have never intentionally swerved,—and that is, that no man that ever breathed, ever did or could treat the sacred scriptures with a more rational reverence, with more entire respect, and with more intense devotion and purpose of heart, to find out and to set forth their true and unsophisticated meaning, than I. And sit a righteous God in judgment between my soul, and the soul of anyone who shall be offended at what he shall hear from me, or between me and the most evangelical preacher of the gospel, who would denounce me as an infidel, or revile me as a blasphemer, and my life, my salvation should be the forfeit, if I had not in every instance treated the sacred text with greater submission, and more becoming reverence, than he.

Upon this principle, then, renouncing all impertinence, all invention, all imagination of evidence, where evidence is not forthcoming.

There is no evidence that these five books, commonly called the Pentateuch, were written by any person who bore the name of Moses. The books themselves assert no such thing, and we have no right to assert it for them.

There is, however, authority which might, to those who jump at conclusions, make it for a moment seem that the person mentioned in the Book of Exodus, under the name Moses, was their writer, and that is where our Saviour says to the Jews, 'If ye had believed Moses, ye would have believed me, for he wrote of me:' and that answer of Philip to Nathaniel, 'We have found him of whom Moses did write, Jesus of Nazarus, the son of Joseph.'

But, Sirs, the day itself is not more apparent than the fact, that if that were the case, these writings could not possibly be the writings of Moses, since, in no part of them is there the least allusion to Jesus of Nazareth, and the only sons of Joseph mentioned in these books are the two heads of the tribes, Ephraim, and Manasseh.

There is no evidence, then, that these books were written by any person of the name of Moses; and though Josephus, Philo, Manetho, Diodorus, Orpheus, Strabo, Longinus, and other exceedingly ancient authors, have spoken of writings ascribed to Moses, or rather, more correctly speaking, to *the* Moses, for the word is plural, and evidently signifies more than *one*,—there is no reason to suppose that by the Moses they meant any particular person. Nor do the books of the Moses, in the language of those ancient authors, mean any thing more than books *according to the Moses*: as our four gospels, which I hope are of quite as good authority as the books of the Moses, are called gospels, not *by*, or *of*, but *according to* Matthew, Mark, Luke, and John.

Neither is there any reason why the number of these books should be confined to five; but there *is* reason why their number should be extended to *nine*, because we then bring in the four books which follow—*i.e.*, Joshua, Judges, Samuel, and Kings, as resting on a common authority, and bearing a common character. For these four books, being perfectly anonymous, as the five of the Pentateuch are, cannot be more honorably considered, than as constituting a continuation of the same great work. As it was a custom, the most ancient and sacred of any that antiquity has preserved, in works of genius and literature, to divide the whole composition into nine books, and *that* in honour of the nine Muses, who were believed to inspire such performances.

And then, the Book of Chronicles, which follows these nine books, being entitled, as it is, in the Hebrew, דברי־הימים, *Debri heyemim;* and in the Greek, παραλειπομενων—that is, *of things omitted*, defines exactly the place of their conclusion, and is a natural appendix to the whole nine books. The reader will see that these *things omitted*, and therefore brought in afterwards into this appendix, at the end of the nine books, are omissions from the Books of Genesis and Exodus, as well as from those of Joshua, Samuel, or the Kings: thus demonstrating, that the whole nine books, to which this common appendix is affixed, must have been considered as constituting but one common and complete work in itself.

And supplying us with a meaning and a reason, where none besides so probable can be assigned, why the books should be called Books of Moses, and why there should be exactly nine of them—that is they are books written under divine inspiration—that is, the divine inspiration of the nine Muses.

It was in Egypt especially that the nine Muses—that is, as these divinities were formerly called the nine *Moses*, received divine honours; their name being exactly the same as Moses, and of the same signification, and for the same reason, signifying *drawn out of the waters*, and even out of the very same waters: those of the Nile, out of which Moses is said to have been drawn. The real exposition of the fable being, that the worship of these deities grew upon the respect shown to the nine emblematical figures which were exhibited among the Egyptians, to denote the nine months of the year, during which that country was free from the inundation of their great river. Hence these Moses were said to be *drawn out*, or *saved from the waters*, and were represented each as holding some instrument or symbol as a pair of compasses, a flute, a mask, a trumpet, &c.,

expressive of the one or other of the months of the year over which they severally presided. And the whole group were represented as dancing round the Sun, who, personified as the god Bacchus, was always represented as attended by the Muses, and presiding in the midst of them; and by that metonomy of language, which always gives a common name to things which have an essential relation to each other. Bacchus himself acquired the name, precisely the same name, MOSES, and was worshipped and adored under that name. It being a matter of pride and pomp, throughout all the forms of Pagan piety, to give their Gods plural names, though with a singular signification: as everyone knows that the name of God, in the Hebrew text of the Old Testament, אלהים, *Eloheim*, is such a plural word, though meaning but one individual: and our Kings and Emperors, and Bishops, imagining themselves to be God's representatives, from the same egregious vanity, always speak of themselves in the plural, as We George, or We William, by the Grace of God, King, and We John, or We Thomas, by divine permission, Bishop or Archbishop.

And thus the plural name Móses, which was first given to the nine Muses, was by metonomy transferred, in its plural form, to the individual god, Bacchus, because he was always attended by the nine Muses, and was believed to have been drawn out, or extracted from the fire, as the nine Muses were from the water.

And as it was in Egypt that so particular honour was paid to the nine Muses, we actually find that the most ancient history of Egypt, that of Herodotus, is divided into nine books in honour of the nine Muses, each of which is inscribed respectively with the name of one or other of these Goddesses: a reason which cannot lose its influence on our reflections, when we compare the striking coincidence of the facts, that the historical books of the Old Testament actually are nine in number,—that the name of Moses is absolutely the same as Muses,—that the books are of an Egyptian character, and refer so eminently to Egyptian history, habits, and customs,—that the Moses to whom they are ascribed absolutely was an Egyptian born and bred, and learned in all the wisdom of Egypt, and was drawn out of the very same river which the nine Muses were drawn out of: and that just as the nine Muses answer to the nine months, saved from the waters of the Nile, and to the nine books of Herodotus's Greek History of Egypt, so do they answer to the nine books of this Hebrew History of Egypt, as the four gospels of the New Testament, for no better reason that anybody could ever yet assign, answer to the four seasons of the year, and are not said to be written *by* Matthew, Mark, Luke, and John, but according to them. It being necessary to the accomplishment of prophecy, that Christ, as well as Moses, should be of Egyptian origin, 'that it might be fulfilled which was spoken of the Lord by the prophet, 'out of Egypt have I called my son.'

'The true pronunciation of the word which we call Moses is,' says the learned Volney, '*Moushah*.'

Philo Judæus—that is, Philo the Jew, tells us that the name of Μως, *Mose*, which is the Egyptian name for water; and Josephus, in nearly the same way, derives it from Mo, water, and Uses, which he says signifies, 'those who are saved out of the water.'

Gregory, of Nyssa, takes the safer way of telling us, out and out, that the whole word μωϋσης signifies water.

But if the more careful Philo be to be depended on, Μως is the Egyptian word for water: and EES, as the learned Bryant shows, is *fire*, and was one of the titles of the Sun: the whole together making *water and fire*, which was the combined name under which the River Nile was worshipped, the Nile being believed to be an immediate emanation from the Sun, which again identifies the character of Moses and the God Bacchus, whom we find worshipped under the name of Hues—Ζευς Ομβριος, or Jupiter pluvialis, or the rainy Jupiter, who is really none other than the same Deity who is addressed in those words of the Psalmist:

'Thou Lord sentest a gracious rain upon thine inheritance, and refreshedest it when it was weary.'

And whose worship has descended to us in those emblematical letters I H Σ, which are falsely read *Jesus Hominum Salvator*, but which really are the name at full length of Hues or Bacchus, the personified genius of the Nile, or of the Sun, considered as the source of the Nile.

These etymologies and analyses may seem strange, trifling, or unnecessary to fanatical ignorance, and to that stupid, uninquiring, and uncurious bigotry, whichever holds, that the way to treat the scriptures with due respect is to be as ignorant as possible, and never to know or to inquire what their true meaning is. But by the sincere inquirer and humble searcher after truth, they will be regarded as of unspeakable importance, as often, very often will it prove, that the very gem and pearl of truth is hidden in the sand that the idle and presumptuous had not deemed worth a moment's sifting.

Thus deriving our knowledge solely from scripture, and not bringing our own preconceived conceits and presumptuous conclusions to it, we shall not have read that Moses was so called, because he was drawn out of water, as if nothing more had been meant than what appears in that statement: but we shall compare that statement with the wonderful coincidence of the God Bacchus Sabazius, having also been called Moses, and also Hydrogenos—that is, *born of water*, for the very same reason, and with reference to the same waters, those of the River Nile.

And knowing as we do, that this Moses was first found on the banks of the Nile, that Christ himself was also called out of Egypt, and that the Egyptians certainly worshipped the Nile as the Supreme God, or an immediate emanation from him: we shall compare this our knowledge with the wonderful, most truly wonderful respect shown to water, and the curious enigmas about water, which run through every part of our Christian scriptures.

When the Egyptians worshipped the river Nile, as they most certainly did, it must puzzle invention to imagine how they could worship the river otherwise than by worshipping the water, or by showing most extraordinary respect, and attaching most extraordinary notions of sanctity and of sanctifying qualities to water; and to that Nilometer or Cross with which they measured the depth of the inundation: which Cross was itself adored in the Temple of Serapis, who was the same as Nilus, and which name Serapis is, in the language of Egypt, the same as *Salvator Mundi*— that is, *the Saviour of the World*.

Who, then, would not seek to know what I am sure no Christian can tell, why and wherefore 'tis that our Christian scriptures abound with such innumerable expressions of supreme respect and mystical honour paid to water, that the idolatrous worshippers of the Nile could not possibly have paid it greater respect.

Why is it that we must all of us be hydrogenous or born of water, or in some way, or for some reason, ducked, or dipt, or sprinkled, or saved, or pulled out of the water, as that 'except a man be born of water he cannot enter into the kingdom of God?' John iii. 10.

Why is it that as 'there is one Lord, one faith, so also there must be one baptism' (Ephesians iv. 4) or general ducking and washing?

Why is our Christ himself called by that very epithet, than which the idolatrous worshippers of the Nile could give to the Nile none more appropriate, even the fountain of living waters?'

Why is it, that when the apostle would define to us who or what Christ was, that he tells us, 'this is he who came by water?'

Why speaks he of himself in the character of the personified genius of a river, when he cried, 'If any man thirst, let him come unto me and drink?'

Why, in the very same character, tells he his disciple Peter 'If I wash thee not, thou hast no part in me?'

Why does the woman of Samaria find him, not merely in the character of the personified genius of water, but as the personified genius of a pump, standing where a pump should do, directly over the well, and speaking as a pump would do, if we conceived it to speak at all. 'If thou knowest the gift of God, and who it is that saith to thee, Give me drink, thou wouldst have asked of him, and he would have given thee living water'—that is, *quite fresh from the spring?*

Why is it that St. John tells us that 'his voice was as the sound of many waters?' or,

Why is it that the same St. John, to put his watery nature beyond all question, describes him as not being able to die upon the cross till he had first been tapt, and let off, and forthwith came thereout *water*, which was the particular essence and life of his divinity?

And why are we said to be baptised *into* Christ—that is, ducked and dipt, and plunged over head and ears into him. Romans vi. 3.

As in like manner, 'all our fathers were baptised unto Moses in the cloud and in the sea.' 1 Corinth. x. 1.

That is, Moses in the cloud, and Moses in the sea, are none other than an hieroglyphical way of meaning the waters in the cloud, and the waters in the sea,—the sea and the clouds being the great and primary reservoirs of all the waters.

And Christna, or Chrishna, absolutely was the Sanscreet name of the River Nile, from which all the waters of the world were believed to be derived: or,

Why, I ask in the name of that respect which is due to these mysterious legends, is baptism, the being dipt or ducked in water, as absolutely necessary to the salvation of a Christian as faith,—as in that solemn injunction, 'Go teach all nations, baptising them, and he that believeth and is baptised shall be saved.' And not being taught merely, nor believing merely, were ever sufficient unto salvation, but there must be a splash for it. No interest can we have in Christ, unless we are baptised into him,—no Lamb without *Duck*.

They who are said to be saved by Christ are said to be saved by water: and when the apostle, as the highest honour that could be conferred on man, was permitted to have a view of Christ in glory, the angel showed him *a pure river*.

So great are the mysteries, but so sure is the key that unlocks them all, involved in the name of Moses, *drawn out* of the waters.

> 'For where, with sevenfold horns, mysterious Nile
> Surrounds the skirts of Egypt's fruitful Isle;
> And where in pomp the sun-burnt people ride
> In painted barges o'er the teeming tide,
> Which rushing down from distant India's lands,
> Its sable waters fructify the sands.'

And Moses' horns are accounted for, in common with those of Bacchus, by the demonstrated fact, that they are both of them personifications of the river Nile. The Nile always being represented and emblemized as wearing horns, and as identified with Bacchus, with Dionysius, with the Ocean, which was believed to flow from it. And with the Sun, from which it was believed to flow, is addressed in those solemn invocations of the Orphic Hymns:

> Ελθε μακαρ Διονυσε πυρισπορε, Ταυριμετωπε,
> Ταυρογενης Διονυσας ευφροσυνην πορε θνητοις.

What reason there shall be to think that such a person ever existed, or that he, or the God Bacchus, or the nine Muses, whose very names are the same: or Jesus Christ, whose character is the same, ever existed, or were either of them anything else than the personified genius of the *Great Father of*

Waters, I shall bring before you in a further prosecution of those sacred studies.

But of thus far as I have proceeded, I dare pledge all the respect which I would wish to hold in men's minds, that if, indeed, the Bible were in every iota of it the Word of God, I could not handle it more faithfully, nor study it more laboriously, nor bring forth the result of those studies more honestly than I have done : as I am sure that even among the ministers and preachers of the gospel, the more learned, candid, and honest anyone were, the less would he be able to withhold his conviction from the truths which I have brought before you.

But if words may deceive us as to their meaning, objects which we see with our own eyes can hardly do so. And who can misread the fact, that the most ancient form of the cross, preserved in the Lateran Palace at Rome, is set in the stream of a river, representing as coming down from heaven? And the Crux Coronata of Pope Nicholas the First, in the Church of St. Clement at Rome, exhibits Jesus Christ nailed on the Cross, the indisputable personification of the river Nile, the four great branches of which river are represented as flowing out of the Cross, as if Christ, and Cross, and all were dissolved in those streams at which the beasts of the earth are represented as drinking.

They who have prosecuted with me this sacred and delightful science, must be conscious that they understand the scriptures infinitely better, see more beauty and significancy in them, and feel a higher respect and reverence for them than the stupid, uninquiring, uncurious, and uncritical millions, who are content to be ignorant, or than their teachers, spiritual pastors and masters, whose great interest and aim it is to keep them in ignorance, who call it treating the scriptures with respect and reverence, to be as profoundly ignorant of them as the ground they tread on, to ask for no more significancy of them, than that which satisfies the curiosity of the boys and girls at a charity-school, and to let anything more of the matter than their infancy had been entertained with, 'pass by them as the idle wind which they regard not,' while they would protect their own ignorance by raising the cry of Atheism, Deism, Blasphemy, and Infidelity against us who are not ignorant, nor will consent to play their fool's game of shutting eyes, and opening mouths, to see what God will send us. With *us words* must have meaning, and if they have been called words of God, the more heedfully, and the more laboriously and carefully do we sift out, examine, and compare; and hesitate and doubt ere we presume to ascribe to the Almighty what may prove to be nothing more than the cunningly devised fables of wicked and deceitful men.

Should we not act in this way, if the matter were only one of temporal interest, if it were a mere legacy, or deed of gift, or title to a property? And shall they have a right to think themselves pious men, or to say that they fear God, who are ready to swallow any sort of nonsense as the dictates of infinite wisdom, and as they say, 'hug the Bible to their hearts, and call it all divine,' without knowing the meaning of a single word of the divine original.

Resuming, then, our science: 'Draw not nigh hither, put off thy shoes from off thy feet, for the place whereon thou standest is holy ground,' are words directly admonishing anybody but a sheer fool, that all this argument of this whole book, is of a wholly different nature, and an entirely contrary character, to that appearance of historical fact and actual occurrence, which it might seem to wear 'in the upturned wondering eyes of the babes of salvation. It never *did* occur, it was never meant nor implied that anything of the kind ever occurred.

Imagination itself could not imagine it: and if it could, the text itself forbids our imagining it: 'Draw not nigh hither'—that is, surely, *never think of such a thing!* Let not such a foolish and insane an idea have place in your mind: 'put off thy shoes from off thy feet'—that is, put off the common and ordinary way of understanding things, according to the mere letter, and first impression they may may make on you. 'For the place whereon thou standest is holy ground'—that is, not surely, holy dirt of the streets, holy gravel and stones, holy muck or mud, or whatever might be the nature of the soil he stood on, or *stand off*, merely because there's a hole in the ground; and you'll get your foot into it if you come nearer.

But all that is herein exhibited is of a holy nature,—you enter here within the vestibule of allegorical astronomy, must understand upon different principles, and must interpret by wholly contrary rules, to those of the gross and common acceptation of the mere words and machinery of the science.

Though, then, the monks of St. Bazil are idiotish enough to think that they are, to this day, in possession of the very bush itself in which God appeared unto Moses, and call it the *holy briar* bush, at the foot of Mount Horeb, and will tell you how it pricked God Almighty's nose, just as the crown of thorns run into Jesus Christ's forehead:

And though the painted windows in the Rev. Edward Irving's chapel present you with pictures of that very bush, with God Almighty said to be sitting in the midst of it, you can see nothing but the bush and the smoke:

And though, in the 33rd of Deuteronomy, God is honoured by that very title, 'Him that dwelt in the bush,' as we know that folks that have no houses must be content to do:

And though the Egyptian people and their descendants, the gypsies among us, to this day, still continue to honour their God, by dwelling as he did in the bush: yet is the sacred text far more honoured, and more honourable in our eyes, when, with becoming reverence, we seek for that more solemn and recondite sense, of which we are admonished in those words, 'the place whereon thou standest is holy ground,' and dismiss from our minds entirely all those grovelling and absurd conceits which our religious dunces and ignoramuses would palm upon people just as ignorant as themselves

END OF PART I. OF EXODUS.

The Devil's Pulpit.

"DELENDA EST CARTHAGO."

No. 21.—Vol. II.] Price 2d.

EXODUS.—Part II.

A Discourse,

DELIVERED BY THE REV. ROBERT TAYLOR, B.A.

AT THE ROTUNDA, BLACKFRIARS ROAD.

' *And when the Lord saw that he turned aside to see, God called unto him out of the midst of the bush, and said, Moses, Moses; and he said, Here am I! And he said, Draw not nigh hither, put off thy shoes from off thy feet, for the place whereon thou standest is holy ground.*'—EXODUS, iii. 4.

I RESUME the sacred subject, in continuation now, from the positions in which I left the convictions of my audience, on Sunday last.

The ground on which all the narratives, both of the Old and New Testament are constructed, is HOLY Ground: as I have shown the exact derivative meaning of that word HOLY, which is SOLAR—that is, *of* or *pertaining to the Solar System*, or astronomical ground. And thus we see at once, that the supposing a real occurrence of the incidents detailed, or an actual existence of the persons spoken of, is as gross and childish a mistake as that of the booby who should imagine that all the figures which he sees depicted on a celestial globe were realities, that the names of the constellations were names of persons who had had a substantive existence, and their risings and settings, their occultations, or goings down into Egypt in the West, and their *Exoduses*, or comings up again in the East, were matters of history.

But I am master of the convictions of all who have attended this course of astronomico-theological science, to the proof, that Moses, the Muses, Bacchus, and Jesus Christ, are each of them but varied, and very slightly varied, personifications of the great Father of Waters, the River *Nile*, the very same as Serapis, Osiris, Sirius, and all the multifariously named personifications of that great river, which was believed by the Egyptian people to be an immediate, emanation from the *Sun*: and whose worship is retained to this day among ourselves, and to be identified beyond all emergence of a doubt, in the extraordinary respect shown, and wonderful efficacy ascribed to water, in every form, and among every sect of Christians and of Christianity.

I showed in my last discourse, that the Christ of the New Testament speaks of himself, and is throughout spoken of in the character of the personified genius of a river.

And that the Sanscreet name of the river Nile is *Christna:* which absolutely is none other than the name *Christ*. And that Serapis, which is another name of the river Nile, is the Egyptian or Coptic for the words *Salvator Mundi*—*i.e.*, the Saviour of the World.

As the very ancient medals of Alexandria exhibit the effigies of the Nile on the one side, and of Serapis on the other, and the legend under each respectively, to the Nile the Holy God, and to Serapis the Holy God.

And that *Hues*, which is another name of the same river, is none other than the very I.H.S. which is inscribed on our Christian altars, and which, read as it should be, as Greek, and not Roman letters, is I H Σ, which, with the Latin termination *us*, is Jesus, the common name of Bacchus, as the personified genius of the Nile, and of the Nazarene, the twice-living demon of the Jordan.

But when Christians are called upon to answer those questions, which any man having the proper spirit of a man would never suffer to remain unanswered, why is so much stress laid upon water throughout the whole Christian system? Why hath a man no part in Christ unless he *wash* him? Why must we be baptised *into* Christ? Why must we be born of water? Why is it only he who believeth and is baptised that shall be saved? Why is it that the new-born infant is not innocent, but is born in sin, and under the wrath of God till it be dipt or sprinkled in water? Why is the second person in the Trinity declared to be 'He that came by water?' Why are the three that bear witness on earth, answering to the Father, the Word, and the Holy Ghost, that bear record in Heaven, none other than the Spirit, the *Water*, and the Blood, where the second person in the Holy Trinity is so expressly declared to be nothing else but water? Why is't that 'tis 'Water wherein the person is baptised in the name of the Father, and of the Son, and of the Holy Ghost? And it is my baptism wherein I was made a member of Christ, a child of God, and an inheritor of the Kingdom of Heaven.'

Christians can only stare and look angry at you: they could only say that so it *is*, but wherefore it should be so, you have come to a better school than theirs to learn.

If we are to renounce all privilege of having ideas and to attach no meaning to words, why there's an end on it, and one religion is neither better nor worse than another, but 'tis all a drunken jargon, and an idiot's ramble together: but if we may be reasonable and consecutive in our train of thought, we cannot if we would shut off the observance of the good chemistry that prevails throughout the Christian theology, there is nothing but what will mix and amalgamate.

But the whole Christian world have never yet hit upon one single metaphor or form of speech, save that of a pigeon or a dove: nor is there one, in any part of scripture, where the third person in the Godhead is alluded to, but in which he is spoken of as a *fluid;* as something that may be drank, something that you may carry in a bottle, the *comforter*, of which the apostle speaks: 'Be not drunk with wine, wherein is excess, but be filled with the Spirit.'

It is always the *pouring forth* of the Spirit, or the *outpourings* of the Spirit, or the Holy Ghost *poured forth*, or some predication that could only appertain to what was essentially fluid, and might be drank or taken *internally*—that is, the figure or metaphor of speech when it is the third person of the Deity that is intended.

So that in the cure of our souls we have both an external and internal application. We are baptized into Christ, and the Holy Ghost is baptized into us: the one as a bath, the other as a balsam. We are taken into Christ, and the Holy Ghost is taken into us; in *that* we bathe, and this we drink.

Nor is it enough that we be born of water; but 'Except a man be born of Water and of the Spirit, he cannot enter into the Kingdom of God.'

Now, Sirs, would it be in any other case that a man would suffer his reason to be so stultified, his understanding so insulted, and write himself such an ass, such a stark-staring fool, and show so much of the water and so little of the spirit in his composition, as not to say to a clergyman who used such language, Good God, Sir, what do you mean? Know we not what water is? Do we not wash in it? Do we not drink it? Can anything be more material, more palpable to feeling, sight, and taste? And if this essential agent in your theory of salvation be thus material, can the other be less so? Certainly not! the Spirit is literally AIR, and the allegorical worship of the elements, is thus the real secret of your Christian Trinity. And you are baptized in the name of the Father, of the Son, and of the Holy Ghost, as those three personifications are, and never were, nor meant anything else than the imaginary genii of Fire, Water, and Air. As 'I indeed baptize you with Water,' said John the Baptist, 'but he who cometh after me shall baptize you with the Holy Ghost, and with Fire.'

And as 'tis the second person of the Holy Trinity who gives his name *Christ* to the whole Christian mythos, which from him is called *Christianity;* and Christna was absolutely the Sanscreet name of the river *Nile;* and Moses is absolutely the Egyptian name for *Water;* and all our Fathers were said to be *baptized into Moses,* and all we their sons are *baptized into Christ:*

We have discovered the meaning where your preachers of the gospel could find no meaning at all for their own language. For this is what it means: Christianity is *hydrolatry,*—water-worship. Your Moses and your Christ are but what Bacchus, Serapis, and Osiris were, diversified personifications of the genius of the river Nile.

Put back every expression, every sentence, every sentiment, every action, every attribute ascribed to Jesus Christ in the New Testament into its proper congruity! read your gospel as it should be read, as *the allegory of the* NILE, and all becomes intelligible, harmonious, beautiful. The Christian or *New* Testament is but an improved edition of the Mosaic or *Old* Testament; as that Old Testament was but an attempted revision of the still older Testament of the self-same hydrolatry or water-worship, in which it was still none other than the river Nile, who was worshipped under the names of Osiris, Bacchus, and Serapis.

Those names were by the Egyptian monks changed into those of Moses and of Christ, of the same significancy and veiling, the self-same eternal allegory, under precisely the same doctrines, mysteries, and ceremonies.

In all which, 'tis still the Deity of the second person— that is, the *second* personification of the elements, the Deity of Water, the personified genius of the river Nile, who is propounded to our faith, and is the object of our adoration.

Our Christian ministers, the most ignorant of all ministers that ever were on earth of what the true origin and real meaning of their religion is, have monstrously imagined a history, where all was allegory, and have taken the very grossest and most apparent metaphors of speech as literalities, not allowing to the most figurative language upon earth the common use and license of a figure.

And where the Egyptian people, who are known to have been all imagination and vivacity, and the genius of whose language was so full of trope and metaphor, that they could hardly speak of anything without personifying it, nor describe the most ordinary phænomena of nature, without falling into the language of an apparent history.

Our Teutonic stupidity has stumbled on the wild conceit that history it must needs be, that real personages were intended, and absolute facts occurring to those personages, the ultimate gist of their language.

So when Eastern eloquence spake of wine, as 'the blood of the grape,' our Western dulness interpreted that most obvious figure of speech, as if the grape, to be sure, had been a man that had been pressed, and squeezed, and crucified, and gone through all the sorrows and calamities of our own famous friend *John Barleycorn*.

When the Egyptian people, by the same figure of speech, called the water, 'the blood of the river:' as the river was their God, they who were washed in the river were spoken of as washed in blood.

Their river deity was imagined to be a man who *had* blood: the annual inundation was the shedding or pouring forth of his blood: and as that inundation was the source and vegetation and fertility to all the provinces through which it flows, it was the language of gratitude, as well as of allegory, to speak of it as his 'most precious blood-shedding, his blood that was shed for the life of the world.'

They put the allegorical language into the mouth of their allegorical God, and it was the language of God himself: 'My blood is drink indeed.' And hence the eternal confusion between the metaphorical and the literal term, the *blood* and the water, observable through the whole Christian allegory. Our Christ is he that came, 'not by water only, but by water and blood.' Sometimes we are said to be saved by water, sometimes redeemed by blood. And as *this* could not be without the idea of violence and death, the interesting romance of the *Man of Sorrows*, 'who for us men and for our salvation came down from heaven,' as the Nile was believed to do, veiled the physical history of the annual inundation of that great river.

As the Nile was believed to be a fluxion of Osiris, as the Sun, and to flow down directly from heaven, the time of the Sun's appearance in the constellation of the Lamb, when the point of the Vernal Equinox was in that sign, having been observed to mark the beginning of the swell, the benefit of the inundation was ascribed to the supposed influence of that constellation, and the waters of the Nile were therefore called 'the blood of the Lamb.'

Thus, that mystical language of the Apocalypse, that he 'saw a pure river of water of life, clear as crystal, proceeding out of the throne of God and of the Lamb, had no other reference than to the river Nile, proceeding, as it was believed to do, from the Sun in the seat or sign of the Lamb.' And they who 'washed their robes, and made them white in the blood of the Lamb,' were merely the washer-women and laundresses that took in linen, and washed it in the waters of that sacred stream.

Well spake the Lord by the prophet, saying, 'out of Egypt have I called my Son.' For it is none other than the language of Egyptian hydrolatry or water-worship, which, disguise it as you may, we detect in every figure of speech, in every mode of language which your Christian poetry could invent, or Christian prose could mean:

It is the idolatrous worshipper of the Nile, who would find that language, and none other than that which you have adopted, more apposite to the expression of his sentiment than yours, when he would say:

> 'There is a fountain filled with blood,
> Drawn from Emanuel's veins;
> And sinners plunged beneath that flood,
> Wash out their guilty stains.'

That fountain, that flood, is *the Nile*. It is of the river Nile, and of the river Nile alone, that its passionate idolater would exclaim:

> 'Jesu, thy blood and righteousness,
> My beauty are—my glorious dress,
> 'Midst flaming worlds in these arrayed,
> With joy shall I lift up my head.'

Or,

> 'Jesu, lover of my soul,
> Let me to thy bosom fly;
> While the louder thunders roll,
> While the tempest still is nigh.
> Hide me, O my Saviour hide,
> Till the storm of life be past;
> Safe into the haven guide:
> O receive my soul at last.'

The only difference between the Egyptian and the European idolator is, that the Egyptian could tell you the meaning of the language which he uses, while the Christian uses language for which he has no meaning at all.

On the *one* hand, the language of theology is a beautiful veil, enveloping the science of natural history, signifying the absolute relations which really exist between the visible heavens and this terraqueous globe: on the other, it is a tale told by an idiot full of sound and fury, signifying nothing.

Thus, when we study deeply the learned languages, and trace out the first meanings and subsequent variations of senses which the nomenclature of theology has undergone, we find evidence of an identity of the very names, as well as of the allegorical histories, of Moses, Bacchus, Jesus, and the Nile.

According to Diodorus Siculus, the most ancient name of

the Nile was Ὠκεανης, from whence our word *the ocean*. The Nile, as the father of waters, being believed to be the source of all the waters on earth, the sea, and all that in them is. In that word, we find the confusion of the Greek and Syriac terms. *O-Kuone-ees**—that is, the *dog*, the *fire*, by the very same analogy that Osiris, the Egyptian name of the same river is composed of Οσυρ—is, which is literally the *Star*, the *Fire*.

The ancient Ethiopians, by whom are meant the Indians, always called the Dog Star (Sirius), and the river Nile, by the same name:

'Because,' says Sir Wm. Drummond, 'the heliacal rising of the Dog Star (Sirius) was observed to take place nearly about the time when the inundation is approaching to its greatest height. As the flood became greatest when the Dog Star (Sirius) emerged from the Solar rays, superstition imagined a necessary connection between the Dog Star and the river. And upon allegorising this phænomenon in the fabulous history of the Indian Bacchus, they represented this deity as always accompanied by a DOG.

Christna, the undoubted origin of the name Christ, was the Sanscreet name of the Nile; while the name *Moses*, composed of *Mose*, which is the Egyptian word for water, and EES, which is the Syriac for *Fire*, presents precisely the same combination as the most expressive epithet for the personified genius of the waters, emanating, as was believed, from the Sun, and having their inundation always indicated by the position of the Dog Star, as Moses, in the allegory, in all his peregrinations through the wilderness, is represented as accompanied by his faithful and trusty friend *Caleb*, who 'stilled the people before Moses'—(Numbers xiii., 30)—that is, made them be quiet by his barking.

Caleb, being the literal Hebrew for a dog, and Caleb, the son of Jephunneh, literally meaning Caleb, the son of a something that is too funny to be mentioned.

But the identity of the characters of Moses and of Bacchus is not alone that of names as resting on the indisputable evidence of Orpheus, who expressly calls Bacchus Moses, and ascribes to him the character of a legislator who wrote his laws on two tables of stones.

And this evidence, be it observed, was before the world 950 years before the Christian era, whereas the claim of any Israelitish or Jewish people to any interest or connection with that story, was not made till 600 years after that time. But the whole fictions of Bacchus and of Moses run through every incident, like linked horses in a chariot, step for step, and stage for stage together, with no more difference in any respect than what would appear in any two carelessly compiled editions of one and the same story:

Both Bacchus and Moses were of Egyptian origin.
Both of them brought up in Arabia.
Both of them distinguished by a wonder-working rod.
Both of them crossing the Red Sea.
Both of them fetching water out of the rock.
Both of them leading armies through deserts.
Both of them lawyers.
Both of them parsons.
Both of them soldiers.
Both of them conquerors.
Both of them conjurors.
Both of them married: and
Both of them wore horns.

For look, I pray ye, at the pictures of Moses and Aaron on your Christian altar-pieces at this day, and you will find Moses is distinguished by two rays of light coming out of his temples, according to the vulgate rendering of Exodus xxxiv., 29, which says, 'his face was horned.' Of which distinction Bacchus was so far from being ashamed, that he was expressly adored and worshipped under the epithet Ταυροκερως Υης, which literally signifies Bull-headed Jesus.*

But ask of the Christian world why their Moses wore horns, they cannot tell you: they have no idea what it can mean. It is enough for them that Moses has said, 'I the Lord thy God am a jealous God:' and so you must not say anything about his horns if you love him. The prophet Habakkuk indeed has endeavoured to put a better grace on the matter, by saying that 'the horns grew in his hands, and *there* was the hiding of his power.' But it was a mistake; the horns grew in their proper place, upon his forehead, and there was no hiding 'em at all. The Apostle

---

* Bryant's Analysis, Vol. III., p. 310.

Paul pretends that Moses put a veil over his head; but this, again, betrays its reference to the hidden sources of the Nile, and involves another of the distinctive epithets of Bacchus, Κρυφιον, *the veiled prophet.*

Upon the stupid mistake of taking the Bible for a history, and its personifications for persons, we may safely defy all the Christian learning in the world, to find out the meaning of this mysterious language; but with the clue of astronomical science in our hands, we can wind our way through the whole maze.

And this is its significancy: remembering the rule of that figure of speech, the metonomy which I have so often explained, and which you will remember by that simple rhyme:

'A metonomy doth new names impose,
And things for things by near relation shows.'

You see how the waters of the Nile come to be spoken of as the *blood* of the Nile. You see how the Nile, arriving at its crisis of inundation, when the Sun is in the sign of the celestial Lamb (of March) comes to be considered as identical with that Lamb; and, consequently, the inundatory waters being believed to flow down from the Sun, when in that constellation, are the blood of the Lamb—that is, 'the river of the water of life, flowing out of the throne of God and of the Lamb'—that is, of the SUN of the Lamb.

You see how Moses, being literally the name of the waters of the Nile, thus wonderfully influenced by the Sun in the constellation of the Lamb, makes the heavenly song, or incantation, or *singing-in* of the inundation, to be called, as it is in your scriptures, 'the song of Moses and the Lamb.' And Moses in the Mount of God—that is, the waters of the Nile, considered as in the Lamb before their descent to this earth, by the same metonomy, is the Lamb, or the Sun in the sign of Aries, just at the point when the horns of the Bull of April begin to emerge over the out-going month of March: and Moses therefore appears as if the horns of the Bull were just beginning to peer over his forehead.

The image or figure of the signs in which each season commenced, became the form under which the ancient astronomical priests painted the Sun of that season. So the skin of the Lion of July was represented as the mantle of Hercules, and the horns of the Bull appeared on the forehead of Bacchus, and of Moses, and of Christ, whose only difference from the other two is, that his character as the Nile is more distinctly marked, as a 'Lamb that had been sl in,' whose blood constituted the waters of the Nile, thus believed to flow down from the throne of God and the Lamb.

And he had seven horns in express designation of the seven great branches of that mysterious river, as described by Virgil.

Thus, by that natural metonomy of language, and that irresistible association of ideas, which forces us to give the same name to things that are observed to have inseparable relations to each other, the Sun in the constellation of the Lamb, the Lamb itself as the constellation in which the Sun is, when the first appearance of the swelling of the waters of the Nile takes place,—the Nile, and the waters of the Nile, was believed in, addressed and worshiped as the one, only, and Supreme God.

And though the name of the Nile does not once occur in our sacred scriptures, that name having certainly been given to the river since the time of Homer, yet we know that the most ancient Coptic name, *that* given to it by the Egyptians themselves, was יאר, JAR!

And under that very name *Jah*, and under that very meaning of that name, *the river of God*, and under all the ascriptions and attributes that could indicate a river, and none but such a river do our Christian churches, to this day, resound with the praise and glory of our God, the Nile. Who, whether worshipped as the *Lamb of God* who washes us from our sins in his baptismal waters, or as the Spirit of God, who baptizes us with his holy fire, is still none other than the river Jar.

And all the mistake and confusion that appears to appertain to the matter, has originated only in the fact, the melancholy fact, that Christians are and ever have been the most ignorant of what the real origin and meaning of their religion is, of any people that ever lived.

Or how else could it have been, that the very ceremonies, the very names, nay, the very words, the psalms, the hymns, the prayers and praises, the everything that was said, the everything that was done, the everything that was meant, in the idolatrous worship of the Nile, should have been adopted in every church and chapel in Christendom; and

Christians have been persuaded that there was an essential distinction where no Christian upon earth has been able to show an essential difference.

It is the language of the worshippers of the Nile, their very forms of prayer, their very ascriptions of praise and gratitude to the God, the JAR, for fertilising their lands, which none but they could use, than which they could use no other, which are plagiarized in our psalms, sung in our hymns, and typified in our ceremonies.

What can be plainer in terms, what can be sublimer in meaning?

'O praise God in his holiness, praise him in the firmament of his power. Praise him in his name JAH! (that is, the Nile) and rejoice before him.'

In what other language could they invocate the descent of the waters from their celestial source, than ' O thou that wouldst rend the heavens and come down!' In what other language could they express their gratitude, when, as they believed in answer to their prayers, the waters *had* come down?

The River of God is full of water, thou preparest their corn, for so thou providest for the earth, thou waterest the ridges thereof abundantly, thou settlest the furrows thereof, thou makest it soft with the drops of rain, and blessest the increase of it. Thou crownest the year with thy goodness, and thy clouds drop fatness,—the folds shall be full of sheep, the valleys also shall stand so thick with corn that they shall laugh and sing.

To whom, to what but to the river Nile, in whom and in which alone all these sublime images of speech have a meaning, and all these attributes concentrate, could that stave be applicable:

> 'Praise Nile, from whom all blessings flow,
> Praise Nile all creatures here below:
> Praise Nile above, ye heavenly host,
> Nile, Father, Son, and Holy Ghost.'

Three persons, or three thousand, all meant but one God, and that God was the river Nile, for in the channel of that river dwelt all the fulness of the Godhead—that is, all the beneficial influence of the Sun's rays '*bodily.*'

If it were one or two, or only a few of such analogies that supported our theory, it might seem the work of curious conjecture merely; but they who shall have followed this course of science, throughout, will have found that there is no part of scripture but what we can by this science clearly and entirely explain, which is what, without it, we are authorized in saying, is more than the preachers of the gospel, of any denomination whatever, are able to do. The question for your choice is, whether you will continue to go to schools where you will be sure to hear nothing but the echo of your own opinions, from which, if you were schooled for ever, you could learn nothing, or join with us who take every day a new lesson!

Delenda est Carthago.

END OF PART II. OF EXODUS.

The Devil's Pulpit.

"DELENDA EST CARTHAGO."

No. 22.—Vol. II.]   [Price 2d.

AARON:

A Discourse,

DELIVERED BY THE REV. ROBERT TAYLOR, B.A

AT THE ROTUNDA, BLACKFRIARS ROAD.

> 'And the Lord said unto Moses, See I have made thee a God to Pharaoh, and Aaron thy brother shall be thy prophet.'—EXODUS, vii. 1.

HAVING, in my last discourse, entirely demonstrated the mythological character of MOSES, and shown his place, relations, and affinities in that sublime system of occult science under which the astronomical priests so ingeniously veiled all that they knew of the phænomena of the universe, we come now to the study of the place and character of his brother AARON, in the same astronomico-theological sytem.

Aaron is distinguished in this system as the first individual that every held the priestly office,—the first of priests. He it is, from whom all the priests derive their title, and take the example of their character. 'For no man,' saith the apostle, 'taketh his office upon himself, but he that is called of God, as was Aaron,' as he is still more distinguished by that peculiar epithet applied to him in the 106th Psalm: 'Aaron, the Saint of the Lord.'

Aaron, be it observed, the very proverb of a man in the

odour of holiness, is spoken of as being in so perfect a state of grace, that the precious ointment whereby he was anointed with the oil of gladness *(Sheshun)* above his fellows, 'poured upon his head, ran down his beard, yea,' says the luxuriating Psalmist, 'it ran down Aaron's beard, and went down even to the skirts of his clothing. It was like the dew of Hermon, which fell upon the hill of Sion. For there the Lord promised his blessing, and life for ever more.'

Our Christian poetry catches a sympathetic smoothness, in describing the greasy subject; and, we who might not have preserved our gravity at the thought of a reverend divine, with a whole dripping-pan emptied on his head, are charmed into becoming seriousness on reading—

'That it was like that precious oil,
 Which poured on Aaron's head,
Ran down his beard, and o'er his robes,
 Its costly moisture shed.'

Now, Sirs, I pray ye observe! this is all the difference of the mode of instruction which we follow here, and which you would find in any of your churches, chapels, or synagogues, throughout this miserably priest-ridden country. If you were to attend their preachments all your days, not one of them could or would tell you a word about the oil, or point out any significancy, or meaning, or relevancy in this mystical anointment. But to conceal their own ignorance, your spiritual pastors and masters would endeavour to persuade you that it was a sin to inquire: and that *we* forsooth are impious blasphemers, because we are not such dunces, nor so ignorant and stupid, as they are.

The analogy that will strike the curious critic in the comparison between Moses and Aaron, and indeed they are most curious, are, that as Moses was a type of our salvation by *water*, Aaron was so by *oil*. That as Moses was a type of Christ, by his being drawn out of the waters of the Nile, and so answering to the character given to Christ in the New Testament: 'this is he that came by water.' So Aaron was yet more significantly a type of Christ, in being, in reality, what Christ was only in name, the 'Anointed.' For Christ, as we are told, signifies the 'Anointed,'* or the smeared or begreased.

---

* Χριστος, from Χριω, *Ungo, lino,* to besmear.

And if to have been the first that was anointed, and to have been anointed head, and beard, and all, from top to toe, till he was all over a complete sop in the pan, be any evidence of being the Anointed, and the Anointed means the Christ, it is certain that not Jesus, but Aaron was *the Christ:* not of Jesus, but of Aaron alone could it have been truly said, that God had anointed him with the oil of gladness above his fellows,—though Jesus might have been in a state of salvation, it was Aaron that was in the state of grace.

And if being in a state of grace should mean being in a state of favour and acceptance with God; still less will the claim and title of Jesus admit of comparison with the paramount honour and distinction of the both holy and oily Aaron.

For, notwithstanding all the favour and grace that Jesus might be believed to stand in, it amounted to no more than such as left him, to be a dependent wanderer all his days, for he had not where to lay his head,—whereas Aaron was Archbishop of the Tabernacle.

Thus Aaron bears to Moses, in the Old Testament, precisely the same relation that the Holy Ghost bears to Jesus Christ in the New,—the one is emblemized by water, the other by oil, with that we must be besplashed, with *this* we must be besmeared.

When we come into life we must be baptized, when we go out of it we must be anointed. We are baptized into Jesus Christ, and greased into the Holy Ghost.

If he wash us not we have no part in Jesus Christ. If he besmear us not we have no part in the Holy Ghost.

And both of these operations are so equally necessary, that we are almost assured that the one is of no use without the other,—for when the Ephesians had not so much as heard that there was any Holy Ghost, the Apostle exclaimed, ' unto what, then, were ye baptized?' And 'when Paul had laid his hands upon them, the Holy Ghost came upon them, and they spake with tongues:' though all the difficulty of this glorious miracle is to imagine how they could have spoken without tongues.

The idea of the Holy Ghost (account for it who may) never occurs but in immediate association with some notion of grease, oil, lard, suet, or soap, which being mixed up or used in proper combination with the waters of baptism, makes what our church calls the *laver of Regeneration:* and the effects ascribed to the Holy Ghost bear the same analogy to the effects of material oil or grease. It was always attended with a peculiar glibness and fluency of utterance, setting men's tongues running nineteen to the dozen, and was therefore supposed to be peculiarly inherent in preachers, priests, and prophets,—so that it was called the gift of tongues: and prophets famous for speaking of things before they happened, and preachers as famous for speaking of things that never did happen, are always said to preach and to speak with unction.

The subject, you see, is exceedingly dangerous: and our Bible Society, and Bible circulating fanatics, have put a book into our hands which they impiously and temerariously call *the word of God*, of the meaning of which they are as profoundly ignorant as the wallowing swine, and for which, like swine, they are ready to turn and rend us when we offer to lay the pearls of true knowledge and real understanding of its meaning before them; they bid us examine it, and they dared not examine it themselves; they pretend to teach it, and they cannot so much as read it in the original tongues; they know and feel that, in the gross first sense and apparent letter, it is monstrously absurd and nonsensical, while they can give no other meaning to it, and dare not trust themselves to listen to those who can.

The sacred mythologist, whoever it was that wrote this mythology, in only proceeding so far as from the second to the sixth chapter of this Exode, has forgotten the story he had told about Moses in the bulrushes, and makes both Moses and Aaron, to have been the sons by an incestuous marriage of Amram: ' Amram took Jochabed, his father's sister, to wife, and she bare him Moses and Aaron.' And with curious iteration he repeats, ' These are that Aaron and Moses to whom the Lord said, Bring out the children of Israel from the land of Egypt, according to their armies, these are they which spake to Pharaoh, King of Egypt, to bring out the children of Israel out of Egypt: these are that Moses and Aaron.' Exodus vi., 27.

And Aaron took him Elisheba, daughter of Aminadab sister of Naashon, to wife. Of this Aminadab we find no more than the name which literally signifies Prince of the people.

But it must not escape our observance, that this first priest of the Old Testament is represented as a married man, and that the name of his wife Elisheba is precisely the same as Elizabeth, the wife of Zacharias, who is in like manner the first-mentioned priest of the New Testament.

The characteristic feature, however, of this be-christed or anointed Aaron, this first of priests, this Saint of the Lord, is, that after his most intimate acquaintance with the Lord God of Israel, after having heard the voice of God in the thunders of Mount Sinai, proclaiming himself a jealous God, and in his second commandment, forbidding the making 'of any graven image, or the likeness of anything that is in heaven above, or in the earth beneath, or in the waters under the earth.' After having been himself the distinguished individual to whom alone it was permitted to enter into the holy of holies, and conjointly with his brother Moses, having seen God face to face, and conversed with him as a man converseth with his friend. After having been an eye-witness of all the miracles which God wrought in Egypt; nay, himself the immediate agent in performing them, possessing the very wand, by whose mystical uplifting God rained all his plagues on the head of the devoted Pharoah.

Yet this Reverend Mr. Aaron, this anointed of the Lord, took the opportunity, when his brother's back was turned, of turning infidel at last, and telling the congregation that he had been preaching to so many years, that all that he had been preaching was mere gospel—a hoax, a rhodomontade that did well enough to preach, but not a word of truth in't. And as for the pompous fling of 'worshipping the Lord thy God, that made heaven and earth, the sea and all that in them is,' he substituted a calf.

O day and night, but this is wondrous strange! 'They made a calf in Horeb, and worshipped the golden image.' The ladies lent their earrings to make him, the priest of God burnt incense before him, all Israel worshipped him. And none other than Aaron himself it was who made this golden calf, who expressly called it *God*, and Lord, the most awful names of the God of Israel. And Aaron built an altar before it,—and Aaron made proclamation, and said, to-morrow is a feast unto the Lord—that is, unto Jehovah, the calf. 'And the people rose up early in the morrow, and offered burnt offerings, and brought peace offerings, and the proclamation was אֱלֹהֶ-אֱלֹהֶיךָ-יִשְׂרָאֵל, 'these be thy Gods, O Israel'—that is, this calf is thy trinity, O Israel.'

The apology which Aaron afterwards made to his brother Moses, for this flagrant idolatry, is scarce less mysterious than the idolatry itself: 'Let not the anger of my Lord wax hot, thou knowest this people that they be set on mischief. For they said unto me, Make us Gods which shall go before us, for as for this Moses which brought us up out of the land of Egypt, we wot not what has become of him. And I said unto them, whosoever hath any gold, let them break it off: so they gave it me, then I cast it into the fire, and there came out this calf.'

One might bravely say at the first glimpse of the matter, that if it were so, these children of Israel must be the stupidest people that ever lived.

But flinging of stones is never a safe game, when they fly back into our own faces. If there were no other people who ever gave their gold to the priests, and no other people that worshipped the golden image that the priest set up, one might enjoy one's full fling at them. But there is a country which I have visited in my travels, where the golden calf is worshipped to this day, in the shape of a calf's head set in gold, and surrounded with an inscription expressive of his eternal power and Godhead, *Dei Gratia Rex*, as much as to say this is the true God and eternal life. It being an acknowledged maxim among the people, that the Rex, or Basileus (which was originally one of the titles of the Sun) never dies. And by a most curious analogy, the ancient coins and pieces of money of Crete and Athens actually bore on them the impression of a Calf or Bull's head, as the object of their idolatry, from which *pecus*, the general name of cattle, our word *pecuniary* is derived: thus discovering, what we in vain attempt to conceal, that money is the universal God, and religious matters, and pecuniary matters, are but different names for one and the same thing.

But we must not condemn the greasy priest unadvisedly,—for though his calf-making was a grievous sin, and his brother Moses was so excessively provoked at it, that in a fit of violent rage he broke the tables of stone on which the second commandment which Aaron had so flagrantly violated, was written; yet, as if on purpose to make sure of breaking the commandment too, he made *four* calves himself, and set 'em up, not merely on the mount of God, but in his very sanctuary; and there they stood each upon one leg, like a cock upon a hen-roost, on the four corners of the mercy-seat of Yahou.

Nor was the worship of the calf abolished in Israel, even *after* the reigns of their greatest and wisest kings. It was Jeroboam who reigned over ten tribes out of the twelve, who set up two calves of gold, and repeated with respect to them the proclamation of Aaron, 'Behold thy gods, O Israel, which brought thee out the land of Egypt.' 1 Kings, 12. So invincible was this *moscholatry*, or calf-worship, that their most zealous King, Jehu, who in his zeal for the Lord of Hosts, the God of Israel, destroyed the worshippers of Baal, in the good old orthodox way, of a general massacre.: yet from the sins of Jeroboam, the son of Nebat, who made Israel to sin, Jehu departed not,—to wit, the golden calves that were in *Beth-el* and that were in Dan. 2 Kings, 10. But not alone the ten tribes that seceded with the usurper Jeroboam, but the two tribes of Judah and Benjamin, that remained true to their legitimate sovereign, adopted calf-worship, and Rehoboam, the son of Solomon. it was, who ordained him priests for the high places, and for the devils, and for the calves which he had made, and such as set their hearts, says the sacred text, to seek the Lord God of Israel, came to Jerusalem to sacrifice unto the Lord God of their fathers, when that Lord God of their fathers was nothing but a calf.

And, indeed, with what reason can Christians who worship a God that was born in a stable, complain of the Jews for worshiping one that was born in a cowhouse.

But not alone in Judah and in Israel was calf-worship the true and universal religion,—but not the prevalence of Christianity upon earth: no! nor the presence of God himself in heaven (say the scriptures) has yet set aside the divine honors paid to the godhead of a calf. For even there, in heaven, before the throne of God, we are assured by St. John, that *there* was *a beast like a calf.* Nor was that calf merely *before* the throne, but it was *in* the throne,—not merely was the calf *with* God, but the calf was God. And now I trust the plot is thick enough about us.

Can your Christian ministers explain all this? You

know they cannot! But is not the probability, at least, that it might admit of explanation?

And are we to suppose that the Egyptian people, among whom this calf-worship originated, clever and accomplished as they were in arts and sciences, in literature and poetry, could have meant no more by these strange types and figures than that gross sense, which is all your Christian preachers can attach them?

Would it be held unfair, unjust, and ungenerous to take the Christian in the grossest sense of his words, when we heard him address his God, as a *beast*, and call him ' a dear and bleeding lamb,' and sigh out his plaintive piety in such dolorous ditties as, ' O Lamb of God, that taketh away the sins of the world, have mercy upon us.' And can it be fair to ridicule the equally sublime and mystic language of the worshippers of that dear sacred Bull, who, with his everlasting horns, did break the mundane egg out of which creation sprang.

Or how is it possible to obey that mystic command of John the Baptist, 'Behold the Lamb of God that taketh away the sins of the world;' and not at the same time behold the calf of God who taketh away the sins of the world, still more effectually, who is the very next constellation, as April is a more glorious and sunshiny month than March? And why is it that we could not be redeemed by the blood of Bulls and Goats, but with the precious blood of Christ as of a Lamb without blemish and without spot? But for that reason, written in the stars of heaven, that it was *not* when the Sun was in the constellation of the Goat, though that be properly the beginning of the year, that the waters of the Nile, whose Sanscreet name was *Christna*, were observed to begin to swell for the inundation, and so, not the blood of the Goat, that was the blood of Christ. Nor was it when the Sun was in the constellation of the Bull of April, though very near that time that the swell began, and so, not the blood of the Bull. But it was exactly when the Sun entered the celestial sign of the Lamb or Ram, that the mighty river began to rise from its bed, or, as the Egyptian people believed, to descend from heaven: and hence the blood of Christ—that is, the water of the Nile, was the blood of the Lamb.

Now perpend, I pray, the solution of this astronomical

enigma. Compare your absolute date,—the name of Aaron literally signifies lofty or mountainous. Your Moses, Aaron, Joshua, Elijah, and Jesus Christ, all contrive to die, or to set or to disappear from the top of mountains, or eminences, the most convenient for observing the last glories of the setting Sun, or the moment of the occultation or sinking below the horizon of particular stars. Moses died as he deserved to do, with his shoes on, on the top of Mount Nebo, though he appears again, none the worse for such a death, in company with Elias, who never died at all, on the top of the Mount of Transfiguration—that is, literally, the Mount of Metamorphosis, talking with Christ, who was metamorphosed on that occasion into the Sun. While poor Aaron died, or rather his brother Moses killed him on the top of Mount *Hor* (Numbers xx. 28), which literally signifies the *Mount of Light*.

For as Aaron had been so abundantly be-christed, it wouldn't have done to have let him off without a little be-crucifying with. And his brother Moses wanted his clothes, so he stript him stark naked, in order to make him a type of the first Adam as well as of the second.

And Christ died on Mount Calvary (called, for some reason which we may guess at, more safely than we may tell, *the place of a skull*), yet he appears again in the same regimentals that Aaron died in, to make his last grand ascension into the heavens, from which he had descended.

And where was it that Aaron had set his calf, but in Horeb?

Why is Jeroboam said to have set up two calves, ' to wit, the calves that were in Beth-el and in Dan,' when one calf must have answered all the ends and significancies of the sacred hieroglyph? Why, but that by a mistake precisely similar to that of St. Matthew, who has represented Jesus Christ as riding upon two asses, he has mistaken *Beth-el*, which literally signifies the *house* or mansion of the Sun, and is nothing more than an interpretation of what the word *Dan* means for a distinct name, and has thus supposed, that because the calf was in that *mansion of the Sun*, which is called Dan, there must needs have been two calves. *Dan* (as I have heretofore shown), being literally the name of that mansion of the Sun, which is the sign of the Zodiac which we call *Taurus:* and where, as you see, the celestial

That Latin word *Taurus*, divested of its mere Latin termination *us*, being none other than *Taur* or *Thor*, the name of the Supreme God of Egypt, from whom our fourth day of the week derives its name, Thor's-day, or *Thursday*,—as the Latins have it, Die Jovis, or Jupiter's day.

There was indeed, then, but one calf in the matter, and that calf never was any other than the beautiful constellation Taurus, the Bull, which you may see this evening in the eastern part of the heavens—that is, in Horeb, the *East*, the Calf in Horeb, which you will easily distinguish by the little group called the Seven Stars, or the Pleiades, which are in his forehead, and that most magnificent shining red star of the first magnitude, which is the Bull's eye, and commonly called Aldebaran, that name literally signifying the shiner.

Nor will it seem quite so monstrous, that Aaron, the Saint of the Lord, should have set up a golden image of this celestial calf in Horeb, in the East, in the Mount of God, in Bethel, in Dan,—all these definitions, as you see, identifying the place of *Taurus*, the Bull of the Zodiac. When, to this very day, you have only to go to the top of Ludgate-hill, and without a microscope, you will see *Beth-el*, the house of God, which we call *St. Paul's;* and in that *Beth-el*, even upon the western pediment of that Cathedral you will see an image of that very Calf, couchant at the foot of the figure of St. Luke the Evangelist. And that it can by no possibility be other than an image of that very calf of the Zodiac, your own eyes shall certify you, when, as you shall see, that calf is a peculiarly religious calf,—he is in the very act of saying his prayers, he is down upon his knees, he is just going to say—*(but I must not say what he is going to say).* You see only his head and shoulders, and his two fore legs, while his hind legs and all the rest of his body are invisible, which is precisely the form and attitude of the Bull in the Zodiac, of which all the hinder parts lie back in the regions of infinite space which no telescope can reach, leaving only to the eye of man a view of so many of the stars as fall within the imaginary outline of a Bull's head and shoulders.

And thus have our Christian architects, in the construction of our most magnificent Cathedral, set up the Calf in Bethel, and observed the plan of building which the great astronomical priest, who performs the character of God

Almighty in the sacred drama, proposed to the builders of the Temple : 'for see,' said he, 'that thou make all things according to the pattern'—that is, according to the pattern of things in the heavens. And there they are, indeed, according to the pattern.

And by a most wonderous analogy, as a Calf is a young Bull, so a chapel, the house in which the calf was worshipped, is a young church, and all our religious words, as well as our religion, being derived from Egypt, as the most learned Bryant has proved. Our religious word *chapel* is directly traceable to the Egyptian CALF-EL, like the Hebrew Beth-el, signifying the *house of God, the Calf*.

Our Christian edifices are but improved eidouranions, in which the astronomical errors and blunders of the Old Testament, or Old *Covenant*—that is, constellarium or groupings together of the stars, as that word Covenant literally means, are corrected. And, ' the same stone which the builders rejected is become the chief stone of the corner.' Now, if ye have eyes to see, do, I beseech ye, open them upon our Christian *Bethel*, and see whether the stone which represents the calf at the foot of the Evangelist, St. Luke, on that edifice, is not literally and absolutely the chief stone of the corner.

And as you shall see the undoubted image of Taurus, the Bull of the Zodiac, on the outside of the edifice, pay your two-pence, and go in, and you will see, or ought to see, a magnificent painting of Aaron, the Saint of the Lord, who is none other than the personified genius of the star Aldebaran in the Bull's forehead, standing there on the south side of the altar of God, and basking in the rays of glory, which glance off from the tetragrammaton. Aaron was first distinguished as a priest by the Hebrew name *Cohen;* but this name was that which the Greeks gave to the stars of the first magnitude, as Cohen Sehor, Cohen Sirius ; and of these the most eminent, the Cohen Aldebaran, the Priest Aldebaran, who was the tutelary star of the Arabian tribe of *Misa*, presents us with a palpable version of the *Kohen Aherun*, the Priest Aaron, the tutelary star of the sacerdotal tribe of Levi.

Then look upon the starry heavens, and see the relations of that beautiful star, that anointed prophet, priest, and king, to the stars about him, to those beautiful princesses, the seven stars, and to the beneficial effects which all nature experiences on the rising of that star with all his shining train. And then you will be able to see the meaning, where none of your gospel-preachers can show any meaning at all, of that astrolatrous language which you are taught to repeat, every ninth day of the month, in your 46th Psalm: 'Thy seat, O God, is for ever and ever,—the sceptre of thy kingdom is a right sceptre. Thou hast loved righteousness, and hated iniquity, wherefore God, even thy God, hath anointed thee with the oil of gladness above thy fellows—*i.e.*, more oil on Aaron than on any other priest, emblematical, as more of the Sun's rays on Aldebaran than on any other star, physically.

'All thy garments smell of myrrh, aloes, and cassia, out of the ivory palaces, whereby they have made thee glad.'

Arabia, famous for its spices, myrrh, aloes, and cassia, thus associates the fragrance of those drugs with the influence of the beautiful star, their tutelary Aldebaran of the month of April, when these odorous plants are in full blossom, and when, upon the grateful senses of the voyagers in the Levant,

'North east winds blow
Sabæan odors from the spicy shores
Of Araby the blest.'

Kings' daughters are among the honourable women—upon thy right hand doth stand the queen in a vesture of gold/ wrought about with divers colours; and so stand the Pleiades, the daughters of Atlas, in the court of the star Aldebaran. And even so doth stand the Queen Star among the Pleiades, twinkling with variegated light, with purple and gold, 'sky-tinctured grain, and colours dipt in heaven.'

Nothing in nature likes to be reckoned old,—nothing would be old that could help it,—and therefore in personifying God either as man or beast, care was always taken to represent him as a young one of the sort.

Thus the Lamb of God, 'the precious bleeding Lamb.' was considered a most sublime and decorous expression of true piety.

The attribute of immortal youth could never be dispensed with. An old God would not have been relished.

For this reason the Pagan priests filled their Pantheon

with boy-divinities: Osiris, Horus, Helios, Bacchus, and Apollo himself were all of them young.

And I dare appeal to all the hymns and prayers, and all the sermons and religious tracts, all that is said, sung, read, or heard in any of our churches and chapels to this day, whether God the Son does not take precedence of his Father, and whether the doctrine is not continually, 'Believe in the Lord Jesus Christ, and thou shalt be saved?'"

The divinity of the Father is only subsidiary to the convenience of appropriating the exclusive idea of youth or boyhood to the Son: for which the writers of the New Covenant have strained the point so ridiculously, that, forgetting that they had represented him as about thirty or thirty-one—that is, a number answering to the number of days in a month—that is, to the length of time during which the Sun continues in any one of these twelve signs (as *that*, 'as you see in this allegorical language), may be said to be the age of that sign, the age of the Lamb of March, of the Calf of April, or of the two Boys of May, the spring month so necessarily associated with an idea of youth and boyhood,—they have spoken of him as being still like Bacchus and Cupid eternally,—a child using the epithet, *the holy child Jesus*. For of a truth, they say (that is, in a true understanding of this enigmatical astronomy) against thy holy child Jesus, whom thou hast anointed, both Herod and Pontius Pilate, with the Gentiles and people of Israel, were gathered together—that is, grouped into constellations, through which the infant son has to pass or *overcome* in his annual progress through the year.

The people of Israel (or *Benni Yesroile*), as I have heretofore abundantly demonstrated, being none other than the stars which constitute the twelve tribes, or twelve signs of the Zodiac. All the controversy between the merits of the Calf of Aaron and the Lamb of Moses is the chronological question, whether the point of the Vernal Equinox was in one or other of those signs; and whether, therefore, the honour of being the Supreme God or leading constellation should be assigned to the Calf or the Lamb. The constellation which first rises above the Equator, at this equinoctial point, being always said to lead or bring up the twelve signs which follow out of the land of Egypt, or house of bondage —that is, from below the horizon, where they are *supposed* to pass through a state of misery and servitude into the land flowing with milk and honey.

And hence the significancy of that never-varied, and as I may say, before the development of this great science, that never-understood, predication which always accompanies the name of the *Elohim*, which we translate God. None was God, or worshipped as God, but that constellation which was the leader to the rest, and brought them up out of Egypt.

Thus the astronomical language of the Lamb of Moses was, 'I am the Lord thy God, which brought thee up out of the land of Egypt.' While Aaron would have had it, that it was the Calf or Bull of the Zodiac that was the leading constellation, and said, therefore, of the stars that constitute that group, these are thy Gods, O Israel, which brought thee up out of Egypt.' While Jeroboam, 800 years afterwards, fell into the same astronomical mistake, when he said of the same golden or starry calf *in Dan* (that is, in the sign Taurus): 'Behold thy Gods, O Israel, who brought thee up out of Egypt.'

Neither of those astronomers being acquainted with the precession of the Equinox, which had removed the character of leader-up out of Egypt out of the sign Taurus, backward into that of Aries, as that fact was known to the priest who personated the character of Moses, and who consequently endeavored to correct the ancient Egyptian theology according to his more accurate astronomy.

The Egyptian name of the Lamb of God—that is, of the *Sun in Aries*,—was Amon, to which was added the glorious title Jupiter, forming the God Jupiter Ammon variously sounded as Amen, Aman, Amoun, and sometimes dropping its initial article,—becoming *Mon* and *Man*, was ridiculously naturalized into the language of the various nations which adopted the Egyptian superstitions without any reference to its original signification, which is AM-ON, *the Fire, the Sun*. And Jesus Christ gets the title, not merely of the Lamb of God, but of the Amen, the faithful and true witness, in the Revelations of St. John: and of the *Son of Amen*, or *Son of Man* in the gospels.

But as the wonderful order and regularity of the motions of the heavenly bodies presented the most magnificent type of faithfulness to engagements of fidelity and truth, the name of the chief of them, AM-ON, *the Fire, the Sun*, became a name for *truth*, and the utterance of that name was the most solemn protestation of sincerity or consent.

Ammon was the same as Bacchus, as also was Yes. And thus, to this day, we pronounce the names of our God, the Sun. When we say *Amen*, and yes, Ammon, or Amen, for verily, or so be it, or so it is, and yes, for *it is so*, or *it shall be so*, or *I will*.

This yes is only pronounced in the vocative, or ablative, instead of the nominative case, when the Quakers call it *yea*, which literally signifies *by God*.

As the French, who cannot distinctly utter a y, call it *Oui*, which is still the same, the common name of Ammon and Bacchus, and bearing the same signification as an appeal to Bacchus or Ammon, *by God*.

But the Greek word for yes or yea, by a curious anomaly, is Nαι. Hence the eternal quarrel between yea and nay, and people continually being apt to say nay when they mean yea: and hence the apostle's decision in the matter. The Son of God, Jesus Christ, was not yea and nay, but in Him was yea—that is, in Him was Bacchus. For all the promises or puttings forth of God in Him are yea, and in him Amen—that is (than which words could be no plainer), Bacchus, Jupiter, Ammon, Amen, Yea, and Jesus, are all one and the same God, the personified genius of the Sun in the sign of Aries. And verily I say Amen, Yea, Oui, and by God, it is so.

END OF THE DISCOURSE ON AARON.

The Devil's Pulpit.

"DELENDA EST CARTHAGO."

No. 23.—Vol. II.]   Price 2*d*

MIRIAM:

A Discourse,

DELIVERED BY THE REV. ROBERT TAYLOR, B.A,

AT THE ROTUNDA, BLACKFRIARS ROAD.

'*And Miriam, the prophetess, the sister of Aaron, took a timbrel in her hand, and all the women went out after her with timbrels and with dances. And Miriam answered them, Sing ye to the Lord, for he hath triumphed gloriously: the horse and his rider hath he thrown into the sea.*'—EXODUS, xv. 20, 21.

IT is in this truly sublime and beautiful passage, that we have first mention of the *august* personage, with whom I am now to bring you into better acquaintance.

Both the Greek and Latin versions which I have read to you, are honester and fairer than the English, which in this instance, as in many others, egregiously PROTESTANTIZES— that is, it gives a false or strained rendering, in order to put a Protestant complexion on a Catholic sense, and has actually changed the name of the original text in this and in every passage where it occurs, into *Miriam*, in order to prevent our suspecting or discovering that this Miriam, this first of prophetesses (as her brother Aaron was the first of prophets), was not a mere *Miriam*, which might be a name for anyone, but is indeed Maria, even none other than that blessed

Virgin Mother of God, and Mother of us all, eternally a Virgin, holy as God is holy, and pure as God is pure!

What confidence, then, can or ought a sensible man to place in our Protestant translation of the Bible, when he discovers that it has been translated so fraudulently, so deceitfully, and would have concealed from him so important, so grand a fact? Or what confidence in any of our Protestant clergy or preachers, of any one of whom, from the Lord Archbishop in a cathedral to the preacher in a tent, were you either by writing or the most respectful inquiry, to call for an explanation of what they preach, they would cover their inability to give it by treating you as an infidel, and an enemy, and a rebel against God, for presuming to ask for it.

But observe: This Mary, the prophetess (for *that* is her true name) is introduced in the sacred ode very abruptly, as a personage with whom the reader is supposed to have been previously, and from other sources, sufficiently acquainted. There was no occasion explicitly to state who the Lady Mary was, or whence she came, or what part she bore in the bringing up of the children of Israel out of Egypt.

Know ye not Mary? not to know Mary argues an ignorance of the theological system, too gross to be hopeful of instruction.

Mary, the prophetess, the foreteller, the forerunner, the announcer, the indicatress, the harbinger and herald, as that word הנביאה, *He Nebiaiah, the prophetess*, signifieth.

And what signifies that name מרים *Miriam*. It is in the singular, *Mare*, the sea. It is in the plural *Maria*, by false quantity pronounced MARIA, the sea. It is μια, the feminine of εις; in the Greek noun of number, for *one*, or the Sun. And *Maia*, the mother of Mercury; and Myrrha, the mother of Adonis. Its symbol or cypher, from the earliest formation of letters, M, Y,—an *m*, with the downstroke of a jod, or y, affixed to it,—M, for MARE, and Y, or J, for Yes, or *Jesus*,—Mary being the mother of Jesus. And none other than that very hieroglyph (as the shapes of all our letters were originally hieroglyphical) constitutes, as you see, the monogram of the Celestial Virgin of the Zodiac, who, like all the other constellations, is sprung out of the sea: as all the twelve signs of the Zodiac appear to rise out of the sea, and to set in it, as they rise above the horizon on the East, and set again in the West: and thus acquire the allegorical character of the twelve fishermen.

And where does this Lady Mary make her first appearance, but where she *should* do, and as her name imports?

Παρα θινα πολυφλοισβοιο θαλασσης, by the shores of the much resounding splashing sea? Πολυφλοισβοιο θαλασσης, the epithet of *multitudinous* always being appropriated to *Mare*, the sea, the multitudinous ocean, the genius, goddess, or lady of the sea, as Venus, Miriam, and Mary, severally were, acquired the name of Myrionimous, and Polyonomous —that is, of *a thousand names*, and of *many* names, for which reason Mary and Polly are still synonymous names among ourselves, Polly, Molly, Mary, Maria, and Moll, each alike signifying the lady or mistress of the sea.

And why had we no mention of her before, when the children of Israel were *in* Egypt? Why, but because the stars, of which she takes the lead, were *then* below the horizon; and *she* must necessarily come up *first*, for them to follow.

And why is she a prophetess (*Nebaiah !*)? But because *all* the planets and groups of stars are prophets and indices in turn of the stars which come after them; and the constellation of Venus, in the Zodiac, is a foreteller, in like manner as the Stars in the Ram are called the Rams of Nebaioth, which minister unto the coming God of Day, and are therefore stars of *augury*, or divination, whose allegorical language it is which we read in the 60th of Isaiah, 'Arise, shine, for thy light is come, and the glory of the Lord (that is, the brightness of the Sun) is risen upon thee.'

And who is this 'horse and his rider,' of whom this Lady Mary is so pleased to have him 'thrown into the sea.' See ye not *there*, in the Sagittarius of November, that very 'horse and his rider,' who must necessarily sink into the sea, when the Lord triumphs gloriously—that is, when the Sun shines brightly; and bringing up the children of Israel into the regions of long days and summer months, throws 'the horse and his rider' (the gloomy genius of November) below the horizon.

For had there been any *real* drowning of a *real* army in a *real* sea, *that* army must have consisted of many horses and riders; and the singular number and the definite article, 'the horse and his rider,' would have been a very feeble synecdoche for the greatness of the triumph.

Nor, if there had been any intended historical congruity in its being an Egyptian army, could there have been any horse at all thrown into the sea; for sure we shouldn't forget our lesson so fast, as not to remember that all the horses in Egypt had just before died of the murrain. And it must have been rather hard to kill 'em first and drown 'em afterwards.

So woefully bestead are they who would attempt to make a history of an allegory, and to represent the sublime machinery of astronomical science as a detail of real occurrences.

But the Lady Mary joins with her brother Aaron in a sedition against Moses, because of the Ethiopian woman whom he had married. Of which enigma, the solution *is* a reference to an union, or adoption of an Indian mythology, into the Coptic, or Egyptian *Exode*,—Ethiopia being the theological name of India.

On this occasion, we read, that 'the Lord came down from heaven in the pillar of the cloud, and stood in the door of the tabernacle,—and his wrath was kindled against Aaron, and against his sister Miriam, to such an extent that he smote the young lady with the leprosy, and she became leprous white as snow, even as one dead of whom the flesh is half consumed, and insisted that she should be shut out of the camp seven days.' (Numbers 12.)

Now, Sirs, see, I beseech you, the injustice, see the oppressive tyranny and cruelty of your ministers and preachers of the gospel, and say if any Pharaohs, Neros, or despots of kingly name that ever held men's bodies in so grevious a bondage as these priestly tyrants would impose upon our minds.*

These filthy spurcities, these atrocious follies, from which the mind of an innocent child, if not held down by authority, would turn with contempt, and cry *Shame! Shame!* are the text, the literal text, of your holy Bible, your word of God, of which a thousand evangelical dunces, not knowing a word of the original text, nor ever exercising the faculty of

---

* They foist on us what is in the latter the grossest trash and sheerest idiotcy that ever was in the world, as the word of God; and when we quote it in the most respectful manner, they feel that that quotation itself is sarcasm, and to repeat it in any way is to treat it irreverently.

guessing at its meaning, will sing me that pretty madhouse melody:

> 'Should earth, or hell, or men, or fiends,
> Against my faith combine;
> I'd clasp the Bible to my heart,
> Convinc'd it is divine.'

But can they tell the meaning of it? They cannot. Can their Christian ministers instruct them? They cannot; for they do not know themselves; and therefore, with that united cunning and cruelty which ever characterises priestcraft, they endeavour to raise the general squeal among the savages, against the general learning with which they cannot compete, and the superior honesty which would employ that learning to unravel the mystery of antiquity, to free them from the yoke of ignorance, and tame the fierce barbarians into men.

But how beautiful—how charming is science! how delightful are the investigations of the occult treasures of ancient learning—how irresistible the conviction which still progressing evidence forces upon us, in the course of these sacred studies!

It is not the common people whom I address, or whom I wish to address. It is those alone who love knowledge, who follow reason as the supreme guide, and seek truth as the great end, to whom I appeal.

> 'Ye generous few, who love this sacred shade,
> How rich a scene is to your view displayed;
> Knowledge for you unlocks her classic page,
> And virtue blossoms for a better age.'

Ye have seen each person of the eternal trinity, Adam, Eve, Noah, Abraham, Sarah, the Patriarchs, Moses, Aaron, each falling into their exact astronomical relations.

And now! the planet Venus, whose domicile is in the pavilion of the Zodiacal Bull of April, whose very name was Mary, as that name signifies, *sprung from the froth of the sea*, presents the solution of the leprous whiteness that covered the beautiful form of Miriam, and of the sea, from which she sprang, her father, Neptune, seeming to throw up his froth, or spitting in her face. When she rises as the planet Venus, in her domicile of April, out of the sea, her direct adversary, the horse and his rider, of the gloomy month of November, is thrown into the sea, as a necessary consequence, on the opposite side.

ים סוף, the Sea of Surph! As in the Pagan allegory, it was the month of April when Venus rose out of the waves, and landed in her favourite island of Cyprus, from whence she was caught up into heaven.

Thus every island had its Venus Anaduomene, sea-born goddess, or tutelary saint, imagined to have sprung out of the main, to be its protecting or guardian genius.

And thus our own most popular British air is but a version of the song of the Egyptian Miriam, and the Cyprian Venus. For,

'When Britain first, at heaven's command,
Arose from out the azure main,
This was the charter—the charter of the land;
And guardian angels sung this strain:
Rule, Britannia! Britannia rule the waves!'

And thus alike Miriam, Venus, and Britannia,—the song, the songstress, and the occasion of the song, are all a fiction, the mere creation of a poet's fancy, as e'en thus. 'The poet's eye, in a fine frenzy rolling, doth glance from earth to heaven, from heaven to earth. And as imagination bodied forth the form of things unknown,' the poets' pen turned them to shape, and 'gave to airy nothing a local habitation and a name.'

And hence (as the fabulous history of the church on earth was devised upon the plan of a *picture in words*, of the phænomena of the visible heavens) you have the idea of eternal persecutions, or *followings* of one sign or star after another, which is the signification of that word, presented you in the *wordy picture*, or fabulous allegory, answering exactly, and even to the most extraordinary minuteness, to the celestial original. As they go up on one side, their adversaries, the opposite signs, must go down on the other. They are eternally pursuing, but never overtaking each other.

Hence the meaning of those mystical words of the apostle, ' yea, and all that will live godly in Christ Jesus, shall suffer persecution,' as to be sure they must, 'they fall successive, and successive rise.'

And this same *Venus*, who is triumphing over the horse and his rider in her *Exodus*, or coming out of Egypt, will be in turn persecuted by the great red dragon, Sagittarius, or

Serpentarius, for they are one and the same; and 'the string of his bow hath he made ready against her.' But she will be caught up with her man child into heaven, and so neither he nor she be any the worse for such a persecution.

But when *the woman*, who, as the planet Venus, had been a wanderer (as that word signifies), was caught up into heaven, even to the throne of God, of course she became *fixed*,—she was settled for life. And *there* is that same eternal Venus fixed for ever in the Virgin of August. Of which astronomical sense, the allegorical enigma is *that* which we read in the 20th chapter of Numbers—that is, in the 20th lesson of allegorical arithmetic, where you read that 'Miriam died in Kadesh, and was buried there.' While it does well enough to sound on the uncurious and uncritical ear, as if Kadesh was the name of a place, and as if Miriam died in Kadesh, or in *Kadesh-Barnea*, had meant no more than as if she had been a real person who had really died in a place of as real a geography as our Spitalfields or Smithfield. But it makes a little difference when the innumerable other astronomical indications are backed by the criticism which discovers that קדש Kadesh, is the name for glory or brightness, and *Kadesh-Barnea* is the brightness of corn. So that Miriam dying, and being buried in Kadesh-Barnea, is an evident enigma for the Virgin, the genius of the harvest month, being absorbed as she is in the brightness of the Sun, which renders even the bright star, or sheaf of corn in her hand, invisible.

Which analogy is so wonderfully preserved in the new mystery, that St. Luke first mentions the Virgin Mary by express association, as a Virgin *in the sixth month*, which, reckoning March the first month, can be none other than the Virgin of August, who, when the angel Gabriel paid his addresses to her, was found at home (as she always will be found) in the sixth month. While her husband Joseph, *Io sepe*—that is, *the manger of Io*, which is in the stable of Augeas, on the 25th of December, is expressly declared to be (the Son) of Heli, which is literally (the Son) of *the Sun*,—Jesus being, *as was supposed*, says the evangelist—that is, all this allegory was supposed or imagined merely,—Jesus being, *as was supposed*, the Son of *Io sepe*, ως ενομιζετο. While the Virgin is still more astronomically defined by Matthew, as being the *Virgin of Bethlehem*, which is the

House of Bread, a direct definition of the pavilion of the Virgin of August.

Now, Sirs, resist this demonstration who can, it is no less than mathematical demonstration. Turn to your almanac, turn to your calendar by which you find the lessons in your Prayer Book, and you find that there, even there, your Christian chronologers have fixed the 15th of August as the sacred festival of the ASSUMPTION of the Blessed Virgin, or taking up of the Virgin into heaven. It ever having been a tradition, that the Virgin Mother of God never died, but shared with Enoch and Elijah the honour of being translated or *assumed*, and taken up into heaven. As in the Liturgy of the Catholic church for that day are the words, 'This day the Virgin Mary ascended the heavens. Rejoice ye, for she reigns with Christ for ever.' The Virgin Mary is taken up into the heavenly chamber in which the King of Kings sits in his starry seat. That very 15th of August, in the Roman Calendar of Columella, is the very crisis of the disappearance or evanescence of the Virgin of the Zodiac. That very 15th of August is the day which the ancient Greeks fixed as the day of Assumption of the blessed Virgin *Astrea*. And the seven days during which Miriam was shut up, and not allowed to show her leprous face in the camp of Israel, is precisely the length of time during which the Virgin of the Zodiac absorbed in the effulgence of the Sun's rays, as he is passing through her, is *shut up*, so as to be rendered wholly invisible in the stars of heaven.*

But it is three weeks before the Sun appears to have made sufficient progress to suffer the stars which form the constellation again to become visible to the naked eye, and just at the end of that three weeks, when her beautiful head is seen on the other side emerging out of the Sun's rays, have your Christian Almanacs fixed the festival of the nativity of the blessed Virgin—that is, September 8th.

And as she was born, I suppose she had a *mother*. Well, then, her mother, the mother of the blessed Virgin, the

---

* And hence the solution of the fable of Exodus is expressed in that motto of our Earls of Balcarras, Astra, Castra, Numen, Lumen, *the Stars, the Camp, the Sun, the God*,—on the assumption, which all astronomers admit, that the Vernal Equinoctial point was in the first degree of Aries, in the year 388 before Christ.

grandmother of Jesus Christ? is not that a question that a man may with propriety ask?

It is ANNA? and what is Anna? it is the actual feminine of the well-known word Annus, *the year*: and thus the Virgin Mary is proved to be none other than the Virgin of the Zodiac, which is 'the Daughter of the Year;' and Anna has the festival of *her* nativity fixed on the very day when the ancient year of the Egyptians was reckoned to begin.

The Gospel of St. Luke, cautious of letting in too strong a light on the astronomical allegory, has not told us directly who the mother of the Virgin Mary was, but has only mentioned Anna, the prophetess, the daughter of Phanuel—that is, of the tribe of Aser, when the words are translated into their meaning, 'the year, the daughter of our shining God, in the constellation of Virgo.' The 26th of July, our *St. Anne's day*, being the beginning, or standing upon the first degree of that sign, when that point was the point of the Vernal Equinox: which, upon the calculation of the motion of precession, on principles recognised by all astronomers, at seventy-one years, eight or nine months for a degree, and consequently 2160 years for a whole sign, gives us 13,060 years, when St. Anne's day was the first of the Egyptian year. Any time in the infinite ages before which time, but demonstrably *before* which time, this allegorical Almanac must have been in being. And thus, while we are not able to say exactly how old the gospel *is*, we are able to assign a time, than which it is demonstrated to be much older. It is older than 13,060 years ago—that is, more than 11,230 years older than the period assigned to Christianity, and more than 5,393 older than the period which has been dreamed of, as that of the creation of the world itself.

While our Christian chronologers have fixed the birth of Christ in the stable of Nazareth, at the very day,—nay, to the very minute, to the accuracy of the setting of a chronometer, to that minute of midnight, between Christmas Eve and Christmas Day,—when, for the same reason, the ancient Egyptians fixed the birth of their God Osiris, the Persians that of their God Mithra, the Greeks that of Bacchus—that is, when the Sun, having passed his lowest point of declension at the winter solstice, enters the first degree of Capricornus, the Goat, where, exactly in the visible heavens is the stable of Augeas, in which he is said to be born, at the moment when the middle of the Virgin was on the eastern border of the horizon, which constellation was therefore said to be his mother. As in the meditation of the third mystery of the Rosary, are these words: 'Let us contemplate how the blessed Virgin Mary, when the time of her delivery was come, brought forth our Redeemer, Christ Jesus, at midnight, and laid him in the manger.' As Justin Martyr boasts that Christ was born on the day when the Sun takes its birth in the stable of Augeas—that is, in the station of the celestial Goat, where the stable of Augeas is found in the Sixth Labour of Hercules. And Albert the Great is great in his admission. We know that the sign of the celestial Virgin did come to the horizon at the moment where we have fixed the birth of our Lord Jesus Christ. All the mysteries of his divine incarnation, and all the secrets of his marvellous life, from his conception to his ascension, are to be found in the constellations, and are figured in the stars.

But the famous picture of the *Marine Venus*, admitted to have been the finest work of art which the world had ever seen, the work of Apelles, in the execution of which, that artist is said to have used his mistress, Campaspe, for his model, who had been given him by Alexander the Great, came at length into the possession of the Roman Emperor, Augustus, who placed it in the Temple of his God.

And thus have we the Augustan era, as the supposed epoch of the origin of Christianity, when art lent its aid to superstition: and the beautiful Virgo Marina became the no less beautiful Virgin Mary, the genius of the month which derives its name from Augustus. That the Virgin Mary, the Planet Venus, and the Virgin of the Zodiac, are absolutely the same, and consequently that Jesus Christ, the Son of the Virgin Mary, is none other than the same kind of allegorical and imaginary figment, as they were, is demonstrable from the absolute identity of all the epithets and doxoligies, prayers and praises ascribed to Venus in the Pagan, and to Mary in the Christian theology.

And not alone to Venus, but to Adonis, the well-known paramour of Venus, in the mythology, are the prayers of the Christian church, under that very name *Adonai* (which only differs from Adonis by the addition of the pronoun suffix, which makes it *our Adonis*), to this day addressed. The collect for the 18th of December is: 'O Adonai, come and redeem us, with a stretched-out arm.'

The only difference between Christians and Pagans being, that the Pagans had some sense, and kept in view the sublime physical science, in the words which they used: they knew, and they could tell the meaning,—while Christians use even the very same words, and have no meaning at all for them.

Though we read in the Old Testament the most terrible denunciations of God's wrath against those idolaters, who worshipped *the Queen of Heaven* (Jeremiah 44). By whom all agree to have been meant none other than the planet Venus, or the first constellation of the Zodiacal Virgin. Yet have the very words, epithets, titles, attributes of this Queen of Heaven been adopted into our Christian liturgies.

I repeat you now the hymn of the Pagan Lucretius to the Cyprian Goddess, in juxtaposition with the hymn to this day retained in the Litany of the blessed Virgin Mary. And if there *be* a difference, the wit of man is yet unborn that can show what that difference is:

> 'O thou, from whom the Æneadæ arose,
> Source of delight, the joy of Gods and men,
> Bright Venus! thy imperial sway extends
> O'er the wide seas, and all th' expanded fields
> Of teeming nature. By thy power of old,
> The various tribes that rove the realms below
> Issued to life, and filled the vacant world.
> O lovely Queen of Heaven! at thy command
> The whirlwinds die away, the storm is still;
> And the big clouds dissolve in limpid air.
> To thee we owe the beauties of the field,
> And Earth's rich produce. At thy mild approach
> The dimpling waves put on a thousand smiles,
> The sky no longer lowers; but calm and clear
> Spreads its pure azure to the world's extreme.'

But such were the forms of Pagan piety.

And where is the difference,—where, I pray, the shadow of a difference? when, in ten thousand Christian Churches throughout all Christendom, you shall hear them in the holy office of the Virgin, to this day, thus addressing our Christian Venus.

'O holy Mary, mother of our Lord Jesus Christ, queen

of heaven, and lady of the world, Virgin most miraculously fruitful,—hail star of the sea—morning star!

> 'Bright Mother of our Maker, hail!
>   Thou Virgin ever blest;
> The ocean's star, by which we sail,
>   And gain the port of rest.
>
> Hail, lady of the world,
>   Of heaven bright queen;
> Hail Virgin of Virgins
>   Star early seen.
>
> Hail flourishing Virgin,
>   Chastity's renown;
> Queen of clemency,
>   Whom stars do crown.
>
> Mother of grace, hope
>   To the dismay'd;
> Bright star of the sea,
>   In shipwrecks aid.'

And then the following ejaculations—

> 'O lady, hear our prayer,
>   And let our cry come unto thee!'

Or, if words can be clearer:

> 'Hail, Virgin most prudent,
>   House for God placed,
> With the sevenfold pillar,
>   And the table graced.
>
> Saved from contagion
>   Of the frail earth
> In the womb of thy parent,
>   Saint before birth.
>
> Mother of the living,
>   Gate of Saints' merits,
> The new state of Jacob,
>   Queen of pure spirits.
>
> To Zebulon, fearful
>   Armies array:
> Be thou of Christians,
>   Refuge and stay.'

And there is that Virgin, which literally is the domicile, or house, placed for the reception of the Sun, whose summer's seat it is.

And even there, in that tabernacle of the Sun, is that beautiful furniture, the sevenfold pillar and the table; and that constellation, known to the Phœnicians and Hebrews, under the name of *Succoth Benoth,* or tabernacle of the girls, was softened in the Greek utterance into Succoth *Venus,* or pavilion of Venus.

And thus have we a clear and intelligible explanation, where none of your Christian teachers can give any explanation of those words of the angel of St. John, in the 21st of the Revelation: 'Come up hither, and I will show thee the Bride, the Lamb's Wife,' as any astronomer can say the same as well as he: 'Come up hither, and *I* will show thee the Bride, the Lamb's Wife!' There she is, Myrrha, the daughter of Ammon, daughter, mother, and wife too. And there is her woolly-headed husband, him of whom the same St. John instructs us, that 'the hair of his head was like wool,' as I suppose the hair upon a lamb's head is in general very much like wool.

But where was it that the inspired apostle saw this Lamb, and the Lamb's wife? He tells you, 'from the top of a great and high mountain,' the most convenient for making astronomical observations: and then explicitly defines them in that great heavenly city, the Zodiacal band, which had twelve gates, or twelve great entrances, and names written thereon, which are the names of the twelve tribes of Israel, as those twelve names really are the names of the twelve signs of the Zodiac. And the wall that surrounded the city had twelve foundations, and in them the names of the twelve apostles of the Lamb, which again, not only in number, but in character, answer to the twelve signs of the Zodiac.

Of which, the 6th, or harvest month, called by our Catholic brethren, *the gate of the Saints' Merits,* is yielded to the miraculously fruitful Virgin, which was never any other than the Virgin of the Zodiac.

But if any of you shall ever visit Paris, and will be at the pains to look on the architecture of the church of *Notre Dame,* dedicated to the honour of the mother of our Lord Jesus Christ, you shall see in characters, which you must shut your eyes not to see, and renounce the faculty of understanding to avoid understanding, that that *Notre Dame,* that Virgin Mary, to whom that church is dedicated, is, and was, and never meant any other than the Virgin of the Zodiac.

For there, over the great gate which presents itself on the left, as you enter at the north, is carved the twelve signs of the Zodiac, from among which, the 6th, or sign of the Virgin, is thrown out, and its space occupied by the figure of the statuary who erected the building, and the Virgin set above them all, as the Goddess to whom the edifice is dedicated.

And if such were the nature of the mother, such must have been that of the son, and such also that of the whole eleven apostles.

Heaven and earth, and all the bright squadrons of the twinkling night, bear witness; and the Sun himself, the glorious King of Day, evidences the fact.

END OF THE DISCOURSE ON MIRIAM.

www.ingramcontent.com/pod-product-compliance
Lightning Source LLC
Chambersburg PA
CBHW022102150426
43195CB00008B/238